The Transition from Socialism in Eastern Europe

Domestic Restructuring and Foreign Trade

WORLD BANK

REGIONAL AND

SECTORAL STUDIES

The Transition
from Socialism
in Eastern Europe

Domestic Restructuring
and Foreign Trade

EDITED BY

ARYE L. HILLMAN

AND

BRANKO MILANOVIC

The World Bank
Washington, D.C.

The World Bank Regional and Sectoral Studies series provides an outlet for work that is relatively limited in its subject matter or geographical coverage but that contributes to the intellectual foundations of development operations and policy formulation. These studies have not necessarily been edited with the same rigor as Bank publications that carry the imprint of a university press.

The findings, interpretations, and conclusions expressed in this publication are those of the authors and should not be attributed in any manner to the World Bank, to its affiliated organizations, or to the members of its Board of Executive Directors or the countries they represent.

The material in this publication is copyrighted. Requests for permission to reproduce portions of it should be sent to the Office of the Publisher at the address shown in the copyright notice above. The World Bank encourages dissemination of its work and will normally give permission promptly and, when the reproduction is for noncommercial purposes, without asking a fee. Permission to copy portions for classroom use is granted through the Copyright Clearance Center, 27 Congress Street, Salem, Massachusetts 01970, U.S.A.

The complete backlist of publications from the World Bank is shown in the annual *Index of Publications*, which contains an alphabetical title list and indexes of subjects, authors, and countries and regions. The latest edition is available free of charge from Distribution Unit, Office of the Publisher, The World Bank, 1818 H Street, N.W., Washington, D.C. 20433, U.S.A., or from Publications, The World Bank, 66, avenue d'Iéna, 75116 Paris, France.

Arye L. Hillman is William Gittes Professor of International Economics at Bar-Ilan University in Israel. Branko Milanovic is a senior economist in the Country Economics Department at the World Bank.

Cover design by Sam Ferro

Library of Congress Cataloging-in-Publication Data

The Transition from socialism in Eastern Europe : domestic
    restructuring and foreign trade / edited by Arye L. Hillman and
    Branko Milanovic.
        p.   cm.—(World Bank regional and sectoral studies)
    Includes bibliographical references and index
    ISBN 0-8213-2148-X
    1. Europe, Eastern—Economic policy—1989– 2. Exports—Europe,
Eastern.   3. Privatization—Europe, Eastern.   4. Post-communism–
Europe, Eastern.   I. Hillman, Arye L.   II. Milanovic, Branko.
III. Series.
HC244.T6988 1992
338.947—dc20   92-1684
                                                                    CIP

Contents

II. Foreign Trade

Introduction

Arye L. Hillman and Branko Milanovic

The transition from socialism to a market economy in Eastern Europe encompasses a variety of economic, political, and social dimensions. Transformation in some of these dimensions, once under way, is easier to achieve than in others. Political change—a prerequisite for economic change—once seemed difficult, if not impossible. Yet once circumstances permitted political change, the political transformation in East European countries was relatively swift. Democratic institutions were introduced to replace those established by the Communist party, free elections took place, and new parliaments and presidents were chosen. There were some differences among countries, but the main components of political change—a multiparty system, representative democracy, and a free press—were readily instituted.

Economic transformation is, on the other hand, more complex. A modern functioning market economy is not only difficult to achieve: it is also often not clear what is meant by "market economy." Everybody agrees that a market economy should somehow lead to a greater availability of goods and services, but there is disagreement as to how this is to be achieved. For some, the idea of a market economy implies job protection and a broad social welfare system. For others, the concept of the market economy implies a competitive environment and unbridled free enterprise. For a third group, the state would aid the market by identifying enterprises with the greatest potential for success and steering the targeted enterprises toward the most profitable activities. Adherents to each of these positions can point to an actual market economy that, at least superficially, embodies the principles they espouse: in the first case, Sweden; in the second case, the United States; and in the third case the Republic of Korea.

Throughout this volume, $ signifies U.S. dollars.

1

An economy that has for decades been planned or which has experienced decentralized redistributive socialism cannot instantaneously be transformed by decree, or by good wishes and declarations of intentions, into a Western market economy. This volume addresses the complexities that are encountered in economic transformation from socialism to a market economy. Part I is concerned with issues of domestic restructuring, and Part II with issues of international trade and payments.

At the outset we are obliged to define two terms. The first is "socialism." Socialism is a system where a dominant share of assets (outside agriculture) is nonprivately owned. In such a system, most nonagricultural labor is also employed by the nonprivate sector. As long as East European economies display such features, they can be considered "socialist," even if politically they have been transformed into democracies. Our definition of socialism is negative ("nonprivate"), in order to include not only canonical centralized Stalinist-type economies, but also those decentralized economies in which public corporations or labor-managed firms predominate. In these decentralized socialist economies—beginning in Yugoslavia, then Hungary, and later Poland—ownership is undefined other than being manifestly not private, and management rights are divided among the state, management and workers. Most chapters in this volume address issues of transition in the context of such decentralized socialism, where central planning has been formally abolished but private property rights to productive assets have not been broadly instituted.

The second term that requires clarification is "Eastern Europe." This was, until recently, an accepted term describing the European countries of the former Soviet bloc plus Yugoslavia and Albania. A new term has appeared in the aftermath of the political change: Central and Eastern Europe. We have decided to adhere to the old term for two reasons. First, this volume is concerned not with a geographical but with a conceptual entity. Reference is made to Western Europe as encompassing Finland or Sweden, although both lie as far east as Poland or Hungary and, in a geographical sense, belong to Northeastern Europe. Similarly, Japan is considered to be part of the West. Second, if a geographical approach were used, we would be obliged to make distinctions between Central, Eastern, and Southeastern Europe (or the Balkans). Clearly this would be unnecessarily cumbersome.

Domestic restructuring

The requisites of domestic restructuring are identifiable from the attributes of *centrally planned socialist* economic systems. *Centrally planned* and *socialist* are two distinct conceptions. Central planning can be abolished all but instantaneously by decree, just as it was introduced. This action, however, is not in itself sufficient to introduce a market economy. The central theme of this volume is that the elimination of central planning does not necessarily imply an immediate—or even a delayed—transition to a market economy. The abolition of central planning alone merely results in decentralized industry without the incentives provided by private property rights, and characteristically entails imperfect markets with heavy state interference and *ex post* redistribution designed to equalize outcomes.[1]

Because in the Eastern European countries the departure from central planning preceded the departure from socialism, a phase of a nonplanned, decentralized *socialist* economy was inevitable. While the abandonment of central planning takes place through the relaxation and elimination of mechanisms of direct control, the transition from socialism to capitalism occurs through a change in property rights from social or collective ownership to private ownership. This transition is more arduous and time consuming than the transition from central planning to decentralized socialism, if only because of the distributional connotations. During the transition from socialism, rights to a society's wealth are reassigned and future income flows are thereby, to a large extent, determined. This is practically a world built anew.

It is accordingly of interest to direct attention to circumstances where central planning was eliminated, but property rights were not assigned and *ex post* redistribution remained pervasive. The Yugoslav economic system of self-management provides a laboratory, as does post-1968 Hungary, and, to a lesser extent, the experience of Poland in the 1980s. Yugoslavia abolished central planning in the early 1950s, but not social ownership of the means of production, while after 1968 Hungary sought to combine, in its own version of "market" socialism, the efficiency of the market with the social security and egalitarianism of socialism. In Poland in the 1980s, the state gradually divested itself of responsibility for planning the economic activities of individual enterprises. In all these instances, decentralized socialist enterprises were left to make independent economic decisions in an environment in which social ownership, but not formal state directives, persisted.

It is the experiences of (the former) Yugoslavia, Hungary, and Poland which form the core of the studies in this volume. The experiences of these countries are supplemented by an account of economic transformation in China, which also moved away from planned socialism in the 1980s; here, too, socialism persisted without central planning.

The first issue that arises in a consideration of the economic transition from socialism is the effectiveness of government policies in indirectly

---

[1] It is useful to distinguish between *ex ante* redistribution, which occurs when a government protects an industry or gives it preferential treatment, and *ex post* redistribution through taxes and subsidies, where the sole objective is to equalize outcomes (for example, making all enterprise profit rates more or less uniform). *Ex ante* redistribution gives rise to the usual rent-seeking behavior; *ex post* redistribution stunts incentives as outcomes become independent of actions. Socialist economies were characterized by both types of redistribution; *ex post* redistribution was particularly pernicious.

regulating economic activity. Stabilization and other macroeconomic policies are required to replace the central allocation and distributive mechanisms of the centrally planned economic system. In Chapter 1, Hinds demonstrates that when decentralized socialist enterprises are left to manage themselves, either the effectiveness of government stabilization policies is seriously compromised or policies are rendered ineffective. The self-managed socialist economy is, as both experience and the supporting logic of theoretical analysis demonstrate, intrinsically susceptible to macroeconomic instability—an instability that cannot be contained by policies effective in a private ownership market economy. This is because traditional instruments of macroeconomic policy are not effective in nonprivate ownership settings. A more restrictive monetary policy in a capitalist environment leads to higher interest rates, increased bankruptcies, higher unemployment and the redeployment of labor and capital toward more efficient sectors and enterprises. It stimulates what Schumpeter called "creative destruction." In a socialist setting, higher interest rates lead to distress borrowing, interenterprise financing, decapitalization of assets, and no bankruptcies or firing of workers. The structure of production remains more or less unchanged, as it is expected that the government will honor its implicit obligation to bail out nonviable enterprises. Moreover, the greater is the magnitude of the problem (that is, the more enterprises are threatened), the greater is the perceived likelihood that all endangered enterprises will ultimately be rescued, because a major collapse of industry would be politically unsustainable.

This is but one example of how in the absence of privatization classical macroeconomic instruments can be blunted, or their effects become perverse. Hinds presents a policy sequence that he proposes should be adhered to in the transition to capitalism. Since macroeconomic instruments developed for a private economy cannot be effective in an economy dominated by socialist enterprises, early and fast privatization is essential. Privatization thus becomes a key not only to the incentives and efficiency associated with private ownership, but also to the effectiveness of policies directed at achieving macroeconomic stability.

Another crucial issue is the manner in which privatization will be accomplished. What are the options and possibilities? How have economies emerging from socialism met the challenge of reassigning private property rights? These issues are addressed in Chapter 2 by Milanovic. He reviews the developments that transformed firms from socialist enterprises—small cogs with precisely defined duties and rights in a centrally planned economy—to independent enterprises where workers and managers vie for power under the often meddling eyes of local bureaucracies. The failure of the decentralized socialist experiments underscores the need for unambiguous private property rights with no further experimentation. Milanovic evaluates the merits and disadvantages of different privatization procedures. No single approach dominates all others. Each procedure requires trade-offs. If widely spread ownership is sought, free distribution of shares is the best approach.

Dispersed ownership, however, all but severs the essential monitoring link between owners and managers that underlies incentives for efficiency. Managers would remain uncontrolled and unresponsive to the possibly millions of small shareholders. If state revenues are to be maximized, sale by auction appears the best approach. This approach, however, could lead to concentration of ownership, perhaps in the hands of foreigners or those who enriched themselves in the previous system. Milanovic examines these trade-offs against the background of experiences in Hungary, Poland, Yugoslavia, and Czechoslovakia.

In privatization issues, politics and economics interact. One approach to privatization is the employee ownership model. Transferable private property rights are initially assigned to workers; enterprises, however, can subsequently evolve into more common private firms owned by external investors. Bogetić, in Chapter 3, investigates the case for privatization by employee ownership as a means of diffusing initial political opposition to private ownership. He reviews the experiences of worker ownership in developed market economies and asks if this ownership system is appropriate for socialist economies in transition.

Chen, Jefferson, and Singh ask in Chapter 4 if China's economic reforms can provide lessons for East European countries. As a consequence of decentralization in the 1980s, incomes rose substantially in China. Yet China's experiences are idiosyncratic in a number of respects—China's great size, for example, mandated administrative decentralization. In addition, Hong Kong and Taiwan (China) acted as ancillary agents, providing direct foreign investment and experience with international marketing. In contrast to recent experience in Eastern Europe, political liberalization in China did not accompany economic decentralization. Many enabling aspects of economic liberalization in China occurred not as the result of concerted policies, but were legitimized, in an *ex post* fashion, in reaction to diverse decentralized initiatives.

A more pertinent laboratory for evaluating the performance of decentralized socialism is the self-management system of Yugoslavia. Workers in Yugoslavia managed social capital on behalf of society without either central planning or private ownership. (As a noted French sociologist, Jacques Ellul, put it in 1954, this was "liberalism without capitalists, that is anarchy.") Although workers did not have ownership claims to the enterprises in which they worked, they were in principle residual claimants to the enterprises' profits. Insofar as workers had an interest in maximizing profits, at least in the short run, incentives should have been present for relatively efficient operation of the enterprises. However, because profit appropriation was contingent on continued employment in the enterprise, incentives for investment and profit maximization over time were severely distorted. Yugoslav market socialism was consequently not a success story.

Chapter 5 by Saldanha and Chapter 6 by Vodopivec present perspectives on the Yugoslav failure. Chapter 5 describes how the self-management system in its pure theoretical form leads to misallocated capital and labor, overly capital-intensive and highly leveraged investments, unduly risky projects, and, as emphasized in Chapter 1, macroeconomic instability. The state interference that then appears is not only the adjunct of the socialist environment, but is inevitable given the nature of the economic system. Saldanha proposes that were the world inhabited by the best and most self-denying bureaucrats, they would still have to intervene in the operation of Yugoslav-type enterprises, because of the inappropriate incentives.

Chapter 6 takes a different view of the Yugoslav failure. Vodopivec proposes that self-management was a veneer behind which the political bureaucracy engaged in massive redistribution in order to preserve its power through patronage. The chapter focuses on this redistributional aspect of the Yugoslav system and empirically documents the means and extent of redistribution among a sample of enterprises. Redistribution is explained from a public choice perspective that includes the activities and motives of political as well as economic agents.

The Yugoslav experience provides pertinent lessons for countries on the path of transformation from socialism to a market economy. The persistence of social capital in a decentralized market economy implanted distortions that called forth large-scale government intervention, which in turn negated the concept of a decentralized market economy. The explanations offered by Saldanha and Vodopivec thus have complementary elements.

Did the market socialism of post-1968 Hungary fare better than the Yugoslav variant? In Hungary, the overt unemployment and price instability of Yugoslavia were avoided. Factor markets that might facilitate allocative efficiency were, however, also absent from the Hungarian version. Although the central planner had been formally dismissed, substantial administrative regulation of the socialist enterprises persisted, again imposing the heavy hand of government on the economy. "Socialist" markets had few of the efficiency characteristics of markets in a capitalist economy. Chapter 7, by Hillman, provides an account of the Hungarian experience, and describes the domestic restructuring needs that were present when market socialism and the political monopoly of the Communist party came to an end. He describes the responses of large enterprises to the twin shocks of domestic economic transformation and change in the manner and terms of conducting international trade.

Gelb, Jorgensen, and Singh, in Chapter 8, study the adjustment of a small sample of Polish enterprises to the radical Polish liberalization and macroeconomic stabilization package known as the "Big Bang." Poland had been dismantling central planning during the 1980s. As decentralization progressed and enterprises became more independent (often run by workers' councils), problems similar to those of Yugoslavia appeared, including hyperinflation. The Big Bang captured worldwide attention as the first attempt by a country to achieve macroeconomic stabilization while at the same time ushering in a new liberal economic system. Gelb, Jorgensen, and Singh recount how the Big Bang affected the economic environment in which Polish enterprises functioned. Although domestic and often foreign demand had declined dramatically, the enterprises in the sample generally fared well in the aftermath of the Big Bang. This was largely because past hyperinflation had eroded their liabilities. Yet, still under the socialist spell, these enterprises trusted that the government would rescue them should their economic condition further deteriorate. There was little evidence of the restructuring through relocation of labor that in a Western market economy would result from the same magnitude of demand shock. The system exhibited remarkable stability, or, from another perspective, remarkable rigidity.

The conclusion that emerges from the discussion, analysis, and evidence presented in Part I of this volume is that the elimination of central planning is only an initial, incomplete step. For the transformation to be effected swiftly and with minimal meandering, the key institution of a market economy, pervasive private property, must be established. Only then can markets be operative and government policy addressing macroeconomic instability be effective. Without privatization, without the incentives of the capitalist market economy, economic agents will fail to replicate the behavior of real market participants.

International trade

The end of socialism in Eastern Europe was also accompanied by an end to the socialist system of conducting international trade. Socialist international trade had been regulated through the mechanisms of the Council for Mutual Economic Assistance (CMEA) The institutional framework of the CMEA system of trade and payments, which is described in Chapter 9 by Schrenk, provides the point of departure for change, and demonstrates the extent to which change is necessary if international transactions are to be consistent with a restructured market economy based on private property rights. Schrenk shows how the CMEA system was the logical adjunct for the international transactions of a centrally planned economy. The system was based on government-to-government negotiations regarding the content of trade and prices. The actual conduct of trade was undertaken by state monopolies. The trading mechanism was bilateral, with the U.S.S.R. having a dominant role in sequenced strategic trade negotiations. No recourse was available for multilateral balancing of deficits and surpluses among CMEA participants, nor was there a formal mechanism that facilitated or compensated for bilateral trade imbalances. This was highly regulated, planned-in-advance international trade that assured foreign sales and at the same time protected enterprises by eliminating the possibility of unplanned, disruptive competitive imports.

The extreme protectionism of the system perpetuated a technology gap that is reflected in the distinction between "hard" and "soft" goods. This distinction, made frequently in this volume, is neither discrete nor absolute; rather, it applies to a continuum of quality differentials. The hard/soft distinction reflects the inferior quality of goods produced in CMEA economies (and traded between them), relative to close substitutes produced and internationally traded in the West. CMEA manufactured goods were for the most part soft goods, that is, goods that could only be exchanged within the planning framework of CMEA and which, because of quality deficiencies, were practically nontradeable for hard currency. The production of soft goods was perpetuated by the highly conservative CMEA system, where the quality standards of yesterday's deliveries set the precedent for those of today, with little or no specification for quality improvement attached to the physical units in which traded quantities were defined. The persistence of soft goods reflected the technological inferiority of socialist enterprises.

Chapter 10, by Hillman and Schnytzer, spells out the implications of the CMEA system of international trade for socialist comparative advantage and domestic enterprise incentives. Comparative advantage was reflected broadly in a pattern of trade in which the U.S.S.R. provided hard goods—oil, natural gas, raw materials—in exchange for soft manufactured goods, at terms of trade favorable to Eastern Europe. The soft/hard goods exchange reinforced the dependence of East European economies on Soviet trade. From the enterprise perspective, however, the system was beneficial, because soft good sales were assured and domestic markets were protected from competition of higher-quality imports—or indeed from import competition of any sort. This was also the case under Hungarian market socialism, for after abolishing central planning, Hungary remained entrenched in the planned socialist CMEA system of international trade.

The attraction of the CMEA system to the socialist enterprises of Eastern Europe is illustrated by Terrell's case study in Chapter 11. In the 1970s the Polish government, cognizant of the technology gap and its implications, embarked on a concerted program of importing Western capital equipment embodying up-to-date technology. This attempt to bridge the technology gap failed. The empirical evidence presented by Terrell reveals that imported Western capital was not efficiently utilized; Polish enterprises preferred to maintain the status quo of a pattern of production that made use of CMEA-specific capital equipment. Enterprises were comfortably ensconced in the CMEA system, and incentives were such that there was no reason for change, notwithstanding the availability of more technologically sophisticated imported Western capital.

The incentives for enterprises to maintain their CMEA orientation were in direct contrast with the need for adjustment and restructuring evoked by the end of the CMEA system. With the demise of CMEA in 1991, not only did the prior assured soft good export demand disappear, but there were additional significant changes. Trade with the hard good supplier, the U.S.S.R. (or the republics thereof), was to be conducted in hard currency rather than under the conditions of the prior clearing system, and also the East European economies' terms of trade would substantially deteriorate as a consequence of a switch to world prices for oil and natural gas. The costs imposed by trade-related aspects of transition therefore compounded the problems of domestic restructuring.

The end of the CMEA system of trade had far-reaching consequences that extended to the government budget. Associated with the CMEA system was a price equalization scheme that arbitraged the prices of internationally traded goods through a system of implicit and explicit taxes and subsidies. The end of the CMEA meant the end of these taxes and subsidies. Chapter 12 illustrates the impact of this change in Hungary. Abel, Hillman, and Tarr ask the counterfactual question: what would the effect on the government budget have been, had the end of the CMEA and the elimination of the associated trade taxes and subsidies occurred one year earlier? The result would have been a substantial decrease in government revenue that would have increased the magnitude of the budgetary deficit by a multifold factor. The broader point is the illustration that departure from the CMEA system can have a substantive budgetary impact that calls for offsetting fiscal policies in the former CMEA economies.

With the demise of the CMEA, issues arose concerning the adaptation of East European countries' international trade and payments mechanisms. Chapters 13 and 14 set out proposals and suggest options for post-CMEA trade and payments arrangements. Proposals by Michalopoulos and Tarr in Chapter 13 are directed at three issues: (a) identifying interim arrangements to facilitate international trade in the post-CMEA regime; (b) confronting the need for hard currency payment for imports at a time when a substantial terms of trade loss has been incurred because of the switch from CMEA to international prices; and (c) specifying the nature of interim international payments arrangements, given that full convertibility will not have been achieved.

With respect to specification of a post-CMEA trade regime, the authors recommend that enterprises conduct their international transactions without attendant state obligations, that enterprises alone bear the risks of doing international business, and that all transactions take place in hard currency. With respect to payments mechanisms and the problem of payments imbalance, the advantages and disadvantages of regional clearing arrangements, with and without the enhanced credit arrangements of a payments union, and with and without the participation of successor states of the U.S.S.R., are considered. Because of the less than full convertibility of currencies, it is proposed that there would be benefits from clearing arrangements with short settlement periods: short-term liquidity constraints that could inhibit trade would thereby be circumvented. More generally, however, clearing and payments arrangements that tie former CMEA economies to each other by discriminating in the ease with which these economies can transact among themselves rather than with others, are judged to be undesirable. It is held that the former CMEA economies should be outward looking, focusing on participation in the international trading system, rather than on prior CMEA trading partners. Regional arrangements imply allocations of externally provided credit in ways that are not necessarily efficient, because credit assists in financing intraregional balances rather than overall trade imbalance. A further reservation is that formalized regional clearing arrangements could become mechanisms for regional protectionism.

Chapter 14, by Ethier, presents an alternative, more eclectic view of regional payments mechanisms. Ethier suggests that there may be substantial unrealized gains from trade among East European countries. In particular, he proposes that the possibility be entertained that a marginal diversion from East-West trade to restructured East-East trade could be beneficial because of the distorted and centralized manner in which CMEA trade was conducted. This view suggests that there is potential benefit from a maintained post-CMEA relationship among East European countries that is not overly encumbered by constraints of hard currency payments. The CMEA payments system could be replaced by either bilateralism achieved by default, by a multilateral settlements system, or through the addition of credit facilities by an East European Payments Union (EEPU). Under default bilateralism, no institutional arrangements replace the former CMEA system and bilateral arrangements evolve that ignore multilateral aspects of trade. Incentives arise for governments to negotiate bilateral trade agreements as under the CMEA system. Incentives to discriminate then arise as governments seek to limit exports to trading partners with whom they have a trade surplus, and to limit imports from trading partners with whom they have a trade deficit. A multilateral settlements system does not have such associated incentives to engage in trade discrimination, because of automatically canceling triangular balances. The addition of credit arrangements to the multilateral system establishes a payments union in which credits have an insurance function by pooling hard currency balances.

Chapters 13 and 14 both compare the case for an East European Payments Union with the circumstances of the European Payments Union of the early 1950s, and note the similarities of "dollar shortage" and gains from multilateralism. While Ethier acknowledges the case against an EEPU that is stressed by Michalopoulos and Tarr—namely that such arrangements might become a "cocoon" for the old system, and might attract outside credit that would be inefficiently allocated by discriminately fostering intraunion trade—he also observes that the case for an EEPU rests on the nature of the alternative, whether this is default bilateralism or a multilateral trading system. An EEPU dominates the former, but not necessarily the latter.

I. Domestic Restructuring

A. Economic Policies as Requisites for Systemic Change

1

Policy Effectiveness in Reforming Socialist Economies

Manuel Hinds

Socialist economies have traditionally suffered from grave inefficiencies in resource allocation. In recent years, the inefficiencies have been accompanied by macroeconomic instability. These problems have been attributed largely to the deficiencies of central planning. As a result, there is a perception that the problems confronting these economies can be solved by policies that introduce prices as the main mechanism to allocate resources and that impose conventional stabilization programs.

The solution, however, is not so simple because the main source of the problem is not central planning, but the absence of private ownership of the means of production. Without private ownership, factor markets essential to the functioning of market economies are absent. As a result, the socialist system creates an economic environment in which resources are misallocated and in which there is chronic excess demand, even after central planning is eliminated and prices are liberalized.

With these considerations as a basis, this chapter investigates policy effectiveness in reforming socialist (or former socialist) economies. The basic proposition is that massive privatization is a prerequisite for the introduction of market forces; if massive privatization is not included in the policies implemented, stabilization policies will be ineffective, unless the economy is prepared to tolerate a huge cost in terms of unemployment and output losses. Privatization is the core policy element of economic reform; without it, market mechanisms will not improve the allocation of resources, and stabilization of the economy is not feasible.

Quite frequently, a policy approach that is based on massive privatization is dismissed as impractical on the grounds that privatization is

13

too gradual a process. While true in many cases, this view should be strongly qualified. First, privatization can be carried out relatively quickly.[1] Second, while stabilization can be achieved in the short term without privatization, it is likely that instability will return if privatization is not carried out immediately thereafter.

There are substantial differences among the reforming countries of Eastern Europe and between them and other countries in the region. Thus, the following discussion of policy options is based on stylized facts common to most of them.

Self-management

The end of central planning in East European countries came either through its formal elimination or because central planners could no longer enforce their authority. In practice, these economies became decentralized in different degrees. The establishment of a decentralized economic system without private ownership of the means of production requires delinking the ownership of enterprises (by governments) from enterprise management. There are two principal varieties of decentralized enterprise: one managed primarily by workers' councils, called the self-managed system, and one managed by independent managers, or the public corporation type.

Self-management spread through those countries that spearheaded reforms in the 1980s. Initially established in Yugoslavia, it was adopted in conjunction with Hungarian market socialism and also in Poland as it began the transition from planned socialism. In this system, workers became the de facto masters of the enterprise. Although they did not own the enterprise de jure, it was expected that they would behave in the manner of owners in capitalist economies because formally they could increase their incomes only in proportion to the profits earned by the enterprise.[2]

Incentives in a self-managed enterprise are different, however, from those in private enterprises. In capitalist economies, investors are entitled to enjoy the returns to capital whether or not they work in the company. They can sell their entitlement, transforming their claims on real capital into cash, and they can bequest ownership to heirs. They know that capital formed with their investment, and its returns, will benefit them or their heirs.

Such an assurance, however, does not exist in the self-managed enterprise. Under that system, workers have access to the rents of capital through their power to decide on the allocation of the surplus of production. They do not, however, own the capital. This is an extremely important

---

[1]For a discussion of some of the mechanisms that could be used for this purpose, see Hinds (1990a, 1991) and Milanovic (this volume).

[2]See Milanovic (1989), Saldanha (this volume), and Hillman (this volume).

difference. Incumbent workers run a high risk of not being able to enjoy the benefits of today's proposed investments because they cannot cash in their claims to future benefits and they cannot transfer their entitlement to their heirs. Workers enjoy the benefits of investment only as long as they remain in the company, a condition that they can fail to meet as a result of death, enterprise restructuring, or other causes.

Thus, workers can immediately appropriate the rents of capital, but they cannot be assured of the ability to do so in the future. Given a choice between certain and uncertain earnings, the incentive is to increase current individual earnings at the expense of the enterprise's financial viability.

Governments have tried to prevent decapitalization of enterprises by imposing restrictions on the use of enterprise net income—by forcing the allocation of a certain percent of profits to investment and by imposing taxes on excessive wage increases. With time, however, these measures have proved largely ineffective. Workers learned that if they increase their salaries to excessive levels—so that the enterprise incurred losses—the government would bail them out and would ensure continuing resources to invest. This dependence, in addition to returning the power to allocate investment to government, creates inflationary pressures.

As a result of the linkage between wages and profits, wages tend to be positively related to the capital intensity of the enterprise, as more capital-intensive firms tend to have higher profits per worker. To avoid a source of inequality that would create political problems, governments intervene to equalize the rate of profit per worker in different enterprises, taxing the most profitable to subsidize less successful firms. This destroys the meaning of profits.[3]

Because of the disadvantages of workers' control, other countries acted in early 1990 to prevent the establishment of this system in their newly reforming economies.[4] They were unable, however, to prevent workers from obtaining effective power within enterprises because the independent managers (public corporation) system is inherently weak. When this system was tried in socialist economies in the past, it gave way to either central planning (as in the U.S.S.R. in the 1920s and mid-1960s) or self-management (as in Poland and Hungary in the 1980s).

The weakness of the independent managers system derives from the isolation of the manager who represents an absent and silent owner. Under a system where the owner (the government) has agreed not to intervene in the management of an enterprise, managers confront powerful forces (labor) that fill the void left by the absent owner. Rather than combatting these

---

[3]See the evidence presented by Vodopivec (this volume).

[4]For example, the Soviet Union reestablished the role of the government in appointing and firing managers (1990 Law on Enterprises), after having given those rights to workers in 1987. In other countries, proposals to give power in the enterprises to workers were not formally adopted.

forces, managers accommodate them, fearing the political consequences of worker discontent. Labor conflict or strikes are indicative of management failure and lead to Communist party intervention.

Furthermore, in the absence of owners, managers begin to identify their interests with those of the workers. Like their subordinates, they are salary earners and they benefit from increasing salaries to the point of enterprise insolvency, trusting an eventual state bail out. Managers become political beings who survive by appeasing others while furthering their own ambitions. Workers are appeased by raising wages, politicians by increased hiring, and managers benefit from expansion, regardless of the profitability of capital invested. The tendency to accommodate workers' demands leads, for the purposes of macroeconomic stabilization, to equivalence between the system of independent managers and the self-management system.

Thus, in these two varieties of decentralized socialism there is no advocate for capital in the enterprise; problems with both the allocation of resources and for stabilization result. Solutions designed to address these problems—such as having the government decide on the allocation of resources, and equalizing profits per worker across enterprises—destroy the ability of the market to allocate resources.

Macroeconomic instability

Monetary creation in Eastern Europe was excessive while strict price controls were in place. As a result, the population accumulated large stocks of money that it could not spend. There is thus a stock of money, called the overhang, that would be used to bid prices upward if a liberalization of prices were to take place.[5] This would cause a strong macroeconomic imbalance. The following section reviews this problem.

Inflationary flows

In a monetary economy, the symptoms of macroeconomic imbalance are inflation and current account deficits. These are means of financing excess nominal domestic demand caused by a deficit somewhere in the economy. In order to be sustainable, stabilization policies should include both a reduction of the proximate cause of the imbalances—monetary creation—as well as the establishment of measures aimed at eliminating their ultimate cause—the deficit of real resources. If the need for those resources is not eliminated, tendencies for inflation or balance of payments problems arise. In conventional stabilization packages, this is achieved by balancing the

---

[5]Not all countries have had an overhang. The classical example of a country with a large overhang was the U.S.S.R. Yugoslavia never had one and Poland eliminated its overhang through hyperinflation.

budget. If any deficit remains after the budget is balanced, stabilization requires that it be financed without recourse to monetary creation.

In Eastern Europe, deficits leading to macroeconomic instability are rooted in the current and cumulative effects of price and institutional distortions that have prevailed for decades. During this period, pervasive price controls have aimed at reducing the prices of essential goods and services regardless of production costs. These distortions have had two main effects. In the short run, markets do not tend to clear because the low official prices encourage consumption while discouraging production. To solve this problem, governments have resorted to widespread subsidization, compensating producers for losses incurred from selling at official prices.

Fiscal deficits caused by these subsidies became the proximate cause of macroeconomic instability. Reducing subsidies brings about heavy losses in enterprises—at any price level—because of the long-term effect of price distortions. The prolonged artificial separation between prices and costs broke the link between installed capacity and consumer preference. For decades, investment decisions were based on the preferences of planners or enterprise managers rather than consumers. As a result, the structure of supply corresponds neither to comparative advantage nor to the structure of demand.

Thus, when the government cuts subsidies and liberalizes prices, enterprises incur losses. Governments that have faced this problem—Yugoslavia, Hungary, and Poland—have chosen not to send lossmakers into bankruptcy because of the enormous social problems that widespread bankruptcy would cause. At the same time, they decided not to subsidize the enterprises explicitly. Rather, they allowed them to survive by lending money through the financial system, and printing money (or borrowing abroad) to allow the financial system to absorb the consequent losses. Through this mechanism, the deficit was shifted from the central government to the financial system. For stability purposes, however, the location of the deficit is not important. What matters is validation of the deficit by printing of money.

As a result of these events, accounts that should be balanced are not only those of the fiscal budget, but, very importantly, those of the enterprise sector and, because it absorbs a substantial portion of enterprise losses, the banking system. The magnitude of these losses is significant. In Poland, Hungary and Yugoslavia, losses incurred by the central bank alone amounted to more than 30 percent of gross domestic product (GDP). These losses were gradually monetized, leading to hyperinflation in Poland and Yugoslavia and inflation in Hungary.

Losses in the banking system are just the reflection of losses in enterprises. Banks absorbed these losses in three ways. First, they absorbed losses caused by real devaluations of enterprises' external debts; banks in Eastern Europe have done this both *ex ante* (assuming the foreign exchange risk at the moment of borrowing) and *ex post* (picking up the tab after their customers failed to service their external obligations). Second, the banking system also provided subsidies to enterprises in the form of loans at highly negative real interest rates. Third, banks took large losses in uncollectible loans. Central banks financed the absorption of all these losses through monetary creation.[6]

Relative prices and the overhang

Monetary overhang complicates stabilization. Because of the overhang, governments may fail to achieve macroeconomic balance by simply stopping monetary creation. Monetary expenditures would remain excessive as a result of the unloading of the overhang. Prices would continue to increase until real cash balances held by the population declined to an equilibrium level.[7]

Thus, it would appear that removing the overhang is essential to avoiding a burst of hyperinflation in these countries. This is not quite true, however. Removing the overhang may not preclude the outburst of inflation. In fact, as I shall argue below, removing the overhang would in many cases be uneconomical because the liquidity absorbed in its removal would shortly have to be reinjected into the economy. This is so because of the need to adjust relative prices.

Sustainable stabilization programs should include shifts in relative prices to elicit a movement of resources toward those activities that would lead to economic recovery, as well as to eliminate the inflationary pressures created by price controls. In most market economies, the needed shift in relative prices is only a real devaluation because the most significant price distortion is that of tradables relative to nontradables. In socialist economies, however, price distortions are more pronounced and widespread. Sustainable economic recovery requires both devaluation and substantial price liberalization.

The need to redress relative prices in reforming socialist economies complicates stabilization. To shift relative prices, some prices have to rise while others have to fall. If this is done at a constant average price level, the prices of goods and services that are relatively overvalued will have to fall in nominal terms. It is widely recognized that prices tend to be sticky downwards. As a result, there is an asymmetry: while understated prices rise immediately, overstated prices take a long time to fall. In the meantime, the

---

[6]The first two forms of transmission of losses to the banking system—absorption of the foreign exchange risk and subsidized credit—allowed loss-making enterprises to survive, and even to appear profitable. When estimating the total extent of enterprise losses, the banking system's losses on these accounts should be added to those of the enterprises. The banking system's loan portfolio losses, however, appear in both the enterprises and the banking system. They should be counted only once when estimating total losses.

[7]Another source of pressure on the price level would be the introduction of check payments that would likely accompany the establishment and strengthening of the banking system. The introduction of check payments will undoubtedly increase the banking system multiplier, thereby increasing the supply of money even if the creation of reserve money is stopped.

markets would not clear efficiently. Pressure for excessively high prices to fall would be exerted through a fall in demand. A depression would result, with high rates of unemployment. The magnitude of depression and unemployment would depend on the original degree of distortion in relative prices and the inflexibility of the economy. On both counts, socialist economies rank high.

It seems, therefore, that an increase in the official price level is unavoidable. If distortions in the economy are moderate, no compensation in the wage level would be needed to compensate for the jump in price levels. In this case, it would be feasible to control the process and avoid excessive inflation. If distortions in relative prices are extreme, however, wages would have to be increased and high rates of inflation could be unavoidable. Furthermore, an effort to avoid these effects could in itself be quite damaging to the economy. In such cases, it would be best to allow a burst of inflation, and, once the configuration of relative prices becomes more reasonable, to take measures to stabilize prices.

Moderate cases of relative price distortions

In cases where relative price distortions are moderate, the main problem is that the nominal value of the supply of goods and services is too low relative to nominal money incomes (mainly wages). The problem could be solved merely by allowing prices to jump ahead of wages. If governments were committed to limiting monetary creation, the main inflationary risk would be posed by the overhang, which would have to be removed. Part of the overhang would be eliminated by price increases. The rest could be managed by extracting the excess nominal money balances in several ways. The best of these methods is a lump sum tax imposed through a confiscatory monetary reform. This can be done quickly. If coupled with control on the flows of new monetary creation, it can reduce inflationary expectations substantially, thus reducing the costs of adjustment.

Other ways of reducing excess nominal money balances could prove too difficult and too slow to implement. One such method is the selling of nonmonetary assets to the population and sterilizing the proceeds (that is, not spending or giving credit with the proceeds of the sale). These assets could be of a financial or nonfinancial nature. Selling financial assets to the population would be the faster of these two methods. It would be more expensive, however, for the government to sell financial than nonfinancial assets. This is so because the government has to pay interest on financial assets. On the other hand, selling houses, land, or enterprises would not entail a loss of revenue to the government because the government receives no net income from the ownership of these assets.[8] Selling the stock of

---

[8]The government receives mainly taxes from the users of those assets, which would still be collected.

housing would be cheaper, but would take a long time; the legal and technical problems of selling land and office buildings are as great as those associated with selling housing units. The problems of selling enterprises are even greater.

Another possibility would be to liberalize interest rates in order to equilibrate demand and supply of monetary assets. This strategy has risks, however, because interest rates cannot be relied upon to equilibrate the credit market in an atmosphere of pervasive distress borrowing. Credit would increase as much as deposits. Equilibrium could come only after considerable instability.

Extreme cases of relative price distortions

The relative prices of goods and services are so distorted in some East European countries that, in order to correct these distortions, some prices would have to increase ten or twenty times. Individual price increases influence the overall rate of inflation in inverse proportion to the price elasticity of demand. The most distorted prices are those of essential goods. If these goods become unaffordable, the process of reform would be politically infeasible.

An example combining a tradable and a nontradable good in Russia demonstrates this principle. The average monthly wage in 1990 was 250 rubles and the monthly rental for an apartment was approximately 10 rubles, which was also the price of a bottle of vodka. The cost of one month's rent is the same as the cost of a bottle of vodka—or about 4 percent of the average monthly wage. These relative prices are clearly unsustainable. Since the comparison involves two nontradables—work and rentals—and one tradable—vodka—it is not possible to use relative prices in other countries to estimate appropriate relative prices in Russia, were Russia to open its economy. The magnitude of the obvious distortion is so great, however, that even conservative estimates of the adjustments that would have to take place result in very large adjustments in the price level.

The price of an apartment in a Western city comparable to Moscow would be at least $400, or 80 bottles of vodka.[9] If these relative prices were applied to Russia, the price of an apartment in Moscow would be 800 rubles, or 320 percent of the average wage. Western financial institutions apply a simple standard to determine the ability of a potential borrower to pay a mortgage: the installment on a housing unit should not exceed 25 percent of a family's income. To reach an equilibrium similar to that of the

---

[9]This estimate allows for the small size and low quality of the apartments. The price, however, would be probably much higher if these apartments were the only ones available, as is the case in Russia. The high price charged in Russia for hotel rooms that would be quite cheap in the West shows how nontradables depend only on the local supply and demand. To be conservative, however, the calculation assumes that the prices of apartments would approximate those in a market where better dwellings are available.

West, the average wage would have to rise to 3,200 rubles, or 1,600 rubles for families with two earners.

The increase in wages would also increase the price of vodka, as well as that of all other goods bought with the remaining 75 percent of the wage earners' income. The price of apartments would continue to rise in a trial and error process that would eventually approach equilibrium in an asymptotic way, if two conditions were met. One is that all prices were free to move. The other is that monetary creation remains absolutely passive, in the sense that it cannot go ahead of the relative price adjustment. This second condition is difficult to realize. Most likely, the shift in the price level would turn into hyperinflation. Once relative prices were close to normal levels, a stabilization program would be required.

The alternative to hyperinflation would be to cause the price of vodka to fall to one-eightieth of its value while keeping the nominal wage constant. This process would take a long time unless the government were to revalue the ruble eighty times in nominal terms, so that imported vodka would force the domestic price down. This would mean that the production of vodka would cease in Russia, together with that of all tradable goods. For a short while the country would enjoy a consumer boom, supplied by foreign producers. Then, the country would go into a deep depression.

Several Western economists have proposed the use of international reserves to import tradables from abroad in order to equilibrate demand and supply while the economy is in the process of being stabilized. Such a program would unwittingly cause the results discussed above. In the process of importing tradables, the exchange rate would be overvalued, and local industries producing goods equivalent to those being imported would be wiped out, causing extremely high unemployment rates. With foreign exchange and borrowing possibilities exhausted, the country would go back to square one, but with a huge external debt. It would have depleted its international reserves and its creditworthiness by importing consumption goods. Instead of using foreign savings to finance investments needed for recovery, the country would have to use its own savings to service the debt.

Hyperinflation has tremendous social and economic costs. It would, however, adjust relative prices much faster than the alternative fall in nominal prices. This would at least establish a basis for recovery. Furthermore, the extent of distortions involved clearly suggests that a downward individual price adjustment in conditions of an overall stable price level would be unrealistic. In the end, the certainty of hyperinflation would still be present. The problem of adjusting relative prices thus cannot be solved without accepting at least a short period of hyperinflation.[10]

The attempt to control prices during a period of hyperinflation can only result in an aggravation of macroeconomic imbalances, prolonging the period of trial and error that eventually results in an equilibrium of relative prices. The best strategy to follow when the rates of inflation become high, therefore, is to free prices completely and avoid indexation. This can be done only if the period of high inflation is quite short (not exceeding, say, six months). After this period, a stabilization program should be imposed.

The costs in terms of unemployment would in any case be high. High rates of inflation would reduce layoffs relative to the opposite strategy, but it would not eliminate them. For this reason, a social safety net is needed.

It is clear, then, that when hyperinflation cannot be avoided, there is no point in seeking to remove the overhang; for shortly thereafter the government would have to reinject liquidity to finance the jump in nominal prices and wages needed to adjust relative prices.

Trade reform

Price reform requires an accompanying trade reform. The economies of Eastern Europe have been able to maintain distorted structures of relative prices through the extensive use of quantitative trade restrictions. In the absence of trade liberalization, free relative prices would settle at distorted levels because they would correspond to domestic demand and supply conditions that diverge from those of international markets. For example, with a monopolistic industrial sector, the price of industrial goods tends to increase relative to the price of agricultural goods, which experience greater competition in most socialist countries.[11] Falling profitability of agricultural goods would prompt a decline in supply during the next agricultural season, aggravating food supply problems. Actual or potential competition from abroad would provide guidelines for the domestic relative prices of tradable goods, thus avoiding these problems.

Initially, trade reform should consist of replacing quantitative restrictions with equivalent uniform tariffs that have an identical aggregate effect on the balance of payments. Subsequently, tariffs should be reduced according to a

---

[10]A real revaluation would most likely need to take place anyway; the inflation of nontradables has to exceed the rate of devaluation to make nontradables relatively more expensive (in Eastern Europe, the prices of nontradables tend to be too low relative to those of tradables). At the same time, however, the nominal price of foreign exchange has to be increased to attain equilibrium in the balance of payments.

[11]Damaging shifts of relative prices against agriculture have happened at least twice as a result of price liberalization programs in socialist economies. One instance is the "Scissors Crisis" of the early years of the New Economic Policy in the U.S.S.R. Also, during January–March 1990 agricultural prices in Poland stayed constant or fell, while industrial prices increased substantially.

preannounced schedule. This action would give enterprises time to adjust to the newly competitive environment and it would reduce pressure on the exchange rate (and therefore on domestic prices) relative to what would have been the case with more sudden liberalization.

There is another reason to liberalize trade early in the process of economic reform. It is well known that the structure of production in socialist countries is biased toward a heavy industry that produces capital and intermediate goods. Socialist industrial sectors use more capital and more material inputs to produce final goods than do developed market economies.

Soviet authors point to this feature of the Soviet economy to stress that the structure of production should be reoriented toward consumer goods. This is not necessarily a valid argument. If the country is opened to international trade, the extent of the adjustment needed could be substantially less than if the country remains closed because many enterprises would find enough external demand to keep them in operation. A significant number of enterprises that produce capital and intermediate goods should be able to transform themselves into efficient operations capable of exporting to international markets. The technical ability of engineers is not in question, nor is the level of education of the work force. Difficulties arise because of inadequate incentives and lack of access to state-of-the-art technology; these problems would be solved by privatization and price liberalization, and by trade liberalization, respectively. Rather than become producers of consumer goods, enterprises engaged in the production of capital and intermediate goods could concentrate their efforts on improving efficiency. If they are unable to become more efficient, then it is better that enterprises be closed. The enterprise as it exists, however, with its current technical cadres, location, work force, and so on, may not be suited to efficient alternative production. International trade would quicken this process of resource reallocation.

Trade liberalization has to be coordinated with the demise of the Council for Mutual Economic Assistance (CMEA). These actions will help bring relative prices closer to international levels. Trade liberalization by itself, however, does not eliminate the need for a jump in price levels, nor does it reduce inflationary pressures resulting from the price reform process. Currency devaluation to achieve external balance should be combined with price liberalization, thus reducing the number of necessary price level adjustments to one.

Options for stabilization

Even if excessive monetary stocks are reduced, the greatest problem—that of excessive expenditures—remains. The stabilization of an economy suffering from a deficit in the enterprise sector is conceptually equivalent to the stabilization of an economy with a deficit in the public sector. This is clearly understood. There seems to be confusion, however, between two approaches to reducing nominal domestic demand. One approach is to reduce domestic demand at the source, eliminating enterprise losses. The other approach is to establish a surplus in another sector of the economy—that is, the budget—that compensates for these losses.

These two solutions may appear identical, but only if one identifies the subsidies that the state provides to lossmakers, both directly and through the banking system, as the source of macroeconomic instability. This, however, is not the case. When a government raises taxes or reduces government expenditure in an effort to cover enterprise losses, the result is a misallocation of resources such as earlier plagued East European economies. It is the same misallocation as results in market economies when instability is combatted by crowding out the private sector from the financial system even though the deficit is in the government sector. This procedure is not sustainable in the long run.

Transferring current losses to the budget and balancing the budget can be used only as a temporary device to stabilize the economy while enterprise losses are being reduced. It can also be used as a device to mobilize public support for the drastic and painful measures needed to reduce enterprise losses. If people understand that they are paying higher taxes to keep loss-making enterprises in operation, they are likely to exert pressure on the government to stop these subsidies. A sustainable solution requires that such losses be eliminated.

How can a government reduce enterprise losses? Losses result from excessive financial costs, excessive cost of material inputs (including capital) or an excessive wage bill (which could be the result of excessive wages, overstaffing, or both). A fourth cause of losses is the consistent understatement of output prices relative to wages (that is, the use of subsidies). East European enterprises incur losses from all of these sources. They have excessive debts, suffer from serious inefficiencies that result in excessive material costs, and they are overstaffed. In the short term, however, a government has only a limited scope for action.

Losses arising from excessive debt cannot be reduced except by default. This would involve defaulting on external creditors, banks' depositors, or both. Governments have refused to do this. They sustain the operations of bankrupt banking systems and service external debt without obtaining the resources to do so from debtor enterprises. For stabilization purposes, the best a government can do is finance these expenditures in a noninflationary way.

Noninflationary financing requires that governments include the service of these debts in the fiscal budget and then balance the budget. To spread the impact on the budget over time, governments can issue bonds in local currency to recapitalize institutions that have incurred losses as a result of the servicing of external debt. In Poland, losses are concentrated in Bank Handlowy; in Hungary, in the central bank; in Yugoslavia, losses were spread among the central bank, commercial banks, and enterprises. The same solution can be applied to cover the portfolio losses of commercial banks. The monetary impact of this operation on the budget would be the service (payment of principal and interest) of these bonds. Governments should thus either raise taxes or reduce other expenditures in amounts equivalent to the service of these bonds.

Losses due to inefficient use of material inputs and excessive wage bills can be avoided. Governments should concentrate on reducing these losses. Increasing the overall efficiency of enterprises requires a deep structural reform: a substantial portion of socialized enterprises must be privatized and the efficiency of public sector enterprises must be improved. Although these reforms are essential in the medium term to provide sustainability to the process, the stabilization of inflation-prone economies cannot await completion of this process. The only course open to governments in the short run is to reduce the wage bill by reducing overstaffing, real wages, or both. Self-management presents serious obstacles to accomplishing this.

Decentralized socialism

Decentralized socialism presents two serious problems for the stabilization of the economy. Socialist enterprises lack incentive to react positively to the monetary mechanisms used to achieve macroeconomic stabilization. Socialist economies also lack mechanisms for avoiding the contractionary effects of reduced domestic demand on the country's production and employment.

Absence of stabilizing forces

The first problem relates to the feasibility of stabilization itself. It is very difficult for decentralized socialist enterprises to adjust efficiently to financial discipline. In the very short run, enterprises could adjust by reducing the size of their labor forces, reducing wages, or both. Both solutions when applied in a market economy result in a lower real wage in the short run. Workers who are dismissed seek jobs at a lower wage rate, thus lowering the economy's overall wages. In a decentralized socialist system, however, the availability of people offering their labor for lower wages does not affect the wage level in enterprises.

As a result, wage resistance is fierce in decentralized socialist enterprises. If enterprises were forced by macroeconomic instruments to reduce expenditures, workers would reduce investment or decapitalize their enterprises rather than reduce their own wages. If the government's stabilization program is not credible, workers will continue to increase their own wages in order to maintain or improve their purchasing power vis-à-vis the rest of the economy. If they are convinced that the government is serious, and their enterprise faces bankruptcy (or they may be fired), their best response is again to increase wages and extract as much as possible from the enterprise before they are dismissed. Because enterprises in Eastern

Europe tend to be grossly overstaffed, individual workers perceive the risk of being fired as high; this perception strengthens their incentive to decapitalize the firm.

Decentralized socialist enterprises are very rigid concerning the size of their labor force. Incumbent workers have an incentive to oppose the hiring of new staff because this would dilute profits and cause a fall in the income of all workers. They are also reluctant to fire redundant workers. Although some principles, such as the rights of seniority, could be used to fire some workers, there have been few examples of workers firing fellow workers on a large scale.

Also, enterprises can finance wage increases without credit from the banking system. Enterprises can lend to each other even if credit is not available from banks. This would increase the velocity of money, reducing the effect of contractionary monetary policies.

Why would cash-rich enterprises lend money to lossmakers? They do so because enterprises experience little competition. Monopolies and monopsonies abound. Enterprises cannot function without customers, and if their only customer fails, they will fail as well. Thus, it is in their interest to give credibility to financial paper issued by clearly insolvent companies. The more widespread is the practice, the more an externality effect against the central bank is created. When possibilities to trade on paper end, the central bank faces a situation in which continuing with contractionary credit will mean the bankruptcy of both profitable and loss-making enterprises because the former hold large amounts of financial paper issued by the latter. The central bank responds by opening the gates of monetary creation.

This is a stylized description of what has happened several times in Yugoslavia. Interenterprise credit has also been pervasive among state enterprises in Hungary and Poland.

The supply response

The second problem with stabilizing a decentralized socialist economy relates to the possibility of reactivating the economy after stabilization. In market economies the contractionary effects of reducing the rate of growth of nominal domestic demand are minimized by a shift in the allocation of resources from nontradables to tradables, elicited by a real devaluation. Larger exports and increased import substitution provide new markets that compensate for the reduction in domestic demand. For this to happen, however, factor markets are required. Because factor markets do not exist in socialist economies, this shift in resource allocation is hindered.

Decentralized socialism is not conducive to investment in the creation of new firms and activities because entrepreneurs cannot enjoy returns from capital. Further, because the remuneration of labor is higher in capital-intensive firms (which tend to be older firms), workers do not have incentive to move out of old firms to become partners in new ventures. Existing firms are in operation because they already existed when control was given to workers. Laid-off employees would not find new jobs.[12] This could raise the costs of adjustment to high levels in terms of output and unemployment. As a result, the government's motivation to stabilize the economy may falter.

The implications for a stabilization program

Under decentralized socialism there are formidable obstacles to reducing the wage bill through macroeconomic measures. These obstacles threaten the success of a stabilization program. Regaining control of socialist enterprises is a minimum requirement for a successful stabilization program. This control would help governments overcome obstacles even if they are unable to establish an ideal way of managing public enterprises. Regaining control, however, seems to be an elusive goal because there is no way short of massive privatization to avoid the principal-agent problems that endanger stabilization.

Sequencing

Because of the interdependence between stabilization and structural reform, reforms should be undertaken simultaneously with stabilization. This, however, is not possible; the time needed to complete the processes differ. Governments have two options. One is to attempt a conventional sequencing, first stabilizing the economy and then carrying out structural reforms; previous experience in East European economies, however, suggests that the probability of failure in this instance is high. The other option is to combine stabilization and structural reform and recognize that the economy will remain unstable for some time.

Optimal sequencing would allow for the maximum sustainable rate of economic growth during the transition period. This sequencing would minimize fiscal expenditures, leaving maximum resources available for efficient investment and production. The previous analysis suggests that to achieve these objectives, governments should maximize the speed at which they carry out both the reduction of losses through enterprise and bank restructurings, and the substitution of noninflationary for inflationary means of financing losses incurred but not realized.

The dynamics of fiscal expenditures

Fiscal expenditures are affected by at least three factors: first, the speed at which banks and enterprises are restructured; second, the way in which restructuring is carried out (that is, how the burden is allocated and how the

---

[12]This effect is magnified by the labor immobility caused by lack of housing markets. Unemployed people living in one city will not move to another city even if offered a good job because of the impossibility of securing new housing.

restructuring of banks and enterprises is sequenced); and third, the speed at which inflation is reduced.

The speed of restructuring and the fiscal expenditures

Fiscal expenditures during the transition period are affected by the speed of the restructuring process. Once losses already incurred have been transferred to the budget and financed in a noninflationary way, reductions in current enterprise losses allow governments to further reduce inflationary financing and to restructure the banking system, thus stabilizing the economy. The faster the elimination of losses, the lighter the fiscal expenditures needed to absorb them.

In the extreme case of an instantaneous elimination of lossmakers, fiscal expenditures would be minimized because fiscal resources would only be used to finance losses already incurred. Because restructuring increases unemployment, however, governments will confront social safety net requirements that substantially add to fiscal expenditures. The amount required, however, is less than the amount "saved" by reducing fiscal outlays through fast restructuring.

The trade-off between speed of restructuring and total fiscal expenditure is illustrated in Figure 1.1. The present value of total fiscal expenditure is shown on the vertical axis as the sum of the cost of financing losses already incurred, plus the burden of avoidable losses, plus the cost of the social safety net. The horizontal axis depicts the speed of the process. As the speed of the process increases, the cost of the social safety net increases, but at a rate slower than the rate of decrease of the burden of losses. Consequently, the faster is the restructuring, the higher is the unemployment, but the lower is the overall fiscal expenditure.

The manner and sequence in which restructuring is carried out

The manner in which restructuring is carried out also has an important effect on the magnitude of fiscal expenditure. If banks are owned by governments, then governments do not have recourse against shareholders. In the former Yugoslavia, on the other hand, banks have been owned by enterprises, and the law imposed unlimited liability on founding members in the event of bank insolvency. The law empowers the government to write off the bad assets of insolvent banks not only against the equity that the founding members invested in the banks, but also against the totality of the founding members' net assets. If the government wanted to reduce fiscal expenditure, it could take advantage of this legal provision.

Another aspect of restructuring that has an important effect on fiscal expenditure is the way in which bad loans to borrowers other than founding members are collected. In an environment of financial crisis, even debtors with full capacity to repay may refuse to service their debts, and collections from restructured enterprises may be lower than possible.

Figure 1.1 Speed of restructuring and fiscal expenditures

Present value of fiscal burden

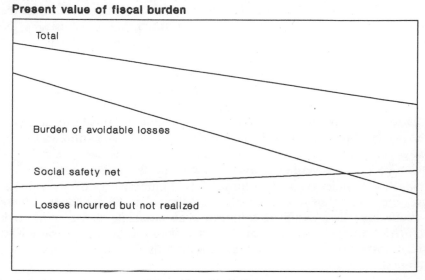

Total

Burden of avoidable losses

Social safety net

Losses incurred but not realized

Speed of restructurings

The sequence in which restructuring and liquidation of banks and enterprises is carried out also affects the magnitude of fiscal expenditure. The reduction in fiscal expenditure caused by restructuring comes primarily from the elimination of losses at the enterprise level. When banks and their debtor enterprises are restructured at the same time, the elimination of enterprise losses reduces fiscal expenditure while the simultaneous issuing of bonds to recapitalize banks finances the remaining losses in a different way. The net effect is a reduction in fiscal expenditure.

If, however, bank restructuring takes place before enterprise restructuring or liquidation, there will be no reduction in fiscal expenditure. Instead, the present value of fiscal expenditure would increase. Governments would issue bonds to recapitalize banks but would have to continue financing enterprise losses until restructuring occurred.[13] Governments would *both* have to service the bonds and subsidize the lossmakers. This would duplicate the flows coming from the government. The service of bonds would be used to finance new activities, while old activities would still be financed, thereby increasing inflationary pressures in the economy. If governments were unable to absorb the burden of the service of the bonds in a noninflationary way, the rate of inflation would increase.

The decision of whether to restructure banks at the same pace or more quickly than enterprises is an important one. Bank restructuring should

---

[13]The fiscal budget would be affected because lossmakers would continue making losses that would eventually be covered by the government.

precede enterprise restructuring *only* if the government is able to mobilize the resources needed to service the recapitalization bonds in a noninflationary way. Otherwise, the inflation rate would rise. If this were the case, it would be preferable to delay the restructuring of banks (and the economic recovery) until it can be synchronized with the elimination of losses resulting from enterprise restructuring.[14]

Inflation and fiscal expenditures

Inflation has both positive and negative effects on net fiscal expenditure.[15] The principal positive effect is the reduction of real expenditure caused by delays in paying government expenditure. The negative effect is the reduction in real government revenue caused by delays in tax collections as well as by subsidies transferred through fixed interest rate loans granted at low nominal interest rates. Reliable information on the net result of these two effects in East European countries is not available. Evidence in other countries, however, shows that inflation causes substantial government budget losses in real terms. A reduction in inflation improves the budget situation.

Some warnings are due in this respect. One is that several countries attempting stabilization have grossly overestimated such gains, among them Brazil and Argentina during the Cruzado and Austral Plans, respectively. Another warning is that only minor gains may result from reducing the subsidization of already granted loans because the real value of such loans will have declined by the time stabilization programs are under way. A third warning is that gains will result from reduced subsidies to loss-making enterprises only if these enterprises are either restructured or closed, so that their losses, and therefore their need for subsidies, disappear. If the government is not prepared to take those actions when an inflation reduction program is implemented, then subsidies will have to be conveyed in other ways.

Stabilization and structural reforms

The three-stage process

Governments should start by planning an increase in budget revenues over expenditures sufficient to compensate for enterprises losses. This would provide a fundamental reduction in nominal domestic demand. To minimize

---

[14]The creation of some private banks under proper regulation will help finance the emerging private sector. These new banks, however, will be totally different from those of the past system.

[15]These are revenues separate from revenues obtained by the government from the inflation tax, which is a way to finance fiscal expenditures.

the negative effects of the self-management system on the efficacy of a stabilization program, governments should try to regain as much control as possible over self-managed enterprises.

It should be stressed that heterodox measures can be useful if orthodox fiscal and monetary measures alone cannot remove the fundamental causes of inflation. If, however, governments are not prepared to implement fully the heterodox program, then heterodox measures will surely backfire. If sizable inflation is still fueled by monetary policies accommodating enterprise losses, then an effort to fix the nominal exchange rate would lead first to an inflow of speculative capital, and then to an unsustainable drain on international reserves. There would also be an explosion of inflation at the end of the fixed wage and price period.[16]

There are two further points. The first is that stabilization and structural reform should be seen as two aspects of the same problem; the sequencing of policies to achieve both has to be closely coordinated. In conventional stabilization programs, the government focuses its efforts on quickly stabilizing the economy. Structural reforms are viewed, at least initially, as a lesser priority. If this approach is consistently maintained, no reduction of losses will take place. The combined strategy, on the other hand, leads at least to incremental advances in the reduction of losses.

The second point is that policymakers should not expect that inflation will be reduced to zero or close to it. Rather than a short battle, they should expect a long war. This realization should also affect the sequencing of measures. For example, it would affect the timing of the use of heterodox measures. Heterodox measures are useful mainly as a way of changing expectations. They cannot be used continually because they lose credibility. If heterodox measures are used, they should be reserved for the final assault on inflation.

A stylized description of sequencing, with a three-stage economic program, is presented below. (A preparation stage, involving the privatization of a critical mass of enterprises is discussed in the next section.) In the first stage, stabilization relies on the fiscal adjustment the government is willing to undertake, combined with actions taken by government-appointed managers to reduce enterprises' wage bills. The government gives these managers targets for wage bill reductions. One segment of the enterprises would already be privately owned and the government would not have to deal with those enterprises other than through macroeconomic policy. In the second phase, the remaining enterprises are privatized and restructured by their new owners. In the third stage, the government executes a final inflation reduction program. The three stages are shown in Figure 1.2.

---

[16]This was the experience of Argentina and Brazil with their respective Austral and Cruzado plans; Poland and Yugoslavia were on the same path in 1990–91.

In the first stage (which would last approximately six months), the government would aim at a drastic reduction in the rate of inflation, based mainly on a budgetary adjustment and a restructuring of the most insolvent banks. The rate of inflation at the end of this stage would be much lower than the initial rate, but would still be quite high. In the longer second stage, the government would concentrate on further restructuring enterprises and banks while carrying out price reforms. This would not only reduce fiscal expenditure (and therefore the rate of inflation given a certain level of fiscal revenues) but would also prepare the way for economic recovery. In this stage the government would try to improve the effectiveness and efficiency of taxation. It is possible that inflation would still be excessive because of a budget deficit at the end of this second stage. The third stage would rectify this problem.

Figure 1.2 A possible three-stage path of adjustment

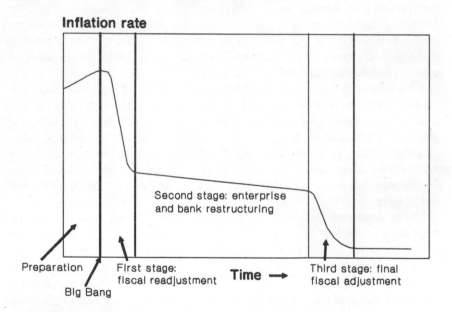

There are several advantages to this approach. First, inflationary financing would decline at approximately the same rate as the source of inflation is reduced. Second, mechanisms to force economic agents to react to restrictive monetary policies would gradually be put in place, improving the grasp of such policies through time. Third, flexibility in the allocation of resources would improve, facilitating economic recovery.

This approach, however, entails substantial risks. The first stage faces the same kind of risk as would the alternative approach of pursuing stabilization before structural reform; during the first stage, moreover, the risk is aggravated by the fact that heterodox measures to break inflationary expectations cannot be used. With inflationary expectations running high, the only way to enforce the necessary contraction of nominal domestic demand would be to immediately bankrupt companies encountering liquidity problems as a result of credit contraction. This would give credibility to the program, introducing wage and price discipline, and interrupting the process of spontaneous privatization. Of course, pressure not to follow this policy could be overwhelming. Central banks could eventually be forced to print money to keep losing enterprises alive, thus nullifying the effects of the program.[17]

Another risk is that it may not be possible to carry out price and ownership reforms and enterprise restructuring in a highly inflationary environment. The probability that the government will lose the motivation and political support for this long process of stabilization is high.

The sequencing of structural reforms

At the simplest level, the challenge in Eastern Europe is to solve five problems. The first problem is that prices are currently distorted. The second problem is that enterprises do not react appropriately to prices because of the perverse incentives in the system. The third problem is that enterprises make economic losses causing widespread misallocation of resources; some losses are apparent, but many are hidden by the distorted price system. The fourth problem is that subsidization of lossmakers causes inflationary pressures. The fifth problem is the lack of a financial system capable of mobilizing and allocating resources efficiently.

One way to solve these problems is first to reform enterprises so that they can react to market mechanisms, and then to solve the remaining problems through market mechanisms. This approach has three components: facilitating the creation of new private enterprises, privatizing a majority of the now socialized enterprises, and devising a mechanism to manage the remaining public enterprises in a way that mimics private enterprise. Improved management of public enterprises would not eliminate the need for the privatization of a majority of enterprises; an efficient simulation of private entrepreneurship in the public sector requires a strong private sector.

Thus, for example, a restructuring and modernization of enterprises can be better accomplished by private entrepreneurs than by state agencies. Private entrepreneurs can enforce needed closures and layoffs with fewer political pressures than the government. Private entrepreneurs also have a stronger incentive to make the right decisions about the refurbishing of factories.

This approach suggests the following sequencing. First, after a period of preparation, it will be necessary to privatize rapidly a large portion of socialized enterprises, thus creating a critical mass of private enterprises that

---

[17]In the recent past, the only country to eliminate hyperinflation successfully without adopting heterodox measures was Bolivia.

can react appropriately to prices (see the preparation phase in Figures 1.2 and 1.3). This can be accomplished through any of the privatization methods that involve giving away enterprises.[18] Second, once privatization has been achieved, prices can be liberalized. This liberalization (known popularly as the "Big Bang") would include domestic price liberalization coupled with the substitution of tariffs for quantitative restrictions to trade. The tariffs would be reduced subsequently under a clearly defined schedule. Third, once most enterprises are privately owned and prices are free, financial discipline—the removal of subsidies and the enforcement of financial contracts—can be introduced. Financial discipline is thus imposed when an appropriate set of incentives is established at the enterprise level.

Figure 1.3 Sequencing of reforms and stabilization

			Financial discipline	Privatization of banks
Enterprises	Holdings created, downsizing	Giving away enterprises; creating new management system for socialized enterprises	Bankruptcies; restructurings	
Prices	Controlled		Liberalized	
Interest rate	Controlled		Controlled	Liberalized
Banks	State-owned		State-owned	Privatized
Budget	Surplus		Declining surplus	Balanced
Monetary policy	Restrictive		Nominal anchors	According to demand
	Preparation		◄———Big Bang	

Enterprise restructuring makes explicit the losses hidden in bank portfolios. After writing off bad loans, governments can recapitalize banks and then privatize them. To keep inflation at manageable levels while still subsidizing lossmakers (prior to a privatization of banks), governments

---

[18]For a discussion of how this can be achieved while solving the problem of enterprise control, see Hinds (1990b).

would have to run fiscal surpluses. If these surpluses fall short of enterprise losses, some inflation is unavoidable.

Paradoxically, in order to minimize the rate of inflation in these circumstances, moderately negative real rates of interest (at least in the preparation phase) are required.[19] Governments would be able to collect inflation taxes from depositors. If interest rates were positive in real terms, a higher inflation rate would be needed to collect the same real revenue from the inflation tax (in 1989 the introduction of positive real interest rates in Yugoslavia caused a large increase in the rate of inflation).

In the post-Big Bang period, interest rates would have to be increased to positive real levels. Control, however, should be maintained to avoid upward pressures on the interest rates by distressed borrowers. Access of distressed borrowers to credit should be curtailed through the regulation and supervision of banks, and not through interest rates, which are ineffective for this purpose. Later, when lossmakers have been eliminated through enterprise restructuring and bankruptcies, interest rates can be liberalized.

The economy would be under substantial inflationary pressure from the subsidization of losses during the preparation phase and from price liberalization after the Big Bang. To stabilize the economy, governments must combine the imposition of financial discipline with restrictive monetary policies.

According to this model, enterprises are first privatized and then restructured, while banks are first restructured and then privatized. This is because enterprises are the ultimate source of losses in the economy, and the bankruptcy of nonviable firms is necessary. However, banks have been passive recipients of losses; their bankruptcy would serve no purpose and would cause considerable harm.[20] Banks are needed, but not loss-making enterprises. If banks were privatized before restructuring, they would have to be nationalized again to be recapitalized, and then privatized a second time.

However, the private sector is required for enterprise restructuring. The question is, then, how can governments justify privatizing enterprises that are sure to fail immediately after privatization? Either entrepreneurs will refuse to buy these enterprises, or they will buy them in ignorance of their adverse condition, and could then sue the government. There are two answers to this question. First, privatization can be implemented by giving away enterprises. Second, private entrepreneurs can save enterprises that would otherwise fail.

---

[19]Interest rates, however, should be unified during the preparation phase, eliminating preferential credits.

[20]Depositors in these countries certainly cannot be blamed for not choosing their banks prudently. In most cases they did not have a choice. Forcing these banks to go under and creating others would serve no disciplinary purpose. Furthermore, if depositors lose money, it would undermine the public's confidence in the nascent banking system.

The experience of Poland and former Yugoslavia

Poland and Yugoslavia initiated stabilization programs on January 1, 1990. In both countries, inflation fell—in Yugoslavia to a rate of zero and in Poland to levels that, although high, were considerably lower than those of 1989. This experience appears to belie the arguments presented in this chapter; it has led to the argument that socialist economies can be stabilized by using market mechanisms proven in the West. This, however, is not the point. If the government is able to control monetary creation, then inflation must come down. The issue is how sustainable can stabilization be if its effects include a large fall in GDP and if there are no forces leading to economic recovery?

In the case of Poland, a national consensus allowed the government to enforce a wage freeze. The impact on the real wage is difficult to estimate; because excess demand for a number of products existed, the real wage was overstated before the program was instituted. Nevertheless, it is clear that the real wage fell. Nominal domestic demand declined to the extent of causing substantial trade surpluses.

There were other encouraging signs. The trade account improved not only as a result of declining imports but also because of increased exports. Some enterprises were able to compensate for part of the decline in domestic demand by selling abroad. Also, most enterprises reduced their inventories. Some enterprises sold equipment. These are normally signs of increased efficiency in the use of inputs.[21]

Some indicators, however, were not encouraging. Despite increased exports, industrial production fell 30 percent in the first quarter of 1990; production remained at that level with no sign of recovery. At the same time, the rigidities of the labor market were evident. After an initial lull, unemployment hardly rose, but then increased to approximately 6 percent of the labor force by October 1990. This figure was low for an economy in which output had fallen by 30 percent; it should be compared with unemployment in western Germany, which in April 1990 was 7.3 percent, raising concerns of economic overheating. Also, unemployment in Poland was concentrated in the trade and construction sectors. In the manufacturing sector, employment decreased much less. In industry, the needed reduction of the real payroll took place almost exclusively through reductions in the real wage. Labor did not exhibit mobility, remaining more or less where it was at the onset of the program.

The supply response would therefore have to come from increased production in the same firms engaged in the same activities. That is, the composition of production would have to return to what it was before the onset of the program. In an open market, this could happen only if today's

---

[21]For a detailed study of Polish enterprises' responses, see Gelb, Jorgensen, and Singh (this volume).

relative prices coincided with those prevailing before the reforms. This indeed is not the case, since relative prices have changed. Resource allocation, however, did not change: resources were still locked in inefficient activities.

Inefficient enterprises could not be easily identified for at least three reasons. First, some prices had not been liberalized, including energy prices. Second, monopoly pricing was pervasive, so excessive costs were passed onto buyers; this practice would not be possible with effective trade liberalization. Third, enterprise accounts were unreliable: lack of liquidity, which could be a sign of trouble, was not yet perceptible because enterprises whose debts had been wiped out by inflation were still able to raise cash by reducing inventories, maintaining arrears with other enterprises, exporting at a loss, and selling equipment. Enterprises were also borrowing from banks. According to the National Bank of Poland, in the period of January to May 1990, nominal bank credit to state enterprises grew 107 percent (or 32.6 percent in real terms).

This suggests that the reduction of inventories and the increase in exports may have represented not increased efficiency, but rather desperate bids to delay illiquidity. If this were true, then these enterprises would fail once their inventories and other sources of cash were depleted. The real adjustment would be still to come. The real test of the reform program would take place when inefficient enterprises reach illiquidity.

The government would have to carry out the structural reforms needed to elicit mobility of resources within the socialist sector and between it and the rest of the economy. These reforms include demonopolization, privatization, and a redefinition of the role of the state in economic activity.

In Yugoslavia, enterprises that were unable to pay their bills were supposed to be sent into bankruptcy and then automatically become candidates for privatization. Enterprises, however, delayed adjustment in an even more dramatic way than in Poland. The fall in production was much less than in Poland, or approximately 8 percent. Enterprises started to become illiquid faster in Yugoslavia than in Poland because the real value of their debts was not reduced (as real interest rates were positive for some time) and because wages were increased substantially after having been frozen by the government (salary increases in January 1990 averaged 24 percent).

In order to stay current with their bank loans, while at the same time avoiding layoffs, many enterprises simply stopped paying salaries. By April 1990, about 1.6 million workers were not being paid. The government was finding it difficult to handle the number of enterprises that had become illiquid and that were supposed to be sent into bankruptcy. The monetary program was relaxed in May 1990 to help enterprises survive. Between June and September, enterprises raised salaries again, this time by 40 percent. This increased losses in enterprises, which, in the first six months of the year, had been equivalent to 12 percent of GDP on an annual basis.

The experiences of the stabilization programs in both Poland and Yugoslavia do not necessarily mean that stabilization programs in any socialist country in transition will fail. Programs will almost certainly fail, however, if needed structural reforms—including privatization—are not undertaken. In fact, the reduction of inflation that took place in Poland and Yugoslavia during 1990 may have occurred during what was described above as the period of still high but manageable inflation. The respite that lower inflation provided should have been used to place the economy on a sustainable growth path.

In summary, under the pressures of stabilization programs, labor-managed enterprises went to extremes (falling in arrears with the banking system and with each other, selling needed assets, and giving license without payment to their employees) to avoid laying off workers. With these measures, enterprises avoided the permanent adjustments needed to improve production, expecting the government eventually to bail them out. As a result, adjustment programs failed to achieve necessary gains in efficiency. In the long run, the striving of labor-managed enterprises to maximize wages at the expense of capital will continue to result in inefficient investment and inflationary pressures.

Even in Poland and Yugoslavia, programs could have succeeded if governments had been tough enough to resist countervailing pressures. The costs of resistance, however, are high for two reasons. First, in the absence of an effective social security system, large-scale unemployment would cause pain to a substantial portion of the population. Second, without a strong private sector, a supply response will not be evoked. The experiences of Poland and Yugoslavia suggest that the reform process should center on privatization and private sector development.

References

Gelb, Alan, Erika Jorgensen, and Inderjit Singh. 1992. "Life after the Polish Big Bang: Episodes of Preprivatization Enterprise Behavior." This volume.

Hillman, Arye L. 1992. "Enterprise Restructuring in the Transition from Hungarian Market Socialism." This volume.

Hinds, Manuel. 1990a. "Issues in the Introduction of Market Forces in Eastern European Socialist Economies." Europe, Middle East and North Africa (EMENA) Discussion Paper. World Bank, Washington, D.C. Processed.

——. 1990b. "Privatization of Agro-Industrial Enterprises." In Polish-European Community-World Bank Task Force, *An Agricultural Strategy for Poland*. Report of the Polish-European Community-World Bank Task Force. World Bank, Washington, D.C. Processed.

———. 1991. "Markets and Ownership in Socialist Countries in Transition."
    In Arye L. Hillman, ed., *Markets and Politicians: Politicized Economic
    Choice*. Boston and Dordrecht: Kluwer Academic Publishers.
Milanovic, Branko. 1989. *Liberalization and Entrepreneurship: Dynamics of
    Reform in Socialism and Capitalism*. Armonk, N.Y.: M. E. Sharpe.
———. 1992. "Privatization Options and Procedures." This volume.
Saldanha, Fernando. 1992. "Self-Management: Theory and Yugoslav
    Practice." This volume.
Vodopivec, Milan. 1992. "State Paternalism and the Yugoslav Failure."
    This volume.

2

Privatization Options and Procedures

Branko Milanovic

The study of economic liberalization and privatization in formerly socialist or centrally planned economies lacks a conceptual framework within which to locate and assess alternative ways of transforming the state sector. The first section of this paper outlines such a framework. The second section uses this framework to show how present-day socialist economies differ from Western market economies. The next two sections discuss the origins of reforms and present stylized facts of privatization. They are followed by a discussion of the merits and disadvantages of different privatization options. The paper ends with a description of privatization efforts in Hungary, Poland, former Yugoslavia, and Czechoslovakia.

Modes of production

At its most abstract level, all economic activity can be regarded as an interaction of the three factors of production: labor, capital and entrepreneurship. A focus on quantities of inputs and outputs provides an idea of the physical characteristics of the process; when we look at quantities and prices, we obtain a picture of the profitability or efficiency of the process. If we focus on (a) ownership of capital (that is, whether capital is owned by the state or private individuals), and (b) agent(s) who make decisions about how much capital and labor to use, what to produce, where to market, and so on (that is, who fulfills the entrepreneurial or managerial role), we obtain Table 2.1.

An earlier version of this paper was published as Milanovic (1991). I am grateful to the publisher (Centre for Research into Communist Economies, London) for permission to reprint parts of the paper.

Table 2.1 Combination of different modes of production

	Labor	
Capital	*(1)* *Entrepreneurial role*	*(2)* *Hired out*
Privately owned (1) Entrepreneurial role	Cooperative 1 (self-employed)	Capitalist
(2) Hired out	Cooperative 2	Entrepreneurial
State-owned (3) Entrepreneurial role	n.a.	State socialist (centrally planned)
(4) Hired out	Labor-managed	Public corporation

n.a. = not applicable.

Each cell in the table denotes a particular combination of ownership of capital and entrepreneurship. We shall first consider the upper part of the table, which includes all ideal cases (in a Weberian sense) of private ownership of capital. Cell (1,2) represents the capitalist mode of production:[1] capital is privately owned, labor is hired out, and the entrepreneurial role is reserved for the owners of capital.[2] In cell (1,1) we have a mode of production where the laborer owns the capital he uses in production and makes all entrepreneurial decisions. This is the situation of small-scale proprietorships particularly common in the early phases of economic development. If instead of one individual owner we have a group of worker-owners, we can talk of a partnership or cooperative. We can refer to this a mode of production as Cooperative 1. The mode of production in cell (2,1) differs from that of Cooperative 1 only in so far as capital is owned by outside investors. Workers who borrow the capital make all entrepreneurial decisions. We call such an arrangement Cooperative 2.[3] Finally, in cell (2,2) we have the neoclassical entrepreneurial firm wherein the entrepreneur hires both capital and labor.

---

[1]We refer to each particular combination of ownership and entrepreneurship as a mode (or type) of production.

[2]To the extent that managers have an entrepreneurial role, entrepreneurship is shared between them and the capitalists.

[3]It is a relatively infrequent arrangement, probably because of the risk involved: absence of the collateral and moral hazard faced by the lender due to the possibility of default by the cooperative (see Eswaran and Kotwal (1989)). In the United States, for example, this model is found in certain taxi companies: the car is owned by an outside investor who receives a certain return on his capital, whereas management decisions (where to drive, how many hours to drive per day, and so on) are made by the driver.

We can now move to the lower part of Table 2.1, which displays different modes of production with state ownership of capital. Again, the simplest method is to begin with the prototype, which is the state socialist (or centrally planned) mode of cell (3,2): here capital is owned by the state and the state makes all entrepreneurial decisions (about prices, quantities, and investments), and labor is hired. This is the situation of a firm in a classical centrally planned economy, where firms are simply administrative units of the national economy (*masterstaya*, in Bukharin's terminology). Firms do not exist as separate legal entities and all decision making takes place at the center. This is the only mode of production where coordination of economic decisions is entirely centralized. In all other modes, even when capital is state owned, the decision-making function is exercised at the level of the enterprise and the coordination of economic decisions is by necessity decentralized.

Cell (4,2) represents the public corporation mode: capital is owned by the state, which by virtue of its status as owner receives a certain return (in the same way a private bond holder receives a guaranteed return on money he lends an enterprise). Entrepreneurial decisions, however, are in this case made by a management board that remains, in principle, independent of the state. Finally, in cell (4,1) we find the labor-managed enterprise. It differs from the public corporation only in that it is the workers and not the management who exercise the entrepreneurial function. Capital is still owned by the state. It is the mode of production that has been most extensively studied in the labor management literature, beginning with Ward's (1958) model.

The role of this conceptual framework is to systematize our intuitive grasp of different modes of production. Real-life examples can readily be identified. A 100 percent Employee Stock Ownership Plan (ESOP) and the Mondragon cooperative are examples of the Cooperative 1 mode.[4] As these cooperatives are leveraged, we move toward the Cooperative 2 mode. The public corporation, as defined here, is almost exactly the same as the British public corporations of the forties, or similar state-owned concerns in market economies. The difference between the labor-managed firm (whose capital is owned by the state) and the Cooperative 1 (where capital is privately owned) is also apparent. In real life there are, however, combinations of our ideal types. For example, joint stock companies where most business decisions are made by management are closer to the entrepreneurial than the capitalist mode. In the extreme case when a firm is 100 percent leveraged, it becomes a neoclassical entrepreneurial firm.[5]

---

[4]For a discussion of ESOPs and the Mondragon cooperative, see Bogetić (this volume).

[5]Recent management buy-outs represent an opposite tendency. As management comes to own all (or a majority of) shares, it reestablishes the identity between the owner of capital and the decision maker that existed in early capitalist firms.

It is important to realize that (a) the position of a social group will differ with the mode of production: workers, for example, will have more rights in a labor-managed than in an entrepreneurial firm; and (b) different social groups will consequently tend to prefer different arrangements. This fact forms the basis of a study of the political economy of ownership transformation (or economic liberalization) in centrally planned economies. Once a centrally planned economy begins to transform, different coalitions will support different modes of productions. Before we move to this part of the discussion, however, it is useful to briefly describe, in the same framework as was used above, the key differences between state-dominated (until recently, centrally planned) and market economies.

How centrally planned economies differ from market economies

Each country has a combination of different modes of production. This combination will be called the *structure of production*. At its most abstract, this structure gives a picture of property and management relations in an economy. The dominant mode of production (the most common in the country) will impart its essential characteristics to the whole system.

Table 2.2 presents a comparison of the structures of production in Great Britain and Poland in 1985. The structure of production is calculated in terms of total employment, although the same analysis could also be conducted in terms of gross output, value added, value of capital assets, or some other variable.

Table 2.2 Structure of production: United Kingdom and Poland, 1985
(percentage of total employed)

	United Kingdom	Poland
Cooperative 1	10.2	23.1
Capitalist	62.5	5.4
Privately owned capital	*72.7*	*28.5*
State socialist	22.0	71.5
Public corporation	5.3	0.0
State-owned capital	*27.3*	*71.5*
Total	*100.0*	*100.0*

Source: Milanovic (1989, p. 23).

We can see the main differences between the two countries. The percentage of people who work on state-owned assets is only 27 percent in the United Kingdom, and more than 70 percent in Poland. For each person in the United Kingdom who works in a state-owned company there are 2.7 people who work in privately owned companies. The situation is reversed in Poland, where the ratio is 2.5 to 1 in favor of the state sector. Labor is twice as likely in Poland to exercise an entrepreneurial role than in the United Kingdom, mostly because of the prevalence of small agricultural holdings in Poland.

If we rank socialist and market economies by the percentage of value added (or output) produced in the state-owned sector (see Table 2.3) we obtain a pyramid that is almost exactly inverted. On average, about 90 percent of the output of socialist economies is produced in the state-owned

Table 2.3 Importance of state-owned sector in different countries
Percentage of total value added

Czechoslovakia (1986)	97.0
German Democratic Republic (1982)	96.5
U.S.S.R. (1985)	96.0
Yugoslavia (1987)	86.6
Hungary (1984)	85.8
Poland (1985)	81.7
China (1984)	73.6
Unweighted average	*90.6*
France (1982)	16.5
Austria (1978-79)	14.5
Italy (1982)	14.0
New Zealand (1987)	12.0
Turkey (1985)	11.2
Germany, Federal Republic of (1982)	10.7
United Kingdom (1983)	10.7
Portugal (1976)	9.7
Australia (1978-79)	9.4
Denmark (1974)	6.3
Greece (1979)	6.1
Spain (1979)	4.1
Netherlands (1971-73)	3.6
United States (1983)	1.3
Unweighted average	*9.3*

Note: Data for Yugoslavia and Hungary include worker-managed firms and cooperatives, respectively, as part of the state sector.
Source: Milanovic (1989, pp. 15, 20).

sector, whereas in capitalist economies the share of state enterprises and public corporations is, on average, less than 10 percent.[6] In the least privately oriented economies among the capitalist countries (France in 1982,

---

[6]Government services are excluded from these figures; only commercial activities are included.

for example, or Austria in the late 1970s), the state sector accounts for about 15 percent of the value added. The most reform-oriented socialist economies (for example, China) produce less than 30 percent of gross domestic product (GDP) in the private sector. No socialist economy has increased the share of the private sector to over one third of GDP.

Analysis of the structure of production may be conducted not only to throw light on the difference between two systems or two countries, but also to measure the changes taking place in a single country. Table 2.4 shows such a comparison for Poland. Between 1985 and 1989 the importance of the sector with state-owned capital (measured by its share in total employment) declined by about 0.5 percentage point, whereas the share of the capitalist sector (outside agriculture) expanded by more than 1 percentage point. Total

Table 2.4 Structure of production in Poland, 1985 and 1989
(percentage of total employed workers)

	1985	1989
Cooperative 1	23.1	22.4
Capitalist	5.4	6.5
Privately owned capital	*28.5*	*28.9*
State socialist[a]	71.5	28.6
Labor managed[a]	0.0	14.0
Public corporation[a]	0.0	28.5
State-owned capital	*71.5*	*71.1*
Total	*100.0*	*100.0*

a. Estimate for 1989. It is generally held that approximately 20 percent of socialized firms are effectively controlled by workers' councils. The rest of the socialized sector is divided evenly between state socialist (controlled from the center) and public corporation modes.
Source: Poland, *Rocznik Statystyczny* (Statistical Yearbook), various issues.

employment in the capitalist sector (admittedly from a low base) grew by 32 percent, as it attracted both workers from state enterprises and farmers migrating to cities. The formerly centrally planned sector was to a large extent dissolved as central planning disappeared and workers' councils or managers acquired greater rights.[7]

It is within this framework that we study recent attempts to privatize in Eastern Europe. Until 1990 the main change in East European socialist economies was the change in the *proportion* of the centrally planned sector to other sectors. This change occurred through liberalization that abolished

---

[7]This, however, is only a rough estimate: Polish statistics for 1989 list all state-owned enterprises together, regardless of the level of control exercised by the state.

many barriers to the creation of private sector enterprises and the formation of cooperatives. The structure of production changed as these modes of production expanded, while the absolute size of the state socialist sector remained constant. This was still true in 1991 in the former Soviet Union, where laws on cooperatives and individual labor led to an expansion of the private sector (our Cooperative 1 mode). Total employment in cooperatives in the U.S.S.R. in April 1989 was 2 million of a total labor force of 130 million (including *kolkhozniki*) (U.S.S.R. 1989, pp. 34, 321). China has experienced similar changes: the private and quasi-private sector (outside agriculture) increased from almost zero before 1978 to account for 14 percent of industrial output by 1987 (China 1989, p. 267).[8]

When the intention is to reduce the state socialist sector in *absolute size*, the most important economic problem is the direction in which the state sector will evolve. In the following sections, I shall discuss options for the devolution of the state sector, and will show how the interests of different social groups involved in this process diverge.

What will replace the state sector?

The idea of eliminating the centrally planned (state socialist) sector is not new. Early opposition to Stalinism voiced demands for greater enterprise autonomy. This was true of Yugoslavia in the early 1950s, Poland in 1956, the Hungarian economic reform of 1968, Liberman's blueprints for the U.S.S.R. in 1962, and, in a certain sense, even Kosygin's reforms of 1965. The problems created by central planning—notably excessive centralization, absence of flexibility, stifling of technological progress, political dictatorship, and so forth—were understood even in these early years. The reaction to central planning took two principal routes: movement toward the labor-managed type of enterprise or toward public corporations. As is apparent from our classification, both modes imply decentralized decision making and in both modes the state ownership of assets is preserved. The difference between the two modes is that in labor management, the entrepreneurial role is exercised by workers (through workers' councils) whereas in public corporation mode, decision making is reserved for managers, and enterprises resemble the British or French model of public corporations (*sociétes d'état*).

This movement toward an arrangement in which the state exercises its role as the owner of assets but does not interfere in management explains why two new features appeared in East European countries as they reformed. First, in order to obtain a return on its capital (the capital that the state originally transferred to enterprises in the form of grants) the state

---

[8]The quasi-private sector includes the cooperative sector below the level of township. See also Byrd and Gelb (1990, p. 33).

began to require enterprises to pay an amount on the value of their assets; examples include the compulsory interest paid on fixed assets in Yugoslavia (introduced in the 1950s and abandoned in 1971), the so-called dividends still paid on assets in Poland, and the assets taxes paid by enterprises in Hungary.[9] Management contracts in China (in existence since 1981) fulfill the same function: the state supervising agency and the enterprise negotiate not only the interest rate charged on the state-owned portion of assets, but also taxes and prices (see Nagaoka 1989, pp. 15, 29).

Second, because enterprises became autonomous, the state could no longer treat them as subdepartments of the national economy, taking all profits from profitable firms and automatically covering the losses of others. For the first time in socialism the taxation function of the state appeared. Enterprises were supposed to pay a tax on profits; in principle, lossmakers could no longer depend on the state to bail them out. The level of the corporate tax rate is thus to some extent an indicator of the decentralization of an economy, or more exactly the distance the economy has traveled from the centrally planned model (where the tax or subsidy rate is by definition 100 percent).

Social groups which together opposed centralized state ownership very soon disagreed about what should replace state socialism. Workers (particularly the more conscious and organized groups, such as workers' councils and genuine workers' trade unions) tended to support labor management whereas technocratic groups, engineers, economists, and businessmen tended to support a devolution toward public corporations. Technocrats considered efficient functioning of the enterprise to be of foremost importance, and were less concerned with ideological issues such as worker control. They also may have been aware that worker control of industry could lead to runaway wage inflation, decapitalization of assets, low labor discipline, and so forth—in short, to what Jacques Ellul in 1954 described as "noncapitalist liberaⅼism, that is to say anarchy" (p. 210). This conflict persisted in Polish Solidarity in the early 1980s.[10] It was resolved in Yugoslavia in the 1970s by the summary political dismissals of all accused of "technocratic leanings" and the imposition of "integral labor management." In Hungary the labor management concept triumphed as a

---

[9]The existence of compulsory returns on assets also has another function in labor-managed enterprises: it prevents workers from decapitalizing the firm. It is well established, both in the economic literature and in practice, that workers in labor-managed firms have an incentive to pay themselves high wages and to invest little of their own funds in their firms. Ultimately, if they can expect to find employment elsewhere or are approaching the end of their active life they might try to decapitalize the firm altogether. On the same point see Saldanha (this volume).

[10]Lewandowski and Szomburg write: "The concept of board of directors . . . [was regarded] in the years 1980–81 . . . as an alternative to the self-management philosophy" (1989, p. 259).

result of the 1984 reforms; these reforms, as we shall see, later proved an obstacle to faster privatization.[11]

I have described the mechanics of this conflict elsewhere (Milanovic 1989, Chapter 5). In the 1970s the bureaucracy used the conflict between technocrats and workers to retain power at the enterprise level by allying itself with large groups of conservative workers and thus fending off a potential challenge by technocrats. It is important to note that even in countries or firms where devolution away from centralized state ownership occurred, no significant improvement in performance was registered; at the same time, state interference, although now somewhat less oppressive, did not decrease as much as the proponents of the labor management and public corporation models had expected. Most problems present in a centrally planned economy remained—overstaffing, low efficiency of investment, and slow technological progress.

The economic crisis that deepened in the 1980s, despite continuing decentralization and further reformist moves, heightened awareness of these shortcomings. Ultimately, it led to a fundamental reassessment of the original model. If all changes toward decentralization compatible with the retention of state property were found wanting, then a more radical solution to the problem was required. The root of inefficiency of socialist economies may lie, then, not in the absence of the market (since both the public corporation and labor management models included markets), but in the form of enterprise ownership.[12] This line of reasoning has led to a more radical proposal, namely that the state-owned sector be privatized.

The fundamental reassessment and abandonment of socialism has broadened the area of discussion by including different types of privatization as alternatives. In geometrical terms, the area of feasible options now extends to the upper portions of Table 2.1; no longer are options confined to solutions where state ownership of capital is assumed. In the next section, I shall discuss different privatization proposals, examine their logic and genesis, and identify their likely supporters.

An important clarification must first be made. The term privatization is used here to refer to the transfer of ownership from the public sector to the private sector; according to this definition, the ultimate owners of net assets

---

[11]Among economists, the main proponent of the labor management concept was Tamas Bauer; Marton Tardos is associated with the idea of public (or holding) corporations.

[12]Tardos describes the view prevailing at the time of these early reforms: " . . . once liberated from the shackles of plan directives and central distribution of material, the enterprises were supposed to be able to meet the efficiency demands of the market; at the same time, the national economy was to retain those economic advantages that were promised by a transformation to socialist property relations. There appeared to be no need to examine the proprietary problems of state enterprises and cooperatives; after all, they had been independent legal entities all along whose independence could not be exercised earlier merely because of the plan directives" (1990, p. 8).

are identifiable, physical persons.[13] The implication of our definition is that state-owned holding companies (as in Algeria) would not fall under the heading of privatization, although they might represent decentralization. On the other hand, the transformation of a state-owned enterprise into a Cooperative 1 whose assets are owned by workers is here considered an example of privatization.

Stylized facts of privatization

The first legal change in the privatization process involves the introduction of laws that allow for the transformation of state-owned enterprises (SOEs) into joint stock companies. These new joint stock companies may still be entirely owned by the state, but the act of identifying an enterprise's unambiguous owner nevertheless opens the way for the enterprise's eventual privatization. Shares initially held by the state can later be purchased by either other state-owned institutions or private individuals. The way is thus legally cleared for the transformation of SOEs into mixed, and eventually privately owned, companies. The transformation of state-owned enterprises into joint stock companies is often referred to as commercialization (that is, the process by which enterprises become autonomous and profit-maximizing entities) or corporatization. Corporatization laws are normally accompanied by legal changes that establish (at least in principle) a uniform economic treatment of different sectors of ownership. Ceilings on private sector employment, bans on certain private sector activities, limits on the ownership of land or capital, and so on, are abolished. Commercial transactions between the two sectors are liberalized.[14]

In reforming socialist economies, the still nominally Communist governments and legislatures have generally passed corporatization laws. Thus, in Poland the Law on Economic Activity that abolished virtually all limits on private enterprise was passed in January 1989 by the Rakowski government. In Hungary, the Economic Association Law (also called the Company Act) allowing the transformation of enterprises into joint stock

---

[13]This definition is narrower than that offered by Hemming and Mansoor (1988, p. 1), who include transfer of control in their definition of privatization. Transfer of control is not an appropriate indicator of privatization in socialist economies: for, according to this definition, the transfer of control from central authorities to public corporations or workers is privatization. The evolution of the state sector toward public corporations or labor management, however, characterized an earlier phase of reform. Yarrow's definition of privatization—the "transfer from the public to the private sector of entitlements to residual profits" (1986, p. 325)—is inadequate for the same reason.

[14]Prior to these changes, such transactions were either banned or severely circumscribed because of a fear that interaction between the two sectors would lead to an erosion of state (social) property. As we will see below, these fears are not unfounded. The legal changes embodied in corporatization are, however, only a reflection of a deeper ideological change: the state no longer views the state sector as the preferred sector.

companies was passed in 1988 under the Communist government. In Yugoslavia, the Enterprise Law was passed in 1988 while Mikulic's staunchly Communist government was in office. A constitutional amendment guaranteeing the equal treatment of all sectors of property ownership was adopted by the Communist-dominated legislature in Bulgaria in April 1990, and in the U.S.S.R. in August 1990. These changes represent a break with the past, but it is useful to note that they were supported (and the laws may have been drafted) by those who believed that the laws led the way not necessarily toward a privately owned economy, but rather allowed for the transformation of centrally planned (or labor-managed) enterprises into public corporations. They held that by creating fully autonomous share enterprises (*sociétés anonymes*), one of the essential mechanisms of capitalism, the capital market, would be replicated in a setting characterized by nonprivate ownership of capital.

Some economists (Horvat 1989, p. 40; Bajt 1988, p. 152ff; Iwanek and Swiecicki 1989; and Nuti 1987) envisioned a situation of interlocked ownership between firms and institutional investors that would then, not unlike corporate investors in the West, trade shares or bonds on a capital market. Instead of individual A selling his shares in company X to another individual, we would have company A trading its shares in company X with yet another state-owned company. Obviously, for a capital market to emerge, property claims have to exist; these property claims, however, need not be held and exchanged between private individuals or privately owned institutions. The concept was still consistent with the absence of private property, even if it is doubtful that a capital market not ultimately anchored on private property could ever function efficiently.[15]

Recent political developments in most East European countries have made the idea of a capital market in which nonprivately owned firms would trade shares largely irrelevant. Political changes have opened the way much more widely to privatization. Corporatization laws made possible the creation of joint stock companies and defined property claims to the new capital in a relatively clear manner (for example, if a new infusion of capital were privately owned, the enterprise would become part private and part

---

[15]A similar idea was that of state-owned holding companies. It was propounded by Iwanek and Swiecicki (1989) in Poland; Tardos [1982 (quoted in Mizsei and Tarok 1989), 1988] in Hungary; and Kovac (1989) in Yugoslavia, among others. It was implemented in Algeria. The same idea for China was argued by Singh (1990) and, to some extent, by Gu and Liu (1988). The initial idea, before privatization became popular, was to create national holding companies (NHCs) that would either have stakes in different enterprises or, preferably, an equal stake in each enterprise. Holdings would be free from state interference and would try to maximize profits (dividends received from SOEs plus capital gains). Because a holding company would need to state its selling and buying prices for the shares of different enterprises, competition between NHCs would ensue. An NHC believing that shares of a particular enterprise were underpriced would attempt to mount a takeover bid in the same way that private capitalists do.

state owned). The laws failed to unambiguously identify the owners of existing assets or to prescribe a procedure for their privatization.

This happened because of two factors. First, privatization was not considered a priority issue when the laws were drafted. Thus, writing in 1988, Tardos claims that ". . . direct methods [for reprivatizing] property . . . cannot be employed in our country. When it comes to this, we may learn from the experiences of conservative governments succeeding socialist ones in Western countries, but we cannot imitate them" (1990, p. 25). Second, the ownership problem itself is extremely difficult to solve as both the state and employees have strong claims on enterprise assets. In effect, state ownership is (was) a fuzzy concept in all socialist countries. As long as the state was the sole owner, there was no need to formalize the relationship by giving all shares to the state. In some cases, as in Poland, enterprise assets were formally divided into two funds: a state fund and an enterprise fund[16] (at the end of 1989, the latter was almost three times as big as the state fund). The rationale was that assets acquired through state grants should in principle be distinguished from those financed by workers out of retained earnings. Even when financial obligations were imposed only on the first part of capital (for example, by requiring that a prescribed rate of return be paid on the state portion), the division of capital was arbitrary and the legal position of the two funds remained unclear.[17]

These reforms occurred together with rapid changes in the rules of economic behavior, the distribution of political power, and the mechanisms of economic coordination. The transformation of enterprises into joint stock companies was in its early stages; the control of enterprises by the state, on the other hand, was weakening daily. Confusion over enterprise ownership led to a clash between two approaches to privatization. The first, "privatization from above," advocated that the state be identified as owner, temporarily centralizing assets in the hands of the state, and then selling (or freely distributing) these assets to private individuals. The second approach, "privatization from below," or spontaneous privatization, suggested that the real owner of all, or at least part, of the assets was the enterprise itself—that is, workers or management—and that workers and management should decide how and to whom those assets should be sold.

---

[16]In other cases, as in Yugoslavia and the U.S.S.R., the situation was even more legally complicated. Capital assets in Yugoslavia were defined as social property, that is, the property of all, available for workers to use. The situation in the U.S.S.R. was similar: assets were deemed to be "the property of all people." The difficulty of such a position, from the point of view of prospective privatization, is well illustrated by asking who would receive the proceeds in the case of sale. When this question was posed for the first time in Yugoslavia in 1988–89, no one could provide an answer. Workers could not receive the proceeds since they only have a usufructuary right over the assets, nor could the state because the system was based on the fiction that the assets belonged to society and not to the state.

[17]Legal specialists claim that the enterprise fund is also state property. Workers and management reject this.

The first approach was advocated by governments that had reached a political consensus in favor of privatization, as well as by liberal economists. This approach, it was argued, is more logical and would lead to quicker privatization. It was based on the following premise: if ownership belongs to the state, then the state has the right (like any private owner) to alienate it. Privatization would proceed more rapidly, as the consent of individual enterprises would not be required. Centralization of property claims in the hands of the state thus came to be advocated by the most ardent supporters of privatization.

Hungary and Poland were pushed in the apparently contradictory position of seeking to recentralize assets only a few years after some assets had become quasi-owned by workers, and after management rights had been transferred to workers' councils. The speed of change in these countries meant that they moved in about five years from a centrally planned socialist mode of production to a decentralized labor-managed mode (see arrow A in Table 2.5), and then had to retrace their steps and return to unambiguous state ownership so that they could speed up privatization (see arrow B). It is ironic that "privatizers" tried to undo what the original "nationalizers" had done some 40 years ago using the same instrument: the state.

Table 2.5 Transformation of the state sector

Capital	Labor	
	Entrepreneurial role	*Hired out*
Privately owned		
Entrepreneurial	Cooperative 1 (self-employed)	Capitalist
Hired out	Cooperative 2	Entrepreneurial
		B
State-owned		
Entrepreneurial	n.a.	State socialist centrally planned
		A
Hired out	Labor-managed	Public corporation

n.a. = not applicable
Source: Milanovic 1991

The political problem that arises with this approach is that it presumes that ownership rights unambiguously belong to the state—a position contested both by the management and workers in enterprises to be privatized. Employees argue that decentralization had transferred many management rights to them (including the right to invest retained profits) and that they should be able to claim property rights over at least a portion of the enterprise's assets. They point out that if an enterprise were autonomous (as they had previously been assured), it could enter into any legally permissible contract, and it could issue its own shares and sell them to anybody (including private persons). Using this rationale, workers and managers engaged in "wild" or spontaneous privatizations.

This attitude was supported by those still in positions of influence who believed privatization to be a means of converting their dissipating political influence into economic power. They supported managements' and workers' independent privatization attempts. The decision to privatize, contract out services, or lease firms' assets thus often reverted to management or to workers' councils, depending on their respective strengths. Managers sometimes took this opportunity to appropriate parts of the firm cheaply, or to guarantee themselves good jobs in exchange for arranging favorable deals for foreigners (Springer's purchase of regional newspapers in Hungary is one example) (see Kaufmann 1990).[18] The process became known in Poland as the *embourgeoisement* of the *nomenklatura*.

The wave of spontaneous privatization started in Hungary in 1988; by 1989 it was common in Poland; and in Yugoslavia it began in earnest in 1990. It took numerous forms. For example, a private firm owned by, say, a former manager, would lease almost the entire capital of an enterprise at favorable terms; the former manager would then rehire enterprise workers and continue production, thereby circumventing ceilings on wage growth imposed in the state sector. Higher wages made the whole scheme palatable to workers. Or a state enterprise might agree to sell output at official prices to a private company that would later resell the same goods at higher free market prices. Profits would be shared between management and workers. Transactions were sometimes mere paper formalities, with goods never leaving the premises. In some instances, enterprises were bought at low prices by former managers, or by anyone with sufficient influence and interest to do so.

Predictably, spontaneous privatizations provoked a public outcry. The consequence of that outcry was an attempt to codify the process of privatization through the introduction of privatization laws. In the meantime, governments either attempted to ban spontaneous privatization (as in Poland) or introduce some control over the process by creating watchdog agencies (as in Hungary).

Privatization laws represent the second major legal change required to relaunch the process of privatization on a larger scale while still insuring some transparency and social acceptance of the process. In the next section, I discuss the advantages and disadvantages of different privatization options.

---

[18]The same phenomenon is occurring in eastern Germany.

Typology of privatization

The number of firms privatized in Eastern Europe during 1990–91 can be considered both great and too few. It can be considered great if we take into account the absolute number of privatizations (particularly of small enterprises), the rapid growth of the private sector even in a context devoid of the essential infrastructure of market economies (problems include an archaic banking system, unreliable accounting practices, disputable asset valuations, and a shortage of qualified personnel). The number is too few, however, if we consider the enormity of the task that still lies ahead. The percentage of state assets privatized in 1990 and 1991 was (at the most) between 5 and 6 percent in Hungary,[19] between 3 and 4 percent in Poland, and less in other countries. A vast share of output is still produced in state-owned enterprises.

The task is enormous and probably without precedent. The only possible precedent is the Japanese government's sale of state assets to the upper classes after the 1867-68 Meiji revolution.[20] In modern times the largest privatization program (in terms of GDP) has been that of Chile where enterprises producing approximately 25 percent of GDP were privatized between 1974 and 1989.[21] The second largest privatization was probably the one undertaken by the Thatcher government in Britain, affecting firms producing approximately 4.5 percent of GDP and employing about the same percentage of the labor force. The British process took almost ten years in conditions characterized by sophisticated capital markets, and a long-running capitalist tradition. In contrast, the task of post-Communist governments is to privatize SOEs that account for at least 50 percent of GDP; before the process began it was hoped that it could be accomplished in 5 to 10 years despite the absence of a capital market. It is understandable that the actual results thus appear meager. I shall here consider several ways in which privatization can be accomplished.

All privatizations can be divided into three conceptual types, according to the potential ownership group targeted by the procedure. Internal privatization occurs when primarily workers in a firm are eligible for ownership. External (sale) privatization occurs when the eligibility criterion

---

[19]Calculated from data in OECD (1991, p. 71).

[20]In social terms, it was not very different from the *embourgeoisement* of the *nomenklatura*: in both cases, a class that had lost political power tried to compensate for the loss by increasing its economic power.

[21]It may be noted, however, that some of the early Chilean privatizations were relatively easy to administer: they involved returning assets to owners from whom they had been nationalized only a year or two earlier. Also, the process suffered a reversal in 1982–83 when the state had to renationalize banks due to a financial crisis (see Luders 1990).

is the ability to pay for shares. Free distribution occurs when any citizen is eligible to receive a portion of the assets for free or at a nominal charge.[22]

With internal privatization, shares are given or sold to workers employed in a firm, including those who have worked there in the past. Workers can also acquire shares gradually, first borrowing money from a commercial bank, and later acquiring shares as they repay the credit (the ESOP model). There may be restrictions on the transfer of shares. If shares have to remain with the work force, the enterprise is of the Cooperative 1 type. The main difference between employee buy-outs in the West (for example, the National Freight Corporation buy-out) and internal privatization in post-Communist countries, is the absence of a capital market in the latter (see also Bogetić, this volume). If shares, on the other hand, are freely transferable, enterprises tend to become capitalist (limited liability or joint stock) companies.[23]

With external privatization, shares are sold to the highest bidder. Bidders can be divided into several noncompetitive groups to prevent one group (for example, foreign buyers) from securing all shares or to spread the potential capital gain as widely as possible. Special regulations for small investors are introduced with the same objective in mind.

The free distribution of shares is a form of privatization where certificates exchangeable for shares in state-owned firms are given to all eligible citizens of a country (republic, city). The size of the target group increases along the continuum of internal privatization to distribution of shares.

Another privatization technique is privatization through holding companies (or mutual funds). This method introduces an additional step in the process of privatization: firms to be privatized are first taken over by several funds. The funds later bring these firms to the market and sell them by auction (as with external privatization) and/or they distribute shares in the funds themselves (and thus indirectly in the enterprises they own) to all

---

[22]A fourth type of privatization occurs when users of a particular service are eligible (regardless of whether the shares are sold or distributed). An example is the privatization of British Telecom where some shares were sold at nominal prices to telephone subscribers. We omit discussion of this type of privatization as no particular interest in it exists in Eastern Europe.

[23]The French experience, described in Uvalic (1989, pp. 47–48), suggests that workers sell shares quickly. For example, during privatizations held in 1982, approximately 10 percent of shares of a dozen large companies were reserved for employees. Most shares were bought by management. Workers bought shares principally for speculative reasons (to realize capital gains) and sold them quickly. The same seems to have been the case in the United Kingdom: the number of shareholders in British Aerospace fell from over 150,000 on the first day of quotation, to 27,000 shareholders less than a year later (Santini 1986, p. 42). This implies a first-year shareholder attrition rate of 87 percent. For a few other privatizations (for example, Amersham, British Gas, British Telecom, and British Airways), the attrition rate ranged from 12 to 75 percent per year (see Milanovic 1989, p. 166).

eligible citizens.[24] Privatization through mutual funds thus represents a technique that ultimately reduces to either external privatization or the free distribution method. Table 2.6 summarizes these relations.

Individual privatizations, however, often consist of a combination of privatization models. For example, 50 percent of an enterprise could be sold to the highest bidders, 30 percent distributed to all citizens, and 20 percent given to workers.

I shall now review the key advantages and disadvantages of the different options.

Table 2.6 Target groups of different privatization models

	Internal	External
Sale of shares	Workers	Private persons Institutions Foreign investors
Giveaway	Workers	Private persons

Internal privatization

Advantages. The main advantage of internal privatization is that administratively it is easy to implement and is popular at least among the employees (workers and managers) of successful enterprises. These employees expect to make capital gains because the market price of the company is likely to be higher than the price at which the shares are acquired (which may often be zero). Implementation problems are minimal: workers must agree on a formula for distributing shares (for example, they must decide if pensioners or previous employees are eligible) and they must decide under what conditions, if any, shareholding will be open to outsiders.[25] The transformation process is indeed spontaneous: the state remains largely uninvolved.

Finally, if existing assets are the product of earlier decisions by workers to reinvest their earnings, then internal privatization may be regarded as equitable.

---

[24]Note that in order to qualify as privatization, this option must include transfer of ownership in holding companies and firms to private individuals.

[25]In some internal privatizations envisaged in Poland (see Walkowiak, Breitkopf, and Jaszczynski 1990, p. 67), shareholding would be open to external investors but their shares would carry one vote, while shares held by employees would be worth two or three votes.

Disadvantages. The main problem with internal privatization is a reflection of one of its advantages: spontaneity. No external party can control abuses in the process. For example, if the management tightly controls workers' councils, it can ensure—through bribery, coercion or manipulation of information—that workers accept a privatization proposal favorable to management. This lack of external control is precisely the feature of the *nomenklatura* takeovers in Poland and Hungary that attracted public criticism.

A more general problem with internal privatization is that it favors workers from profitable firms; those employed in loss-making or mediocre firms, as well as those in state administration or social services, will not receive anything.[26] (A way to placate some of these constituencies may be to give to those employed outside the enterprise sector the right to buy shares at discount.) In countries where agriculture is private, farmers would also not benefit. When a firm's self-investment has been less important than state grants, and when employment in a better enterprise appears unrelated to any particular merit of the worker—basically, when the enterprise has not been very autonomous in the past—it is more likely that differences in capital gains will be viewed as inequitable. Internal privatization would consequently be viewed as less inequitable in the former Yugoslavia, where, by and large, enterprises had greater autonomy and for a longer period of time than in Poland or Hungary. Internal privatization would be least recommended for Czechoslovakia or successor states of the U.S.S.R.

The equity problem can be alleviated to some extent by progressively taxing capital gains (once they are realized—that is, once the shares are sold), to minimize after-tax differences in capital gains. The objective of the government, however, must be to allow some capital gain, so it can marshal support for the policy. Some nonuniformity in gains among different groups will persist.[27] Internal privatization more or less implies an absence of

---

[26]As Polish Minister of Industry Tadeusz Syryjczyk argues: "What can be said to the argument that an enterprise belongs to its workers? That farmers who through a long period carried the burden of industrialization now do not have any right to national capital? And teachers and doctors? That a greater right on shares has a young man who works in a factory for one year than a pensioner who worked there for 30 years? If this idea were put in practice workers of rich enterprises would acquire huge capital, and others nothing" (quoted in Baczynski 1990, p. 4). The response of those in favor of workers' ownership is the following: "Should workers of state-owned enterprises have in this revolution the same role as machinery, buildings and land, just changing one owner for another?"

[27]It is argued that giving unequal capital gains to workers in different enterprises is not different from the situation of labor-managed enterprises where gains are appropriated through capital rents. Consequently, it is said, concerns with equity are misplaced. Instead of allowing workers to appropriate the rent through higher wages, internal privatization gives them the net present value equivalent in one lump sum. However, internal privatization is "neutral" only in comparison with a labor-managed economy as it currently exists; it is not neutral in comparison with a free distribution of shares. Workers in nonprofitable firms would surely be better off with free distribution than with internal privatization.

revenues for the state (except from the taxation of capital gains). Revenues generated by enterprises may similarly be low, because most shares will be distributed free or for a nominal charge; if the objective is that every worker become a shareholder, the price of shares must be affordable. Internal privatization is thus unlikely to generate substantial new funds for a capital expansion of enterprises.

Later evolution. Internal privatization will, if there are no obstacles to the trading of shares, eventually lead to "normal" external privatization (that is, the creation of a capitalist firm) where the majority of shares are held by nonemployees. This evolution occurs through the departure from the firm of shareholding workers, the sale of shares to outside investors, or the bequest of shares. One of the defects of the Cooperative 1 model—the absence of risk diversification—would be solved in the medium term.

Support for internal privatizations in Eastern Europe is weaker than one might expect. Although the American ESOP organization has established contacts in Poland, Slovenia, Bulgaria, and several successor states of the Soviet Union,[28] no strong political backing for internal privatizations seems to exist. In Poland, for example, workers' pressure in favor of internal privatization is not particularly strong, although a few new parties are apparently trying to capitalize on what they hope could become a popular issue. In Czechoslovakia and, particularly, Hungary, internal privatization is rejected. The political weakness of the idea may also derive from the fact that it is seen as an extension of workers' self-management, which was influential in the early 1980s but later discredited.

External privatization

Advantages. The main advantage of external privatization is that it allows the state to collect money through the sale of enterprises at realistic prices.[29] If a country suffers from a liquidity overhang, as do many in Eastern Europe, external privatization should allow some excess money balances to be absorbed (assuming that the government sterilizes that money). Also, if the existing distribution of income is taken as given, the model allows for an optimum allocation of shares because, as with any other good, shares are purchased by those willing to pay the most. The implementation of external privatization is relatively simple. Several rounds

---

[28]In 1990 more than 1,000 Soviet enterprises leased their assets from the state. They paid only a fixed amount to the state and made all decisions independently. At least one of these enterprises (Moscow Agricultural Combinate, with 800 employees) has purchased assets from the state and has organized itself into an employee cooperative with private ownership of capital.

[29]External privatization can take one of three forms: fixed price offer for sale (where shares are offered at a predetermined price), auction, or placement (where shares are taken over by a broker who later sells them to the public). In developing countries the most popular technique is sale to single owners (see Nankani 1990, p. 44). Its efficiency is dubious; it is not considered a serious alternative in Eastern Europe.

of sales can be organized and/or investors can be divided into several groups (small and big investors, domestic and foreign, institutional and physical persons) to allow capital gains to be more widely spread. Price discrimination, whereby preferred investors (for example, small domestic investors) pay less for shares, can be realized.

Disadvantages. The greatest difficulty with external privatization is determining the reservation price below which the state refuses to sell shares. At first it might seem strange that price determination could be a problem in an auction. Yet, in socialist economies just beginning to privatize, there is no stock market; information about companies can thus be incomplete or misleading. For example, the accounting system is adjusted to the demands of a state-regulated or centrally planned economy and independent auditors do not exist. It is therefore difficult to assess the worth of a company.

If one of the objectives of the state is to sell "national patrimony" at a reasonable price, then setting an appropriate minimum price becomes very important; this is especially true because capital gains, if significant, would accrue to those who already have enough money to bid for shares. It is difficult to argue that already better-off people should receive greater capital gains. The process, as in the United Kingdom and France, becomes open to the charge that it favors higher income groups.[30] The experience with a few sales in Eastern Europe shows that this may become a major problem. A Hungarian parliamentary commission investigated the sale of Ibusz travel agency whose shares were oversubscribed 23 times; the opening price on the first day of trading was 3 times higher than that paid by investors. The government was accused of arranging "sweet deals" and squandering national wealth.

A solution to the problem is either to slow the pace of sales to avoid egregious pricing mistakes (as the market develops, pricing presumably becomes more "correct") or divide investors into groups and use information from one auction to set the reservation price for the next auction. This is the idea underlying Kawalec's (1989) proposal: foreign investors would only be allowed to bid for the first 20 percent of shares (so the price would be relatively high and the capital gain small). The price from the first round of auctions, reduced perhaps by 10 to 20 percent, would then be used as the reservation price for the second auction, which would be

---

[30]For the first eight French privatizations (up to May 1987), underpricing of shares, calculated as the percentage difference between the offer price and the actual price on the first day of trading on the Bourse, ranged between 5 and 80 percent (calculated from Durupty 1988, p. 67). The average weighted capital gain in the United Kingdom amounted to 18.4 and in France to 14.9 percent (Jenkinson and Mayer 1988, p. 487). In nominal amounts, capital gains from privatizations up to the end of 1987 were 3.3 billion pounds (approximately $4.3 billion) and FF 12 billion (about $1.5 billion). The capital gain accrued disproportionately to better-off households. Whereas only 2 percent of low-income French households bought shares, the proportion among top income groups was 30 percent (Durupty 1988, p. 114).

open to domestic investors only. Unsold shares would be kept by the government (as preferred shares) and sold at a later time. This suggests that external privatization would need to be conducted through several rounds of auctions, each geared toward a different class of buyers.

Another objection to external privatization is that those able to purchase the shares, and hence benefit from any capital gains, are not necessarily "socially deserving," either because they were too closely associated with the previous undemocratic regime or because they made their money through foreign exchange deals, smuggling, or other semilegal or illegal activities. With massive external privatization there may be an imbalance between the number of enterprises offered for sale and the funds of ordinary citizens; prices may, therefore, turn out to be low regardless of any intentional mispricing. The fact that capital gains will indeed accrue to the rich segment of the population, and that concentration of wealth will increase, is a serious argument against auctioning as the only form of privatization.

The role of institutional investors. External privatization will be open to individual investors as well as to institutional investors (such as pension funds, insurance agencies, and so on). It is difficult to prescribe an optimal blend between the two. In market economies institutional investors have tended to become more important. The percentage of publicly quoted equity held by institutional investors grew in the United Kingdom from 47 percent in 1975 to 63 percent in 1990; in the United States it grew from 33 percent in 1980 to 45 percent in 1990. In both countries, pension funds alone hold 30 percent of total listed shares. In Japan and Italy the role of institutions is even greater: they hold more than three quarters of all shares; on the Tokyo stock exchange individuals' holdings accounted, in 1991, for only 21 percent of all shares (*Economist* 1990b, p. 96; Emmott 1991, p. 8).

According to some views, the key advantage of institutional investors is their ability to monitor firm's managers. Because institutional investors tend to be large shareholders, they have more to gain (or lose) from a firm's good (or bad) performance and they can more easily replace a poor management team. Institutional investors are better able to track and assess enterprise performance; their greater professionalism (compared to the individual investor) allows institutional investors to make more informed decisions and to process information at a lower unit cost.

It is also argued, however, that because institutional investors work with other people's money they display the same weaknesses inherent in any principal-agent relationship. They may not be very efficient "policing" agents for enterprises in which they own shares simply because they themselves are imperfectly controlled by shareholders. Institutional investors may thus be even less effective in enforcing proprietors' interests than diffused shareholders. Recent changes in ownership patterns in some market economies (primarily in the United States, Britain, and France)—for example, management buy-outs and the shunning of publicly quoted in favor of privately held companies[31]—lend some credence to this view. These changes have better realigned the interests of owners and managers. In terms of modes of production, the changes represent a move from entrepreneurial to capitalist firms.[32] They also affect the role of institutional investors. As the place of external owners is taken by internal owners (managers or employees), institutional investors also tend to become less important as shareholders.

On the other hand, the growing share of private placements—whereby companies sell debt or equity directly to institutional investors without making public offerings—increases the importance of institutional investors as shareholders.

The recent trend away from publicly quoted companies in the West, however, does not seem relevant for Eastern Europe. Conditions there are vastly different. One of the objectives of privatization in socialist economies is the creation of a market economy; this requires the development of the stock market. Another objective is diffused ownership. Neither a market economy nor diffused ownership can be achieved unless a number of companies become public (in the sense of "publicly quoted"). A more relevant issue, then, is the distribution of shares between individuals and institutions.

An insufficient accumulation of wealth in the hands of individuals, as is the case in Eastern Europe, improves the prospect of an important role for institutional investors. It could also be contended that institutional investors in Eastern Europe are more likely to understand the operation of stock markets than private individuals. Yet in many instances the role of institutional investors is severely circumscribed by the current economic system. For example, with the present system of pay-as-you-go funding of social insurance and with current pension rules, pension funds (even if they become truly independent of the state) would not have sufficient resources to invest in newly privatized firms.[33] Similarly, the take over of a part of an insolvent firm's assets by commercial banks (as happened in Hungary and Yugoslavia) does not indicate that banks are assuming a more market-oriented approach; rather, it is reminiscent of the old practice of writing-off

---

[31]In 1989 and 1990, the number of new U.S. firm listings on stock exchanges was 50 percent less than the annual average in the previous seven years (*Economist* 1990a). Also, since 1980 more than 1,000 U.S. firms have become privately held as result of leveraged buy-outs (*Economist* 1988, p. 75).

[32]Management buy-outs represent an interesting stage in the evolution of capitalism. In early capitalist firms, owners were managers simply because they owned the capital. Dissociation between ownership and management occurred later as result of the increased scale of operations and the division of labor. Management buy-outs reestablish the initial identification of owner and manager, but this time through a different route: the manager becomes the owner.

[33]One way to circumvent a lack of funds, suggested by Kovac (1989), could be to allow cross-ownership similar to Japanese *Keiretsu*. Several firms form an apex enterprise, which they own; the apex in turn holds shares in each of the firms. No money is needed for the deal: shares are exchanged through barter.

nonperforming loans by converting them into equity. Finally, institutional investors are currently almost all state owned. They need to be converted into private companies (which would require that their portfolios be cleaned up) before they can assume a meaningful role as stockholders of other firms.[34]

In conclusion, short-term prospects for institutional investors in Eastern Europe appear mixed: they possess some advantages (for example, professionalism), but an excessive reliance on them could slow the privatization process and fail to create a sufficient constituency that supports privatization. More ominously, the process could fall prey to the old idea of entrepreneurship exercised by state-owned institutional investors.

Free distribution of shares

Advantages. The key advantages of a free distribution of shares are that it is egalitarian, it circumvents the problem of fund shortages or the concentration of funds in the hands of foreigners or former *nomenklatura*, and it solves the difficult and politically explosive issue of enterprise valuation. These advantages can be reviewed in turn. It is also the simplest formula for privatization: it dispenses with arguments about the contribution of different groups to the accumulation of an enterprise's or nation's wealth. It gives concrete meaning to the vague term *social ownership*.[35] The resources for privatization (that is, vouchers) are, as it were, produced by the government, and no group or individual enjoys any privilege. Foreigners are excluded from at least the first round. Because proper enterprise valuation is difficult in socialist economies, the government may prefer to issue vouchers and have the population determine the correct value. The government cannot be accused of intentionally underpricing some assets—an accusation that, because of the complex and often arbitrary nature of valuation, can be difficult to rebut. If the government freely distributes shares, it cannot be accused of favoritism. Voucher privatization can be completed relatively quickly (from 6 to 12 months), although it probably involves higher administrative costs than the other two options.

Disadvantages. The free distribution of shares, by definition, involves almost no revenue to the state. Abstracting from increased subsequent revenues through the taxation of firms expected to become more profitable as a result of privatization (so that the faster privatization proceeds, the greater will be the net present value of taxes), the process could even imply a net cost to the state because of administrative expenditures that may not be fully recovered. The trade-off between the breadth of privatization and level of revenues is very much in evidence in this scheme.

---

[34]On the sequencing of enterprise and bank privatization, see Hinds (this volume).

[35]One of the first proponents of widespread distribution, Edgar Feige (1991), even called this process "socialist privatization."

Another problem is that wide distribution of shares will fail to strengthen the link between a shareholder's income and the performance of the enterprise in which he holds shares. The absence of this link was one of the reasons why the state was not an efficient owner. If private ownership is dispersed with many people owning small stakes (as it would necessarily be in the beginning), the monitoring of enterprise management would be weak. The cost of monitoring for the individual small shareholder may be higher than the expected loss of income caused by poor monitoring. Monitoring would be particularly difficult in the new environment, which would be full of uncertainty. As Demsetz and Lehn (1985) argue, shareholding in such an environment must be more concentrated. In addition, an underdeveloped auditing system will make it easy for managers to make false reports. This could erode confidence in the system and discourage the formation of a stock market, without which distribution of shares could become a meaningless exercise.[36]

The problem of overly dispersed ownership would, however, be alleviated through time as holdings become more concentrated. When this happens, both the equity consideration (that all members of a community should have equal access to privatized assets) and the efficiency consideration (that a clear group of owners of each company must emerge) come close to being satisfied.[37]

Mutual funds (holding companies)

Advantages. The main advantage of the mutual fund model is that it may result in both relatively fast privatization (if shares in holding companies are distributed to the population), and fast improvements in the allocation of capital and in firms' efficiency. Introducing a layer of mutual funds run by professional managers between enterprises and the population could lead to the quick creation of a capital and stock market (at which only institutional investors or mutual funds would initially trade). The mutual funds could probably make the best use of scarce managerial skills, improving the

---

[36]Similar problems have limited the development of a stock market in capitalist countries like Turkey.

[37]Another problem appears in some early distribution schemes (see, for example, Feige 1991). Shares in all firms are given in "bundles" to eligible citizens. If one wants to acquire more shares in enterprise A, he must also buy more shares in enterprises B, C, and so on, from people with similarly bundled shares. Shares, however, can be unbundled using certificates (issued in the same amount to all eligible citizens) with which to bid for and buy shares of different firms. This is the substance of proposals put forward by Lewandowski and Szomburg (1989), Hinds (1990), and Saldanha and Milanovic (1990), as well as of the Czechoslovak voucher scheme whose implementation began in October 1991. One of the first such proposals was offered by Milovanovic (1986, pp. 116–17).

functioning of the economy and assisting enterprises with their restructuring.[38] If enterprises are brought to the market by mutual funds, and the level of the population's financial knowledge improves, then the individual stockholder will become an increasingly important player on the stock market. For those unfamiliar with the stock market, shares in mutual funds would provide a less risky asset than stocks of individual companies, the values of which can be expected to fluctuate greatly, especially in the beginning. Mutual funds will enable a "soft landing" in the transition from socialism to capitalism.

Disadvantages. The principal problem with this model is the danger that slow privatization could become "no privatization at all." Groups opposing privatization might prefer this proposal for that reason, believing that through inertia mutual funds will remain in state hands. This scenario represents a reversal of the idea of "simulated" capital markets, in which nonprivately owned companies try to behave like capitalists. In order to preempt such developments, revised proposals for privatization through mutual funds insist that all (or most) shares in mutual funds be immediately distributed to the general population. An immediate distribution would achieve two objectives: it would introduce some control over the managers of funds (so that funds did not turn out to be relabelled state ministries), and it would open the stock market to the population (even if trade would initially take place only in mutual fund shares).

Country experiences

Hungary

Hungary's privatization process was similar to the model described in the section on stylized facts of privatization. Major decentralization took place in 1985. This change represented a move toward the model of a labor-managed enterprise. Decentralization was preceded by an important development: beginning in 1982, worker teams were allowed to rent machinery and equipment from their enterprises and work on their own account after work hours. Enterprise Business Work Partnerships, as this form of organization was called, was a prototype of the labor-managed enterprise: labor and entrepreneurial income belonged to workers who paid a rental to the state (or SOE). This model initially affected only a portion of workers, but was generalized in 1985. The role of enterprise councils was expanded: the state only retained the right to nominate directors and

---

[38]Yarrow (1990) has recently pointed out that restructuring in the United States and Britain, following the oil price rise, was accompanied by a move away from conglomeration toward more dispersed forms of organization.

influence policies of large and "strategic" enterprises.[39] The distribution of power within the enterprise, however, was such that management (allowed by law to occupy only half the seats of enterprise councils) was able to wrest control from workers, and transform state socialist enterprises into public corporations.[40]

When the Hungarian government wanted to change course in the late 1980s and to begin with a serious privatization, it became embroiled in a political conflict with enterprises whose managers and workers resisted the attempt to strip them of property rights. In particular, they did not want to lose the ability to appropriate a portion of the return on capital in the form of higher wages and bonuses, nor did they want to lose the entrepreneurial role they had only recently acquired. The original anti-Center coalition between workers and management—which had been in danger of collapsing with decentralization because workers, in contrast to management, supported an expanded role for enterprise councils—reasserted itself when both groups felt threatened by the state's attempt to regain control.

In October 1988 the Hungarian parliament passed the Economic Association Law allowing state enterprises to become joint stock companies. This led to a spurt of employee and management buy-outs, often at terms quite advantageous to employees and management. Foreign companies also became involved, securing some extremely favorable purchases. The decision of whether to convert enterprises into joint stock companies rested with enterprise councils. The process had two major flaws: first, the process was not equitable because privatization took place at prices that were too low, and second, the state was not entitled to the proceeds of sales, even if sizable portions of the firms' capital had been acquired through state investment or subsidized credits.

At the same time, a curious political coalition formed that supported the process of spontaneous privatization. The coalition was composed of economic liberals, who held that spontaneous privatization was the most natural and quickest way to dismantle the state sector, and parts of the old *nomenklatura* who saw in spontaneous privatization an opportunity to acquire economic power. The first group viewed the inevitable social costs of spontaneous privatization as the unavoidable cost of the transition to a private ownership economy. The second group expected to profit from these social costs.

---

[39]Classical state-managed enterprises accounted for 27 percent of Hungarian firms in 1987. More than half of that number were public utilities. The remaining 73 percent of enterprises were managed by enterprise councils, composed of employees and management, or, in the case of enterprises employing less than 500 workers, by workers' assemblies. See also Mora (1991, p. 2).

[40]The process, of course, was not tidy. In October 1987 the government allowed the issuance of property notes, which were nontransferable workers' shares. Firms that availed themselves of this opportunity became Cooperative 1.

The Transformation Law passed in June 1989 was designed to address some of the abuses of spontaneous privatization and to establish more rigorous procedures for future privatizations. In order to limit undervaluation of assets, privatizations were to be overseen by the State Property Agency (SPA). This agency, in operation since March 1990, was empowered to bring cases of fraudulent privatization to a court, which could overrule a decision to privatize (as it did with the sale of the Hungarhotel hotel chain). Valuation problems with the first flotation of a Hungarian firm on the Budapest and Vienna stock exchanges (shares were traded at approximately three times the issue price) led to recrimination between Parliament and the SPA, and the resignation of its first director.

Initially, the SPA could begin privatization only for enterprises unambiguously owned by the state—that is, those enterprises whose self-management rights were not expanded in 1985. These enterprises, however, were mostly utilities. In the case of worker-managed enterprises (which comprised about 70 percent of all enterprises and 50 percent of assets), the SPA required parliamentary authorization to initiate privatization. This provision was eventually changed and the SPA was given authority to initiate privatization regardless of the opinion of workers or management. In September 1990, dissatisfied with the relatively slow pace of privatization, the Hungarian government established a new vehicle for privatization. It introduced the concept of investor-initiated privatization: an investor could approach the SPA directly and negotiate the sale of a firm.

Three types of privatization were thus in existence in Hungary by 1991: privatization initiated by the SPA (or "privatization from above"), expected to account in the years to come for the sale of between 6 and 9 percent of state assets per year; investor-initiated privatization (or "lateral privatization"), expected to account for the sale of 5 percent of assets; and spontaneous enterprise-initiated privatization (or "privatization from below"), also expected to account for 5 percent of asset sales. According to this somewhat optimistic scenario, more than 15 percent of state assets would be privatized annually.

Data on the extent of privatization activity are not fully reliable. What is known about spontaneous privatizations mostly concerns individual cases and these cases were often "wild" or fraudulent privatizations that attracted popular interest. Under the Transformation Law only a dozen enterprises were privatized by the end of 1990 (Mora 1991, p. 11). At that time, it was estimated that assets worth $1.8 billion (or roughly 6 percent of the total gross accounting value of state assets) were sold or were in the process of sale (OECD 1991, p. 73).[41]

The transformation of the structure of production in Hungary has probably proceeded faster than in other formerly socialist economies.

---

[41]According to SPA criteria, an enterprise with at least 20 percent private ownership is considered wholly privatized.

Spontaneous privatizations have eroded the state socialist and labor-managed sectors, while private sector activities have increased significantly. In the beginning of 1988, private sector employment (including the self-employed) accounted for 6.3 percent of the nonagricultural labor force; two years later that proportion was about 11 percent (Hungary 1989, pp. 65–66).

The Antall government, which came to power after the first free elections in March 1990, appears to have a less permissive attitude toward spontaneous privatizations than the previous Communist government. The government believes that the main beneficiaries of "wild privatizations" have been managers and *nomenklatura* associated with the previous regime. The government is also more wary of uncontrolled foreign purchases of existing assets in Hungary than the main opposition party.

Poland

The process of privatization has been similar in Poland. The 1981-82 reform (partially undertaken during a State of War) attempted to satisfy some workers' demands, referred to during the years of the Solidarity movement as the three *S*'s: self-management, self-financing, and self-rule. The role of workers' councils, which in Poland had existed in an incipient form since 1956, was reinforced. Workers acquired the right to elect directors, although the state continued to appoint the directors of about 100 enterprises deemed of national importance. In early 1988 the so-called second stage of reform,[42] was launched, beginning the movement toward labor management. One of the principal objectives was to further decentralize decision making, thereby strengthening the role of employees through workers' councils or trade unions.

It was only in 1989, during the last months of the Rakowski government, and, of course, when the non-Communist government came to power in September 1989, that privatization rather than labor management became the preferred solution.[43] This preference did not simply reflect the new government's ideological stance; it was also due to a gradual disenchantment with the idea of labor management, particularly in light of the unsuccessful

---

[42]The first stage was the 1982 reform.

[43]Some argue that the privatization movement started even earlier, during the Rakowski government. It could also be argued, however, that the move toward privatization was made only because Communists expected an imminent loss of power. The *nomenklatura* that controlled enterprises tried, according to this view, to preserve at least some economic power by engaging in unfair privatizations through management buy-outs. It is difficult to know if Rakowski's government intended from the beginning to privatize enterprises, or if it was pushed in that direction by unfolding events. Popular outcry at such privatizations led the Mazowiecki government to bar further privatizations, pending the passing of new legislation. See also Milanovic (1992).

Yugoslav experience.[44] According to some in the Mazowiecki government (for example, Deputy Prime Minister Leszek Balcerowicz and Minister of Industry, Tadeusz Syryjczyk),[45] labor management represented an improvement over the centrally planned system only when the capitalist option was not possible; when the latter became politically feasible, labor management lost its appeal.

The Mazowiecki government quickly realized that the labor management system was probably the worst basis from which to begin privatization: workers are not likely to relinquish rights gained under the labor management system. Before privatizing, the state had first to lay claim to all enterprise assets; only then could it sell the assets to private investors. The government tried to pass a law on the transformation of state enterprises (which would have allowed enterprises to reconstitute themselves as joint stock companies with the Treasury as sole owner),[46] and then pass a law on privatization that would have defined how privatization was to be conducted. The transformation law encountered opposition from workers and their representatives, who rejected the government's attempt to claim sole ownership of state enterprises.

After several months of stalemate, the government abandoned its attempt to pass a separate transformation law. Most key elements were instead included in the State Enterprise Privatization Act, which after several months of parliamentary debate was passed in July 1990. The first step mandated by the Act is the transformation of state-owned enterprises into joint stock companies, which would be entirely owned by the Treasury (what we earlier referred to as corporatization). This transformation, however, will require the agreement of, or can be initiated by, the founding organ (most often a government ministry), the firm's management, and workers' councils. To counteract the possible resistance of workers' councils and prevent a stalling of the privatization process, a provision was included in the Privatization Act giving the Ministry of Ownership Transformation

---

[44]In arguing in favor of privatization, several government documents explicitly refer to the failure of the Yugoslav model. It is not accidental that several members of the Polish government with liberal economic views have studied labor management. Prominent examples include Marek Dabrowski, Deputy Minister of Finance in the Mazowiecki government, and Jan Mujzel, an influential economic adviser.

[45]Baczynski (1990) writes: "Deputy Prime Minister Mr. Balcerowicz and Minister of Industry Mr. Syryjczyk have publicly declared their opposition to the concept of labor management. According to them, this was a purely political idea, launched in the past by the opposition in a situation where other systemic changes appeared impossible. Self-management organs, as counterweight to *nomenklatura*, have fulfilled their role in the majority of enterprises. But when the possibility of a 'normal' privatization opened, some self-management organs did not realize that the situation has changed. Labor management is better than *nomenklatura*, but private enterprise is better than labor management."

[46]After an amendment to the Law on Enterprises was passed in 1987, it became possible for enterprises to become joint stock companies. It was under the provisions of this amendment that spontaneous privatizations took place in 1989.

the right to transform an enterprise into a joint stock company without the approval of management, workers' council or the founding organ, provided the Ministry receives a special authorization from the Council of Ministers.

The next step mandated by the Act is the sale of Treasury-owned shares to all interested parties, which must occur within two years of corporatization.[47] Workers can buy shares at a discount of up to 50 percent, but this form of participation cannot exceed 20 percent of all shares, and the average per worker discount may not exceed the average annual wage in the socialized sector.[48] Different methods of external privatization are acceptable under the Act. Indeed, virtually all options appear possible, as the law specifically allows sales by auction, public offers to sell, private placements, and the distribution of privatization vouchers to citizens.

During the transition period—that is, between corporatization and privatization—enterprises will be managed (as in the past) by directors who are overseen by a supervisory council. Employees would hold one third of the seats on the council, and they would enjoy the same level of protection as they would in state-owned enterprises. Once more than 50 percent of shares are owned by entities other than the Treasury, however, the composition of the supervisory council would be determined by shareholders.

Because of Poland's negative earlier experience with spontaneous privatizations, the law was written to ensure an orderly privatization process. The process is managed by Ministry for Ownership Transformation.[49] Annual targets regarding the number and size of enterprises to be privatized are established by Parliament at the recommendation of the Council of Ministers.

In September 1990 a list of 40 enterprises to be sold by public subscription was drafted. The first five enterprises on that list were sold in January 1991 (see Table 2.7). The sale was not considered a success. By the time the sale should have been terminated, shares of only one enterprise (a construction company) were oversubscribed. The deadline was extended, and all five enterprises were eventually sold, netting about $31.5 million.[50] Almost half that amount was received in the form of earlier-issued Treasury bonds, which gave holders the right to a 20 percent discount. The issue price closely tracked the accounting value of the firms (it was, on average, 6

---

[47]The enterprise is taken off the register of state-owned enterprises at the time of corporatization and is added to the commercial register. Firms functioning under the latter are subject to the Commercial Code.

[48]It is not clear if both (a) 20 percent of all shares and (b) a discount worth less than a yearly wage are binding constraints.

[49]Originally, an agency for ownership transformation was to have been established as part of the state administration. Parliament decided, however, that a ministry could be more easily controlled.

[50]The total face value of shares to be sold was $55 million. Of that amount, $31.5 million was earmarked for sales to the public, $10.7 million for employees, and $12.8 million for private placements (see Table 2.7).

percent less). Approximately 130,000 people bought shares. The high cost of promotion and marketing (a French firm designed the marketing strategy) attracted unfavorable publicity: marketing costs represented almost 10 percent of privatization receipts (Brzeg-Wielunski 1991). Ten months after the sale, share prices for four of the five firms were less than the issue price. The average capital loss was 14 percent.

Table 2.7 Poland: data on the first five privatized enterprises

| Firm | Activity | Ownership structure (percent) | | | Price (thousands of zlotys) | | |
		Public sales	Employees	Private placement	Accounting value	Issue price	October 1991
Exbud	Construct.	45	20	35	163	112	207
Krosno	Glass	50	20	30	72	65	30
Kabel	Cables	83	17	0	65	70	60
Prochnik	Garments	80	20	0	46	50	36
Tonsil	Audio equipment	50	20	30	52	80	40
Weighted average		*57.6*	*19.6*	*22.7*	*76.2*	*72.2*	*62.1*

Source: Private communication from the Ministry for Ownership Transformation, Warsaw, and Czekaj (1990).

By the fall of 1991, a total of eight companies were sold in full by public offering and were quoted on the Warsaw stock exchange which had opened in April 1991. By that time, according to data supplied by the Ministry for Ownership Transformation, privatization had begun in 170 enterprises, accounting for 20 percent of industrial sales (153 SOEs were commercialized). More than 100 small and medium enterprises were privatized using the so-called privatization by liquidation method, whereby firms were taken over by other firms or sold to workers. The single most important success was the transfer to private ownership of approximately 80 percent of retail trade outlets by mid-1991.

The somewhat disappointing performance of the first public sale and a slow overall process of privatization led the government to propose a faster track approach. In July 1991, it announced plans to combine privatization through mutual funds with privatization through the free distribution of vouchers to citizens. Four hundred enterprises would be privatized: 60 percent of equity would be held by mutual funds that would, in turn, be owned by citizens who would acquire their shares by vouchers; 30 percent of equity would remain with the state; and 10 percent would be sold to workers at a discount. In order to insure a strong presence of at least one core shareholder, a minimum of 33 percent of shares would have to be held by a single mutual fund.

According to government forecasts (which, as in Hungary, have not proved very reliable in the past), the state sector's share of Poland's GDP would be halved within 10 years (currently the state sector produces 80 percent of GDP). In comparison, it took Chile and Britain 15 and 8 years, respectively, to privatize enterprises that produced 25 percent (in Chile) and 4.5 percent (in the United Kingdom) of GDP. At these rates, Polish privatization would take between 30 and 50 years to accomplish.

Former Yugoslavia

Until the outbreak of civil war in June 1991, Yugoslavia's path to privatization resembled that of other East European countries. The "battle lines" in the Yugoslav case, however, were more clearly drawn because of the strong tradition of self-management that, in one form or another, existed in Yugoslavia since the early 1950s. Self-management was entrenched in workers' attitudes, the country's ideology, its constitution, and the whole battery of laws designed to protect the management rights of workers (most notably, the Associated Labor Act of 1976).

Both workers and the political bureaucracy that came to power in the 1970s resisted any encroachment of these rights. It became clear, however, that without a significant abrogation of workers' self-management rights, there was not even a theoretical possibility of having a stock market as envisaged by the early reformers (that is, one limited to nonprivately owned public corporations). In effect, if workers from enterprise A own one part of enterprise B, and thereby acquire the right to manage it, the self-management rights of workers in enterprise B are limited. At the extreme, when enterprise B is entirely owned by enterprise A (for example, if it is founded by enterprise A), then its workers are simply hired laborers and not managers. This problem (the link between ownership and management) frustrated attempts to introduce clear ownership titles.

The Enterprise Law passed in 1988 represented a breakthrough: it limited the self-management rights of workers, allowed the transformation of self-managed firms into joint stock companies (that could accept private capital and become mixed firms), and formally equalized the treatment of all forms of property. Also, limits on private activity were gradually lifted, although unevenly in different republics.

A decisive move toward privatization came with the enactment of the Law on Social Capital in December 1989. The law attempted to identify the owner of "social capital," and to establish procedures for the sale of assets. It identified republican state organs (the so-called Development Funds) as the owners of social capital because these entities are supposed to receive proceeds from sales. The fact that the state would receive the proceeds from sales certainly helped to reduce political opposition to privatization. The decision to initiate the privatization process was left with workers' councils. This provision was politically motivated to avoid antagonizing workers. It was also ideologically acceptable because the bureaucracy could feel relieved that privatizations would take place only with worker agreement, and not merely because capitalists express an interest in a firm.

The law, however, was not very effective during its first six months (until June 1990). No sales took place under the law, and no Development Funds were created. The main reason for this failure seems to have been a lack of enthusiasm on the part of workers to transform their firms into private companies. The available incentives (workers could buy shares in their own firm at preferential terms) were not sufficiently attractive.

Faced with this lack of response, Markovic's federal government proposed a more radical approach in July 1990. The main elements were contained in several laws. First, the rights of workers were severely curtailed, as a number of prerogatives (including those of hiring and dismissal) were transferred to management. Labor-managed firms were practically transformed into public corporations (a development not unlike that which took place in Poland). With the loss of self-management rights, workers should be more amenable to privatization: their position would be virtually the same after privatization. Second, management rather than workers' councils would make decisions about "corporatization" (that is, the transformation of an enterprise into a joint stock company) and the sale of shares. Third, privatization was to be essentially of the internal type. Capital was to be sold at its accounting value, with workers (including former workers) receiving a flat discount of 30 percent, plus a variable bonus equal to 1 percent for each year with the firm. The total value of shares sold to an individual worker could not exceed his three-yearly wage, meaning that the total value of shares sold to all workers must be less than or equal to a three-yearly wages fund. The percentage of shares sold to workers would thus vary from enterprise to enterprise as a function of worker interest in the shares and the capital intensity of the firm. For example, if the accounting value of capital were equal to three times the wages fund (that is, the capital-labor ratio of three), and if all workers wanted to use their entitlement in full, all shares would be sold to workers. Enterprises with a capital-labor ratio greater than three would have to sell a portion of shares externally to pension funds and private investors at a 30 percent (flat) discount. Fourth, privatization was linked to stabilization: it was envisaged that wage increases above the norm would have to be paid in internal shares and not in cash (in Brazil, a similar scheme required commercial banks to buy privatization certificates).

The law's main virtue was its explicit recognition of workers' interests. It attempted to compensate workers for their loss of self-management rights by offering them shares at preferential prices. Self-managed enterprises would thus be converted mostly into Cooperative 1 firms and then, as shares became tradable, into limited liability or joint stock companies.

The July 1990 federal laws were shot down by political disagreements between the republics. By the end of 1990, Slovenia had decided to abrogate all federal laws, including the privatization law. Enterprises that had been privatized were threatened with sanctions. Croatia followed suit, thus effectively halting the transformation of the social sector in Yugoslavia's two most developed republics. Other republics continued to accept the validity of the federal law, and internal privatizations became relatively numerous in Serbia and Bosnia. This outcome was somewhat ironic, as the quasi-Communist government in Serbia was certainly less keen on privatization than the more liberal Slovenian government.

As the republics drifted farther apart and clouds of impending war gathered, almost all republics decided to pass their own privatization laws. In April 1991, after much dispute and the resignation of a number of top officials, Croatia became the first republic to pass a privatization law. For enterprises subject to privatization (60 percent of Croatian economy), the republican law allows a discount for workers. Privatization is supposed to be initiated by enterprises, and is subject to approval by the Agency for Ownership Transformation (successor to the Development Funds). Serbia followed in August 1991 with a law that, although similar to the federal law, is somewhat less supportive of privatization; it offers lower discounts for workers; there is no compulsory privatization; and large areas of the transportation, oil, and telecommunication sectors are exempted from privatization. The Serbian government still appears to prefer public corporations to privately owned firms.

By mid-1991, however, privatization—indeed, economics as a whole—had been relegated to the back burner, as political conflicts expanded into military confrontation. Moreover, authoritarian and nationalistic governments in both Serbia and Croatia regarded privatization with suspicion. Not only would an effective privatization undercut their political power, but it would offer economic opportunity to those "ethnically undesirable" people whom both governments took great pains to oppress. Finally, because of the civil war, both governments needed to further centralize decision making and reinforce their economic control. Thus, although Yugoslavia initially exhibited the most decentralized decision making, by 1991 Yugoslav enterprises had, by and large, less autonomy than enterprises in the other East European countries discussed here.

Czechoslovakia

Until the November 1989 change of government, the Czechoslovak economy was one of most centralized in Eastern Europe. In 1989 the state sector and cooperatives accounted for 96 percent of net value added and 90 percent of employment. Although some decentralizing measures were undertaken after 1987—including the introduction of workers' councils—the key features of the centralized command system remained unchanged. Czechoslovakia's economic transformation began from a starting point significantly different from that of its neighbors. For 10 to 20 years before the political changes of 1989 and 1990, Hungary, Poland, and Yugoslavia had experienced economic decentralization and there was a relatively active private sector.

Czechoslovakia's pretransformation experience had both drawbacks and advantages from the perspective of the eventual privatization of the state sector. Among the drawbacks were a lack of management culture and entrepreneurial skills, and an inappropriate industrial structure from the point of view of comparative advantage. On the other hand, a relatively unambiguous definition of ownership (enterprises belong to the state and not to workers and/or management) can be an advantage, as we saw earlier. In April 1991 enterprises were formally "renationalized"; they were allowed to begin their transformation from state-owned enterprises to corporations, and workers' councils were abolished. At the same time, equality of treatment for all types of property became constitutionally guaranteed (Mejstrik 1990, p. 14).

The privatization process was somewhat slowed, however, by the government's decision to restore ownership to people whose properties had been nationalized during the period of Communist rule (that is, after February 1948). This decision was motivated by the desire to establish a precedent of legal respect for private property. It was also motivated by the desire to assure foreign investors, whose interest in Czechoslovak enterprises is expected to be significant, that their property rights will be legally protected.

With its emphasis on restitution, Czechoslovakia has adopted a route similar to that taken in the former Democratic Republic of Germany. In other countries (for example, Hungary, Poland, and Slovenia), restitution is either fairly symbolic or it involves only small enterprises in the retail and service sector. This difference can be explained by the different economic traditions that prevailed in these countries before the beginning of Communist rule. Czechoslovakia was traditionally distinguished by its egalitarian distribution of income and wealth. Unlike Poland and Hungary, it was a nation with few large landowners. The industrial sector had a more modern class structure, with a sizeable urban middle class and relatively well-paid blue-collar workers. It was, moreover, one of the few functioning democracies in the period between World War I and World War II. The nationalization that occurred in Czechoslovakia during the 1940s was thus less socially acceptable than nationalizations in Poland and Hungary, which affected a smaller segment of the population.

A number of difficult issues arose in Czechoslovakia with respect to restitution. One issue concerned eligibility for restitution: from what date would nationalization be deemed illegitimate—the end of the war (May 1945), or the Communist takeover (February 1948)? Enterprises were often nationalized between 1945 and 1948 in reprisal for collaboration with the Nazis (as with Renault in France). Assets that had previously been appropriated by Nazis and given to Nazi supporters were also nationalized during this time. In the case of Jewish owners, entire families had perished and many assets could not be assigned to anybody.

There was relatively little question that nationalizations of this nature should not be reversed. Even if there is agreement that the eligibility date should be the date of the Communist takeover, however, the issue is not solved: some nationalization laws were passed by the democratic parliament (in which the Communists were the largest party) prior to the Communist coup, but they took effect only in 1948 when the democratic government was no longer in existence. Should such laws be treated as if they occurred before or after the cutoff date?

Another issue concerned the manner of restitution. Restitution in kind, even when possible, is often a restitution of objects that might have changed substantially in the intervening 40 years: factories, buildings, and shops had expanded, improved, or, in some cases, deteriorated. Cash restitution is an expensive option. The government would not have the resources for a large-scale cash restitution. Restitution could also be made by distributing vouchers to former owners, entitling them to purchase shares in privatized companies. This alternative was favored by the Slovak government because it involved no financial cost.

After a long process of legislative drafting, the restitution bill was passed in February 1991. The two issues mentioned above were resolved in the following manner. The cutoff date for ownership eligibility was set at February 25, 1948. Restitution would be made in three ways: in cash, in vouchers and in kind. Most of the roughly Kcs 300 billion ($11 billion) of property subject to restitution would be restituted in kind. In cases where property was deemed to have deteriorated, the former owners would be entitled to a cash compensation not to exceed Kcs 30,000 (or about $1,100), as well as compensation in securities (shares of privatized companies or vouchers).

A few days after the restitution bill was passed, federal Parliament adopted the Large Privatization bill[51] (called *large* to distinguish it from the so-called small privatization of restaurants, shops, and retail stores). The privatization law combines enterprise-initiated privatization and state control in an ingenious way. Individual enterprises can, of their own accord or in response to a request by their founder (Ministry), draft privatization proposals. These proposals must include all relevant information about the enterprise, a designation of the part of property subject to privatization, a valuation of the enterprise, a proposal for the enterprise's future corporate form (joint stock or limited liability), a privatization time frame, and finally, a discussion of individuals or companies that have expressed an interest in buying the enterprise (or its part). The proposal is submitted to the enterprise founding organ. After further discussion between the founder and the enterprise, the proposal is submitted for approval to the federal Ministry of Finance (if the enterprise was founded by a federal body) or to the appropriate republican body (if the enterprise belongs to the republic).

After the privatization project is accepted, the enterprise is officially transferred to the Fund of National Property (at the federal or republican

---

[51]The bill is officially entitled the Law on Transfer of State Property to Other Persons.

level, depending on the founding organ). The Fund proceeds with the privatization process. The law allows two types of privatization: privatization by private agreement between the buyer, enterprise, and state administration, or by auction. No workers' discounts are mentioned in the law, although the enterprise can, in planning its privatization project, propose a discount for its employees (or even a full employee buy-out). The state administration can either accept or reject the proposal. The proceeds of privatization are received by the Fund and can only be used to assume the debts of privatized firms, to pay the cash portion of restitution, or to cover the operating expenses of privatization. By mid-1991 approximately 2,500 enterprises in the Czech part of the country had submitted privatization proposals.

Another interesting feature of the Czechoslovak process is that the two phases, corporatization and privatization, are practically combined. As discussed above, a common feature of privatization laws in other East European countries is that state- or labor-managed enterprises first become joint stock companies (with the state holding all or most shares), and are later offered for sale. According to the Czechoslovak privatization law, both phases occur simultaneously when the enterprise defines its privatization proposal.

The privatization law does not address the issue of foreign ownership. The implication is that foreign entities will not be treated differently from domestic entities. The process, however, is designed to provide a check on foreign ownership. Because privatization proposals have to be accepted by government bodies, the government can reject a proposal if it considers it to be detrimental to the national interest.

Some of Czechoslovakia's key economists and government officials originally proposed to proceed with privatization through the distribution of virtually free vouchers to all citizens older than 18 years of age. The distribution of vouchers began in October 1991. Vouchers worth $33 each can be purchased at more than 5,000 locations throughout the country and, as of May 1992, voucher holders have been able to invest in the companies of their choice.

Because small privatization (the privatization of shops, retail outlets, restaurants, and so on) is easier to accomplish, it has progressed further. According to the October 1990 law, private property nationalized by a series of acts in 1959 will be returned to its former owners. This property includes approximately 70,000 workshops, restaurants, pubs, rental houses, and so on.[57] As for small properties that belong to the state and were not

---

[52]Mladek (1990, p. 13) relates an amusing story that illustrates the problems associated with restitution. Former owners requested the restitution of 170 villas in Prague that presently house foreign diplomats. Some foreign embassies protested, threatening to nationalize Czechoslovak embassies in their own countries. The law was amended to exclude diplomatic villas from the list of property that could be restituted in kind.

previously nationalized, they will be sold to Czechoslovak citizens by auction; the proceeds of these auctions would accrue to republican or local bodies.

Auctions of workshops, restaurants, and service outlets started in January 1991. All Czechoslovak citizens are allowed to participate (foreigners are allowed only if the property is not sold). Auctions have almost invariably been successful, with sale prices often exceeding the threshold price set by the government by several times[53] (although some argue that threshold prices have been set unrealistically low). Small privatizations continue apace, with auctions taking place on a weekly basis in numerous cities. By the end of 1991, approximately 16,000 small businesses had been sold; the average value per small business was $27,000.

Even small privatization is not devoid of problems, however. In Czechoslovakia, unlike in Poland, less of the retail trade has been privatized. Prospective buyers are deterred by a number of factors: high real interest rates (for financing of inventories), the obligation of new owners to continue carrying some items (for example, food) for at least two years after privatization, and the absence of incentives for workers to "self-privatize."

New private investments in retail outlets are also hampered by the absence of commercial space; in many newly built residential areas in Czechoslovakia, for example, a single large supermarket serves an entire neighborhood. Such supermarkets cannot be readily bought by private individuals because of their value. On the other hand, space for small stores is scarce or even unavailable. As in other countries, disputes over the ownership of land also complicate privatization.[54]

Conclusions

The process of privatization in Eastern Europe has been characterized by (a) a lifting of all or most limits on private sector activity, and the introduction of constitutionally guaranteed equal treatment of the private and state sector; (b) the legal transformation of many SOEs into corporate (joint stock) firms; and (c) the privatization of some former SOEs. In almost all countries, liberal attitudes toward the private sector have resulted in the fast growth of that sector. In Poland, Hungary, former Yugoslavia, and Czechoslovakia, private nonagricultural employment has expanded between 15 and 20 percent a year, against a decline of employment in the state sector.

---

[53]In the first such auction in Prague on January 26, 1991, the ratio of sale price to threshold price was 10 to 1.

[54]In Czechoslovakia, land was never officially nationalized even if it was used de facto as state property. All ownership titles thus still exist. Yet the number of claimants exceeds the original number of plots severalfold because of the branching of families.

In contrast to the fast growth of the still small private sector, the transfer of state (nonprivate) enterprises to private ownership has proceeded rather slowly. Most transformations have been of the so-called spontaneous type. Spontaneous privatizations are generally inequitable and nontransparent, and they create social tensions. However, they are also faster. Hungary, which exhibited a greater willingness to allow spontaneous privatizations, also recorded more instances of privatization than other East European countries.

A government can choose among several privatization options, all of which have their disadvantages. External privatization through sales (the British model) is too slow; the process is also hampered by the absence of capital markets, a lack of private savings, and problems of enterprise valuation. The free distribution of vouchers has been considered too radical; the defects of this model include ownership that is too dispersed to effectively monitor managers, and an absence of revenue for the state. Spontaneous (internal) privatizations, involving employee buy-outs, can also be inequitable. Mutual funds may slow privatization to a crawl.

It is becoming clear that the process that is actually adopted will consist of a combination of different options; the relative importance of these options will vary between countries. Countries with a history of decentralized decision making and with more skilled management may be more willing to accept spontaneous privatizations. This is the example provided by Hungary and Slovenia. Strongly unionized labor (as in Poland) or a long history of labor management (as in Yugoslavia) renders the adoption of some incentives for worker ownership imperative. Countries with no history of decentralization, and a high abhorrence of the *nomenklatura* (for example, Czechoslovakia and Romania) put greater emphasis on the free distribution of shares.[55] External sales are more easily accomplished in richer countries (like Hungary) as well as in those less concerned with a possibly high foreign stake (for example, Hungary and the Czech lands).

References

Baczynski, Jerzy. 1990. "Dla ubogich" (For the Poor Ones). *Polityka* 3:4.

Bajt, Aleksander. 1988. *Samoupravni oblik drustvene svojine* (Self-Management Form of Social Property). Zagreb: Globus.

Bogetić, Željko. 1992. "Is There a Case for Employee Ownership?" This volume.

Brzeg-Wielunski, Stanislav. 1991. "Efekt Sniezniej Kuli" (The Snowball Effect). *Gazeta Bankowa* 23, 9 June.

---

[55]I am grateful to John Nellis for pointing this out to me.

Byrd, William, and Alan Gelb. 1990. "Township, Village, and Private Industry in China's Economic Reform." Policy, Research and External Affairs Department Working Paper 406. World Bank, Country Economics Department, Washington, D.C. Processed.

China. 1989. *Statistical Yearbook of China 1988*. Beijing: State Statistical Bureau and Economic Information and Agency.

Czekaj, Jan. 1990. "Jak wyceniono pierwsza '5'?" (How the First Five Were Valued?) *Zycie Gospodarcze* (December).

Demsetz, Harold, and Kenneth Lehn. 1985. "The Structure of Corporate Ownership: Causes and Consequences." *Journal of Political Economy* 93:1155–77.

Durupty, Michel. 1988. *Les Privatisations en France* (Privatizations in France). Notes et Etudes Documentaires, No. 4857. Paris: La Documentation Française.

The Economist. 1988. "How LBOs Are Shaping Up." 26 November, p. 75.

———. 1990a. "Survey of Capitalism: In Triumph, in Flux." 5 May.

———. 1990b. "Common Fodder." 10 November, p. 96.

Ellul, Jacques. [1954] 1964. *The Technological Society*. Reprint. New York: Vintage Books.

Emmott, Bill. 1991. "Gamblers, Masters and Slaves." *The Economist*, 27 April.

Eswaran, Mukesh, and Ashok Kotwal. 1989. "Why Are Capitalists the Bosses?" *Economic Journal* 99:162–76.

Feige, Edgar. 1991. "Perestroika and Ruble Convertibility." *The Cato Journal* Winter:631–53.

Gu, Peidong, and Xirong Liu. 1988. "Study on Turning State-Owned Enterprises into Stock Companies." *Social Sciences in China* 9:25–45.

Hemming, Richard, and Ali Mansoor. 1988. "Privatization and Public Enterprises." International Monetary Fund Occasional Paper 56, Washington, D.C.

Hinds, Manuel. 1990. "Issues in the Introduction of Market Forces in Eastern European Socialist Economies." Europe, Middle East and North Africa (EMENA) Discussion Paper. World Bank, Washington, D.C. Processed.

———. 1992. "Policy Effectiveness in Reforming Socialist Economies." This volume.

Horvat, Branko. 1989. *ABC jugoslavenskog socijalizma* (The ABC's of Yugoslav Socialism). Zagreb: Globus.

Hungary. 1989. *Statistical Yearbook of Hungary*. Budapest: Statistical Office.

Iwanek, Maciej, and Marcin Swiecicki. 1989. "Socialist Stock Company: The Missing Link in Economic Reform." In C. Kessides, T. King, D. M. Nuti, and C. Sokil, eds., *Financial Reform in Socialist Economies*. Washington, D.C.: World Bank.

Jenkinson, Tim, and Colin Mayer. 1988. "The Privatization Process in France and the U.K." *European Economic Review* 32:482–90.

Kawalec, Stefan. 1989. "Privatization of the Polish Economy." *Communist Economies* 3:241–56.

Kaufmann, Sylvie. 1990. "Les Nouveaux 'Raiders' à l'Est" (The New Raiders in the East). *Le Monde*, 20 April.

Kovac, Bogomir. 1989. "Nacionalizacija i privatizacija" (Nationalization and Privatization). *Ekonomska politika*, December 11.

Lewandowski, Janusz, and Jan Szomburg. 1989. "Property Reform as a Basis for Social and Economic Reform." *Communist Economies* 3:257–68.

Luders, Rolf J. 1990. "Chile's Massive SOE Divestiture Program: 1975-1990: Failures and Successes." Paper presented at the World Bank Conference on Privatization and Ownership Changes in East and Central Europe, 13–14 June, Washington, D.C. Processed.

Mejstrik, Michal. 1990. "The Transformation of Czechoslovakia to a Market Economy: The Possibilities and Problems." Processed.

Milanovic, Branko. 1989. *Liberalization and Entrepreneurship: Dynamics of Reform in Socialism and Capitalism.* Armonk, N.Y.: M. E. Sharpe.

———. 1991. "Privatisation in Post-Communist Societies." *Communist Economies and Economic Transformation* 3:5–39.

———. 1992. "Poland's Quest for Economic Stabilisation, 1988–91: Interaction of Political Economy and Economics." *Soviet Studies* 44:511–32.

Milovanovic, Milic. 1986. *Kapital i minuli rad* (Capital and Past Labor). Belgrade: Savremena administracija.

Mizsei, Kalman, and Adam Torok. 1989. "Modified Planned Economies at the Crossroads: The Case of Hungary." Processed.

Mladek, Jan. 1990. "Privatisation, Liberalisation and Foreign Participation in Czechoslovak Economy: Current Situation and Proposals." Processed.

Mora, Maria. 1991. "The (Pseudo-) Privatization of State-Owned Enterprises (Changes in Organizational and Proprietary Forms, 1987–1990)." *Acta Oeconomica* 1–2:1–17.

Nagaoka, Sadao. 1989. "Reform of Ownership and Control Mechanisms in Hungary and China: Recent Developments and Future Directions." Industry Series Working Paper 7. World Bank, Industry and Energy Department, Washington, D.C. Processed.

Nankani, Helen B. 1990. "Lessons of Privatization in Developing Countries." *Finance and Development* 27:43–45.

Nuti, Mario D. 1987. "Feasible Financial Innovation under Market Socialism." Paper presented at the Workshop on Financial Reform in Socialist Economies, European University Institute, October, Florence, Italy. Processed.

OECD (Organisation for Economic Co-operation and Development). 1991. *Economic Surveys: Hungary.* Paris.

Poland. Various years. *Rocznik Statystyczny* (Statistical Yearbook). Warsaw: Central Statistical Office.

Saldanha, Fernando, and Branko Milanovic. 1990. "Proposal for a Fast and Efficient Privatization of the State Sector." *Privatization Review* Fall:20–29.

Santini, Jean-Jacques. 1986. "Les Denationalisations au Royaume-Uni." In Broclawski, Longueville, and Santini, eds., *Les Privatisations à l'étranger: Royaume-Uni, RFA, Italie, Espagne, Japon*. Notes et Etudes Documentaires No. 4821. Paris: La Documentation Française, 25–62.

Singh, Ajit. 1990. "The Stockmarket in a Socialist Economy." In Nolan and Fureng, eds., *The Chinese Economy and its Future: Achievements and Problems of Post-Mao Reform*. Cambridge, U.K.: Polity Press.

Tardos, Marton. 1990. "Property Ownership." *Eastern European Economics* 28:4–29.

Uvalic, Milica. 1989. *Profit Sharing Schemes in Western Europe*. Florence: European University Institute.

U.S.S.R. 1989. *Narodnoye Khozyaystvo SSSR v 1988* (National Economy of the U.S.S.R.: 1988). Moscow: Goskomstat.

Walkowiak, Witold, Mikolaj Breitkopf, and Dariusz Jaszczynski. 1990. "Private Sector and Privatization in Poland." Paper presented at the World Bank Conference on Privatization and Ownership Changes in East and Central Europe, 13–14 June, Washington, D.C. Processed.

Ward, Benjamin. 1958. "The Firm in Illyria: Market Syndicalism." *American Economic Review* 48:566–89.

Yarrow, George. 1986. "Privatization in Theory and Practice." *Economic Policy* 1:323–77.

———. 1990. "Holding Companies as a Means of Accelerating Privatization in Poland: Some Comments." Processed.

3

Is There a Case
for Employee Ownership?

Željko Bogetić

Enterprise reform and privatization (or divestiture by the state)[1] are the mainstays of a strategy to liberalize East European economies in transition from socialism. Because of the large size of the state or social sector in former socialist economies, privatization is a formidable task.[2]

The many methods and techniques that have been proposed for implementing privatization programs (Milanovic, this volume) draw on theoretical literature that expounds the merits of privatization, and on the experience with privatization in industrial (primarily the United Kingdom and France) and some developing countries (Chile, Malaysia, Sri Lanka, among others). The evidence, however, does not lend itself to generalizations about which privatization strategies work best, and in what circumstances; consensus on how to privatize is difficult to achieve because privatization is a highly politicized topic.

In order to avoid charges that the privatization process is arbitrary or unjust, agreement about the method of privatization is required at all levels of society, industries and firms. In multiregional, multiethnic political

---

[1]See Berg and Shirley (1987) for a distinction between privatization and a narrower concept of divestiture involving the transfer and/or liquidation of ownership of state firms.

[2]Thorough surveys of issues of transition are found in Hinds (1990), and Fischer and Gelb (1990).

I am indebted to Martha de Melo, Wafik Grais, Arye Hillman, Dennis R. Heffley, Barbara Lee, Branko Milanovic, Alanson Minkler, and Stephen R. Sacks, who provided extensive comments on an early draft of this paper. Also, I am grateful to Michael Conte, Nils Fostvedt, Robert Myers, Stephen Smith, and Fernando Saldanha for extremely useful comments or discussions. I am, however, solely responsible for the final product and any remaining errors.

entities, regional and ethnic dimensions impose additional political constraints on the privatization process: will central governments or the authorities of individual republics or provinces be responsible for privatizing state enterprises? Who will receive the proceeds from these sales?

Because of the variety of constraints and circumstances experienced by countries wishing to privatize state-owned enterprises, programs must be tailored to the conditions of a given country, region, or industry, with particular attention to "the critical role of political will" (Nankani 1990, p. 45). Firm-specific characteristics—such as firm size, internal labor-management relations, age and job-length structure of the work force, monitoring costs, uncertainty, and so on—may influence the outcome of a privatization strategy.[3]

Evidence from Eastern Europe supports the view that it is not possible to generalize about privatization strategies. Although these countries embarked on the design and implementation of privatization programs almost at the same time, they have approached the process very differently. In no country, however, has privatization proceeded at a pace that might allow quick replacement of socialist or state industry with the private sector. In Poland the "Big Bang" approach to stabilization and to opening the economy did not provide a big bang for privatization because of political disagreements about how to privatize. In Hungary privatization also stalled. In the former Yugoslavia an employee-oriented strategy for privatization was legislated in the Law on Social Capital (1990) and the Law on Distribution of Personal Incomes (1990), but the results were scant.

The objective of policymakers is to quickly privatize a substantial portion of the state sector and to create a competitive market economy.[4] Internal privatization (employee buy-outs) assures that employees[5] have a stake in the privatization process; for this reason it may prove the most efficient and least contentious method available. In contrast to external privatization (which involves the sale or granting of enterprises to external owners), internal privatization occurs when an enterprise is bought by its own workers and/or managers.[6] Mixed privatization, combining internal and external privatization through the sale of enterprise shares to both outsiders and employees, may facilitate the privatization process because it also allows

---

[3]In a recent review of the World Bank experience with privatization in developing countries, Nellis (1989) stresses the uncertainty surrounding privatization, and argues for a careful and flexible handling of the Bank's conditionality regarding privatization. In particular, rigid deadlines for the sale of enterprises can be counterproductive.

[4]For a different view see Vanek (1989) who argues against employee ownership unless it is accompanied by participation in decision making. It should be noted that employee ownership, as understood in this paper, does not exclude the possibility that some employee-owned firms, if they so choose, will indeed become truly cooperative in the participatory sense, but it does not impose this possibility *ex ante*.

[5]By "employee," I mean both workers and managers.

[6]See also Lee (1991) for an analysis of employee ownership in the context of privatization.

employees to acquire a stake in the enterprise's assets (and hence profits).[7] Without this stake on the part of employees, the process of privatization will be impeded.[8]

In the following section, I discuss why employee ownership may foster privatization in the initial stage of the transition from socialism. I then discuss the internal structure and performance of two employee ownership schemes: Employee Stock Ownership Plans (ESOPs) in the United States, and Mondragon cooperatives in Spain. The final section (on prospects for privatization through employee ownership) considers the prospects for using similar employee ownership schemes in Eastern Europe.

Privatization through employee ownership

The literature on privatization abounds with detailed analyses of privatization methods; the arguments for and against these methods will not be repeated here.[9] Given what is known about various privatization techniques, I argue that schemes involving employee ownership minimize the political, transaction, and monitoring costs. This is not to suggest that there is a need for a uniformly sanctioned and protected system of compulsory employee ownership. Rather, employee ownership is proposed as a means of speeding up the privatization process in socialist economies.

Politics

Privatization is a political process with many opponents. Nankani (1990, p. 45) observes:

> *Employed labor opposes divestiture for fear of job loss. Government officials may resent it because their jurisdiction becomes restricted. And the intellectual community may oppose it because privatization tends to be perceived as primarily benefitting the rich and the privileged.*

Labor is typically a prominent opponent of privatization. Government officials and the intellectual community may be divided along ideological lines, but the workers have the most at stake: job security and salaries which were ubiquitously guaranteed by the state.

---

[7]Recently, Great Britain and Chile successfully implemented the mixed privatization of a number of major firms.

[8]For arguments based on the extension of democratic community in the political sphere to the democratic, participatory (or cooperative) firm in the economic sphere, see Vanek (1989) and Ellerman (1989); a similar view, albeit with different arguments, is held by Minkler (1990, 1989).

[9]For recent surveys of the advantages and disadvantages of various privatization options, see, for example, Milanovic (this volume), Dhanji and Milanovic (1991), and Vuylsteke (1988). Also, Pirie (1988) discusses 21 different privatization methods, primarily with regard to the British experience of the past decade.

Managers of state enterprises[10] may also oppose privatization because of uncertainty concerning their jobs, the expectation that their authority will be restricted by the new private owners, and the fear that the enterprise's budget constraint will "harden" after privatization. If managers of socialist enterprises are to be judged solely by their performance, then managers chosen by political selection may feel vulnerable. For decades the state and/or Communist party assumed the role of market in choosing corporate managers: the invisible hand of competition for managerial jobs was replaced by the "visible" hand of state and party.[11]

The recognition that employees of state firms are a powerful political constituency capable of bringing privatization to a halt has encouraged some countries to try various employee ownership schemes. In Britain cases of successful divestiture featuring employee ownership include the British National Freight Corporation divestiture in 1982, and the Vickers shipyard divestiture in 1986. Both divestitures were examples of a blend of internal and external privatization, and they demonstrated the benefits that can be realized with an eclectic approach; in both cases, too, a substantial number of employees participated in the transfer of ownership. Labor-management relations and productivity improved as a result of the transfer (see Pirie 1988, pp. 124–37). Shares of British National Freight Corporation that were sold to employees and external investors for one British pound in 1982 were worth 70 pounds five years later. Vuylsteke (1988) also notes examples of successful privatization with substantial employee involvement in Italy and France.

In developing countries, the Chilean privatization program (involving privatization of over 400 enterprises since 1973) has, particularly in its later stages, emphasized the twin objectives of spreading ownership while at the same time providing "at least one ownership group with a relatively high stake in it, to make monitoring of management a worthwhile effort" (Luders 1990, p. 24). In at least two instances (Ecom, a computer firm, and Emel, a power generation and distribution firm), employee involvement in the buy-

---

[10]I use the term *state enterprises* to denote firms that are truly state firms in Eastern Europe as well as the "social" firms in the former Yugoslavia. The latter can be viewed as a special case of the former: the state in Yugoslavia appeared as a franchisor of "social" capital to franchisees-worker collectives at zero price, with the capital maintenance requirement.

[11]One may argue that the "animal spirits" of entrepreneurship and managerial initiatives have been somewhat released in the Yugoslav decentralized economy. Yet, even here, "too much" entrepreneurship and initiative has been effectively censured through (semi)official purges, as was the case with a number of successful managers of large firms in Serbia in the early 1970s. For recent analyses of the Yugoslav experience, see Saldanha (this volume) and Madžar (1990).

out was 100 percent;[12] following privatization, the financial performance of both firms improved substantially (Vuylsteke 1988, pp. 31–32).

In Poland, on the other hand, attempted employee buy-outs under Rakowski's government resulted only in management or *nomenklatura* buy-outs (Walkowiak, Breitkopf, and Jaszczynski 1990), provoking immediate public opposition and effectively halting privatization. The public apparently does not want to see former state managers benefit the most from privatization; this resentment appears to be another important constraint on privatization in formerly socialist countries.

In the former Yugoslavia, the Law on Social Capital (1990) gave enterprises the option of selling shares to their employees (as well as to former employees and pensioners) at a discount. The Law on Distribution of Personal Incomes (May 1990) supported this strategy by obliging profitable firms to pay part of their employees' salaries in the form of internal shares. Although the law tried to quicken the pace of internal privatization, unions viewed this measure as a form of incomes policy and as a means of passing the risk of privatization onto employees. Again we see how privatization is a delicate political process, requiring a careful balancing of the interests of employees, managers, external investors and the state. Therefore, the upshot is that political feasibility is one argument in favor of combining employee ownership with other forms of external privatization (for example, sale to individuals, banks, pension funds, and foreigners).[13]

The need for some concentration of ownership

In an environment characterized by a high degree of uncertainty and imperfect functioning of the market for corporate control, owners will want to exercise tighter control over management.[14] In the words of Demsetz and Lehn, "the profit potential from exercising a . . . degree of owner control is, we believe, correlated with the instability of the firm's environment" (1985, p. 1160). Demsetz and Lehn, in an empirical test based on a sample of over 500 U.S. firms, found, among other things, that ownership

---

[12]Nankani (1988) reports on the sale of Ecom, Chile's largest computer firm, to its employees. She notes that "the only group that showed interest was its employees . . . . This decision [to sell to employees] satisfied two other goals . . . [of] privatization program: avoiding liquidation and redistributing ownership among a large group of investors" (p. 37).

[13]Milanovic (1989), in a tally of anti- and pro-reform forces in transition from socialism, also identifies worker-owners as a force potentially supportive of reform. In a sense, this paper is an elaboration of the same idea.

[14]By concentration of ownership I mean *intrafirm* ownership. This concept is not incompatible with a *broadening* of ownership across a greater number of individuals in the total population. An example of perfect intrafirm concentration and perfect spread would be a society consisting entirely of one-person businesses. Therefore, it is important to realize that concentration of ownership within a firm does not necessarily imply a concentration across individuals.

concentration is systematically positively related to uncertainty (as measured by instability in profit rate) and negatively related to firm size.

Consider the relevance of this finding to the privatization process in socialist economies. The economic environment during the period of transition is highly uncertain, giving rise to a high variance of profit rates across firms. In addition, the market for corporate control, perhaps more than other markets in socialist economies, is either nonexistent, or highly distorted. In these circumstances a principal-agent problem of serious dimensions can arise; managers will work in the interest of the owners only if owners are able to exercise direct control. Such control could be achieved by concentrated ownership. If owners cannot directly monitor managers, they will be unable to ensure that managers act in a manner consistent with the owner's objectives.[15]

Who is to take on the role of a majority owner in privatized firms? Foreign investors may not be candidates, except in a limited number of cases; the owners in most firms, then, must be found among employees and external investors (both individual and institutional investors). Because employees are the largest and most politically vocal group, they are natural candidates for fostering the privatization process, especially during its initial phase.

The government, of course, should not seek to sell all firms exclusively, or even mostly, to employees. This would lead to a form of worker capitalism on a countrywide basis. Rather, when employee interest and labor-management relations allow, internal or mixed privatization can help to initiate the process in certain companies.[16]

Apart from political feasibility, there are two advantages to establishing a closer relationship between owners and workers through a partial (or even full) employee ownership scheme:

• some concentration of ownership is created in the hands of employees, which alleviates the monitoring problem that derives from the usual conflicts of interest between owners and workers; and

• the employees' time horizon (that is, their willingness to invest) is extended because they derive capital income from investments in their own enterprise.

When employees become capitalists, the Furubotn-Pejovich effect is significantly diminished, if not altogether eliminated. Employee-owners will adopt a longer-term horizon because they gain the ability to recoup their

---

[15]"To turn a company around, some core group may need to have and use a large if not controlling stake in the enterprises. While perhaps not a serious issue with well-managed firms, it is of concern where firms to be privatized are weak or underperforming, often the case in the developing countries" (Vuylsteke 1988, p. 125).

[16]Employees (and other shareholders) should be allowed freely to trade their shares immediately after privatization. This would facilitate development of a capital market and speed the process of transition to a market economy. The role of capital market development was stressed in IFC (1991) and Bogetić (1991).

original capital investment. Also, though less tangibly, when employees become the owners of capital, motivation and productivity may be enhanced.

Some authors argue (Jensen and Meckling 1976) that employee-owners may, in fact, *increase* shirking; this was a frequent criticism of the Yugoslav model of labor management. Yugoslav firms, however, are different. They lack the clear ownership rights that distinguish employee-owned firms. Moreover, agency problems, or more narrowly, shirking-monitoring problems, where the product is a result of teamwork (Alchian and Demsetz 1972), are not unique to firms in which employees own shares.

Minimizing administrative and time costs

Employee buy-outs (whether in the form of purely internal privatization or in combination with external sales) are clearly simpler and faster than external sales: there is a readily identifiable group of buyers, and the largest problem is finding the best way to finance the buy-out. The procedure is particularly easy when the employees of small firms (for example, firms employing less than 100 workers) decide, with the consent of the state, to buy the controlling share of their enterprise, while floating the rest for external buyers.

Taking advantage of informational asymmetry

Individual employees are knowledgeable about the internal slacks and technological constraints and opportunities facing a firm. In instances where employees express an interest in investing their own capital in their firm, offering them the opportunity to do so taps this informational advantage. In a recent theoretical paper, Minkler (1990) shows that when employees possess superior knowledge about production possibilities, monitoring costs are minimized by a horizontal (such as a franchise, or even a participatory) rather than a vertical (or hierarchical) form of organization. The same reasoning applies here. When employees (agents) have an informational advantage over the external owners (principals), the latter will not be able to direct the former to profitable activities, even when monitoring costs are zero. The larger the knowledge asymmetry between principal and agent, the greater the potential profitability of making employees co-owners, franchisees, or *coopcrateurs*.

A caveat: the inequity of employee buy-outs

Employee buy-outs may not prove equitable to retired employees, workers in nonprofitable and nonprofit enterprises, and the unemployed. It is, of course, difficult to be equitable in a world of uncertainty, uneven knowledge, and costly information.[17] The problem with all privatization schemes is that each may be viewed as an allocation of property rights favoring certain groups. Even the *ex ante* perfectly egalitarian distribution of shares to all citizens, as is currently being implemented in Czechoslovakia, can *ex post* be nonegalitarian, because of asymmetric information in trading of shares. Pragmatically, to ensure public support for privatization, what matters is the public *perception* of equity, and not the pursuit of an unattainable, perfect equity.

Mixed privatization is different from the mass privatization approach. With mixed privatization, the initial distribution of political power and resources influences the success of privatization. In the case of mass privatization, a new set of rules governing the allocation of power and resources is established, representing a radical break with the previous firm structure. Both approaches, however, attempt to privatize in the fastest and least costly way.

Before I discuss more fully the potential consequences of privatization efforts in Eastern Europe, it is useful to briefly analyze two employee ownership schemes. These schemes provide lessons concerning some of the problems as well as the potential benefits of employee-owned enterprises.

A study of two employee ownership schemes

Employee stock ownership plans

Definition and background. Employee Stock Ownership Plans (ESOPs) are an important and growing form of organization in the United States.[18] Participating employees purchase securities of their firm through stock

---

[17]Only in the case of free distribution of shares (or vouchers) to citizens, will Pareto improvement in privatization be achieved. When shares are traded in the market, no one will be worse off than they were before, and those whose shares command positive prices will be better off. The method, however, is equitable only *ex ante*. It is important to recognize that the voucher method results in *ex ante* low concentration of ownership, while *ex post* inequities could be even more substantial than under the alternatives. See Dhanji and Milanovic (1991).

[18]ESOPs are no longer found only in the United States. Many countries, such as the United Kingdom, Thailand, Costa Rica, and Zimbabwe, are experimenting with ESOPs. The following discussion focuses on U.S. ESOPs because they are the largest employee stock ownership plan sector in the world.

bonus plans or combined stock bonus and money purchase plan trusts.[19] ESOPs originated with the 1974 Employee Retirement Income Security Act (ERISA) and the 1975 Tax Reduction Act, which granted employers and employees certain tax privileges.[20] The goals of ESOP legislation in the United States were (a) to broaden the ownership base of corporate stock, (b) to stimulate capital formation by providing more funds for corporate finance, and (c) to stimulate improvements in the performance of participating corporations (GAO 1986a, p. 3). The U.S. General Accounting Office (GAO) has studied the number, structure, performance, and regional and sectoral distribution of ESOPs, in order to determine the extent to which these goals have been met. They found that the goal of broadening stock ownership has been moderately fulfilled; there is less evidence that the other two objectives have been achieved.

The two important legislative acts (ERISA and the Tax Reduction Act) resulted in two different categories of ESOPs:

• ERISA-type ESOPs, where the employer's contribution to the trust is tax deductible. ERISA-type ESOPs include leveraged, leverageable, and unleveraged ESOPs. Leveraged ESOPs borrow money from financial institutions in order to finance the purchase of employer securities. The employer may contribute to the trust the amount necessary to meet annual principal and interest payments on the loan. The employer can thus borrow from financial institutions and repay the loan with pretax dollars, while fully deducting both principal and interest payments.[21] ESOPs that have the legal option of leveraging, but that have not used it, are called "leverageable," whereas those that do not have this option are "nonleveraged ESOPs." Recent GAO surveys (GAO 1985, 1986a, 1986b) revealed two thirds of ESOPs to be of the ERISA type, with a roughly equal distribution among its various modalities.

---

[19]"Stock bonus plan or stock bonus and money purchase plans are employee benefits provided by employers. The plans receive cash or other assets (generally employer stock) from employers and generally allocate those contributions to accounts in the name of individual participating employees. A money purchase plan has a specific contribution schedule (such as 5 percent of salary per year), whereas a stock bonus plan can determine each year how much, if any, to contribute. Employees receive full or partial distribution of the assets in their accounts when they retire, leave the firm, or at the occurrence of other events as specified in the plan. ESOPs differ from most other employee plans in that they are required to invest primarily in securities of the employer, rather that maintaining a diversified portfolio" (GAO 1986b, pp. 12–13).

However, Blassi argues that ESOPs are not so different from most profit-sharing plans simply because ". . . of the approximately half-million profit sharing plans in the United States 96 percent are *deferred* [emphasis added] profit sharing trusts" (1990, p. 173). Moreover, Blassi (1988, p. 11) notes that employee-owned assets in deferred profit-sharing trusts exceeded those in ESOPs by over two times in 1983. This means that the relevance of ESOP experience extends to a variety of deferred profit sharing plans in the United States.

[20]For more on ESOP legislation, see Blassi (1988) or Conte and Svejnar (1990).

[21]Only interest payments are normally deductible.

• The second type of ESOP is the Tax Reduction Act (1975) ESOP, or a TRASOP: a firm is given a 1 percent tax credit[22] on "qualified investment on plant and equipment, provided it made contribution to an ESOP of an equal amount" (GAO 1987, p. 9). Legislative changes in 1976 and 1983 altered the base of the tax credit from investment to payroll, and created so-called payroll-based ESOPs or PAYSOPs. New legislation in December 1986, however, eliminated these advantages while granting new advantages to the ERISA-type ESOPs.

The opportunities opened by tax advantages were exploited by many U.S. firms: in 1975 and 1976, over 1,500 ESOPs were formed. According to a GAO census of ESOPs in 1985 (GAO 1986b), of a total of 7,000 stock ownership plans, approximately 4,200 were active ESOPs. Using a stratified random sample of approximately 2,000 plans, the census found that more than 7 million employees were participating in ESOPs, and the total value of assets involved was approximately $19 billion. The total cost of tax incentives in terms of the foregone tax revenue for the period 1977–83 was estimated to be between $12 billion and $13 billion, largely attributed to the tax credit type of ESOPs.

Ownership spread, concentration, and performance. A basic goal of ESOP legislation was to broaden the basis of corporate stock ownership in the United States. This goal was established in the belief that a diffusion of ownership of stock among employees would strengthen employee identification with the economic system and provide employees with additional asset-based income. The GAO (1986a) found that participation of employees in ESOPs was three times that of the percentage of U.S. families owning stock. ESOPs would appear, then, to represent a means of broadening ownership and creating workers' capitalism.

This broadening of ownership across the U.S. population did not reduce the concentration of ownership within firms. A 1989 GAO study revealed that the top 20 percent of salaried employees held between 29.4 and 66.7 percent of assets, and in some cases a few "external" investors held a large majority of the stock (GAO 1989, p. 7). Blassi and Kruse (1991) also present evidence of rapidly growing employee ownership in public corporations in the United States. Contrary to some perceptions, they show that employee ownership is quite frequent in large U.S. firms.[23] An ESOP can thus reconcile dominant ownership within a firm with the spread of ownership across employees and the population more generally.

Data comparing the performance of ESOPs relative to non-ESOP firms are inconclusive; studies of the relationship between employee ownership and various performance indicators generally provide either ambiguous or

---

[22]They are sometimes called "tax credit ESOPs."

[23]"The Employee Ownership 1000—the top 1000 [firms] by amount of employee ownership on all stock exchanges—now includes almost a third of the Fortune 500 Industrials and a fifth of the Fortune Service 500" (Blassi and Kruse 1991, p. 242).

contradictory results. Studies of profitability (Conte and Tannenbaum 1978; GAO 1989), productivity (Bloom 1985; Lee 1989; GAO 1989), and growth (Bloom 1985; Quarrey 1986) fail to support unambiguously the conjecture that ESOP firms are more profitable and/or productive than non-ESOP firms.[24] The 1987 GAO study[25] finds no significant difference in the performance between the two types of firms. Quarrey (1986) offers evidence, however, that ESOP firms show faster employment and sales growth than non-ESOP firms.

Recent papers by Weitzman and Kruse (1990), and Cable and Wilson (1989, 1990)[26] conclude that there is a positive relationship between profit sharing and productivity. As noted by Card (1990), however, very little is known about the nature or mechanics of this relationship; this can also be said of the relationship between employee ownership and performance.

Many studies find a significant relationship between performance, and employee participation and perceived influence over a firm's decision-making process. In an extremely detailed and thorough survey of the relationship between participation and productivity, Levine and Tyson (1990, p. 203) conclude that ". . . participation usually leads to small, short run improvements in performance and sometimes leads to significant, long-lasting improvements in performance."

To sum up, points to emphasize are the following:

• Firms with ESOPs are privately owned, with clearly defined property rights. As such, they escape the problem of undefined ownership rights that affects Yugoslav firms. Firms with ESOPs are not self-managed firms, although in some cases they do encourage employee participation in decision making.

• Evidence suggests that the performance of ESOPs is not different from that of other types of private firms. This is hardly surprising because, as Kornai writes, the ESOP sector is not an "independent, 'great' sector of the economy but part of the private sector" (Kornai 1990, p. 96).

• Although they contribute to the overall spread of ownership across the population, ESOPs do not appear to jeopardize the concentration of ownership within an enterprise. This is important because ownership concentration is necessary for an efficient owner-manager relationship.

• Because of the tax advantages often offered to ESOPs, there is a budgetary cost in terms of forgone revenues.

---

[24]For a more detailed discussion of studies of ESOPs' performance and other types of non-ESOP firms practicing employee ownership, see Conte and Svejnar (1990).

[25]This is the only study that examines a random sample from the entire population of ESOPs. Another noteworthy study by Bloom (1985) is limited in that it focuses on publicly traded ESOPs, which may have caused him to overrepresent tax credit ESOPs in his sample.

[26]Cable and Wilson (1989, 1990) used a sample of British engineering firms; a similar study was done for West German firms (Cable and Fitzroy 1980).

• The basic lesson from the U.S. experience of ESOPs is that ESOPs can be utilized by privately owned enterprises as a lever with which to foster and broaden the process of ownership change.

Mondragon

Definition and background. Mondragon is a 100 percent employee-owned[27] and employee-managed complex of firms. The organizational form, which can be viewed as an extreme case of ESOP, goes a step further toward the cooperative form of the firm by making employees both owners and managers.

Mondragon cooperatives came into existence during the 1940s in the town of Mondragon, Spain, in the Basque region of Gupiszcoa, when Jose Maria Arizmendi, a local priest, started a small technical school for teaching basic industrial skills to local youth. In 1956 these students created the first Mondragon cooperative. Mondragon has since become a diversified industrial complex of more than 100 similarly organized firms, with more than 20,000 employees. Only two of these cooperatives ever went bankrupt, compared with bankruptcy rates for new firms of 80 percent and 50 percent in the United States and the United Kingdom, respectively.

Many researchers have found the performance of Mondragon impressive. Thomas (1982), in a summary of a much broader study (Thomas and Logan 1980), reports that Mondragon cooperatives outperformed the noncooperative sector, in measures of productivity and profitability, only lagging in the growth of sales per employee because of the rapid growth of employment. In addition, Thomas reports that the cooperatives have a strong financial position because they are able to self-finance through internal capital accounts (Thomas 1982, p. 141).

The cooperatives survived the hardships of a deep recession in the Spanish economy in the late 1970s and early 1980s. During these years, Mondragon cooperatives expanded sales and relocated workers among cooperatives. These adjustments were made possible by flexible pay and relocation policies that were voluntarily pursued by cooperatives; as a result, there were virtually no layoffs in Mondragon during the recession. These facts led Bradley and Gelb (1987, pp. 82–83) to conclude that, because the employee-owners of Mondragon-type cooperatives share a common interest in the success of their firms, they may be in better position to carry out pay adjustment, rather than labor quantity adjustment, in conditions of severe demand fluctuations. This strategy may prove to be a powerful weapon with which cooperatives can fight stagflationary conditions.

---

[27]Although all Mondragon owners are workers, up to 10 percent of its labor force can be nonowners.

Second order support organizations have been established outside the mainstream of producer cooperatives. These support organizations provide services such as banking, social security, research and development for producer cooperatives. The Mondragon complex is involved in several industries: manufacturing, retail trade, consumer cooperatives. A special role is played by *Caja Laboral Popular*, a cooperative bank that generates ideas and finances new investment ventures. In addition, some Mondragon firms join cooperative groups in vertical-type conglomerates to exploit economies of scale and ensure a steady flow of inputs or services to the core producer cooperatives.[28]

Almost every aspect of life and work in Mondragon has been studied. Oakeshott (1978), Bradley and Gelb (1982), Thomas and Logan (1982), Gui (1984), Cornforth et al. (1988), and Whyte and Whyte (1988) describe a successful and growing industrial complex that blends principles of cooperativism with private ownership. Researchers point to the importance of Mondragon's unique features, such as the high degree of community-based solidarity, the tradition of industrial manufacturing, and the immobility of labor and capital in the Basque region, but they also stress the importance of internal policies in shaping the pattern of Mondragon's development, especially with regard to pay, relocation, internal distribution, and investment. Several authors have explored replicability of this model.[29]

Organization, internal policies, and ownership. The basic internal organization of the Mondragon cooperative does not differ substantially from the Yugoslav labor-managed firm. The General Assembly of all employees (based on the principle of one person, one vote) is the highest authority in the firm; the Governing Board, elected to serve as a managerial body, reports to the Assembly at least once a year (Thomas 1982, p. 135). In addition, there are a few advisory councils that advise and/or monitor management: for example, the Social Council, which addresses employee grievances, the Management Council, which offers management advice, and the Auditing Committee (Whyte and Whyte 1988). This is where the similarity with the Yugoslav model ends: employees in Mondragon truly own their enterprises, whereas employees in the Yugoslav model do not.[30] From this true ownership a number of advantages for the Mondragon firm are derived; most important, Mondragon's *cooperateurs* have a long-term interest in the success of their firms, and Mondragon cooperatives are self financing

---

[28]These groups of cooperatives resemble Japanese production Keiretsu, that is, business groups consisting of a central core firm and a number of subsidiaries. For a discussion of Japanese conglomerates, see Yoshitomi (1990).

[29]Bradley and Gelb (1987, p. 94) report that some work has been done to replicate Mondragon in Wales. The Industrial Cooperative Association of Massachusetts has been promoting the development of Mondragon-type cooperatives in the United States. The ESOP Association of the United Kingdom and the United States has already made some contact with Yugoslavs, Russians, and Poles exploring the issue of replicability.

[30]For a property rights analysis of the Yugoslav firm, see Pejovich (1990).

because the internal capital accounts of worker-members allow for a form of deferred profit sharing.

Each new employee-member of the cooperative pays an entry fee, part of which is used for the firm's collective fund, and part of which is credited to the employee's internal capital account. In addition, this internal capital account is credited during each accounting period with the employee's share of profits (which is calculated in accordance with his salary and seniority). Ellerman (1989) believes that the internal capital accounts are one of the keys to Mondragon's success.

Mondragon's worker-owners agree not to pay out funds accumulated in internal capital accounts before a member retires or leaves the cooperative. Upon leaving, a member can collect his accumulated funds with interest, but he cannot sell his claims to the firm's assets to outsiders. This ensures that the firm will always remain employee owned, and the market for shares will always be restricted to the firm itself (that is, shares will remain internal shares). Ellerman (1989) and Vanek (1989) argue that this innovation solves the time horizon problem of the property rights literature (the Furubotn and Pejovich effect), and they insist that the Mondragon cooperative is the most efficient and just form of enterprise organization. Bradley and Gelb (1982), however, discuss the possible costs of locking-in of capital and labor within an enterprise, and warn of the possibility of a trade-off between static efficiency and dynamic capacity for growth in these firms. In particular, some locking-in of labor (that is, Williamson's firm-specific human capital) and capital, although potentially costly to static efficiency, may yet be necessary to increase and sustain capital formation and growth.

Mondragon's cooperative bank, the *Caja Laboral Popular*, is a major catalyst for new investment projects and new firms. Although the bank has a central entrepreneurial role in the complex, it does not appear to "crowd out" individual entrepreneurship and innovation in Mondragon's small- and medium-sized firms.

The internal distribution of earnings is characterized by: (a) a low salary differential (top earners cannot earn more than 4.5 times the salary of the lowest paid full-time worker), (b) the lowest salaries are comparable to salaries earned for similar work in the private sector, and (c) profits are distributed into the collective fund, reserve fund, and internal capital accounts of individual members. Because of the first two factors, managerial jobs in Mondragon will be underpaid relative to similar jobs in the private sector. This implies a potential problem of adverse selection and, indeed, long-term loss, of managerial cadre for the cooperatives. Mondragon's internal policy of screening membership candidates serves as a filtering device: only individuals with sufficiently similar values, interests, time horizons, and a willingness to invest in cooperatives can become members.

The blend of a cooperative decision-making structure and private employee ownership in Mondragon avoids the incentive problem faced by state enterprises in Eastern Europe, as well as the problems related to undefined ownership rights that are associated with the Yugoslav model.

Moreover, the linking of employee rewards to firm performance in a market economy such as Spain's appears an important step toward a more flexible pay adjustment, in contrast to quantity adjustments in response to demand and supply swings. Private ownership and internal capital accounts as a form of intrafirm capital market provide strong incentives for employee-owners, while the cooperative decision-making structure appears to serve as a cohesive force for the firm.

Privatization through employee ownership: prospects

Are employee-owned firms likely to emerge in the transition from socialism in Eastern Europe? The answer is yes, and particularly so in the early stage of privatization. As markets and other types of firms develop, however, they will probably remain only one form of enterprise organization, much as they are in Western countries. The Mondragon model may emerge in some spontaneous privatizations or in new entry firms when employee homogeneity is high and there is a clear (financial) commitment to this type of firm. The importance of employee-owned firms will vary considerably from country to country. Privatization through employee ownership schemes ranging from the "weak" form of ESOP, with workers as minority owners, to a Mondragon-type, "strong" form of worker-owned and worker-run firm is an option that might be utilized by some countries (for example, Poland, Bulgaria, Romania, Slovenia, or some successor states of the U.S.S.R.) more than others (for example, Hungary).

In the former Yugoslavia the federal government viewed privatization as a long-term process. In order to speed up the process, the government advocated a privatization strategy in which employees and other citizens would be able to acquire shares in formerly "social" enterprises. The emphasis, however, was on transferring most of the shares to employees.

There were a number of successful examples of employee-led buy-outs in Yugoslavia prior to the outbreak of civil war. The newspaper *Ekonomska politika*, for example, reported two cases of internal privatization involving Ohis of Skopje (Macedonia) and Hemoform of Vrsac (Serbia) (*Ekonomska politika*, 19 October 1990).

Ohis-Skopje was one of the first firms to implement the government's internal privatization initiative. Internal, nontransferable shares were sold to 3,500 employees, effectively transforming Ohis into a partly employee-owned firm. The nominal price per share was 1,000 dinars (approximately $83 in October 1990), and the total value of the shares was approximately $1.9 million, or about 30 percent of the value of the firm. Ohis also offered its employee-shareholders guarantees of receiving an annual dividend of 10 percent, with the possibility of higher dividends, depending on the firm's financial performance. Interestingly, Ohis is a rare example of a large firm that has never reported any financial losses.

Hemoform, an enterprise worth approximately $57 million, and which employs 1,000 people, is another example of a large, successful firm that has completed an employee buy-out. In the first issuing of shares, the firm's assets were sold to 700 of its employees. Proceeds from this sale are estimated at $22 million. The minimal dividend in this case was not predetermined and will depend entirely on the firm's financial performance.

The Economist (18 May 1991, p. 82) reports a successful employee buy-out of the Moscow-based ventilator firm Moven, and describes the firm's evolution from a state firm to a cooperative, and then to an employee-owned corporation. The firm's employees first managed to evade state control by reorganizing the firm as a cooperative and leasing the firm's equipment from the state. Soon thereafter, the cooperative was transformed into an employee-owned joint stock company, as management borrowed some $3.6 million (6.5 million rubles) from prospective client firms to complete the buy-out.

Although the ownership transfer was completed by management, Moven soon offered 6,500 shares, each worth 1,000 rubles, to its employees at favorable terms; a down payment of only 20 percent was required, and the balance could be borrowed as a long-term loan. Interestingly, employees are free to sell their shares to outside investors, which also suggests that economic rather than political incentives motivated the buy-out. The initial results of the buy-out in terms of output and profit were reported to be very positive; the buy-out also led to a joint venture with a Western firm. The case of Moven illustrates how entrepreneurial management and employees can turn a state socialist firm into a successful privately owned corporation ready to involve itself in domestic and international competition. More state firms can be expected to follow the example of Moven.

These examples of successful employee buy-outs illustrate that this method of privatization has the potential to be quickly implemented, successful, and socially acceptable.

In the successor states of the U.S.S.R., the complexity of regional, ethnic, and political tensions, as well as the competition between conservative and radical approaches to economic transition, make privatization an even more delicate task. An international agency study of the economy of the U.S.S.R. recommended that privatization of small- and medium-sized enterprises be carried out through direct public auctions to individuals and cooperatives; the process might be accelerated, according to this study, if payments could be made in installments. For large enterprises, two strategies were recommended: (a) privatizing by leasing parts of enterprises to private entrepreneurs, and (b) transforming enterprises into joint stock companies owned by holding companies, and then privatizing these companies through a sale of shares. Only a minority ownership for workers was recommended (IMF et al. 1990). The example of Moven shows, however, that the practice of employee-led buy-outs may clear the path for more extensive privatization in successor states of the U.S.S.R.

In Poland the government's objective is to swiftly privatize most enterprises within five years and to create an ownership structure similar to that in Western countries (Lipton and Sachs 1990). The Law on Privatization (July 1990) defined the basic principles of privatization. The Ministry of Ownership Transformation is entrusted with supervisory and some executive functions in the commercialization and privatization of state enterprises.[31]

The privatization program envisages a two-stage privatization strategy: first, state enterprises will be commercialized and will therefore be autonomous; then they will be privatized, with workers guaranteed 20 percent of shares at a discount. Most employee buy-outs have thus far been *nomenklatura* takeovers, however. This has attracted unfavorable publicity, and was stopped by the first non-Communist government. The speed of privatization has since slowed. It is probable, however, that, given the power of trade unions in Poland, internal privatization will become a key privatization method. In the first public offering of five state-owned enterprises, employees bought their allotted part of 20 percent of equity.

In Hungary privatization politics were similar to those in Poland, especially with regard to the public resentment of *nomenklatura* takeovers. A series of laws (the Transformation Law (1989), the Company Act (1989), the Law on the State Property Agency (1990)) created the legal framework for a transfer of state firms into the hands of private owners and institutional investors. A State Property Agency (SPA) was established to oversee spontaneous privatizations, initiate the privatization process, and prevent abuses or the underselling of state assets (Mizsei 1990, p. 27). The SPA has already launched two privatization programs involving some 20 enterprises each, and is planning to launch similar programs every few months. Prospects for ESOP-like firms in Hungary are, at least initially, limited and smaller than in the former Yugoslavia and Russia, and perhaps in Poland.

In Czechoslovakia the government favors so-called coupon privatization or a distribution of investment coupons to citizens. It is not clear whether employee-owned firms would emerge as a result of this form of privatization. The privatization law, although not specific, allows special preferences for employees if management, workers, and investors all agree.

In Bulgaria and Romania laws on privatization are eclectic, combining several different methods of privatization, which would be subject to strict public control; these laws tend to emphasize the prevention of *nomenklatura* takeovers. In both countries, employee participation in privatization is encouraged by price discounts.

In summary, if privatization through some form of employee ownership is fostered in Eastern Europe, political, administrative, and time costs might

---

[31]For a good review of privatization experiences in certain socialist countries, see Lee and Nellis (1990).

be lowered. Employee ownership provides a means of minimizing political resistance, creating a core class of owners, and broadening ownership across the population. Based on this examination of Eastern Europe's scant experience with privatization through employee buy-outs, I would suggest that

• employee-owned firms will emerge as a minority type of firm organization, much like ESOPs in the United States;

• when voluntary employee buy-outs occur, they can be successful, as they reflect the level of employee commitment and readiness for risk taking necessary for private ventures;

• successful employee buy-outs will be motivated primarily by income-related incentives, rather than ideological considerations;

• successful employee buy-outs will result in firms ready to adapt their organization, internal policies, and ownership structure in response to technological and market opportunities (for example, by allowing free sale of shares to external investors); and

• employee ownership contributes to broadening of ownership across population and thus to development of the capital market.

References

Alchian, Armen, and Harold Demsetz. 1972. "Production, Information Costs and Economic Organization." *American Economic Review* 62:777–95.

Berg, Elliot, and Mary Shirley. 1987. "Divestiture in Developing Countries." World Bank Discussion Paper 11. Washington, D.C.: World Bank.

Blassi, Joseph R. 1988. *Employee Ownership: Revolution or Ripoff?* Cambridge, Mass.: Ballinger.

———. 1990. "Comment by Joseph Raphael Blassi." In Alan S. Blinder, ed., *Paying for Productivity: A Look at the Evidence*. Washington, D.C.: The Brookings Institution, pp. 172–81.

Blassi, Joseph R., and Douglas Kruse. 1991. *The New Owners*. New York: Harper Collins Publishers.

Bloom, Steven M. 1985. "Employee Ownership and Firm Performance." Ph.D. diss., Department of Economics, Harvard University, Cambridge, Mass.

Bogetić, Željko. 1991. "The Role of Employee-Ownership in Privatization of State Enterprises in Eastern and Central Europe." Europe, Middle East and North Africa (EMENA) Discussion Paper. World Bank, Washington, D.C.

Bradley, Keith, and Alan Gelb. 1982. "The Mondragon Cooperatives: Guidelines for a Cooperative Economy?" In D. C. Jones and Jan Svejnar, eds., *Participatory and Self-Managed Firms*. Lexington, Mass.: Lexington Books.

———. 1987. "Cooperative Labour Relations: Mondragon's Response to Recession." *British Journal of Industrial Economics* 25:77–97.

Cable, John, and Felix Fitzroy. 1980. "Co-operation and Productivity: Some Evidence from West German Experience." *Economic Analysis and Workers' Management* 14:163–80.

Cable, John, and Nicholas Wilson. 1989. "Profit-Sharing and Productivity: An Analysis of U.K. Engineering Firms." *Economic Journal* 99:366–75.

———. 1990. "Profit-Sharing and Productivity: Some Further Evidence." *Economic Journal* 100:550–55.

Card, David. 1990. "Comment." In Alan S. Blinder, ed., *Paying for Productivity: A Look at the Evidence*. Washington, D.C.: The Brookings Institution, 140–1.

Conte, Michael, and Jan Svejnar. 1990. "The Performance Effects of Employee Ownership Plans." In Alan S. Blinder, ed., *Paying for Productivity: A Look at the Evidence*. Washington, D.C.: The Brookings Institution, 143–72.

Conte, Michael, and Arnold S. Tannenbaum. 1978. "Employee-Owned Companies: Is the Difference Measurable?" *Monthly Labor Review* 101:23–28.

Cornforth, Chris, et al. 1988. *Developing Successful Worker Co-operatives*. London: Sage.

Demsetz, Harold, and Kenneth Lehn. 1985. "The Structure of Corporate Ownership Causes and Consequences." *Journal of Political Economy* 93:1155–77.

Dhanji, Farid, and Branko Milanovic. 1991. "Privatisation." In Paul Marer and Salvatore Zecchini, eds., *The Transition to a Market Economy*, Vol. 2. Paris: OECD, 13–43.

The Economist. 1991. "Fanning the Spark of Capitalism." 18 May.

Ellerman, David P. 1989. "The Internal Capital Accounts Solution to the Social Property Problem in LM Firms with Application to the Socialist Reforms." Yale University Workshop in Worker Management, March, New Haven, Conn.

Fischer, Stanley, and Alan Gelb. 1990. "Issues in Socialist Economy Reform." Policy, Research and External Affairs Department Working Paper 565. Washington, D.C.: World Bank.

Furubotn, Eirik G., and Svetozar Pejovich. 1974. *The Economics of Property Rights*. Cambridge, Mass.: Ballinger.

General Accounting Office (GAO). 1985. "Initial Results of a Survey on Employee Stock Ownership Plans and Information on Related Economic Trends." Briefing Report to the Honorable Russell B. Long, U.S. Senate, GAO-PEMD-85-11, September. Washington, D.C.: GPO.

———. 1986a. "Employee Stock Ownership Plans: Interim Report on a Survey and Related Economic Trends." Briefing Report to the Honorable Russell B. Long, U.S. Senate. Washington, D.C.: GPO.

———. 1986b. "Employee Ownership Plans: Benefits and Costs of ESOP Tax Incentives for Broadening Stock Ownership." Report to Honorable Russell B. Long, U.S. Senate. Washington, D.C.: GPO.

———. 1987. "Employee Stock Ownership Plans: Little Evidence of Effects on Corporate Performance." Report to the Chairman, Committee on Finance, U.S. Senate. Washington, D.C.: GPO.

———. 1989. "Employee Stock Ownership Plans: Allocation of Assets in Selected Plans." Report to the Chairman, Subcommittee on Labor-Management Relations, Committee on Education and Labor, House of Representatives. Washington, D.C.: GPO.

Gui, Benedetto. 1984. "Basque vs. Illyrian Firm: The Problem of Property Rights." *Journal of Comparative Economics* 8:168–81.

Hinds, Manuel. 1990. "Issues in the Introduction of Market Forces in Eastern European Socialist Economies." Europe, Middle East and North Africa (EMENA) Discussion Paper. World Bank, Washington, D.C. Processed.

International Finance Corporation (IFC). 1991. "Financing Corporate Growth in the Developing World." IFC Economics Department Discussion Paper. IFC, Washington, D.C. Processed.

International Monetary Fund (IMF), et al. 1990. *The Economy of the U.S.S.R.: Summary and Recommendations*. Washington, D.C.: World Bank.

Kornai, Janos. 1990. *The Road to a Free Economy*. New York: W. W. Norton and Company.

Jensen, Michael C., and William H. Meckling. 1976. "The Theory of the Firm: Managerial Behavior, Agency Costs and Ownership Structure." *The Journal of Financial Economics* 3:305–60.

Lee, Barbara. 1989. *Productivity and Employee Ownership: The Case of Sweden*. Uppsala, Sweden: Almqvist and Wicksell International.

———. 1991. "Should Employee Participation Be Part of Privatization?" Country Economics Department Working Paper 664. World Bank, Washington, D.C. Processed.

Lee, Barbara, and John Nellis. 1990. "Enterprise Reform and Privatization in Socialist Economies." World Bank Discussion Paper 104. Washington, D.C.: World Bank.

Levine, David A., and Laura D'Andrea Tyson. 1990. "Participation, Productivity and the Firm's Environment." In Alan S. Blinder, ed., *Paying for Productivity: A Look at the Evidence*. Washington, D.C.: The Brookings Institution, 183–237.

Lipton, David, and Jeffrey Sachs. 1990. "Privatization in Eastern Europe: The Case of Poland." *Brookings Papers on Economic Activity* 2:293–341.

Luders, Rolf J. 1990. "Chile's Massive SOE Divestiture Program: 1975–1990: Failures and Successes." Paper presented at the World Bank Conference on Privatization and Ownership Changes in East and Central Europe, 13–14 June, Washington, D.C. Processed.

Madžar, Ljubomir. 1990. "Restructuring Property Relations in Yugoslavia: Summary." Paper presented at the World Bank Conference on Privatization and Ownership Changes in East and Central Europe, 13–14 June, Washington, D.C. Processed.

Milanovic, Branko. 1989. *Liberalization and Entrepreneurship: Dynamics of Reform in Socialism and Capitalism.* Armonk, N.Y.: M. E. Sharpe.

———. 1992. "Privatization Options and Procedures." This volume.

Minkler, Alanson P. 1989. "Property Rights, Efficiency and Labor-Managed Firms." *Annals of Public and Cooperative Economics* 60:341–57.

———. 1990. "Knowledge and Internal Organization." Working Paper. Department of Economics, University of Connecticut at Storrs. Processed.

Mizsei, Kalman. 1990. "Experience with Privatization in Hungary." Paper presented at the World Bank Conference on Privatization and Ownership Changes in East and Central Europe, 13–14 June, Washington, D.C. Processed.

Nankani, Helen B. 1988. *Techniques of Privatization of State-Owned Enterprises. Vol. 2, Selected Country Case Studies.* World Bank Technical Paper 89. Washington, D.C.: World Bank.

———. 1990. "Lessons of Privatization in Developing Countries." *Finance and Development* 27:43–45.

Nellis, John. 1989. "Public Enterprise Reform in Adjustment Lending." Country Economics Department Working Paper 233. World Bank, Washington, D.C. Processed.

Oakeshott, Robert. 1978. *The Case for Worker Co-ops.* London: Routledge and Kegan Paul.

Pejovich, Svetozar. 1990. "A Property-Rights Analysis of the Yugoslav Miracle." *Annals of the American Academy of Political and Social Science* 507:123–32.

Pirie, Madsen. 1988. *Privatisation.* Aldershot, U.K.: Wildwood House.

Quarrey, Michael. 1986. *Employee Ownership and Corporate Performance.* Oakland, Calif.: National Center for Employee Ownership.

Saldanha, Fernando. 1992. "Self-Management: Theory and Yugoslav Practice." This volume.

Thomas, Henrik. 1982. "The Performance of the Mondragon Cooperatives in Spain." In D. C. Jones and Jan Svejnar, eds., *Participatory and Self-Managed Firms.* Lexington, Mass.: Lexington Books.

Thomas, Henrik, and Chris Logan. 1982. *Mondragon: An Economic Analysis.* Boston, Mass.: G. Allen and Unwin.

Vuylsteke, Charles. 1988. *Techniques of Privatization of State-Owned Enterprises. Vol. 1, Methods and Implementation.* World Bank Technical Paper 88. Washington, D.C.: World Bank.

Walkowiak, Witold, Mikolaj Breitkopf, and Dariusz Jaszczynski. 1990. "Private Sector and Privatization in Poland." Paper presented at the World Bank Conference on Privatization and Ownership Changes in East and Central Europe, 13–14 June, Washington, D.C. Processed.

Weitzman, Martin, and Douglas L. Kruse. 1990. "Profit Sharing and Productivity." In Alan S. Blinder, ed., *Paying for Productivity: A Look at the Evidence*. Washington, D.C.: The Brookings Institution, 95–140.

Whyte, William F., and Kathleen K. Whyte. 1988. *Making Mondragon: The Growth and Dynamics of the Worker Cooperative Complex*. Ithaca, N.Y.: ILR Press.

Yoshitomi, Masaru. 1990. "Keiretsu: An Insider's Guide to Japan's Corporations." *International Economic Insights* 1:10–17.

4

Are There Lessons from China's Economic Policies?

Kang Chen, Gary H. Jefferson, and Inderjit Singh

The recent expansion and acceleration of system reform in Eastern Europe invites closer scrutiny of China's reform experience. Prior to the acceleration of economic restructuring in Eastern Europe in the late 1980s and early 1990s, China had accumulated more than a decade of reform experience. This chapter describes the successes and failures of China's experience that may relate to current issues facing East European and Chinese policymakers.

By a number of statistical measures, China's economic reform program has achieved notable success. These are summarized below:[1]

• *Rapid growth:* During 1965–80 China's real gross domestic product (GDP) grew by 6.4 percent a year; during 1980–88 real GDP growth accelerated to 10.4 percent.[2] Total gross national product (GNP) increased 2.5-fold from 1978 to 1988.

---

[1]Unless otherwise specified, statistics reported in this section were drawn or derived from various volumes of the *Statistical Yearbook of China* (China SSB, various years).

[2]These estimates are likely to be biased upward. Rawski (1991) and Jefferson (n.d.) discuss sources of upward bias in official industrial output statistics ("shuifen") associated with new establishment formation, new product innovation and changes in value added ratios. Their estimates of bias vary widely by sector. Preliminary estimates by Jefferson suggest that during 1980–85 within state industry the bias due to product innovation is 7.5 percent in the electronics and communications equipment industry and 2.3 percent in the machine building industry. Overall, during this period, real growth rate of gross value of industrial output is estimated to be biased upward by approximately one percentage point.

This chapter is adapted and reprinted by permission of the publisher from "Lessons from China's Economic Reform" by Kang Chen, Gary H. Jefferson, and Inderjit Singh in *Journal of Comparative Economics* Volume 16, Number 2 (June 1992). Copyright © 1992 by Academic Press, Inc. The authors deeply appreciate the insightful and detailed comments of Tom Rawski.

• *Accelerated employment growth:* During 1978–88 total employment grew at an average rate of 3 percent, exceeding the rate of 2 percent achieved during 1958–78. As labor productivity in agriculture rose rapidly during 1978–88 allowing for the release of workers from farm production, nonagricultural employment growth accelerated to an average rate of 6.5 percent. More impressively, even as the baby boom generation born in the 1960s was moving into the labor force, the urban unemployment rate which stood at 5.3 percent in 1978 fell to 2 percent during 1986–88.

• *Rapidly expanding external sector:* Under the "open door" policy foreign trade expanded fivefold, from 20.6 billion current U.S. dollars in 1978 to 102.8 billion in 1988. Exports, which accounted for 4.8 percent of Chinese GDP in 1978, expanded to 13 percent in 1988. Equally impressive has been the favorable impact of the growth of trade on the quality, production technology, managerial efficiency and marketing strategies associated with the production and sale of many traded goods.

• *Rising living standards:* During 1978–88 per capita GNP doubled in real terms. During 1978–88 the per capita real income of rural residents grew at a rate of 9.6 percent per year; the comparable rate for urban residents was 6.3 percent. During the 1980s the average urban per person living space doubled to 8.5 square meters, and the average rural living area per capita also doubled from 8.1 to 16.0 square meters (Perkins 1989, p. 13).

Table 4.1 compares the consumption of basic-needs items and consumer durables in 1952, 1978, and 1988. The data show a sharp contrast between the two time periods 1952–78 and 1978–88. Even if the per capita ownership of consumer durables in 1952 had been zero, the gains reported during the ten years of reform are multiples of the gains recorded during the previous 26 years. Not only are the Chinese people enjoying a significant improvement in the quantity and quality of food, clothing consumption and living environment, they are also better informed and more mobile. From 1978 to 1987 long distance telephone lines increased 2.8-fold, urban telephone subscribers 2.5-fold, and the volume of passenger traffic 3.4-fold. The number of private motor vehicles, including trucks, passenger vehicles, wheel tractors, motorcycles, and trailers, increased from almost nil to 4.8 million.

These achievements have not been obtained without substantial costs: growing economic inequality,[3] rising economic insecurity, greater price instability, rising corruption and greater political and social instability. In assessing the cause, magnitude and impact of these conditions, however, it is necessary to consider several factors. First, we must distinguish between

---

[3]The extent to which economic inequality has risen or fallen in the sense of an overall Gini coefficient is debatable. During 1978–84 the rapid growth of output and incomes within the rural sector relative to the urban sector is likely to have reduced overall inequality. Within each of these sectors, however, it is likely that the emergence of wealthy households has increased inequality.

Table 4.1 China: improvement in living standards

	1952	1978	1988	1978 as % of 1952	1988 as % of 1978
Food (kg/person-year)					
Grain	197.7	195.5	249.1	98.9	127.4
Edible vegetable oil	2.1	1.6	5.9	76.2	371.3
Pork	5.9	7.7	14.9	130.5	193.6
Beef and mutton	0.9	0.8	1.6	88.9	198.8
Poultry	0.4	0.4	1.8	100.0	437.5
Fresh eggs	1.0	2.0	5.8	200.0	290.5
Aquatic products	2.7	3.5	5.7	129.6	163.7
Clothing (m/person-year)					
Cloth	5.7	8.0	12.2	140.4	152.1
Woolen fabric	0.01	0.08	0.29	800.0	362.5
Silk and satin	0.05	0.28	0.90	560.0	321.4
Living floor space (sq m/person)					
Urban	n.a.	4.2	8.8	n.a.	209.5
Rural	n.a.	8.1	16.6	n.a.	204.9
Possession of principal durables (units/100 people)					
Sewing machines	n.a.	3.5	11.8	n.a.	337.1
Wristwatches	n.a.	8.5	47.0	n.a.	552.9
Bicycles	n.a.	7.7	30.4	n.a.	394.8
Radios	n.a.	7.8	23.9	n.a.	306.4
TV sets	n.a.	0.3	13.2	n.a.	4,400.0
Tape recorders	n.a.	0.2	8.3	n.a.	4,150.0
Washing machines	n.a.	0.0	6.8	n.a.	n.a.
Refrigerators	n.a.	0.0	1.8	n.a.	n.a.
Electric fans	n.a.	1.0	13.4	n.a.	1,340.0
Cameras	n.a.	0.5	1.7	n.a.	340.0

n.a. = not available.
Source: China State Statistical Bureau (1989), pp. 719, 723–24.

temporary conditions arising from the transition and those which promise to persist, and perhaps grow in magnitude, under the new order. The dual pricing system, intended to be a transitional device, has invited pervasive corruption which should diminish as prices become increasingly uniform and competitively determined. On the other hand, economic insecurity, intrinsic to the market system, may become more, not less, pronounced as labor market reforms proceed. In a risk-averse society, such as China's,[4] incomes must be higher to compensate individuals for the increased disutility entailed by risk. Some portion of the spectacular rise in incomes cited above is therefore needed just to make Chinese citizens feel no worse off as they begin to cope with the rigors of life in a market economy.

Second, some of the problems might have been avoided, or substantially mitigated, if an alternative or revised reform strategy had been chosen; the problems were not the inevitable consequences of transition. Socially corrosive corruption, for example, was made more extensive and visible as accelerating inflation in 1988 and 1989 increased the spread between plan and market prices, thus raising the potential gains from corruption.

Third, economic system reform inevitably raises major issues that challenge the core of Communist ideology and the apparatus of control. Certain problems, however, such as the democracy movement and its subsequent suppression during the spring of 1989 and the decline of political stability, may be as much a reflection of the recurring problem of leadership succession within a highly personalized authoritarian regime as it is a symptom of reform.[5]

In order to understand the underlying economic motivation for reform and establish a context in which to identify key lessons of the reform experience, we must first discuss the initial conditions which set the course of China's reform.

Conditions motivating reform

With few exceptions, most of the world's centrally planned economies had by 1990–91 initiated economic system reform. Here we develop the proposition that prior to choosing reform, all of these countries shared certain similarities with respect to their development strategy and their stage of development. We develop this perspective with the respect to China's experience.

Before 1978 China followed a mobilization model of development, also referred to as the Stalinist or Maoist model, which entailed the mobilization of savings and workers to sustain high rates of growth of output and output per capita. This strategy can be usefully viewed within the context of Solow's Neoclassical Growth Model (Solow 1956) in which two of the three instruments for driving per capita income growth are increasing savings rates and limiting rates of population growth.

---

[4]Note that in a survey of workers only 11.7 percent of respondents expressed a willingness to "accept the risk of being out of a job" in exchange for quadruple wages (Reynolds 1987, p. 156).

[5]See Perkins (1989) for a discussion of the impact of economic reform on political attitudes and the demand for political reform.

During the first three decades of central planning, rising rates of savings were achieved through two important measures: (a) maintaining terms of trade favorable to the industrial sector, and (b) limiting wage growth for industrial workers. Low prices paid to agricultural producers and a state monopoly on the trade of agricultural products sustained agricultural subsidies to the industrial sector—both in terms of the raw material inputs to industries and the inexpensive food which was provided to industrial workers to justify low wages. The extra industrial profits produced by industrial units were collected by the state and used to finance capital construction within the industrial sector. The peasants' disguised (unrewarded) contribution to GNP from 1955 to 1985 has been estimated at over 600 billion yuan or $206 billion[6] (Institute of Development 1987).[7] The effect of these measures was to raise China's savings rate from less than 10 percent in the 1950s to more than 30 percent by the late 1970s.

The Chinese government's second major initiative designed to raise living standards was a reduction in rates of population growth. The total fertility rate, which stood at 6.4 in 1965 (World Bank 1990, p. 230), fell to 2.9 in 1980 (World Bank 1982, p. 144). Annual rates of population growth declined from 2.3 percent during 1960–70 to 1.4 percent during 1970–82 (World Bank 1984, p. 254).

The critical insight of the Solow growth model is that rising savings rates and falling population growth rates result in higher capital-labor ratios and rising living standards. Once these rates stabilize, however, in the absence of technical change, the economy moves toward a new steady state in which living standards stagnate. By the late 1970s, China's savings and population growth rates had approached their respective upper and lower limits. Since rates of savings and population growth cannot be forever manipulated in the "right" direction, only productivity growth in Solow's model is able to provide continuous improvements in living standards.

In China, however, during 1957–78, prior to the reform period, both agricultural and industrial productivity stagnated.[8] In Berliner's terms, enterprises and workers in socialist economies escape the pressure of "the invisible foot," which, in market economies, is "applied vigorously to the backside of enterprises that would otherwise have been quite content to go on producing the same products in the same way . . ." (1978, p. 529).

---

[6]We have used the following yuan official exchange rates for $1: 1.7 (1981), 2.9 (1985), 3.7 (1988), and 5.2 (1991).

[7]One study shows that peasant income accounted for only one ninth of what they produced (Chen 1990). The price scissors imposed an extremely heavy tax burden which contributed to rural poverty. In 1978 more than 200 million rural residents lived below China's official poverty standard (that is, annual per capital income was less than 50 yuan and annual grain consumption was less than 120 kilograms).

[8]Perkins (1988) estimates rates of combined agricultural and industrial total factor productivity growth of –1.41 percent during 1957–65 and 0.62 percent during 1965–76. Chen et al. (1988) find that total factor productivity in the state industry stagnated during 1957–78.

Moreover, when innovation did occur it was often wasteful and ineffective. As one senior engineer at the Beijing No. 1 Machine Tool Factory recounted, innovation was not uncommon prior to the reforms, but it was generally inspired by command from above or by patriotism, and not by relative prices or profits.[9]

The pattern of growth described above was also typical of the centrally planned economies of Eastern Europe and the U.S.S.R. In the decades following World War II, most of these countries maintained high and rising rates of domestic savings (principally government savings) which allowed for rapid rates of capital accumulation. At the same time, rates of population growth in these countries fell to levels below those of countries with comparable income levels.[10]

By the 1980s these countries appear to have reached their political limits with respect to the potential for elevating savings rates and depressing population growth. Against a background of slow or stagnant productivity growth, the possibilities to raising per capita incomes and living standards had become exhausted. Politics—a quest for political freedom in Eastern Europe and an effort by Deng Xiaoping to restore the credibility of the Communist party in China following the Cultural Revolution—may have determined the timing of reform; within the context of Solow's model, however, we can also see that during the past decade, the only route to achieving significant gains in living standards was to raise productivity.

Key lessons of reform

China's reform experience yields many lessons. Here we have chosen to stress the six which we consider to be most salient. These are (a) the significance of a leading sector, (b) the efficacy of gradual and partial reform, (c) the importance of proximate, kindred economies as exemplary models and sources of resource transfer, (d) the importance of the distinction between centrally managed and bottom-up reform, (e) the tendency of flawed institutions and bad policies to obstruct reform, and (f) the need for checks and balances and the uncertain ability of a government with a monopoly of political power to establish such measures.

---

[9]Interview conducted in May 1990.

[10]Note that unlike China, the Soviet and East European governments did not implement aggressive population control programs. Nonetheless, due to efforts to expand labor force participation rates, particularly for women, and residential space constraints, rates of population growth in these countries did decline more rapidly than could have been predicted from the growth of real incomes.

The importance of a leading sector

The achievements and failures of China's reform program cannot be viewed in isolation. Dynamic change in one sector has invariably influenced change in other sectors. To understand the successful features of China's reforms, it is vital to understand the synergy which caused the cumulative impact of reform to be far greater than the sum of its parts.

China's economic reform started with the agricultural sector. The initial success of agricultural reforms is beyond dispute. With the restoration of family-based farming, agricultural production grew rapidly. Crop production grew at 6.8 percent during the period 1979–84, well above the 2.5 percent growth rate during the 1953–78 period. Agricultural productivity and farm incomes rose, and the quality and quantity of food available to consumers improved vastly.[11]

Rather than focus on the success of China's agricultural reforms, this section will discuss the impact of those reforms on other sectors, that is, the role agriculture played as a leading reform sector. While the agricultural reforms greatly increased agricultural productivity, the important lesson to be drawn from their success is their direct and indirect impact on other aspects of the system. Specifically, agricultural reforms must be credited with the impetus they gave to rural industry.

In recent years, rural industries (also called township-village enterprises or TVEs) have become the most dynamic sector of China's economy.[12] In the 1980–88 period, 31.3 percent of the growth of China's total material production was contributed by rural TVEs. The share of output value of rural TVEs in GNP increased from 13 percent in 1980 to 21 percent in 1988. The growth of rural TVEs is even more significant considering that TVEs receive neither budgetary investment allocations nor subsidies from the state.

This remarkable growth would not have been achievable without agricultural reforms—in particular, the impetus the reforms gave to agricultural labor productivity which rose at an annual rate of 4.7 percent during the period 1978–84.[13] The higher incomes and savings and the pool of surplus labor that resulted from rising productivity in the agricultural

---

[11]For a discussion of these gains, see Sicular (1990).

[12]Rural TVEs, called "commune and brigade enterprises" prior to the reforms, were established at the township, village, and below-village levels. Most of the township and some of the village enterprises are collectively owned by their communities. Most of the below-village level enterprises and some of the village level enterprises are owned by individuals or partnerships. In general TVEs face harder budget constraints, have clearer ownership status, and are more independent than state-owned enterprises. For a more in-depth discussion of rural industry, see Byrd and Lin (1990).

[13]This estimate is certain to be low, since many workers who were registered as agricultural workers increasingly allocated a part of their labor to nonagricultural activities or left the agriculture sector altogether.

sector generated abundant sources of capital and labor thereby fueling the dynamic growth of rural enterprises.

Capital. In 1978 the assets owned by Chinese peasants were estimated to be worth 80 billion yuan (Institute of Development 1987); each rural resident owned assets worth, on average, just 100 yuan (equivalent to $60). Almost all rural assets were owned collectively by the people's communes.

After the reforms 800 million Chinese peasants regained the right to accumulate private assets and to engage in nonagricultural activities. By 1985 rural private assets were estimated at more than 700 billion yuan, growing at a rate of 27.4 percent per year (Zhou 1988).[14] In that same year gross fixed assets of the TVE sector amounted to approximately 120 billion yuan ($41 billion), just a fraction of the enormous pool of assets that had been accumulated during the first seven years of rural reform.

Labor. Prior to the reforms China's food allocation system, work point system and resident registration system confined peasants to engaging in agricultural activities only at their birthplaces. In 1978 about 10 percent of the rural labor force engaged in nonagricultural activities. As agricultural labor productivity rapidly rose, enabling the country's food requirements to be produced by a shrinking number of workers, and as restrictions on off-farm work were relaxed, off-farm employment rose sharply. By 1988 a de facto rural labor market was emerging and 21 percent of the rural work force was engaged in nonagricultural activities. In the 1980s more than 67 million rural surplus workers were absorbed by TVE enterprises (*Economic Daily* (*Jingji ribao*), October 1989). The rapid increase of employment in rural TVEs did not give rise to slow labor productivity growth in that sector. During 1980–88 labor productivity in rural industry rose by an average of 12 percent per year, high by any standard.[15]

In sum, rural TVEs have become a pillar of China's economy and are playing a decisive role in rural industrialization and national economic transformation (Byrd and Lin 1990). The rise of the TVE sector has itself become a leading sector generating systemic intersectoral benefits. Specifically, the development of TVEs has (a) mitigated the problem of rural surplus labor and the flight of workers to cities, (b) expanded the scope of market activity, bringing competitive pressure to state-owned enterprises, (c) diffused the potential for a growing division between urban and rural areas, and (d) contributed to the economy's export performance.

The latter consequence is further demonstration of China's virtuous circle of economic reform. Great distances and many sectors initially

---

[14]For the purpose of establishing a more accurate comparison of the real value of private assets in 1978 and 1985, note that the 1985 GNP deflator in 1980 prices was 116.9.

[15]This figure is somewhat overinflated due to the existence of upward bias in TVE "constant price" measures of output growth (see Rawski 1991). China's State Statistical Bureau openly acknowledges that it does not have a reliable output deflator for the TVE sector. Nonetheless, the obvious dynamism of this sector and the growth of its share of total industrial output are testimony to the extraordinary growth of productivity in TVE industries.

separated what are probably China's two most successful reforms—rural reforms and the open door policy. Rural reforms transformed agricultural production while the open door policy has given rise to a growing export sector which, in turn, has financed the purchase of a wide range of new industrial technologies. The success of these reform initiatives, however, is not unrelated. The increase in agricultural labor productivity that generated the surplus labor and abundant savings critical to the expansion of TVEs also served indirectly to finance the growth of industrial exports. In 1989 rural TVE exports grew by 30.1 percent, reaching a value of $10.5 billion, or one fifth of China's total export volume (*People's Daily* (*Renmin Ribao*) overseas edition, 8 June 1990).

While we have stressed the positive role of a lead sector and the potential for intersectoral linkages in generating synergy in the reform process, the intersectoral impacts of individual reforms can also have negative consequences. One such case, also relating to the linkage between agriculture and TVEs, concerns the abrupt slowdown in agriculture growth in 1985.[16] Reasons for the slowdown include the full implementation of the household responsibility system in 1984 as the incremental gains were gradually exhausted[17], the drop in the availability of chemical fertilizers and the rapid outmigration of labor from the cropping sector (Lin 1989).

Sicular (1990) argues that these changes followed the 1984 decision to officially sanction the development of private rural enterprise and to allow rural credit cooperatives to lend more freely to rural industry and services. Together with other nonagricultural measures, and in combination with agricultural price controls, these actions depressed the relative competitiveness of agriculture and accelerated the flow of labor and capital to nonagricultural activities. Hence, controls in one sector may give rise to second-best solutions in which controls appropriate for other sectors capture a disproportionate share of resources.

During the last decade, however, gains made by the mutually reinforcing effect of discrete reforms have outweighed the damage caused by individual reforms. In this sense, the timing and sequence of China's first decade of reforms was fortuitous.[18] It will be difficult for reformers in Eastern Europe and the successor states of the U.S.S.R. to initiate a similar virtuous circle of reform.

---

[16]The growth rate of crop production fell from 6.8 percent during 1978–84 to 1.0 percent during 1984–88.

[17]Under the household responsibility system, farmers were allowed long-term leases on agricultural land in return for which they contracted to provide output quotas of certain crops to the government.

[18]It is unlikely that the benefits of the sequence of reforms described above was anticipated by Deng or his reformers. They seemed not to have followed a grand strategy, instead proceeding by trial and error; in Deng's words, they were "crossing the creek by feeling the stones."

The efficacy of gradual and partial reform

China's urban industrial reforms did not begin formally until 1984. The various piecemeal reforms enacted during 1978–84 were considerably expanded in 1984. The 1984 reform package does not resemble the "Big Bang" or "cold turkey" programs which are being tested in or advocated for Eastern Europe and Russia. One major difference is that China's urban industrial reform program emphasized an expansion of enterprise autonomy and incentives, and the reduction, but not elimination, of within-plan allocations.[19] Among the more important urban industrial reforms were:

• Management targets were established with multiyear management responsibility contracts for profits, profit remittance, and taxes.[20]

• Enterprises were allowed to retain profits and were given the authority to invest and distribute bonuses from retained profits.

• Enterprises were given considerably expanded authority to choose the level and mix of production, to sell output and acquire goods on the market, and to set, or at least to negotiate, prices.

These reforms have had the effect of providing a discretionary source of funds that, within regulated bounds, can be used to reward profit-seeking behavior and to finance new investment. The result is a widespread reorientation of enterprise managers and workers toward profit-seeking behavior and a greater tendency for the more profitable enterprises to capture a larger share of investment resources.

The dual price system (state-mandated and free prices) was able to preserve planned allocation while still drawing incremental output into a market system.[21] The incremental aspect of the two-track system also allowed the government to implement price reform and enterprise reform in tandem.

Although enterprise autonomy and initiative are substantially greater than they were at the outset of the reforms, analysts suggest that the reforms are still incomplete and unsatisfactory. Chief among their shortcomings are (a) the persistence of weak labor markets which exacerbates preexisting problems with insufficient worker discipline and motivation; (b) excessive intervention of local officials in the affairs of enterprises, thereby eroding the authority and effectiveness of enterprise managers (Walder 1989); (c) the persistence of soft budget constraints; and (d) the tendency of local government to inhibit competition and interregional trade for the purpose of accumulating resources and revenues (Chen 1991).

---

[19]See Tidrick and Chen (1987) for a more complete account of the status of China's industrial reforms in the mid-1980s.

[20]See Koo (1990) regarding several earlier applications of the enterprise contract responsibility system.

[21]These objectives of the dual pricing system are discussed by Wu and Zhao (1987).

Moreover, as Perkins observes, "the whole approach was ad hoc and highly experimental with many forward movements and reversals in one area or another" (1989, p. 30). Evidence of these and other problems leads analysts to ask whether the enterprise reform program has indeed caused fundamental improvements in enterprise performance, or if the program has instead simply shifted authority previously held at the center to local governments and complicated the task of management so much that resulting gains will be negligible.

Persuasive arguments can be made on either side concerning the effectiveness of China's urban industrial reform program. Here we focus on the key objective of the urban industrial reforms which is to accelerate productivity growth. Specifically, we investigate evidence concerning two indicators: first, industrial productivity growth and, second, changes in efficiency resulting from a tendency for returns to factor inputs to become more equal, as we would expect if profit seeking behavior were becoming more pronounced and factor and product markets were becoming more complete.

Productivity growth. Evidence that the industrial reforms have raised factor efficiency is reported by Jefferson, Rawski, and Zheng (1992),[22] who find that during 1980–88, total factor productivity (TFP) in state industry rose at an average annual rate of 2.4 percent. The comparable rate for the collective sector (including TVEs) was 4.6 percent.[23] Moreover, Jefferson, Rawski, and Zheng find evidence that, following the expansion of the urban industrial reforms, the growth of TFP intensified somewhat during the 1984–88 period relative to the period 1980–84. This finding of robust TFP growth contrasts favorably with an earlier finding reported by these authors and their colleagues (Chen et al. 1988) that during 1957–78, productivity growth in state industry was virtually stagnant.

While several research programs are under way to identify the contribution of individual reform initiatives to this vastly improved productivity performance, some preliminary evidence is available.[24] Using a small sample of 20 state and collectively owned industrial enterprises, Jefferson and Xu (1991b) find that increased enterprise autonomy, profit retention and market exposure have contributed to higher rates of factor productivity growth. Specifically, their findings show that (a) factories in which managers were empowered to rationalize the allocation of workers,

---

[22]Unlike previous studies of Chinese industrial productivity growth, this study includes intermediate inputs and develops price deflators for investment goods and intermediate inputs, so that these factors, as well as output and labor, can be treated at constant price valuations or physical quantities.

[23]Coverage of the collective sector excludes TVEs at the village and below-village levels.

[24]Relevant studies include those sponsored by the Socialist Economies Unit of the World Bank, the National Science Foundation, and the Henry Luce Foundation (at the University of Pittsburgh and Brandeis University) and the Ford Foundation (at Oxford University, the University of Michigan, and the University of California, San Diego).

showed a greater increase of labor productivity; (b) capital productivity has risen most rapidly in enterprises which have the greatest share of self-financed investment;[25] and (c) enterprises with the highest share of material inputs purchased on the market show evidence of relatively high rates of material input productivity growth.

Convergence of factor (labor, capital, and material) returns. In an economy comprised of profit-maximizing enterprises operating within competitive product and factor markets, we expect uniform prices of comparable goods and factor inputs and a tendency for the equalization of returns to capital, labor and intermediate inputs among sectors and enterprises. Recently, evidence has emerged concerning the convergence of factor returns across sectors and enterprises. Jefferson and Xu (1991a) find substantial evidence of the convergence of factor returns among industrial enterprises. The numbers shown in Table 4.2 are coefficients of variation. Large values are evidence of substantial dispersion in the productivity of a single factor across enterprises.[26] Declining values, such as those shown in the table, are evidence that the dispersion of factor returns is becoming more equal over time. Since the convergence of factor returns implies growth of allocative efficiency, some part of the growth in industrial total factor productivity, reported above, appears to reflect improving resource allocation within China's industrial sector. In order to relax the assumption of identical production technologies across industrial branches, Jefferson and Xu (1991a) investigate the tendency of factor returns to converge within individual branches and find further confirmation of significant patterns of convergence. These data are the strongest evidence we have found that enterprise and market reform are providing new incentives to state-owned enterprises to adjust the level and mix of production and factor inputs to respond to price differences and profit opportunities.

---

[25]This finding may alternatively be interpreted as showing that the higher the rate of growth of capital productivity, the greater the share of self-financed investment. In either case, the finding points to the benefits of increased rates of profit retention.

[26]Jefferson and Xu (1991a) use average revenue products (ARPs) as a proxy for marginal measures. This simplification, however, should not systematically bias the analysis. Because the marginal revenue product is the product of the relevant factor output elasticity (alpha) and the ARP, if we assume that the technologies of all enterprises are similar, then the alpha can be factored out of the numerator and denominator of the coefficient of variation and canceled. Alternatively, if we randomly assign output elasticities to each of the ARPs, differences in technology should not systematically bias the coefficient of variation.

Table 4.2 Convergence of factor returns *(coefficient of variation)*

Sector	Labor	Capital[a]	Intermediate
Wuhan sample			
1978	1.870	0.968	0.226
1984	1.089	0.689	0.400
1987	0.853	0.524	0.169
Sample of 353 enterprises[b]			
1980	1.269	1.281	0.581
1987	0.973	0.789	0.250

a. Capital is measured as net value of fixed assets.
b. Within the initial sample of 400 enterprises, 39 observations are missing and 8 contain implausible values.

During the 1980s, China's strategy for a dual track economy wherein the state sector's share was to gradually decline in favor of alternative ownership forms, including private and cooperatively owned enterprises, appears to have been successful.[27] Arguing for rapid marketization and privatization, some analysts and participants in the economic transformation of Eastern Europe and the successor states of the U.S.S.R. contend that "a chasm cannot be leaped in two jumps." China's industrial reforms offer a vivid example of halfway reform—the first of the two or more jumps required to attain levels of industrial efficiency envisaged by China's reformers. While it is conceivable that success was not as dramatic as it would have been had China implemented a program of complete marketization and privatization, the reforms nonetheless led to significant industrial productivity gains during the decade.

The important role of a kindred model

Since the introduction of the open door policy in 1979, China has moved with remarkable speed from almost complete autarky in the 1960s and early 1970s[28] to a point in 1988 where the share of exports in GDP exceeded that of India, the United States and Japan, the three largest market-oriented economies (World Bank 1990, pp. 194–95). By 1988 exports plus imports had risen to over one quarter of GDP.[29] In addition to direct trade

---

[27] In 1978 the state sector represented 90 percent of the gross value of China's industrial output; this share now barely exceeds 60 percent.

[28] In 1970, for example, exports plus imports were only 5.9 percent of net material product.

[29] We note, however, that many of these exports are based on extensive subsidies. See Jefferson and Zou (1989b) and *The New York Times* (1990, p. 1).

promotion, the opening of China has been greatly facilitated by the expansion of foreign direct investment and the designation of Special Economic Zones (SEZs).[30]

The dominant role of Hong Kong and growing influence of Taiwan (China) have been significant factors contributing to the internationalization of the Chinese economy, particularly the economies of the outward-oriented southeastern provinces. As trading partner, financier, intermediary and facilitator,[31] Hong Kong, in particular, has had a profound and pervasive effect on China's development.

Hong Kong as a trading partner. Because Chinese trade statistics do not distinguish between direct and indirect (entrepot) trade, we use Hong Kong statistical sources.[32] These statistics show that in 1988 exports to Hong Kong represented 40.8 percent of China's total exports. Hong Kong was the final destination for only 10.7 percent of exports; 30.1 percent was re-exported, much of it having been further processed in Hong Kong. In 1988, 30.8 percent of total Chinese imports came from Hong Kong, of which 22.0 percent had been re-exported by Hong Kong.

Hong Kong as a financier. The dominance of Hong Kong in China's external relations is also reflected in the level of its direct investment in China. Two thirds of the $3.19 billion of foreign direct investment in China in 1988 originated in Hong Kong and Macao (China SSB 1989, p. 646). The fact that Guangdong province accounts for 43 percent of China's total foreign direct investment further underscores the importance of proximity to Hong Kong. This is true not only for Hong Kong investors, but also for other foreign investors for whom access to Hong Kong's services, skills, market and infrastructure, unobstructed by language or cultural barriers, is a critical asset. The rapid growth of trade between China and Hong Kong partly reflects Hong Kong's interest in investing in low-wage processing and assembling operations in China. Hong Kong firms supply such operations with necessary raw materials and components, some of which are made in Hong Kong.

Hong Kong as an intermediary and a facilitator. A further measure of the important role of the kindred economy is the spectacularly large number of foreign visits of kindred Chinese living in Hong Kong, Macao and Taiwan (China). Ninety percent of the 31.7 million visitors to China in 1988 were Chinese from Hong Kong, Macao, and Taiwan (China); the balance consisted of foreigners and overseas Chinese (China SSB 1989, p. 650). This figure reflects the frequency with which Chinese investors, managers, traders, technicians, and other economic agents, including discriminating consumers,

---

[30]For an excellent discussion of China's open door policy, the magnitudes of trade and investment flows and their impact on China's export and growth performance, see Perkins (1989).

[31]Sung (1988) identifies these four categories in his analysis of the Hong Kong-China link.

[32]Time lags and differences between freight on board (FOB) and cost, insurance, and freight (CIF) are ignored.

cross into China. With nearly 100,000 cross-border trips per day there is a tremendous volume of resources, skills and attitudes being transplanted from Hong Kong into China.

Yet these statistics still do not fully capture the important impact of Hong Kong on China. The tens of thousands of transactions conducted each day between Hong Kong and nearby areas in China, particularly Guangdong province, challenge the institutions and attitudes of central planning. In particular, the presence of Hong Kong trade, capital, and middlemen

• challenges trade and investment monopolies and substantially reduces transaction costs associated with both trade and investment;

• abets China's thriving black market in foreign trade, forcing planners to maintain a more realistic exchange rate for China's currency; and

• provides a source of rapid feedback on reform initiatives with respect to pricing, investment incentives, and trade measures so that planners can gauge the rationality of reform policy.

As Sung (1988) emphasizes, in the long run the most important role Hong Kong can play in the Chinese economy is to demonstrate the efficacy of the market. During the past decade of reform, it is unlikely that any one area or collection of persons has provided more inspiration and guidance in the ways of spontaneous reform than Hong Kong.

With the relaxation of constraints on travel and investment in China, Taiwan (China) has begun to create the second big push of kindred resources. Since its foreign exchange reserves are second in the world only to Japan, the potential for Taiwan (China) to reinforce and expand the impact that kindred Chinese have made to China's first decade of reform is considerable.

In varying degrees, the countries of Eastern Europe, through their proximity to Western Europe and expatriate communities, have analogous access to resources. This is less true for the successor states of the U.S.S.R. While the Baltic countries maintain stronger links with the West than the Russian heartland, distance, language and culture, as well as nearly 75 years of Communist rule, have attenuated the access of other former republics to the resources, skills and attitudes of market economies.

The critical distinction between centrally managed reform and bottom-up (or spontaneous) reform

The initiatives of China's reform program constitute an impressive list.[33] Notable among the initiatives are the establishment of SEZs, provisions for the retention of profits and the distribution of bonuses, and the management responsibility contract system. The impact of these initiatives from the center has been substantial. Three points, however, require emphasis. First, many of these reforms are enabling reforms; that is, they authorize local initiatives

---

[33]See Jefferson and Zou (1989a) for a chronology of reform measures.

but do not guarantee their actualization. In order for reform initiatives from the central government to be effective, households, enterprises, and localities must respond to these initiatives.

Second, many reforms have followed de facto change; the government consented to or sanctioned important reforms only after they had become widespread. The most dramatic example is China's rural reforms which, contrary to popular belief, were not planned by the central government. In fact, the two most important ingredients of the Household Production Responsibility System—leasing land for household farming and setting quotas on a household basis—were explicitly banned in 1979 by China's leadership.[34] The central government initially opposed land tenure and the household contract system, but gradually recognized that these innovations from below enjoyed wide support and constituted a viable mode of agricultural production. Although these measures were initially authorized for remote regions in 1980, it was not until 1985 that the government sanctioned the key administrative measures that comprised China's successful agricultural reforms. Yet, by the end of 1984 over 93 percent of China's cultivated land had been contracted to households (Sicular 1990), and nearly 100 percent of China's rural villages were fixing quotas on a household basis (Institute of Development 1987). More recent examples of bottom-up initiatives that only later became accepted by central authorities include the establishment of stock exchanges in Shanghai and Shenzhen, and Shanghai's Pudong development zone.

Third, many locally initiated reforms remain unsanctioned. While unsanctioned reform was a widespread phenomenon during the 1980s, it became more important as the government grew more tentative about reform during the recent austerity program and particularly since June 4, 1989. While some of these unsanctioned reforms are well publicized, such as the growth of private banking, most are of a more surreptitious nature. Among these are the establishment in rural areas of Guangdong province of subsidiaries for processing or distributing goods which would otherwise be subject to state allocation and price regulation. More generally, many enterprises consciously develop policies to counter or thwart government policy or regulations which inhibit local initiative or profit.

Spontaneous reform has, at a minimum, been a necessary complement to managed reform and, more likely, has been a prerequisite to managed reform. Among the conditions that have caused spontaneous reform to be so important and effective are

• the tradition of a relatively weak central government, aided by China's geographic size and diversity;

• dissatisfaction with the official system and widespread desire for reform and greater local and individual initiative;

---

[34]See "Resolutions of the Communist Party of China Central Committee on Certain Issues Concerning the Agricultural Development," *Almanac of China's Economy* 1981, pp. 11–100.

- a population which has not lost interest in commerce and entrepreneurship, in part because "classical socialism" had been in force for just two decades (approximately 1957–77); and
- the open door policy and the proximity of kindred models and resources.

Spontaneous economic reform should not be stifled. Such reforms can indicate to the government where the greatest returns are to be gained from official incremental reform.

Spontaneous reform implies that important limitations exist on the ability of the government to manage the reform process. Governments may believe that reform can proceed according to a comprehensive strategy or blueprint. During 1989–91 concern emerged among China's leadership regarding the need to maintain control over the reform process, and in particular to sustain a manageable pace of system reforms. This view of reform is analogous to the view of growth espoused by the "balanced" growth theorists Nurkse and Rosenstein-Rodan: in order to avoid bottlenecks and supply and demand imbalances growth must be centrally managed. This perspective contrasts with the view held by proponents of "unbalanced" growth, most notably Hirschman, who argue that prices and other signals serve to allocate resources through more decentralized channels including markets. China's reform experience, in which bottom-up elements of reform have played a key role, tends to validate a spontaneous or unbalanced reform model.

The challenge to the Chinese government is twofold: first, it must establish the macroeconomic controls and regulatory environment in which spontaneous, unbalanced reform can evolve, and, second, it must be able to formulate, monitor, and evaluate policy initiatives designed to resolve bottlenecks and distortions as they appear in the reform process.

Flawed institutions and bad policy impede reform

Economic reform in China is impeded not only by the lack of an economically feasible strategy, the lack of political will or the fear of economic dislocation, but also, at certain junctures of China's reform process, by flawed institutions (or policy instruments) and bad policies. During the past decade significant examples of obstacles to reform have included flawed instruments of indirect macroeconomic management that have necessitated a reliance on direct, administered measures, and antiemployment policies that accentuate the prospect of vast unemployment.

Macroeconomic management. Key instruments of macroeconomic stability in any market economy include an independent central bank, flexible interest rates and an efficient tax system. The absence of these instruments generally necessitates the use of direct controls. This is the case with China. The implementation of China's macroeconomic stabilization program of 1988–90 required the excessive use of direct administrative means, such as price controls, credit and materials allocations, and forced open market operations (such as the substitution of bonds for workers' cash wages).[35] The effect was a contravention of prior reforms and a more serious hiatus in the reform program, with an attendant loss of confidence in the reform process. These consequences would have been contained had the instruments of indirect macroeconomic stabilization been in place.

The following shortcomings of China's system of macroeconomic management have necessitated direct administrative intervention:

• *Lack of independence.* The independence of China's central banking system is weak for several reasons. First, under the existing structure the financial system, government plans, and state budget are still interdependent. Most loans given by the specialized banks (the People's Construction Bank, and the Industrial and Commercial Bank) are centrally mandated. The State Planning Commission and local planning commissions assign to banks the responsibility of financing investment projects that have been approved by the planning system. The Planning Commission approves projects, the Ministry of Finance pays the bills, and the banks lend money accordingly. When the government does not have enough money in the bank, the usual solution has been to print more. The money supply is, then, endogenous; there is no independent monetary policy.

The independence of China's banking establishment is also compromised by China's system of governance. Operating under the close supervision of local governments, the ability of banks to make independent decisions has been limited. Because local governments effectively control local banks, and hence the careers of bank directors, banks are careful to adhere to local government priorities; acting in the "interest of the region" can then seem more important than banking profits. Local governments do not want local banks to remit excess reserves to the next level in the banking hierarchy or lend excess reserves to banks in other localities—even to branches of the same bank. The rule of the game has been to keep deposits within the local boundary, and to try to annex resources by forcing the hand of the central bank. The effect is to swell the volume of local reserves and credit and, again, to necessitate the use of direct credit controls.

• *Inflexible interest rates.* A prominent feature of China's financial system is the considerable appetite enterprises have for investment resources. This condition is the consequence of low, often negative, real rates of interest. In the 1980s nominal interest charges were gradually adjusted upward, but not as rapidly as inflation rose.[36] The effect was a declining real cost of capital that spurred more investment demand at precisely the time when interest

---

[35] See Naughton (n.d.) for a more complete discussion of the elements and impact of China's recent macroeconomic stabilization program.

[36] During February 1989 loans provided by the Ministry of Finance for within-plan investment carried a rate of 3.2 percent, the discount rate at which the People's Bank of China lends to special banks at that time was 7.4 percent; loan rates of the special banks quoted enterprises and officials generally fell in the range of 9 and 11 percent. During 1987–89, the average official rate of inflation was about 18 percent.

rates should have been used to moderate the demand for credit.[37] Arresting this growing imbalance of supply and demand for investment funds required more credit rationing and greater intervention in the banking system.

• *Inelastic tax revenue system.* China is different from most other countries in that the central government collects very few taxes. Local governments collect all revenues other than customs duties and certain excise taxes. Some portion of locally collected revenues are remitted to the center as specified by a system of financial responsibility contracts. According to this system, the amount of revenue remitted to the center is fixed by the contracts. In some cases a fraction of revenues in excess of the target amount is also remitted.[38]

The problem with this revenue scheme is that it is highly inefficient because it is inelastic with respect to the growth of nominal income. In particular, as inflation accelerates (as it did during 1987–88), the target tax base of the center, fixed in nominal terms, declines in real value. Once localities have satisfied their contracted revenue targets with the center, they tend to hide revenues.[39]

Since expenditures of the central government rise with inflation, the gap between expenditures and revenues grows, therefore requiring deficit financing and the printing of money. Officials also manipulate tax rates to expropriate funds from enterprises, particularly private establishments and rural industry, in order to finance budget deficits.

China's breakdown in macroeconomic stability has many sources but the problem has been aggravated by an insufficiently independent banking system, inflexible interest rates and an inefficient revenue system. The acceleration of inflation and the use of clumsy administrative means to combat it have taken a considerable toll on the reform program, and not only because of the use of various counterreform measures. More importantly, inflation undermined the public's enthusiasm for the reform process, particularly price reform, and damaged the credibility of reformers to effect an orderly transition to a market economy.

Anti-employment policies. Bad policies with regard to the labor market have inhibited critical reform initiatives. Urban labor market reform is needed to enforce greater discipline and efficiency within China's industrial enterprises and to create the flexibility required for the reallocation of workers across sectors, industrial branches and individual enterprises.

---

[37]Jefferson and Rawski (1992) report evidence that the user cost of capital (real rate of interest plus depreciation rate) for enterprises was virtually zero during 1985–88.

[38]Local governments try to hide revenues from the center. There are innumerable ways in which local governments can divert revenues or arrange alternative payments from enterprises, such as accelerated loan repayments, to substitute for revenues, a portion of which may have to be remitted to the Center.

[39]See Jefferson and Zou (1989a) where they describe how an enterprise arranged to accelerate its loan repayment in lieu of taxes with a locality that had already met its minimal revenue obligation.

China has adopted a wide range of policies and pricing conventions that have the unintended consequence of discriminating against labor-intensive activities wherein China's comparative advantage lies. These policies make it all the more difficult to implement meaningful labor market reforms since such reforms would be accompanied by the emergence of the specter of an unmanageable pool of redundant labor.

Jefferson and Rawski (1992) cite five types of China's antiemployment policy: (a) a bias against the agricultural sector that induces labor to leave labor-intensive farming; (b) a bias against the service sector that retards the development of this labor-intensive sector; (c) a bias against labor-intensive forms of enterprise ownership, particularly private enterprise; (d) export policies and practices which prevent the development of labor-intensive sectors; and (e) distorted factor prices that induce enterprises to substitute capital, energy and materials for labor.

The persistence of this formidable set of antiemployment policies generates a legitimate fear among China's reformers and political leadership that a further relaxation of controls on labor allocation and mobility will lead to unacceptable levels of unemployment in urban areas. The government has taken initiatives to pave the way for effective labor market reform. Among these are the optimal labor allocation program to rationalize the allocation of workers within enterprises and the creation of pension and unemployment programs intended to pool the expense of retirement and unemployment among enterprises. These measures do not, however, address the basic problem—a set of policies which make effective labor market reform untenable.

The importance of checks and balances and the difficulty of achieving these under a Communist regime

The intent of China's enterprise reform program was to establish the financial independence and decentralize the administration of enterprises. The devolution of administrative control to local government already begun in the early 1970s, however, has further tended to intensify local administrative interference in enterprise management, as well as to increase price manipulation and corruption.

Administrative interference. Almost every Chinese enterprise reports to numerous supervisory agencies, often at different levels of government. These agencies control production, sales, material supply, investment, working capital, and labor allocations. Local officials resist efforts to curtail the system of perpetual negotiations about taxes, subsidies, allocations and favors; they use a variety of informal mechanisms, as well as their control over geographically immobile factors and resources, to capture power and expand control over local enterprises.

This complex, meddlesome administrative environment seriously undermines the autonomy and operations of factory directors (World Bank 1988; Walder 1989). One enterprise manager (who was a seasoned engineer and manager at the time he assumed the directorship of a state enterprise) reported that it took four years and most of his time and energy just to establish effective working relations with various supervisory agencies. Other managers complain bitterly that they wanted their supervisory agencies "off their backs."

Price manipulation. When the two-track system was established it was anticipated that enterprises would "grow out of the plan." This has occurred somewhat, but not as much as expected. Some government organizations continually increase enterprise quotas and planning targets. In 1988, for example, production in many of Shanghai's industrial enterprises, especially in metallurgy, textiles and some machine building enterprises, was almost entirely planned. Even above-quota products were subject to compulsory local plans (Dong 1988).

Even though the scope of markets continues to expand and capital goods subjected to the state mandatory plan have been reduced from more than 80 percent of total volume of circulation to only 20–30 percent, multiple prices have not shown a tendency to merge. Sometimes the difference between list prices and market prices may not appear to be large on paper; numerous trading units, however, tack on additional margins and demand "handling fees" in cash. Prices of raw materials may rise several times during the distribution process.[40]

The persistence of the two-tier pricing system has created a dilemma for the center. In order to maintain the intended production level of key sectors and products, the center attempted to minimize exposure to market regulations by continuing price control. As a result of these price controls, however, resources are driven away from these sectors, reducing production and creating bottlenecks. While the output of agricultural products whose prices had been decontrolled—such as fruit, vegetables, pork, beef, mutton, poultry, eggs, and aquatic products—grew quickly, the production of grain, cotton, and oil-bearing crops stagnated because their prices were still controlled.[41] "Protected" industrial sectors such as energy, transport and raw material production were squeezed, while processing and consumer durable good industries boomed. Protection in the end proved counterproductive.

Corruption. The existence of multiple prices, while an improvement over fixed state prices, provides extensive opportunities for corruption. Officials with the power to approve distribution targets under state plans often succumb to the temptation of bribes. Acquiring material inputs at list prices rather than market prices can represent the difference between profit- or

---

[40]In early 1988 one government-run company obtained 200 tons of nickel from state stockpiles at the official price of 38,000 yuan per ton, then resold the nickel for 68,000 yuan per ton. Yet the company later regretted the deal because the price of nickel was soon raised to 110,000 yuan per ton (*Economic Reference* (Jingji Cankao), January 28, 1988).

[41]While grain, cotton, and oil-seed prices were substantially increased in 1990–91, price controls remain.

loss-making operations for an enterprise. Government organizations have been using their authority to force enterprises to sell their above-quota products to government-run companies at low prices. Some local governments have gone so far as to close down markets and deliberately create multiple prices for certain products. Profits from high market prices thus fall into the hands of profiteering officials.

Administrative interference, price manipulation and corruption, as well as attempts to monopolize production and trade at the local level, underscore the need for checks and balances in an effective market economy. Among these checks and balances are competitive markets; an autonomous banking system; a comprehensive system of enterprise, commercial and criminal laws; an independent legal system to enforce and interpret the law; and an independent press to monitor and report on instances of economic abuse.

In addition, a key to limiting the ad hoc intervention of the Chinese bureaucracy in enterprise operations is private ownership and a code of property rights. The Chinese government has avoided addressing the issue of the privatization of state and collective enterprises. Because inefficiency within the industrial sector at the beginning of the reform program was so great, halfway measures, including the enterprise (management) contract responsibility system and the dual pricing system, facilitated significant improvements in productivity. Under these halfway measures serious distortions persist. Extensive privatization and more complete marketization will eventually be required, if China is to acquire the capacity to develop new products and technologies and to export at competitive prices.

The list of necessary institutional innovations raises a key question which remains unresolved: to what extent is political reform a prerequisite to a full transition to a market-oriented economy. It may be that the current monopoly of political power precludes the establishment of effective checks on economic power. During the last decade, China's Communist party demonstrated the flexibility to allow economic reforms that would not have been possible in 1978. It remains to be seen if the future leaders of China's Communist party will be able to effect a more complete economic transition without simultaneously effecting political institutional change.

Conclusions

When we attempt to apply the lessons of one country to another we must confront important cross-country differences. This is particularly true for the lessons of reform experience in China, a country of over a billion residents, most of whom worked in the farm sector at the beginning of the reforms in 1978. Because China's industrial sector is neither as developed nor as capital-intensive as that of Eastern Europe and the former U.S.S.R., and because rural savings have been so high, the technical potential for rapid privatization has been higher in China. In 1987 personal savings equalled 43.5 percent of the value of state-owned fixed capital.

Notwithstanding these differences all socialist economies share fundamental conditions on the eve of economic reform which raise a similar set of reform issues. When Hungarian economists Kornai and Daniel (1986) visited China in 1985 they encountered strikingly familiar phenomena: soft budget constraints and extensive underemployment within the state sector, hyperactive bureaucracies, tendencies toward regional protectionism, and heavy reliance upon direct rather than indirect measures of macroeconomic control. These similarities lead us to believe that lessons from China's experience may be relevant to Eastern Europe and the successor states of the Soviet Union.

One of these lessons is the importance of a leading reform sector, a condition which may be difficult to achieve in the more complex industrialized economies of Eastern Europe. Another lesson is the importance of proximity to kindred models.

China's reform program is the model halfway house. Agricultural land continues to be owned by the state, while in industry soft budget constraints and administered pricing persist. Yet China's halfway reform measures have achieved measurable success during the first decade of reform. Part of this success, however, was due to "one shot" gains resulting from the elimination of gross inefficiencies.[42] In the 1990s it is unlikely that China can approach its high output and productivity growth performance of the 1980s without substantially greater market and ownership reform.

References

Berliner, Joseph S. 1978. *The Innovation Decision in Soviet Industry.* Cambridge, Mass.: MIT Press.

Byrd, William, and Qingsong Lin. 1990. "China's Rural Industry: An Introduction." In William Byrd and Lin Qingsong, eds., *China's Rural Industry: Structure, Development and Reform.* Oxford, U.K.: Oxford University Press.

Chen, Kang. 1991. "The Failure of Recentralization in China: Interplays among Enterprises, Local Governments, and the Center." In Arye L. Hillman, ed., *Markets and Politicians: Politicized Economic Choice.* Boston and Dordrecht: Kluwer Academic Publishers.

Chen, Kuan, et al. 1988. "Productivity Change in Chinese Industry: 1953–85." *Journal of Comparative Economics* 12:570–91.

---

[42]Perkins (1989) makes this argument for the agricultural and service sectors. Also, see Lin (1989) for a more formal presentation of this argument for the agricultural sector.

Chen, Yizi. 1990. "Origins of Economic Reforms, Outcomes of the Democracy Movement, and Prospects of China's Politics." In Jia Hao, ed., *The Democracy Movement in 1989 and China's Future* (in Chinese). Washington, D.C.: The Washington Center for Chinese Studies.

China State Statistical Bureau (SSB). Various years. *Statistical Yearbook of China.* Beijing: State Statistical Publishing House.

Dong, Fureng. 1988. "The Reform of Economic Mechanism and the Reform of Ownership." *Jingji Yanjiu* (Economic Research) No. 7.

Institute of Development. 1987. "Peasants, Market and Innovation of the Institution." *Jingji Yanjiu* (Economic Research) No. 1.

Jefferson, Gary H. N.d. "Growth and Productivity Change in Chinese Industry: Problems of Measurement." In M. Dutta and Z. L. Zhang, eds., *Adaptive Innovation in Asian Economies.* Greenwich, Conn.: JAI Press. Forthcoming.

Jefferson, Gary H., and Thomas G. Rawski. 1992. "Unemployment, Underemployment and Employment Policy in China's Cities." *Modern China* 18:42–71.

Jefferson, Gary H., Thomas G. Rawski, and Y. X. Zheng. 1992. "Growth, Efficiency and Convergence in China's State and Collective Industry." *Economic Development and Cultural Change* 40:239–66.

Jefferson, Gary H., and Xu Wenyi. 1991a. "Assessing Gains in Efficient Production among China's Industrial Enterprises." Industrial Reform and Productivity in Chinese Enterprises, Research Paper Series 4. World Bank, Socialist Economies Reform Unit. Washington, D.C. Processed.

Jefferson, Gary H., and Xu Wenyi. 1991b. "The Impact of Reform on Socialist Enterprises in Transition: Structure, Conduct and Performance in Chinese Industry." *Journal of Comparative Economics* 15:45–64.

Jefferson, Gary H., and Zou Gang. 1989a. "China: A Review of Industrial Policy Initiatives, 1979–1989." Background Paper 8 for the Structural Change Project. World Bank, China Department. Washington, D.C. Processed.

Jefferson, Gary H., and Zou Gang. 1989b. "China: Industrial Policy in a Microeconomic Perspective." Background Paper 3 for the Structural Change Project. World Bank, China Department. Washington, D.C. Processed.

Koo, Anthony. 1990. "The Contract Responsibility System: Transition from a Planned to a Market Economy." *Economic Development and Cultural Change* 38:796–820.

Kornai, Janos, and Zsuzsa S. Daniel. 1986. "The Chinese Economic Reform as Seen by Hungarian Economists." *Acta Oeconomica* 36:289–305.

Lin, Justin Yifu. 1989. "Rural Reforms and Agricultural Productivity Growth in China." Beijing: Development Institute.

The New York Times. 1990. "Chinese Trade Practices Raise Concern in U.S." 26 December, 1990, p. 1.

Naughton, Barry. N.d. "Growing out of the Plan: China's Economic Reform, 1978–1991." Cambridge, U.K.: Cambridge University Press. Forthcoming.

Perkins, Dwight. 1988. "Reforming China's Economic System." *Journal of Economic Literature* 26:601–45.

——. 1989. "The Lasting Effect of China's Economic Reforms, 1979–1989." Paper presented at the Four Anniversaries Conference on China, 11–15 September, Annapolis, Maryland. Processed.

Rawski, Thomas G. 1991. "How Fast Has Chinese Industry Grown?" Industrial Reform and Productivity in Chinese Enterprises, Research Paper Series 7. World Bank, Socialist Economies Reform Unit. Washington, D.C. Processed.

Reynolds, Bruce L. 1987. *Reform in China: Challenges and Choices*. New York: M. E. Sharpe, Inc.

Sicular, Terry. 1990. "China's Agricultural Policy during the Reform Period." Harvard University, Cambridge, Mass. Processed.

Solow, Robert. 1956. "A Contribution to the Theory of Economic Growth." *Quarterly Journal of Economics* 70:65–94.

Sung, Yun-Wing. 1988. "The Key to China's Open Door Policy: The China-Hong Kong Connection." Paper presented at the Cato Institute Conference on Economic Reforms in China: Problems and Prospects, 12–15 September, Shanghai, China. Processed.

Tidrick, Gene, and Jiyuan Chen. 1987. *China's Industrial Reform*. Oxford, U.K.: Oxford University Press.

Walder, Andrew. 1989. "Factory and Manager in an Era of Reform." *China Quarterly* 118:242–64.

World Bank. 1982. *World Development Report 1982*. New York: Oxford University Press.

World Bank. 1984. *World Development Report 1984*. New York: Oxford University Press.

World Bank. 1988. *China: Finance and Investment*. Washington, D.C.: World Bank.

World Bank. 1990. *World Development Report 1990*. New York: Oxford University Press.

Wu, Jinglian, and Renwei Zhao. 1987. "The Dual Pricing System in China's Industry." *Journal of Comparative Economics* 11:309–18.

Zhou, Qiren. 1988. "Changes in Property Relationships in China's Rural Areas." In The Rural Development Research Center, ed., *Reforms Facing System Renovation*. Shanghai: Sanlian Publishing House.

B. Experiences with Decentralized Socialist Enterprises

5

Self-Management:
Theory and Yugoslav Practice

Fernando Saldanha

Economic systems do not exist in pure form. The state intervenes at the macroeconomic and microeconomic levels in capitalist countries. Some markets continue to operate in centrally planned economies. The self-managed experiment in Yugoslavia is no exception to this rule.

The free operation of an economic system based on pure self-managed firms would result in high degrees of economic inequality and severe distortions, leading to large efficiency losses. This chapter analyzes how these problems expressed themselves in the Yugoslav economy and what deviations from a pure self-managed system were necessary so that the economy would attain an acceptable efficiency level and a relatively equitable income distribution. However, as will be demonstrated, the multiplicity of regulations through which the Yugoslav authorities attempted to implement a workable self-management system created additional substantive problems. The analysis of the Yugoslav self-management experiment in this chapter is based on the abundant literature on the system, evidence obtained on the field, and statistical data including aggregate income statements for 33 manufacturing branches for the years 1985–87.

Self-management in theory

The self-managed economy

The pure self-managed economy of the theoretical literature is composed of many small self-managed firms. The environment is competitive and decentralized; firms have no market power. Decisions on prices, quantities, decide on entry (firm creation) and exit (bankruptcy), as well as on mergers, acquisitions, takeovers, and so on. Managers are hired by workers.

It is important to distinguish between workers' self-management and workers' ownership of firms. Under self-management, the capital stock is "socially" owned, and is not owned by workers, whereas under the latter system workers do have effective property rights over capital and collect rents therefrom.[1]

In a self-management system, payments to workers take the external form of "wages," but can be conceptually decomposed into wages proper, capital rentals, and flows associated with stock variations. The first two components have traditional economic interpretations.[2] The last component represents proceeds from asset sales,[3] and funds that should have been used for maintenance or to avoid obsolescence but were instead paid as "wages." A worker is not free to buy or sell his rights to earn rents and flows associated with stock variations. As soon as a worker loses his connection to a firm, he ceases collecting rents and flows associated with stock variations from that firm, and is not compensated for these losses. A worker cannot diversify his portfolio by investing in several firms, or in a unit trust; the typical worker's portfolio is a mix of fixed income investments like bank deposits or bonds, and a quasi equity stake in his own firm.

One important feature of self-management is the egalitarianism within the firm. In any given firm, workers in a given skill or seniority class must earn the same wages. Cross-firm wage differentiation is, however, not only permitted, but inevitable, since there is no automatic mechanism that would equalize wages across firms.

The system has many serious inadequacies. Workers confront an inappropriate incentive structure. Several problems are consequences of incentive distortions: barriers to entry and exit, reduced capital and labor mobility, suboptimal technological choices, low individual effort levels, contradictory biases toward under and overinvestment, mismanagement, and reduced entrepreneurial effort. We shall review these inadequacies in turn.

---

[1]Examples of worker-owned firms include Employee Stock Ownership Plans (ESOPs). See Bogetić (this volume).

[2]It is not easy, however, to quantify them precisely. In a pure self-managed economy there is no parametric wage rate that would indicate the value of the first component. One possibility is to define a virtual wage rate as the rate at which the incumbent workers would be able to hire labor if they were allowed to do so.

[3]Workers may be able to appropriate the proceeds from asset sales even though they do not own their enterprises. They cannot sell (or give away) their stakes in the enterprises, but they may gain from assets sales (even if they are done at market value) because the market value of the assets may differ from that of the whole enterprise.

Entry, exit, and investment

Entry and exit are influenced by the decentralization of enterprise decision making in several ways. The costs of firm creation must be borne by the state or the workers and bank financing may or may not be available. The net proceeds from asset sales in the case of exit may go to the state or the workers. In these circumstances viability requires that workers bear the cost of firm creation and collect the revenues from asset sales. If workers cannot collect proceeds from asset sales, then in the event of the closing of an enterprise, workers lose both their jobs and their investment in equities, even when the firm's net worth remains positive. Workers would thus strongly resist plant closures. They would also be unwilling to invest their own funds in their firms. On the other hand, financing of investments by the government on a grant basis or by bank loans gives rise to adverse selection problems. Workers would propose all kinds of investments in enterprises independently of economic merit.[4] Appropriability of revenues from asset sales is necessary for smooth entry and exit under pure self-management.

Permitting workers to collect the proceeds from asset sales does not entirely solve the problem of entry and exit. A functional system requires that workers also bear the costs of firm creation. Entry would be limited, even then, for two reasons. First, the coordination problems involved in firm creation by groups of workers remain considerable; many small workers and investors must together identify a project and agree on implementation details. Second, the adverse selection problems would persist, to the extent that high leveraging of workers' initial investments would be necessary. Each worker would invest only a small sum at the inception of the firm, since all workers are constrained to contribute the same amount; the minimum outlay would determine the common contribution. If workers are risk-averse they will be reluctant to have their wage and nonwage income tied to the performance of a single firm. Conflicts of interest about exit would also arise between old and young workers. Older workers would want to liquidate the firm and collect the proceeds on their exit, while younger workers would prefer to postpone liquidation until they have found an alternative job.

Similar considerations apply to investment. In the most stable form of pure self-management, workers would finance the creation of firms and all investments with their quasi equity;[5] they would also collect the proceeds from asset sales. Decisions on investment and disinvestment would be distorted, for reasons similar to those which would cause distortions in entry and exit decisions.

---

[4]In capitalist economies entrepreneurs who resort to borrowing must invest substantial amounts of their own funds. These investments perform two functions. They signal that the entrepreneur believes in the project, since he would bear large losses in case of failure. And they bond the payments to lenders.

[5]Firm creation would require cash injections, but additional investments could be financed out of retained earnings.

The prediction is that very little entry or exit will take place under self-management, and investment will be distorted by incentives associated with workers' time preferences.

Labor

There is no labor market in a self-managed economy. Workers in low paid occupations or who are unemployed cannot bid for jobs because all workers in a firm must earn the same wage.[6] Instead of accepting a lower wage, an applicant could also offer to pay a joining fee, but this is also forbidden. A self-managed firm thus becomes analogous to an exclusive club that is prevented (by law) from charging admission fees, but is nevertheless allowed to refuse admission.[7] The admission of a new worker leads to the dilution of the nonwage portion of the incumbents' compensation; the hiring will therefore be resisted when it would increase total profits but reduce profit per worker.

These restrictions on within-firm wage differentiation have important consequences for efficiency. There is a high degree of cross-firm wage differentiation for a given skill category. Due to the "club" nature of self-managed firms, labor mobility is impaired, so the best match between jobs and skills is not achieved. Investment decisions are distorted in that workers choose excessively capital-intensive technologies that require fewer workers, and therefore less dilution of nonwage income.

Alchian and Demsetz (1972) have proposed that the capitalist firm be viewed as an institution that provides incentives for monitoring by residual claimants. In a pure self-managed firm workers are the residual claimants, but their stakes in the firm's performance are too small to motivate appropriate monitoring; workers also cannot reduce the costs of monitoring through specialization in that activity. Monitoring in self-managed firms will thus be inadequate. The argument that workers would be motivated by the expectation of gains applies only to very small firms; in medium and large firms, there is a free-rider problem, since the gains from one worker's monitoring will accrue to others.

Restructuring

In a capitalist economy restructuring takes place as firms are merged, liquidated, or broken up. In a pure self-managed economy restructuring activity is inhibited by several considerations, some of which have been raised in the earlier discussion of entry and exit. Sales of equipment that would require shedding excess labor are resisted by those who could

---

[6]Abstracting from seniority and skill differentials.

[7]On the "theory of clubs" that relates to the self-managed firm, see Cornes and Sandler (1986).

potentially lose their jobs. Mergers and acquisitions that may lead to the dilution of workers' rents are also resisted. Workers would refuse to go with new subsidiaries or to stay with the "mother" enterprise, if moving or staying entailed wage reduction. Consider for example the case of an efficiency enhancing merger between two firms, one with high wages, the other with low wages. The workers in the high-wage firm would see their wages drop as their rents would be averaged with those of the other firm, but they would gain due to the efficiencies generated. When worker losses outweigh gains, the transaction would be rejected.

Workers lack incentives to actively seek opportunities for mergers or spin-offs. The gains a worker can expect to make by identifying such opportunities are small relative to the costs of information acquisition. He cannot reap the full gains from his superior information, nor can he lower the cost of information collection through specialization. Managers also have little incentive to look for or propose restructuring. Restructuring may be contrary to their "empire building" strategies, and mergers may lead to dismissals or demotions at the managerial level.

In capitalist systems workers and managers may confront similar incentives to deter restructuring. There are, however, individuals or merchant banks that specialize in restructuring firms, and who, given appropriate incentives, will search for information that could lead to profitable restructuring. Capital markets or private wealth provides financing.

Managerial teams in capitalist economies compete for the right to manage firms in a vibrant market for corporate control.[8] Takeovers, mergers and acquisitions, leveraged buy outs, and spin-offs may be motivated by perceived gains from restructuring not only for capital and labor, but also for management. In contrast, in a pure self-managed economy there is no market for corporate control. Takeovers by capitalists, including leveraged buy outs that turn management into capitalists, are excluded by definition. Takeovers by other groups of workers to replace incumbents are also not possible, as the incumbent workers cannot be fired.

Managers can in theory be replaced. Due to lack of monitoring, however, managers are replaced infrequently, or for the wrong reasons. Managers will not be subject to discipline that the market for corporate control imposes on their capitalist counterparts. The manager of a self-managed enterprise has greater latitude to shirk his responsibilities or to take actions that are personally beneficial at the expense of the firm's value.

---

[8]The value of such transactions in the United States was about $180 billion per year in 1985 and 1986. Shareholders earned $346 billion (in 1986 dollars) from the sale of firms between 1977 to 1986. See Jensen (1987).

The Yugoslav version of the self-management system

In Yugoslavia systems more or less similar to the pure self-management system have been tried for extended periods of time. After a brief unsatisfactory experiment with central planning the Tito government in 1953 shifted the economy to an administered form of self-management. Ten years later centralized controls were further relaxed and there was a movement toward a purer form of self-management. In 1973, however, the tendency toward increased decentralization was reversed and a new system involving more restrictions on the operations of market forces was adopted. This system relied extensively on negotiations, ad hoc regulation by the state, and informal political controls.[9] Table 5.1 illustrates the development of economic mechanisms during the postwar period.

Table 5.1 Yugoslavia: economic mechanisms utilized in the postwar period

1946–53	Administrative socialism
1953–63	Administered market socialism
1963–73	Market socialism
1974–89	Contractual self-management

In the late 1980s legislation further revised the operation of Yugoslav enterprises. The trend was toward private ownership and a decrease in the power of workers' councils. The impact of the legislative changes on the actual functioning of enterprises was minimal however. The traditional self-managed firm was not outlawed and it continued to be the dominant form of economic organization.

Contractual self-management

The Yugoslav "contractual" form of self-management system differs in many ways from the model of pure self-management described in the previous section. Some of these differences represent necessary amendments to the pure self-management system. Other characteristics of the Yugoslav system have their origins in the realm of politics.

Yugoslav contractual self-management differs from the pure self-management model in four important ways.

State intervention. The Yugoslav authorities, aware of the problems that would result from an unfettered self-management system, created a complex

---

[9]See Rusinow (1989).

system of taxation, subsidization and regulation.[10] Direct and indirect pressure was exerted through a variety of channels to implement the policies. Decisions on entry were centralized or were taken by political bodies. The creation of self-managed firms by workers was forbidden. Financial responsibility for initial investments in newly created firms was assigned to the state. Entry and exit was in practice minimal.

Coordinating mechanisms and monopolization. A complex system involving Composite Organizations of Associated Labor (COALs), Work Organizations of Associated Labor (WOALs), Basic Organizations of Associated Labor (BOALs), Social Compacts, and Self-Management Agreements was used to coordinate decision making in enterprises. The BOAL was the fundamental form of organization. WOALs, the approximate equivalents of firms, were usually composed of several BOALs. Social Compacts and Self-Management Agreements were cartel-like coordinating mechanisms involving several WOALs. Due to the prevalence of these cartel-like organizations, the Yugoslav economy remained highly monopolized.

Political divisions. Many decisions at the federal level required consensus among constituent republics. Economic decisions at the republic level were affected by political motives. Strong informal barriers to interrepublic trade contributed to the monopolization of the economy.

Links between banks and enterprises and the lack of financial discipline. Most Yugoslav banks had strong links with one or more enterprises. In many cases the enterprises were founders of the banks. Banks found it difficult to restrict credit to their founders. Banks were also subject to pressure from local authorities.

Notwithstanding the differences between the Yugoslav system and a pure self-managed economy, there were shared problems of income distribution inequities and inefficiency due to misallocation of the factors of production. The next subsections examine these problems in more detail. The analysis is based on data derived from aggregate income statements for 33 manufacturing branches for the years 1985–87.

Income and wage distribution

Table 5.2[11] compares the income distribution of Yugoslavia with some market and centrally planned economies.

Income inequality in Yugoslavia as measured by the Gini coefficient was not particularly small. Two centrally planned economies and four market economies display smaller Gini indexes. Since there are no capitalists in Yugoslavia, the relatively high level of the Gini index is not due to the

---

[10]See also Vodopivec (this volume).
[11]This table is extracted from World Bank (1989a, p. 52).

existence of a class of wealthy rentiers.[12] Inequality can be traced to two causes: wage differentials among employed workers and unemployment.

Table 5.2 Gini coefficients for income per capita for various countries

Country	
United States (1976)	40.3
France (1970)	39.8
Yugoslavia (1983)	31.6
Australia (1979)	31.0
United Kingdom (1973)	30.8
Norway (1970)	30.6
U.S.S.R. (1972–74)	28.8
Sweden (1972)	25.4
Poland (1987)	21.8

Source: World Bank (1989a, p. 52).

Wage differentials were high under Yugoslav self-management; workers with the same qualifications earned widely divergent wages depending on the firm, industry, or republic in which they were employed. The coefficient of variation (standard deviation divided by the mean) of wage rates in the 33 branches studied was 0.30 in 1985, 0.32 in 1986, and 0.81 in 1987. The large increase in 1987 coincides with a deterioration of the financial results of enterprises and was not associated with an increase in the variability of net operating income.[13] On the contrary, the coefficient of variation of net operating income per worker fell from 1.14 in 1985 to 0.41 in 1986 and 0.39 in 1987. The unemployment rate remained very high, despite steady emigration to Western Europe, and in 1990 10 percent of the domestic labor force were unemployed.

Rules determining the partition of an enterprise's net operating income between wages and profits[14] decreed that the amount allocated to wages depended on a performance index which varied directly with net operating income and inversely with the business fund (capital). The rules display hysteresis effects. That is, a firm that was more successful than average in

---

[12]The Gini index may be an inappropriate measure of income inequality in centrally planned economies where shortages are generalized. Indeed, in such economies it is the possibility of access to goods, and not purchasing power per se that determines the welfare levels of consumers. From this point of view the Gini index may underestimate inequality in a shortage economy. On the other hand, there were marked differences among Yugoslav republics with respect to development, and the Gini index captures the inequalities associated with these differences.

[13]Appendix 1 explains some Yugoslav accounting definitions.

[14]Under the stabilization plan implemented in January 1, 1990, there was a need to impose wage controls. Wages were then determined by indexation formulas and negotiation.

the recent past was permitted to pay above average wages even if its current performance had deteriorated. These rules were an important determinant of workers' incomes. It would seem that restrictions on wage payments would simply force workers to save and firms to invest, and thus mainly transfer workers' income to the future. In reality, a firm's retained earnings were subject to informal taxes, including negative interest rates on deposits and forced investments in other firms. It is reasonable to assume that only a small fraction of a firm's retained earnings would be effectively invested so as to provide additional future earnings to workers, and many workers will have retired or quit by the time investments begin adding to income. The division of net operating income between wages and profits was consequently a form of taxation.

The specific methodology for wage determination varied across republics and over time. Appendix 2 describes one such method, the system of wage determination used in Slovenia in 1987. The common and most important feature of such methods is redistributive intervention. This is best presented graphically: Figure 5.1 indicates that there were effective upper and lower bounds to workers' wages.[15] Wage determination systems generally set wages as an increasing function of the ratio between net operating income and the business fund, which meant that variations in the size of the business fund had two effects on wages. First, revenue tended to increase with the business fund, as reflected in the higher net operating income and wages. Second, the larger the business fund the smaller the net income/business fund ratio with all else being equal and hence the smaller wages. Table 5.3 reports cross-section regressions of the wage rate (wages per worker), W, on business fund per worker (B) in the 33 branches of manufacturing for the years 1985 to 1987. The coefficients are positive and significant.

Table 5.4 presents the results of regressions of wages against business fund, revenue per worker and input (material) costs per worker. In these regressions the coefficients of business fund per worker are smaller, and are actually negative in 1987. This is because the two effects are at least partially separated[16] and the coefficient of the business fund more strongly reflects the second ("dilution") effect.

Regressions (not shown here) of wage rates on net operating income per worker and business fund per worker did not yield significant coefficients for the first independent variable in any of the three years considered. On the other hand, substituting revenue per worker (or alternatively material costs

---

[15]The performance indicator in the horizontal axis (the ratio between net operating income and business fund) corresponds to the example in Appendix 2. Other indicators may be used in different republics, but the general shape of the curve remains.

[16]They are not completely separated because, as seen above, the function relating the wage rate and net operating income per worker and business fund per worker is nonlinear.

per worker) for net operating income as an explanatory variable yielded much better fits and statistically significant coefficients (Table 5.4).

Figure 5.1 Relationship between a profitability index and wages

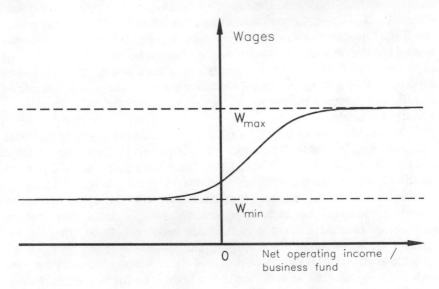

One possible explanation for these results is that there was a movement toward a cost plus system of wage determination during the period.[17] One way to implement this system in inflationary conditions is to index wages to output or input prices.

Table 5.3 Yugoslavia: regressions of wage rates on business fund per worker

W5 = 0.80 + 0.014 B5	$(R^2 = 0.383)$
(0.23) (0.003)	
W6 = 1.41 + 0.030 B6	$(R^2 = 0.700)$
(0.34) (0.003)	
W7 = 3.32 + 0.043 B7	$(R^2 = 0.164)$
(3.42) (0.017)	

Note: Wn = wage rate in 198n. Bn = business fund per worker in 198n. Standard errors of estimates in parentheses.

---

[17]The adverse effects of a cost plus system cannot be overemphasized: in this system, workers have an incentive to maximize costs.

Distortions in the allocation of labor

The section on self-management in theory described the distortionary aspects of the self-management system. Perhaps the most serious distortion is related to the allocation of labor. State intervention did not counteract the reluctance of workers in self-managed firms to hire (or admit) new workers or to make technology choices biased toward capital-intensive techniques. High unemployment rates have been a persistent problem. Intervention by the state created new problems. Layoffs were prohibited and pressure was exerted on enterprises to hire additional workers. Overemployment resulted as a consequence in many enterprises. Absenteeism and sick leave rates were also very high. Workers spent a large part of their time in assemblies where the problems of their firms were discussed. Labor mobility was reduced because workers would not voluntarily quit given the lack of alternative employment.

Table 5.4 Yugoslavia: regressions of wage rates on revenue or material costs per worker and business fund per worker

$W5 = 0.791 + 0.002\ R5 + 0.013\ B5$ $(R^2 = 0.386)$
    $(0.230)\ (0.004) \qquad (0.005)$

$W5 = 0.791 + 0.002\ M5 + 0.013\ B5$ $(R^2 = 0.387)$
    $(0.230)\ (0.004) \qquad (0.004)$

$W6 = 1.324 + 0.014\ R6 + 0.019\ B6$ $(R^2 = 0.787)$
    $(0.289)\ (0.004) \qquad (0.004)$

$W6 = 1.349 + 0.014\ M6 + 0.021\ B6$ $(R^2 = 0.786)$
    $(0.290)\ (0.004) \qquad (0.004)$

$W7 = 1.101 + 0.132\ R7 - 0.031\ B7$ $(R^2 = 0.920)$
    $(1.074)\ (0.008) \qquad (0.007)$

$W7 = 1.560 + 0.134\ M7 - 0.013\ B7$ $(R^2 = 0.904)$
    $(1.177)\ (0.009) \qquad (0.007)$

Note: Wn = wage rate in 198n. Bn = business fund per worker in 198n. Rn = revenue per worker in 198n. Mn = material costs per worker in 198n. Standard error of estimates in parentheses.

Table 5.5 shows the results of regressions of the employment growth rate (DE) on the ratio of net operating income over business fund NYB (an index of profitability) and on the size of the business fund (B) for 1986 and 1987. The coefficients are not significant and the R^2s are low. The same results are obtained if the wage rate is substituted for the profitability index (net operating income over business fund). These results suggest that in Yugoslavia labor did not flow from less to more profitable activities.

Table 5.5 Yugoslavia: regressions of employment growth on net operating income and business fund

$$DE6 = \begin{array}{cccc} -0.01 & + & 0.23 \text{ NYB6} & + & 0.00 \text{ B6} \\ (0.11) & & (0.16) & & (0.03) \end{array} \qquad (R^2 = 0.07)$$

$$DE7 = \begin{array}{cccc} 0.00 & + & 0.01 \text{ NYB7} & + & 0.00 \text{ B7} \\ (0.04) & & (0.01) & & (0.05) \end{array} \qquad (R^2 = 0.06)$$

Note: DEn = one year change (in percent) in employment in 198n. NYBn = ratio net operating income/business fund in 198n. Bn = business fund in 198n. Standard error of estimates in parentheses.

As discussed in the section on self-management in theory, effort levels will probably be lower in self-managed enterprises because of inadequate monitoring. Redistribution, as practiced in Yugoslavia, aggravated the problem. A major difference between the Yugoslav system and a pure self-managed economy is that in Yugoslavia a significant part of the rents of capital was redistributed among enterprises. Net operating income was negative or very small in many enterprises. Workers in such enterprises were likely to earn the minimum allowable wage rate and their marginal gains from effort were zero or very small, since additional income would often be allocated to reduce losses or would be distributed to other enterprises. Thus, workers had little incentive to exert themselves.

Distortions in the allocation of capital

The Yugoslav government pursued an industrialization policy that required high investment levels. Managers were pressured to invest as much as possible. Because the power, influence and wealth of managers depended on the size of the firms they managed, they too favored large investment projects. Workers, on the other hand, wished to see their firm's net income distributed in the form of wages—that is, they wished to consume the firm's capital—while managers (and the government) wished to see a larger portion of income allocated to investment. The incentive for workers to consume the firm's capital compelled authorities to forbid the sale of firm's assets. This restriction proved to be a significant obstacle to capital mobility.

Government redistributive intervention affected investment decisions: workers' incentives to invest were reduced, especially in firms with high probabilities of having either high or low success indicators (that is, in the regions where the curve in Figure 5.1 is approximately flat). A firm's choices in an uncertain environment were distorted: investment projects with significant probabilities of large losses were not rejected, because losses could not cause wages to fall below the minimum level. This problem was specially severe, because workers in the worst firms experienced the lowest risk of wage loss. Large losses would cause better firms to reduce worker wages, but workers already earning the minimum wage had nothing to lose. Similarly, workers in better performing firms avoided projects that would generate large gains with high probability, even when the chances of losses were relatively small. They would gain little in the event of success while they alone would bear the losses. In general, the better is the firm's performance, the smaller is the firm's incentive to invest.

Table 5.6 shows the results of regressions of investment (I) on the ratio of net operating income to business fund, and business fund for 1985 and 1986. The coefficients for NYB are not significant; the opposite is true for the business fund. This suggests that investment was not guided by previous profitability. The evidence is compatible with the hypothesis that managers' objectives were to build personal "empires."

Table 5.6 Yugoslavia: regressions of investment on net operating income and business fund

$I5 =$ $-0.002 - 0.002$ NYB5 $+ 0.076$ B5		$(R^2 = 0.808)$
(0.017) (0.029) (0.007)		
$I6 =$ $-0.002 + 0.004$ NYB6 $+ 0.044$ B6		$(R^2 = 0.775)$
(0.017) (0.028) (0.005)		

Note: In = investment in 198n. NYBn = ratio net operating income/business fund in 198n. Bn = business fund in 198n. Standard error of estimates in parentheses.

Net operating income per worker and income per worker are uncorrelated with credit growth (results not shown here). This is not surprising, given that there is also no correlation between investment and performance. A positive correlation would indicate that credit was being directed to the better performing branches of the economy. A negative correlation would suggest the existence of distress borrowing.

These results indicate that capital did not flow from low- to high-performance branches.[18]

The Yugoslav government attempted to promote investment through centralized mechanisms (at the federal and republican levels). Funds were centrally allocated to large investment projects, and a network of influences and pressures directed bank loans to selected enterprises; in the meantime enterprises with above-average performance usually located in the more developed republics were forced to invest in loss-making enterprises. These efforts were rarely guided by efficiency objectives. In most cases, political considerations predominated.

---

[18]The extremely low rates of entry and exit are also an indication of lack of capital mobility.

The consequences of inefficiency

Losses

Squeezed between high taxes (both through effective taxation and redistribution) and low efficiency, Yugoslav manufacturing enterprises consistently earned low returns. In 1987, which was an exceptionally bad year, the manufacturing sector as a whole had losses. Table 5.7 shows the significance of loss-making enterprises in the economy. Up to 20 percent of workers worked in loss-making enterprises. The general trend toward larger losses can also be seen from Figure 5.2.[19]

Table 5.7 Yugoslavia: loss-making enterprises

Year	Number of loss-making enterprises	Share in the economy (percent)		
		Enterprises	Workers	GSP
1983	2,678	8.9	11.4	3.2
1984	2,195	7.5	8.8	2.3
1985	2,369	8.2	10.2	2.9
1986	2,306	8.0	11.0	3.1
1987	4,218	15.3	22.7	7.4
1988	2,772	10.5	17.5	6.5

Note: GSP = gross social product (a close equivalent of GDP).

The importance of losses is revealed by decomposing the aggregate branch-level data to the enterprise level. Several manufacturing branches were profitable in the aggregate, although a number of enterprises within these branches exhibited large losses.

According to Yugoslav accounting conventions, there are three levels of loss-making firms. First, a firm's net operating income may not fully cover wages. This is the mildest case. When losses are larger, income may not fully cover even interest, taxes, and insurance. In the case of enterprises with the most serious losses, revenue is smaller than the sum of material costs and depreciation (negative net value added at domestic prices); such cases were quite common. In 1985 there were enterprises with negative net value added in 21 of the 33 branches into which the manufacturing sector is divided; in

---

[19]The graph shows the ratio of losses to gross social product (GSP), a Yugoslav equivalent of gross domestic product (GDP), for 1979–81, as given in Knight (1984). The point for 1982 was interpolated.

Figure 5.2 Yugoslavia: losses as a percentage of GSP, 1979-88

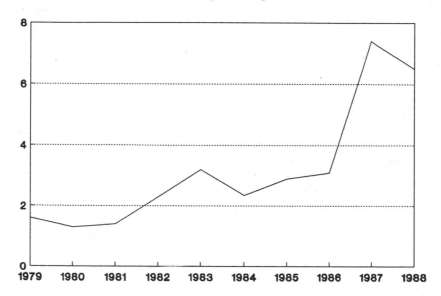

1986 the number of branches with such enterprises had increased to 24, while in 1987 the only branch without such large lossmakers was petroleum and gas extraction. During these three years approximately one third of the manufacturing sector's total losses originated in enterprises unable to cover material costs and depreciation. Because most of the branches were profitable in aggregate in 1985 and 1986, the data indicate large differences in within-branch enterprise performance.

Five branches were among the ten largest loss-making branches in all three years (1985–87): basic chemicals, food products, basic nonferrous metals, animal food, and nonferrous ore mining. Five others were among the largest lossmakers in two of the three years: electricity, furniture and wood products, and coal mining in 1985–86, and petroleum refining and iron and steel in 1986–87. The fact that five branches consistently remained among the largest ten lossmakers in 1985–87 and another five were there for two of three years suggests that no adequate measures were taken to reduce costs or increase efficiency.

Macroeconomic instability

It is possible to identify six macroeconomic strategies pursued by Yugoslavia since the mid-1970s.

• *Import substitution strategy.* The period of 1976–79 was characterized by high investment, large current account deficits, and an approximately fixed exchange rate.

• *First attempts at stabilization.* During 1980–82 price and import controls were imposed, and fiscal discipline was tightened; the external debt continued to grow, reaching $20 billion in 1982. In 1981–82 international banks stopped lending to Yugoslavia and real GDP stagnated.

• *Large real devaluations.* The current account turned into surplus in 1983; measures to deal with enterprise arrears were introduced.

• *Wage increases and dinar appreciation.* Wage discipline was relaxed and the exchange rate was allowed to appreciate in part because of the Congress of the Communist party in 1986.

• *Hyperinflation.* A stabilization program was implemented in May 1988. Ceilings were imposed on credit and wages, and financial instruments were indexed so that real interest rates became positive. In the absence of a significant fiscal adjustment inflation accelerated rapidly, and the program's targets had to be quickly abandoned.

• *Stabilization program.* The stabilization program of January 1, 1990 required a fiscal adjustment of about 5 percent of GDP; in an environment of strict financial discipline, many enterprises became technically bankrupt, or stopped paying wages to avoid bankruptcy. By June 1990 the government relaxed monetary policy by reducing reserve requirements.

Successive Yugoslav governments had been trying to stabilize the economy for more than ten years, but inflation nevertheless gradually accelerated to culminate in the hyperinflation of 1988–89. The 1990 attempt to stabilize the economy, like previous attempts, did not address the fundamental imbalances that were at the root of the inflationary process.[20]

For many years observers had difficulty understanding the source of Yugoslavia's inflation because the government budget was balanced. It seemed that inflation was merely "accidental" and could easily be eliminated through the imposition of nominal anchors.[21] The macroeconomic problems of Yugoslavia, however, were intimately linked to the system of self-management; in 1986 Manuel Hinds demonstrated this connection by noting the chain of causation from self-management to creation of losses at the enterprise and bank level and then to inflation as a way to cover the losses. Hinds argued that "to mobilize the resources needed to service the external debt and to cover the losses of the banking system, the National Bank of Yugoslavia is imposing an inflation tax on the holders of dinar-denominated financial assets" (1986, p. 7).[22]

Table 5.8 shows consolidated enterprise accounts as percentages of GSP. The losses were covered by several mechanisms. Initially the losses were reflected in large current account deficits, as foreign creditors financed the

---

[20]On the positive side, since 1983 Yugoslavia drastically reduced its net international indebtedness through a current account surplus though at the expense of slow or negative GDP growth.

[21]As stated by Jeffrey Sacks and reported by the Yugoslav magazine *Ekonomska politika*, translation by Ljiljana Matic (memo dated 14 December 1989).

[22]See also Hinds (1991) and Hinds (this volume).

Table 5.8   Yugoslavia: consolidated enterprise accounts, 1981–88 *(as percentage of GSP)*

	1981	1982	1983	1984	1985	1986	1987	1988
Gross income	55.9	52.0	48.9	49.9	48.7	51.2	40.1	40.4
Taxes	6.4	5.8	5.7	5.5	5.3	7.4	7.0	6.7
Net income	49.6	46.2	43.2	44.4	43.3	43.8	33.1	33.7
Wages	39.2	37.6	34.9	33.7	34.9	38.4	35.2	34.3
Profits	11.8	10.9	11.2	12.8	11.3	8.3	4.5	5.1
Losses	-1.3	-2.2	-2.9	-2.1	-2.8	-3.0	-6.6	-5.7
Net profits	10.4	8.7	8.3	10.7	8.5	5.3	-2.1	-0.6

Note: GSP = gross social product (a close equivalent of GDP).
Source: Social Accounting Service (Yugoslav government agency).

subsidies that were necessary to avoid the bankruptcy of lossmakers.[23] After the external crisis of 1981–82 these credits were no longer available and inflationary pressures began to mount. Figure 5.3 shows the evolution of the current account and the inflation rate. A high positive correlation is apparent.[24]

Inflation accelerated because the government had to resort to monetary creation to bail out the lossmakers. Some bail-out mechanisms, such as redistribution from successful firms to lossmakers, were not directly inflationary. The principal subsidization mechanism—the extension of credits at negative real interest rates—was, however, inflationary. Ultimately, the sources of the subsidies were the holders of dinar-denominated assets, who were paid even lower real rates. The banking system served as intermediary for the transfer of subsidies. Commercial banks received the portion of the inflation tax that corresponds to demand and time deposits[25] and also received interest rate subsidies on rediscounts from the central bank, which were financed by the inflation tax on base money. The net revenues of the commercial banks were then transferred to enterprises in the form of interest rate subsidies.

Subsidies were also extended in connection with two foreign exchange insurance schemes. The first scheme was associated with a foreign exchange risk guarantee for deposits from residents and nonresidents in the commercial banks; the second involved the central bank's absorbing the

---

[23]This was also observed by Burkett (1989) who states that "the contractual economy is probably less conducive to economic efficiency than either central planning, or a market economy, but living standards continued to rise as long as the external environment was favorable."

[24]Similar developments took place in several Latin American countries in the early 1980s: inflation accelerated dramatically as the current account shifted from a deficit to a surplus.

[25]Part of this tax was transferred to the central bank as an inflation tax on reserve money.

foreign exchange risk associated with enterprise debts in some less developed republics. Both schemes were very costly to the central bank.

Figure 5.3 Yugoslavia: current account (CA) surplus and inflation, 1976–89

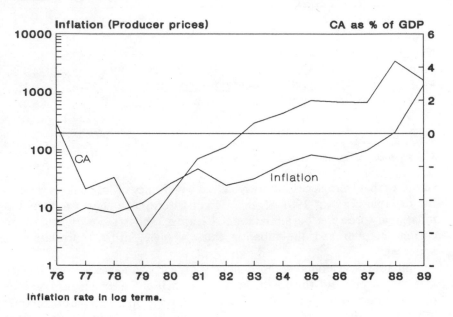

Inflation rate in log terms.

Foreign exchange deposits would normally cause the average cost of funds for commercial banks to increase given the risk of devaluation. This would require upward adjustments of dinar lending rates. The central bank, however, provided full foreign exchange insurance cover to commercial banks, but in turn obliged the banks to charge artificially low interest rates to enterprises. According to this scheme, which was first implemented in 1978, commercial banks redeposited foreign exchange deposits in the central bank,[26] which then extended an equivalent dinar-denominated credit to commercial banks. The real interest rates charged on these credits as well as on credits passed over to enterprises were highly negative.[27]

---

[26]In those cases where the commercial banks had already sold the foreign exchange, a currency swap in effect took place.

[27]See Rocha (1989) for a more detailed account.

Figure 5.4 depicts the transfers between the population, the central bank, the commercial banks, and the enterprise sector. The government is not part of the picture because transfers and loans from the central bank to the government were not a significant source of monetization.

Figure 5.4 Yugoslavia: transfers between sectors

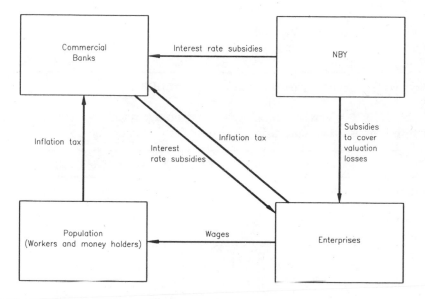

Table 5.9 shows the central bank's seignorage on base money, decomposed into inflation tax and real stock variations. Notice that the inflation tax is a good approximation of the central bank's quasi-fiscal deficit.[28] Table 5.10 shows the banking system's seignorage revenues on broad money, and the net amounts transferred to enterprises.[29]

Although there was no significant fiscal imbalance in Yugoslavia, the consolidated deficit of the public sector was large. This deficit included the quasi-fiscal deficit of the central bank, which was caused by the interest rate subsidies extended to the commercial banks and by the realization of foreign exchange losses.

---

[28]In general, the central bank's quasi-fiscal deficit equals the inflation tax minus the central bank's real net worth variation. See Rocha and Saldanha (1992).

[29]Enterprises had demand and time deposits with the banking system. The inflation tax paid on these deposits was subtracted from the interest rate subsidies received to establish the net transfers. Tables 5.9 and 5.10 are from Rocha (1989).

Table 5.9   Yugoslavia: central bank seignorage revenues on base money, 1981–88 *(as percentage of GSP)*

	1981	1982	1983	1984	1985	1986	1987	1988
Seignorage	2.7	2.7	1.6	3.9	3.6	4.2	4.9	5.7
Of which inflation tax	3.2	2.9	4.3	3.5	4.2	4.3	6.1	6.6
Real stock variation	−0.5	−0.2	−2.7	0.4	−0.6	−0.1	−1.2	−0.9

Note: GSP = gross social product (a close equivalent of GDP).

Table 5.10   Yugoslavia: banking system seignorage revenues on broad money and net transfers to enterprises, 1981–88 *(as percentage of GSP)*

	1981	1982	1983	1984	1985	1986	1987	1988
Seignorage	9.3	7.8	5.2	10.6	7.3	11.2	11.4	10.3
Net transfers to enterprises	3.4	3.2	1.9	4.0	3.8	6.6	6.5	7.0

Stabilization efforts[30]

One might expect that credit ceilings and interest rate liberalization would quickly lead to price stabilization. The program of May 1988 proceeded according to this assumption, but the result was a rapid acceleration of inflation. This may seem a surprising outcome, but a deeper analysis shows the outcome should be expected, since the fundamental imbalances of the economy had not been addressed and no real financial discipline had been imposed. Indeed, interenterprise credits, including a large proportion of arrears, increased rapidly. Enterprises were able to continue incurring losses. To the extent that successful enterprises lent to lossmakers, losses were socialized. As a result of the program the consolidated public sector deficit swelled. The state lost the inflation tax revenues on time deposits when interest rates on individuals' deposits were raised. This loss was to be compensated by a gain due to the elimination of interest rate subsidies. These gains never materialized, however, as they depended on the central bank's adopting a tight monetary policy. Monetary stance, however, remained expansive because losses had increased to such an extent that a tight credit policy would have resulted in widespread bankruptcies. The net

---

[30]For a more detailed analysis of the inflationary process and policy in Yugoslavia, see World Bank (1989b).

result was a deterioration of the fiscal situation that led to an acceleration of inflation. To make matters worse, the central bank continued to incur valuation losses as the mismatch between its assets and liabilities persisted. No additional fiscal resources were generated to compensate for these losses. The program failed and its targets were abandoned later in the year. Inflation continued to accelerate, and reached 2,700 percent per year in 1989.

The stabilization program initiated on January 1, 1990 appeared to have better prospects. After October 1988 the central bank had stopped accepting redeposits of foreign exchange from the commercial banks, a fiscal adjustment had been undertaken, and all interenterprise and enterprise-to-government payments had been centralized in the Social Accounting Service (SDK) so that arrears could be monitored and punished with bankruptcy and liquidation.[31] Credit ceilings and positive real interest rates were integral parts of the program. After so many failed attempts, financial discipline appeared finally to have been imposed in Yugoslavia.

As a consequence of these measures, a large number of enterprises went bankrupt[32] or approached bankruptcy.[33] Before the onset of the program in January, the unemployment rate had been about 10 percent. By April another 6 percent of the work force was either unemployed or at risk of becoming unemployed since their enterprises had been notified by SDK of their bankrupt status. More seriously, 25 percent of the socialized sector's labor force was not paid wages.[34]

These numbers, plus a GSP drop of about 8 percent during 1990, indicated that the program was imposing severe sacrifices on the population. However, inflation had fallen dramatically, and prices actually fell in May 1990. By the end of 1990, however, inflation was still running at 4 percent per month.

The continuation of the inflationary process indicates that financial discipline was not maintained. Bankrupt enterprises were not liquidated; if small, they were placed under the authority of local governments, if larger, republican governments took responsibility for them bailing them out with resources from the Joint Reserve Fund[35] or the republics.

---

[31]A bankrupt enterprise was to be divided between its creditors, which were other self-managed firms. Therefore liquidation did not imply the privatization of enterprise assets. See Atiyas (1990).

[32]Approximately 300 enterprises went bankrupt by June 1990, most in Slovenia where financial discipline had been stricter.

[33]Approximately 7,700 by June 1990.

[34]There were, however, barter arrangements made between enterprises and suppliers of consumer goods, mostly food. The portion of the total wage corresponding to housing subsidies continued to be "paid."

[35]This fund was financed by a special tax on enterprises.

Conclusions

The self-management system distorts incentives to such a degree that an economy left to operate without corrective intervention would most likely collapse. State intervention and the introduction of coordinating mechanisms permitted the Yugoslav economy to achieve a minimum efficiency level, though they created new distortions.

For a while, relatively high growth and consumption levels were achieved through current account deficits and increases in external debt. When external credit became much more difficult to obtain in 1981, the current account improved dramatically. Because the basic problem of low efficiency was not dealt with at that point, domestic imbalance persisted. The consolidated public deficit assumed large proportions and inflation rose rapidly, because of the subsidization of inefficient enterprises. Attempts at stabilizing the economy by imposing financial discipline failed.

No combination of fiscal and monetary policies will be able to stabilize the Yugoslav economy unless there are fundamental changes in ownership structure. A clear demonstration of this is the 1988 stabilization program that raised interest rates to positive levels. Since the enterprises still had to be subsidized, the effect of the program was a reduction of the inflation tax base and an acceleration of inflation.

We have seen that self-managed firms display little entrepreneurial activity (in the Schumpeterian sense) and that they choose overly capital-intensive technology and avoid hiring. The closing of inefficient enterprises therefore only adds to unemployment, as the labor force released would not be able to find alternative employment. A labor overemployment which coexists with a very high open unemployment thus represents a peculiar type of welfare system. If the self-management system is sustained, efforts directed toward imposing financial discipline and enforcing bankruptcy will disrupt economic activity and ultimately fail.[36] The lesson of the Yugoslav experience is that ownership transformation must precede, not follow, the imposition of financial discipline.

---

[36]Knight (1984) provides an interesting account of the difficulties of imposing financial discipline: "Initiation of bankruptcy procedures was a truly rare event, affecting only 14 BOALs (1 percent of all BOALs showing uncovered losses in their annual financial reports) with 1,306 workers in 1982 . . . ." The study proposed that rehabilitation proceedings should be conducted by an independent agency (the Social Accounting Service), and asked for a mobilization of political will to enforce the legislation.

Appendix 1. Yugoslav accounting conventions

The following are the basic accounting identities that relate to Yugoslav enterprises:

Gross material product = Revenue – material costs.
Income = Gross material product – depreciation.
Net operating income = Income – interest – taxes and insurance.
Net operating income = Wages + profits.

Profits can be considered retained earnings, because workers do not receive dividends. Material costs include interest on working capital. Interest is the amount paid, not the amount accrued. Taxes can be decomposed into two parts. First, there are regular taxes that vary with income, including labor costs (wages) according to predetermined rules. Second, taxes have an ad hoc component that depends on income as well, but also on the firm's bargaining power, and on political and social considerations.

Appendix 2. Wage determination: an example

Wages in Slovenia in 1987 were determined according to the following methodology. First, a performance index of the form is calculated:

$$(5.1) \qquad m = \frac{NY}{\alpha L + \beta B}.$$

Here α and β are two positive constants that differ across branches, NY is net operating income, L is size of the labor force, and B is the business fund. Then a function u with the typical shape shown in Figure 5.1 is used to calculate a "correction index" $u(m)$. Finally, the wage (and social services) fund, W^*, is computed as

$$(5.2) \qquad W^* = \gamma u(m)L$$

where again γ is a positive constant that varies across industries.

Manipulating these formulas, we find that

$$(5.3) \qquad w = \gamma u(m) = \gamma u\left(\frac{ny}{\alpha+\beta b}\right)$$

where lowercase letters indicate per worker values, and w equals wage per worker. That is, the wage rate varies directly with the net operating income per worker and inversely with the business fund per worker.

References

Alchian, Armen, and Harold Demsetz. 1972. "Production, Information Costs and Economic Organization." *American Economic Review* 62:777–95.

Atiyas, Izak. 1990. "Notes on the Bankruptcy Process in Yugoslavia." Processed.

Burkett, James. 1989. "Yugoslav Economic Performance and Prospects: An Analysis Based on a Bayesian Vector Autoregression." In *Pressures for Reform in the East European Economies*. Vol. 2 of study papers submitted to the Joint Economic Committee, United States Congress. Washington, D.C.: Government Printing Office.

Cornes, Richard, and Todd Sandler. 1986. *The Theory of Externalities, Public Goods, and Club Goods*. Cambridge, U.K.: Cambridge University Press.

Hinds, Manuel. 1986. "Financial Sector Issues in Yugoslavia." World Bank, Trade and Finance Division, Europe, Middle East and North Africa Department, Washington, D.C. Processed.

Hinds, Manuel. 1991. "Markets and Ownership in Socialist Countries in Transition." In Arye L. Hillman, ed., *Markets and Politicians: Politicized Economic Choice*. Boston and Dordrecht: Kluwer Academic Publishers.

Hinds, Manuel. 1992. "Policy Effectiveness in Reforming Socialist Economies." This volume.

Jensen, Michael C. 1987. "The Free Cash Flow Theory of Takeovers: A Financial Perspective on Mergers and Acquisitions and the Economy." In L. Browne and E. Rosengren, eds., *The Merger Boom*. Proceedings of a conference sponsored by the Federal Reserve Bank of Boston, October, Melvin Village, New Hampshire.

Knight, Peter T. 1984. *Financial Discipline and Structural Adjustment in Yugoslavia*. World Bank Staff Working Paper 705. Washington, D.C.: World Bank.

Rocha, Roberto. 1989. "Structural Adjustment and Inflation in Yugoslavia." World Bank, Trade and Finance Division, Europe, Middle East and North Africa Department, Washington, D.C. Processed.

Rocha, Roberto, and Fernando Saldanha. 1992. "Fiscal and Quasi-Fiscal Deficits: Nominal and Real." World Bank, Trade and Finance Division, Europe, Middle East and North Africa Department. Washington, D.C. Processed.

Rusinow, Denis. 1989. "Yugoslavia: Enduring Crisis and Delayed Reforms." In *Pressures for Reform in the East European Economies*. Vol. 2 of study papers submitted to the Joint Economic Committee, United States Congress. Washington D.C.: Government Printing Office.

Vodopivec, Milan. 1992. "State Paternalism and the Yugoslav Failure." This volume.

World Bank. 1989a. "Poland: Subsidies and Income Distribution." Report No. 7776-POL. World Bank, Washington, D.C. Processed.

———. 1989b. "Yugoslavia, Financial Restructuring: Policies and Priorities." Report No. 7869-YU. World Bank, Washington, D.C. Processed.

6

State Paternalism
and the Yugoslav Failure

Milan Vodopivec

Economic efficiency was a primary goal of the legislation which established so-called social ownership of Yugoslav enterprises.[1] Yet an attempt to implement this legislation through existing institutions proved incapable of achieving even modest efficiency goals. This chapter demonstrates that whatever the other inadequacies of Yugoslav self-management,[2] the system of organization failed to institute an effective appropriation of returns by workers. The failure was intimately related to the system of ownership. Yugoslav social ownership was characterized by a massive and pervasive income redistribution that inhibited incentives for efficiency. Such redistribution is a predictable outcome of bargaining among distributional coalitions in an environment of political autocracy when property rights are nontransparent.

It has never been clear who owns Yugoslav firms, neither to foreigners nor to Yugoslavs themselves.[3] The popular understanding, that social ownership is "ownership by everyone and no one," is not very illuminating. It only suggests that, on the one hand, society at large has some say over the

---

[1] For instance, one of the official rationales for the legislation of the mid-1970s, which introduced the Basic Organizations of Associated Labor (BOALs) was to increase labor productivity by reducing the size of the firm and thus overcoming the free-rider problem. For a discussion of this issue, see Tyson (1979).

[2] See Hinds (1991), Hinds (this volume), and Saldanha (this volume).

[3] The issue of ownership emerged most conspicuously during the privatization drive of 1990, which raised the question, who is the recipient of the proceeds from the sale of "social capital"?

The valuable comments of Peter Murrell and Boris Pleskovic are gratefully acknowledged.

use of the means of production (ownership by everyone) and, on the other hand, that no one person has the right to appropriate the returns and/or make decisions about the use of the means of production (ownership by no one). Nor does studying the voluminous, complex, and often confusing Yugoslav legislation in order to determine how the social and individual components of social ownership are enforced offer any conclusion. It is through an understanding of ownership relations in practice and the actual enforcement of laws that we will understand the nature of social ownership in former Yugoslavia.

A perusal of the Yugoslav legislation might lead one to conclude that social ownership during that period was of a cooperative type, that workers of a particular firm collectively own that firm subject to rules set by society. According to the constitution, Yugoslav workers seem to have had significant ownership rights: (a) they had the right to participate in the decision making of the firm, and (b) they had the right to share the profits,[4] and hence to participate in present and future benefits obtained from economic goods. On the other hand, their rights were not absolute: (a) workers were not allowed to sell a firm's capital assets, (b) they could not recover their investments when they terminate employment, (c) they were required to maintain the book value of capital assets, and (d) the legislation set broad rules about the determination of the firm's wage bill.

Because property rights are also restricted by private contract or law in capitalist countries, one can still understand Yugoslav social ownership to be a form of collective ownership by workers of a firm, with government limiting workers' ownership rights to ensure a socially efficient use of resources.[5]

An interpretation that considers the worker collective of a particular firm in Yugoslavia to have been the owner of that firm is, however, inappropriate: even though the workers were in theory residual claimants, redistribution decisively affected their earnings and de facto voided the provision that workers share the residual. Political elites and bureaucrats were the de facto owners of Yugoslav social property: they benefitted from

---

[4]Apart from the provision on minimal wages, there is no guarantee of earnings of workers—their overall income is tied to the financial result of the firm (The Law of Associated Labor 1976, Art. 116).

[5]Taken to the extreme, the principle of social ownership could thus mean that any enterprise (that is, any group of workers) which does not use "social resources" (that is, the means of production over which the enterprise exercises "social ownership") optimally imposes a negative externality on society and is thus "usurping" the means of production—since resources could have been used more productively by some other group of workers. In this extreme interpretation, social ownership becomes a synonym for efficiency. (This is, of course, a normative definition, since a mechanism to ensure the contestability of the market for means of production is lacking.)

redistribution both directly (through their earnings and perquisites), and indirectly (through advancement in their professional careers).[6]

The failure of the Yugoslav self-managed system, contrary to conventional wisdom, had less to do with worker participation per se than with state paternalism. The essential characteristics of the Yugoslav economic system are thus similar to those of other East European socialist economies. In the search for a model to be applied to postsocialist East European economies, the dismal Yugoslav performance of the 1980s cannot be taken as proof of the commonly asserted proposition that worker (participation in) management cannot and does not work.

This paper analyzes redistribution as practiced in Yugoslavia in the 1970s and 1980s in an effort to empirically substantiate this thesis. The mechanism of redistribution allowed for by the institution of social property is described in the next section. I then investigate econometrically the pattern of redistribution. The redistributive mechanism is described as a confrontation between distributional (special interest) coalitions. The section on alternative explanations of the Yugoslav failure summarizes the efficiency properties of the economic system, and counters the claim that the Yugoslav failure was the consequence of worker participation. Policy implications of this view, particularly with respect to privatization, are considered in the concluding section.

The mechanism of redistribution

The taxation side of the mechanism consisted of the appropriation of financial savings via an inflation tax and the appropriation of resources from the original owner via compulsory financial investments with stipulated negative real returns. The usual counterpart of this form of taxation was subsidization, based on waiving tax payments and allowing exemption from compulsory financial investments. Methods of income redistribution in Yugoslavia thus extended far beyond the standard distribution mechanism of imposing taxes and allowing subsidies to include more important though less visible methods.

---

[6]This conclusion derives from the ability to participate in current and future benefits as the major determinant of ownership, the trait of ownership labelled "economic ownership" as opposed to "legal ownership" by Bajt (1982). While other aspects of ownership (above all, decision making rights) could, indeed, be ultimately regarded subordinate to this aspect, "social ownership" fares no better on the count of decision making: the majority of important decisions (prominently, decisions about investment and the appointment of managers) were made in the political sphere. See Obradovic (1978).

Channels of redistribution

In addition to taxes and subsidies, there were several other channels of redistribution.[7] A broad description of these channels follows.[8]

Proper taxes and proper subsidies (grants). Proper taxes and proper subsidies (grants) are pure income transfers. The category of proper taxes consists of income taxes, other obligations which have the nature of taxes (expenses for environmental preservation), and payments to Self-Management Communities of Interest (SMCIs)[9] for the provision of social services. Proper subsidies are nonreimbursable resources obtained to avoid and/or decrease losses reported in the annual income statement, and payments obtained as additional assistance once a loss has been incurred (at least a portion of grants can be used to pay wages). The sources of such payments are other firms within a Working Organization of Associated Labor (WOAL)[10] and government reserve and solidarity funds (Law on Associated Labor, Article 155). Furthermore, some forms of compulsory interfirm credit (called "pooling of resources" because creditors supposedly retain decision-making discretion over the resources) specify that a creditor must help to cover losses incurred by a debtor.[11]

Quasi taxes (quasi subsidies). Quasi taxes (or quasi subsidies) are complete or near complete appropriations of resources by one agent which are formally accounted for as financial investments by another agent. That is, the investor includes the resources on the asset side of his balance sheet, but usually writes them off after some time (for example, several years).[12] Sometimes they are repaid to the investor, but only at face value or at a small positive nominal interest rate and with a grace period of several years

---

[7]Overall taxes are defined as the sum of proper taxes, quasi taxes, and "losses on money," and overall subsidies are the sum of grants, quasi grants, and "gains on money." Following Baxter (1984, pp. 58–78), "gains (or losses) on money" are defined as real gains (losses) obtained under inflationary circumstances on the basis of owing (or lending and borrowing) money assets.

[8]Precise definitions of accounting data used for empirical analysis can be found in Vodopivec (1989).

[9]SMCIs are independent legal entities providing goods and/or services in the areas of (a) social services (education, health and child care, culture, research and development, employment services, and so on), and (b) energy and infrastructure. They are managed jointly by producers and consumers, and are meant to ensure efficient provision of goods and services in the areas where markets alone fail to do so.

[10]WOALs may be considered the closest counterpart to the Western model of enterprise. It usually consists of several BOALs.

[11]The opposite case, participation in the profits of a debtor, rarely yields positive real gains, because the principal is usually not indexed, and the payment of the profit share in a highly inflationary environment (as in Yugoslavia) generally fails to compensate for the loss on the principal.

[12]Enterprises were advised by the government to accept self-management agreements with such provisions. These agreements acted as a veil preserving the legality and integrity of the system in spite of compulsory and discretionary nature of these transfers.

(in the inflationary environment of Yugoslavia, this means at a substantially negative real interest rate); only a minute portion of the original investment in real terms was, in this case, recovered.[13] Investments of this nature were understood by both parties to be implicit grants, and they were clearly of an involuntary nature.

Channels used for this type of transfer included the following:
- credits to cover losses
- rehabilitation credits
- investments in development funds, SMCIs of material production,[14] special government funds, securities
- investments in solidarity and reserve funds of a WOAL
- foreign loans to enterprises via commercial banks whereby enterprises were relieved of exchange rate risks[15]
- waiver of taxes, contributions, and exemption from the compulsory pooling of resources
- "borrowing" from the firm's own business fund to cover losses (decapitalization of assets).[16]

Most channels of taxation were used selectively. If a firm was unable to pay its obligations without incurring a loss, the obligations were reduced, deferred, or simply waived. Lossmakers (and some other firms, as determined by law) were thus exempted from, partly relieved from, or allowed to defer a variety of obligations.

An enterprise's "ability to pay" is subject to a very important qualification. The income-sharing nature of personal incomes in Yugoslavia made labor costs flexible, at least theoretically. If external obligations (and capital accumulation) had been given priority, and a firm's personal income (wages) fund had thus been treated as a residual, most enterprises would indeed have been able to meet their obligations. The residual that remained for personal incomes would, of course, have been very small, perhaps in

---

[13]For instance, the loan to the Federal Fund for the Acceleration of the Development of Less Developed Republics and Provinces was repayable in 13 annuities, after a grace period of three years and with a nominal rate of 5 percent (Association of Accountants and Financial Workers 1985).

[14]These included natural monopolies (electricity, oil and gas), infrastructure (railroads, roads, ports, airports), and some utilities (broadcasting, telephone, mail) which financed a portion of their investment via direct "contributions" of firms from other industries.

[15]Exchange rate differences stemming from this type of loan (that is, the effects of revaluation of foreign loans denominated in dinars as a consequence of depreciation of domestic currency) were allowed by the authorities to be deferred and thus to be shown in balance sheets of enterprises as the increase of their assets (under "active deferrals"). Consequently, they would not appear among costs when they were due, and so only the original counterpart amount of a loan in dinars was translated into costs, creating large excess final demand. See World Bank (1989).

[16]The firm was obliged to eventually repay these funds, but the "gain on money" clause applied (that is, under inflationary circumstances the firm repaid in its business fund less in real terms than it borrowed).

some cases providing below minimum standards of living. To avoid such socially disruptive and undesirable outcomes, priority was in practice given to personal incomes, and other obligations and accumulation were determined as a residual. It was, therefore, the quasi-fixed nature of personal incomes that determined the size of residual net income and thus the firm's ability to pay its obligations.

Concessionary financing and inflation tax (gains and losses on money). The practice of holding the interest rate significantly below the inflation rate yielded a substantial gain on money accruing to the borrower. Also, there were several general write-offs of debts of the worst-standing firms during the 1970s and 1980s, making the banking system a source of significant redistribution from net creditors to net debtors. Furthermore, the lack of stringent enforcement of penalties allowed firms to default on their debts ("keeping bills in the drawer" as it is called in accounting jargon).

In the empirical analysis which follows, the above channels of redistribution are quantified on the basis of accounting data. There are, however, other important channels of redistribution, whose effects unfortunately cannot easily, if at all, be quantified, and which are consequently omitted from the empirical analysis which follows. The most important channels not accounted for are the following:

• Implicit taxation through regulated prices.

• Redistribution through accounting methods. Firms rely on accountants to bend existing rules to come up with desired results (it is called a "positive zero," that is, the result of an income statement that does not show a loss, but that still avoids taxes on profits). This was particularly important in Yugoslavia, where accounting rules did not take appropriate account of inflation,[17] and where no independent auditing companies existed which could restrict the discretion of firms in their application of the existing rules.

• Depletion of a firm's capital through the irresponsible depreciation of assets in real terms.

Quantification of flows

In this section, I present empirical evidence concerning the redistribution flows as defined and discussed above.

Proper taxes and proper subsidies are calculated as the sum of appropriate flows (taken mostly from income statements). For other variables (quasi taxes, quasi grants, losses and gains on money) the following

---

[17]The treatment of inventories was especially deficient; as one empirical study showed (Lavrac and Cibej 1986), due to the widespread use of the first-in first-out accounting method, material costs were underestimated and income overstated, thus adding to inflationary pressures and creating the potential for higher wage increases.

method is used. The redistribution flow (RFLOW, where RFLOW could be each of the above variables) is calculated as

$$RFLOW = INFLR \cdot (B_{-1} + B_0) / 2$$

where INFLR is an inflation rate (equal to 95.9 percent for 1986 in Slovenia for the retail price index), and B_{-1} and B_0 denote the tax (subsidy) base at the end of the previous and current years, respectively. Note that the redistribution flows are expressed in terms of the money units at the end of the period, and that the equilibrium real interest rate is assumed to equal zero.

In calculating losses on money, the amount obtained by using the above formula is reduced by the sum of interest payments received and income received on the basis of the participation in joint income as stipulated in self-management agreements on pooling of resources. Similarly, in calculating gains on money, the amount obtained by using the above formula is reduced by the sum of interest payments paid by the enterprise and income paid to other enterprises as a dividend on the basis of pooling of resources.[18]

Table 6.1 summarizes data concerning income redistribution for a 1986 sample of 416 Slovenian manufacturing enterprises (accounting for approximately 10 percent of Slovenia's gross national product (GNP)). The

Table 6.1 Yugoslavia: summary statistics of redistribution flows

Variable	Mean	Coefficient of variation	Minimum value	Maximum value
PTAXR	16.4	24.9	0.2	134.1
QTAXR	23.1	93.7	0.0	201.7
MLOSSR	63.1	66.8	1.2	611.8
GRANTR	0.4	821.3	0.0	63.8
QGRANTR	7.4	200.7	0.6	377.3
MGAINR	60.5	89.3	-45.9	852.5
NSUBSR	-34.2	-108.5	-157.5	533.5

Note: All variables are in the form of rates (presented as the percentage of the income of the firm). PTAXR = tax rate proper, QTAXR = quasi-tax rate, MLOSSR = losses on money rate, GRANTR = grants rate, QGRANTR = quasi-grant rate, MGAINR = gains on money rate, and NSUBSR = rate of net subsidies, defined as the difference between the sum of subsidy rates and the sum of tax rates.

---

[18]Although in the 1980s the discrepancy between the inflation rate and dinar depreciation rate was generally not significant, that was not the case in 1986. Consequently, even money liabilities (or assets) denominated in foreign exchange could be a source of gains (or losses) on money. Because of their nontypical nature, these gains and losses are excluded from the discussion that follows.

data are extracted from enterprises' annual income statements and balance sheets (for further details concerning the data, see Vodopivec 1989).

Table 6.1 reveals that proper taxes amounted to 16.4 percent of income, with low variability of the tax rate as suggested by the coefficient of variation (24.9 percent). In contrast, the informal components of taxation, quasi taxes and losses on money, were both more sizable and variable. Quasi taxes were nearly 50 percent larger than proper taxes, with very high variability. The coefficient of variation of losses on money is somewhat lower, while the share of losses on money in income is the highest (63.1 percent).

Grants (nonreimbursable resources) amounted to 0.4 percent of income in the sample. Since most enterprises received no grants at all and some enterprises received quite large amounts (grants were distributed only to a subset of lossmakers), the variability of grants was extremely high, revealing the highest variability among redistribution flows. Quasi grants were considerably higher, amounting to 7.4 percent of income, and were also highly variable. The largest subsidies were gains on money, amounting to 60.5 percent of income; their variability, though the smallest among subsidy flows, still exceeds the variability of proper taxes and losses on money, and is only a little smaller than the variability of quasi taxes.

From the perspective of overall redistribution in relation to the rest of the economy (the sum of taxes minus the sum of subsidies as reflected in the variable NSUBSR), the sample of enterprises was a net tax payer. Net taxes represented 34.2 percent of income. Many social services in Yugoslavia, in addition to general government expenditures, were financed directly from enterprise income (while largely paid from net income in capitalist countries), and hence it is to be expected that enterprises should be net tax payers. Eighteen percent of enterprises, however, received a net subsidy. Significant intraindustry differences confirm that redistribution was highly selective and discretionary.

The above results lead to the following conclusions:

• Informal taxation in the form of quasi taxes was of much greater significance than formal taxation. Moreover, while the latter was based on a uniform taxation rate, the former was selective.

• Grants and quasi grants (reflecting, by and large, pure gifts) together constituted a very significant 7.8 percent of income. The high variability suggests that some firms receive only small and others very large subsidies of this kind.

• Total enterprise taxes (the sum of taxes, quasi taxes, and losses on money) were very large, exceeding total income by 2.5 percent. Total subsidies were significantly lower, but still amounted to 68.3 percent of income. Both rates provide clear evidence of significant resource transfers.

The pattern of income distribution

There was substantial income redistribution among firms during this period. What criteria or patterns of government behavior explain these redistributive transfers? The mechanism of personal incomes control sought to limit the share of the personal incomes fund ("wages fund") in firm's overall income, and was thus explicitly aimed at reducing personal income differentials among firms.[19] Such a system of personal income determination, however, could only be realized through interfirm income redistribution. To be able to pay relatively higher personal incomes as well as meet other obligations, enterprises with below-average income per worker had to receive subsidies. As the description of the channels of redistribution suggests, the donors of these subsidies were enterprises with above-average income per worker, and households (the latter because they were net lenders).

This redistribution mechanism is confirmed by the following regression equation (the OLS method is used; industry dummies are included, but not reported; and t-values are shown in parentheses):[20]

$$\text{SUBS/N} = 5.157 - 0.511 * \text{INC/N} \qquad R^2 = 0.44$$
$$(1.40)\ (-11.29)$$

where SUBS are net subsidies (as defined in the section on the pattern of income distribution), INC is the realized income of the firm gross of depreciation, and N is the number of workers in the firm.[21]

The public choice explanation of redistribution

Studies of the soft budget constraint acknowledge that redistribution takes place through bargaining (Schaffer 1989). Economies in transition from socialism lack institutions capable of preventing soft budget redistribution. To see why this is so, we can consider income redistribution in terms of the confrontation between distributional coalitions or special interest groups. Involuntary redistribution[22] involves a form of contest between two parties with diametrically opposing interests, one advocating and the other opposing the transfer (Hillman and Riley 1989). The reason for pervasive and extensive redistribution lies in the institutional framework, and, in particular, the structure of political (and consequently economic) power in socialist economies.

---

[19]For a more detailed description, see Vodopivec (1989).

[20]The results are based on the same sample of Slovenian enterprises (416 observations).

[21]Because the wage bill is determined on the basis of an exogenously determined "income norm," the coefficient b reflects the variation of net subsidies with regard to firm "profits" (the latter being defined as the difference between firm income and the "income norm").

[22]Of course, there can be voluntary redistribution through charity.

Consider the example of concessionary financing—quantitatively the most important means of redistribution. Consider, for example, a short-term bank loan granted to an enterprise at a negative real interest rate.[23] As is to be inferred from the above empirical analysis, the usual rationale for requesting such a loan is simply to remedy poor enterprise performance. Why, however, would a bank be willing to undertake such an obviously unprofitable transaction? Surely the bank's depositors would oppose it. The bank manager and staff (to the extent that their personal income and the manager's reputation depend on the bank's profitability) also have an incentive to avoid such transactions. But a clearly defined group—the enterprise's workers and managers—favor such loans. For the firm's managers, not only personal income but their career and reputation are at stake.

No matter how reasonable an enterprise's case for seeking concessionary financing, the opposing coalition would, in a market economy, reject this kind of proposal. But in socialist economies the enterprise is supported by local government and Communist party representatives (and for larger operations, high level politicians) motivated predominantly by personal considerations; they all have an interest in preserving employment and social peace, even at the cost of continually subsidizing an unprofitable enterprise. So a coalition is formed for the purpose of obtaining financial assistance for this enterprise. The extent of redistribution reflects the relative power of these two coalitions.

Another example of this conflict is that caused by the granting of formal subsidies, such as the transfer of nonreimbursable resources among sister BOALs to cover losses of one BOAL. The coalition opposing the transfer is composed of workers of the donor BOALs. They usually have little if anything to do with the causes of the economic problems faced by colleagues in a loss-making BOAL. Why should they transfer their income to cover another BOAL's loss? The coalition favoring this transfer consists of workers of the loss-making BOAL, the commune-government, party representatives, and probably the WOAL management. Whatever the reasons for the losses (incompetent management, rigid employment legislation, wrong investment decisions, and so on), it is to the advantage of the coalition to shift income from one BOAL to another, and to persuade and put pressure on workers of the donor BOAL to provide the income for the transfer.

Similarly, making mandatory "financial investments" (for example, in SMCIs of material production and development funds) is clearly not in the

---

[23]In 1986 the average interest rate Yugoslav banks charged on their loans to enterprises was about 32 percent (World Bank 1988). The inflation rate in 1985 was 85 percent, and the government had no serious commitment to contain inflation, so the expected inflation rate in 1986 was certainly the same or higher than the average interest rate on bank loans—which meant that these loans were granted, on average, with *ex ante* negative real interest rate. (The actual Yugoslav inflation rate in 1986 turned out to be 91 percent.)

interest of enterprises, or more particularly managers and workers. Politically, however, these arrangements can be the most appropriate vehicle for implicit subsidization (for example, of big users of electricity); they can be legally imposed on enterprises.

One can suppose that the coalition opposing a transfer may, when its longer-term interests are taken into account, be in favor of a transaction because such transfers represent a form of insurance. In a system such as the one that was in place in Yugoslavia, where labor was meant to absorb all risk, the need to insure against variations in earnings is of paramount importance. Without institutional constraints, workers would probably want to shift some risk onto the shoulders of the owners of capital, who in turn could insure themselves by holding a diversified portfolio. Such insurance, however, does not resolve the associated moral hazard problems. One indicator of the suboptimality is the "premium" payment schedule whereby the least endangered (or historically the best) enterprises pay the highest "premium," and the ones in the worst shape pay nothing at all. Such transfers must be mandatory.[24]

It is important to note that in the first example given above, the commercial bank will probably not bear the full costs of concessionary financing alone. Rather, the commercial bank will request financial help from the central bank (again in the form of subsidized credit). Bargaining between coalitions will then be repeated on a higher level—and again the outcome is predictable. The central bank and possibly the ministry of finance will form one coalition. Another coalition will be formed by the commercial bank and other interested parties such as republican and, in more important cases, federal ministries from sectors that would benefit from loans, and, if necessary, top federal government and Communist party officials.[25]

Social groups differ in their ability to organize for collective action (Olson 1965). The constituency opposing concessionary credit is the population as a whole because it ultimately pays for this subsidy through an inflation tax. A coalition with such a broad base has difficulty representing its interests because of the free-rider problem, and because individuals in the coalition have each only a small stake (Ursprung 1990). Workers at a donor BOAL are similarly unable to organize and block an inter-BOAL transfer. Their formal leaders, the firm's managers, are reluctant to resist the transfer, because they are under direct pressure from advocates of the subsidy (politicians). Individual workers who voice opposition can develop

---

[24]Similar considerations arise in the interpretation of protectionist policies. See Hillman (1989).

[25]Bartlett (1989) describes the struggle between opposing coalitions in the frustrated attempt to enforce restrictive monetary policy in Hungary in 1987–88. He notes that "the National Bank's defeat in this case reflects not merely the specific circumstances which obtained in early 1988. In the Hungarian context, the political position of actors seeking to pursue policies of financial discipline is inherently weaker than that of actors aiming to expand the stock of money and credit" (p. 33).

reputations as troublemakers and thus find it difficult to get new jobs. Similarly, the constituency opposing legally imposed financial investments consists of workers in affected firms, while taxpayers oppose tax waivers because they must pay higher taxes. Because of their large number and the unavailability of selective incentives, these constituencies of workers and taxpayers are unable to organize themselves to defend their interests. Their organizational effectiveness is further reduced because management and political leaders, rather than defending the interests of affected workers and taxpayers, are likely to remain loyal to the center. The same is true for (official) labor unions.

Interfirm redistribution, and the resulting nonappropriability of returns by workers, has efficiency implications. Redistribution provides protection and security, and thus insurance to economic agents, but it gives rise to moral hazard and adverse selection problems. This has a direct bearing on inadequate work motivation[26] and the suppression of entrepreneurship (dynamic inefficiency)[27] in reforming socialist economies.[28] Redistribution also perpetuates the structure of production and contributes to allocative inefficiency, in particular by permitting the avoidance of bankruptcies and layoffs.

The inherent macroeconomic instability of socialist economies also has its roots in redistribution: because of concessionary financing (or soft budgets), socialist economies are extremely prone to expansionary monetary policy.[29] Furthermore, inequities will arise in economies where a substantial portion of GNP is distributed via bargaining among distributional coalitions, because of the different relative effectiveness of distributional coalitions (see, for example, Olson 1982).

Alternative explanations of the Yugoslav failure

Some assign responsibility for the Yugoslav failure to the worker-management system (for example, Hinds 1991), specifically to worker participation in decision making and profit-sharing. Before considering this argument, it is useful to summarize a controversy in the theoretical literature about the effects of worker participation in management on productivity.

---

[26]Using a static framework, my estimate of the dead weight losses which are produced by the redistribution for Yugoslavia in 1986 amounts to between 6 and 7 percent of GNP. See Vodopivec (1990).

[27]Murphy (1990) develops a theoretical model which shows that interfirm redistribution of the type discussed above generates delays in the adoption of new technologies.

[28]A similar view, pointing to the discretionary behavior of bureaucracy as an important cause of inefficiencies in the former U.S.S.R., is taken by Litwack (1991).

[29]For the evidence on the impact of the losses of public sector on inflation in Yugoslavia, see Rocha (1990).

Authors advocating worker participation (most notably Vanek 1970) argue that workers are induced to work harder because of team spirit and enhanced working morale. Monitoring costs are reduced and conflict between management and workers is decreased. Workers are expected to take a more active, innovative role in improving enterprise organization. It is also argued that such worker involvement improves the firm-specific human capital over time, by increasing average job length (as compared with a capitalist firm) and by internalizing some externalities associated with training or workers (Ireland and Law 1982).

Other authors suggest that this form of worker participation does not lead to efficiency gains. Jensen and Meckling (1979) note that there is no well-defined set of procedures for solving the decision-making disputes within a firm. Alchian and Demsetz (1972) believe that profits should be reserved for management because management requires incentives to monitor a firm properly. They predict that worker participation in profit sharing is inefficient, because the incentive of management (or owners) to monitor is reduced. Furubotn and Pejovich (1970) show that ownership rights such as those characteristic of the former Yugoslav system, give rise to a tendency to underinvest because workers have incentive to deplete their firm's capital.[30]

Theoretically there is ambiguity about the effect of worker (participation in) management. One has to review empirical evidence in order to resolve this issue. The conclusion of Alan Blinder (1990), summarizing recent empirical studies of the effect of worker participation in Western economies is unambiguous: there is a consensus in the empirical literature that the effect is weak but positive. Profit sharing, rather than worker participation in management, is more strongly associated with productivity increases. This evidence from developed economies is inconsistent with a view that attributes the failure of the Yugoslav system to worker participation. The proponents of the worker-management explanation of the Yugoslav failure downplay this evidence.

The most damaging feature of the Yugoslav system is, according to critics, the access workers have to the rents of capital through their discretion to decide on the allocation of the surplus of production. Let us, however, respond to these critics by briefly reviewing worker-management literature's findings about the allocative efficiency of the worker-managed firm (WMF) under internal and external financing. While in general the source of financing is not significant (Ireland and Law 1982, pp. 39–42), the

---

[30]This effect is not a necessary consequence of worker participation in ownership, but is a specific conclusion valid for Yugoslavia. Several solutions to this problem have been proposed: Sertel (1982) advocated the introduction of a market for membership. Ireland and Law (1982) were more inclined to offer capital rebates. None of these proposals remedies the problem of the inability of workers of self-managed firms to spread risk by holding a diversified portfolio of assets.

different means of financing lead to markedly different implications once the property rights restrictions of the Yugoslav firm are taken into account.

• *Internal financing:* Self-financing gives rise to the familiar time horizon problem (Furubotn and Pejovich 1970; Jensen and Meckling 1979). Because they are unable to recover their original investments, workers choose to use relatively less capital-intensive methods (a lower capital-labor ratio as compared with the borrowed capital model, but not necessarily lower than in a capitalist counterpart; see Ireland and Law, p. 48). Moreover, if some workers leave the firm, the WMF will be reluctant to replace them: departing workers have lost their original investment; remaining workers have no incentive to share the yields from the original investment with newcomers, who cannot be asked to pay upon joining for their claims to the returns. As a result, in a steady state, self-financed WMFs in the Yugoslav system are of suboptimal size. Note that, according to this model, workers can distribute the residual at will; they thus "have access to the capital rents" which are, of course, generated by the self-financed capital.

• *External financing:* The WMF subject to the Yugoslav type of property rights that finances its investment by bank credits, behaves in a manner identical to a firm of the pure capital rental model (assuming that the principal is repaid at the same rate as the rate of depreciation); that is, it operates on an efficient scale, possibly with a higher capital-labor ratio than its capitalist counterpart. The firm pays its costs (interest on borrowed funds plus depreciation), which equal rental costs (which comprise opportunity costs of capital plus depreciation). There is no time horizon problem in this case, nor are there opportunities to appropriate rents.

One can conclude that (a) in the case of full external finance, workers are not able to extract capital rents, and (b) in the case of self-finance, they indeed make decisions about the residual gross of the reward for capital, but since workers themselves finance the capital, this is analogous to capitalists taking their capital rents. Indeed, only in the case where some workers leave do the remaining workers have the possibility of appropriating rents. This is not the rent that concerns the critics, however.

If indeed workers are not able to extract rents as a result of their ability to decide on what to do with the surplus of production, how can one explain the massive redistribution in the Yugoslav economy? The crucial point is that it is the economic environment that distinguishes the Yugoslav firm from the WMFs described in the literature (and indeed sets it apart from some real-world firms, such as the Mondragon cooperatives[31]). The environment of the Yugoslav firm is one of state paternalism (see Kornai 1980), and is characterized by a political monopoly and a nontransparent, constrained property right structure.

The redistribution—and the perverse effects surrounding the appropriation of returns in this system—arise from the fact that under state

---

[31]On the Mondragon cooperatives, see Bogetić (this volume).

paternalism the rental/interest rate is not established parametrically, but rather varies among enterprises, thereby differentially affecting the value of the residual. The empirical results that I have reported above suggest that (a) workers with below-average income are, as the result of redistribution, effectively charged a below-average rental/interest rate (that is, they are subsidized), and (b) workers with above-average income are effectively charged an above-average rental/interest rate, and so are taxed.[32]

A system entailing large-scale redistribution of this type will generate various types of inefficiencies—such as those discussed at the beginning of this section. It is important to emphasize that it is state paternalism, and not worker participation that is at fault. Note also that the redistribution pattern identified above (the section on the public choice explanation of redistribution) points to compensation as being the driving force behind redistribution. The view that redistribution occurs through the appropriation of capital rents has recently been rejected by Estrin, Moore, and Svejnar (1988) and Estrin and Svejnar (1988), who conclude that, during the period of Yugoslav self-management 1965–72, "less than 0.1% of earnings could be attributed to capital rents" (Estrin and Svejnar 1988, p. 23).

Svejnar and Prasnikar (1990) also question the hypothesis that the poor economic performance of Yugoslav firms is attributable primarily to worker-management, but they decline to identify the forces that are responsible for the failure of the Yugoslav economy. They find that (a) the distribution of power in the Yugoslav firm is more hierarchical than might be expected of pure worker-management, and (b) the behavior of the Yugoslav firm in the areas of employment, returns on factors of production, capital formation and allocation (the rate of savings, capital intensity, regional composition), as well as the structure of industry, are determined predominantly by government policies and/or the nature of social ownership. Svejnar and Prasnikar fail to examine, however, why the government chose such inappropriate policies; they also do not discuss the relationships that underlie social ownership.

Conclusions and policy implications

Income redistribution is an essential characteristic of the Yugoslav social ownership of capital or enterprises. This redistribution allows failing enterprises to avoid bankruptcy and increases the earnings of less productive firms and workers at the expense of more productive enterprises and/or the household sector as a whole. Redistribution results from conflicts between distributional coalitions (special interest groups). Victorious coalitions

---

[32]For similar results, see Kornai and Matits (1987) for Hungary, and Schaffer (1990) for Poland.

typically involve political elites, who should be identified as the de facto owners of Yugoslav "social property."

There are two causes for the large-scale redistribution that occurred in the former Yugoslavia and in other socialist economies. The first is the pursuit of job/wage security, that is, the attempt to perfectly socialize risk. The pursuit of job/wage security conflicts with the official stance in Yugoslavia which has insisted that the labor take the role of residual income claimant. If labor is indeed residual income claimant and capital is nonprivately owned, labor is unable to diversify its asset holdings and thereby minimize risk. In such a system, wage would fluctuate widely. In conditions of high preference for job and wage security, the system becomes nonimplementable and requires income redistribution as a way to mitigate wage fluctuations.

The second cause of this large scale redistribution is the political monopoly which gives to the state power to redistribute income. Political monopoly also prevents the government from making a commitment not to intervene in favor of redistribution. The government is too strong to credibly suggest to ailing enterprises that it cannot rescue them. The government may also pursue its own goals, which may have little to do with the maximization of social welfare, but may be directed toward the preservation of its own political power.

If an autocratic government is an all-encompassing entity concerned with the prosperity of the economy (that is, if that government's benefits depend on the size of the economy's total output) why would it tolerate, it could be asked, or implement an income redistribution that reduces output?

The government may indeed be an all-encompassing entity, but it has several objectives including the ideologically imposed imperative of ensuring full employment. This is the interpretation of Granick (1987), and it is applicable to centrally planned economies. As reforming socialist economies are decentralized, distributional coalitions emerge representing special interests. Some redistribution takes place because bureaucrats extend personal favors expecting to receive favors in return. Managers and bureaucrats interact closely in order to advance their careers. Effective local redistributional coalitions can also emerge when decentralization programs are implemented.[33]

The distributional confrontation between distributional coalitions reflects the absence in socialist economies of mechanisms to curb compensatory (soft budget constraint) redistribution. An end to redistribution requires that new institutions and organizations restore the credibility of the government's commitment not to intervene to redistribute income. Such new institutions would reduce the need of government to intervene by shifting risk to capital owners. The owners of capital, accordingly, would take on decision-making

---

[33]Klaus (1990) refers to "decentralization traps." See also Chen (1991) on the Chinese experience.

roles, and become the residual claimants: this is the basis of the case for privatization.[34]

Marx argued for the negation of private ownership precisely because he was concerned that private property deprives human beings of basic rights—and yet it is precisely the assurance of human rights (not only in the political, but also in the economic sphere) that underlies the privatization impulse in Eastern Europe. With privatization, capital markets emerge; these markets facilitate new entry and efficient investment. Capital markets reduce the involvement of commercial banks in financial intermediation and reduce the government's ability to effect redistribution by influencing these banks. Bargaining among distributional coalitions is replaced by impersonal market outcomes. New institutions would also provide checks and balances (parliamentary multiparty democracy, independent judiciary, and a free press) as additional means to keep governments from engaging in redistribution.

The reassignment of property rights (that is, the change of *legal* ownership) is not in itself enough to effect a transition to a market economy. Firms must also be relieved of political interference.

References

Alchian, Armen, and Harold Demsetz. 1972. "Production, Information Costs and Economic Organization." *American Economic Review* 62:777–95.

Association of Accountants and Financial Workers. 1985. "The Use of the Account Plan for an OAL." *Information on Book-Keeping and Profession* (in Slovene). Ljubljana: Association of Accountants and Financial Workers.

Bajt, Aleksander. 1982. "About Some Open Questions of the Social Property." *Pregled* (in Serbo-Croatian) 72:1345–80.

Bartlett, David. 1989. "The Dilemmas of Socialist Reform: Money and Monetary Policy in Hungary's Two-Tiered Banking System." Paper presented at the Fifth Summer Workshop on Soviet and East European Economics, 10–21 July, University of California at Berkeley. Processed.

Baxter, William T. 1984. *Inflation Accounting.* London: Philip Allan.

Blinder, Alan S. 1990. "Introduction." In Alan S. Blinder, ed., *Paying for Productivity: A Look at the Evidence.* Washington, D.C.: The Brookings Institution.

---

[34]While solving the problem of risk bearing (capital owners can diversify their portfolios), a typical firm in mature capitalism confronts a principal-agent problem. Because of the inefficiency of the markets which function in the role of external policing devices, efficiency considerations call for worker participation in profit sharing, decision making and, possibly, ownership. See Mueller (1976).

Bogetić, Željko. 1991. "Is There a Case for Employee Ownership?" This volume.

Chen, Kang. 1991. "The Failure of Recentralization in China: Interplays among Enterprises, Local Governments, and the Center." In Arye L. Hillman, ed., *Markets and Politicians: Politicized Economic Choice*. Boston and Dordrecht: Kluwer Academic Publishers, 209–30.

Estrin, Saul, Robert E. Moore, and Jan Svejnar. 1988. "Market Imperfections, Labor Management, and Earnings Differentials in a Developing Country: Theory and Evidence from Yugoslavia." *Quarterly Journal of Economics* 102:465–78.

Estrin, Saul, and Jan Svejnar. 1988. "Estimates of Static and Dynamic Models of Wage Determination in Labor-Managed Firms." Discussion Paper 318. Centre for Labour Economics, London School of Economics.

Furubotn, Eirik G., and Svetozar Pejovich. 1970. "Property Rights and the Behavior of the Firm in a Socialist State: The Example of Yugoslavia." *Zeitschrift fur Nationalokonomie* 30:431–54.

Granick, David. 1987. *Job Rights in the Soviet Union: Their Consequences*. Cambridge: Cambridge University Press.

Hillman, Arye L. 1989. *The Political Economy of Protection*. London and New York: Harwood Academic Publishers.

Hillman, Arye L., and John Riley. 1989. "Politically Contestable Rents and Transfers." *Economics and Politics* 1:17–39.

Hinds, Manuel. 1991. "Incentives and Ownership in Socialist Countries in Transition." In Arye L. Hillman, ed., *Markets and Politicians: Politicized Economic Choice*. Boston and Dordrecht: Kluwer Academic Publishers, 137–68.

Hinds, Manuel. 1992. "Policy Effectiveness in Reforming Socialist Economies." This volume.

Ireland, Norman J., and Peter J. Law. 1982. *The Economics of Labour Managed Enterprises*. London: Croom Helm.

Jensen, Michael C., and William H. Meckling. 1979. "Rights and Production Functions: An Application to Labor-Managed Firms and Codetermination." *Journal of Business* 52:469–506.

Klaus, Vaclav. 1990. "A Perspective on Economic Transition in Czechoslovakia and Eastern Europe." *Proceedings of the Annual World Bank Conference on Development Economics*. Washington, D.C.: World Bank.

Kornai, Janos. 1980. *Economics of Shortage*. Amsterdam: North Holland.

Kornai, Janos, and Agnes Matits. 1987. "The Softness of Budgetary Constraints—An Analysis of Enterprise Data." *Eastern European Economics* 25:34.

Lavrac, Ivo, and Joze-Andrej Cibej. 1986. *Valuation of Raw Materials Inventories and Inflationary Income—A Macroeconomic Analysis* (in Slovene). Ljubljana: Raziskovalni center ekonomske fakultete.

Litwack, John. 1991. "Discretionary Behavior and Soviet Economic Reform." *Soviet Studies* 43:255–79.

The Law of Associated Labor (in Slovene). 1976. Ljubljana: Gospodarska Zalozba.

Mueller, Dennis C. 1976. "Information, Mobility, and Profit." *Kyklos* 29:419–48.

Murphy, Michael A. 1990. "The Timing of Adoption of New Technologies and the Regulation of Enterprise Incomes in Soviet Industry: A Game Theoretic Approach." Paper presented at the Sixth Summer Workshop on Soviet and East European Economics, 8–19 July, University of Pittsburg, Pennsylvania. Processed.

Obradovic, Josip. 1978. "Participation in Enterprise Decision-Making." In Josip Obradovic and William N. Dunn, eds., *Workers' Self-Management and Organizational Power in Yugoslavia*. Pittsburgh, Pa.: University Center for International Studies, University of Pittsburgh.

Olson, Mancur. 1965. *The Logic of Collective Action*. Cambridge, Mass.: Harvard University Press.

——. 1982. *The Rise and Decline of Nations: Economic Growth, Stagflation, and Social Rigidities*. New Haven, Conn., and London: Yale University Press.

Rocha, Roberto. 1990. "Inflation and Stabilization in Yugoslavia." Policy, Research and External Affairs Working Paper 752. World Bank, Country Economics Department, Washington, D.C. Processed.

Saldanha, Fernando. 1992. "Self-Management: Theory and Yugoslav Practice." This volume.

Schatter, Mark. 1989. "The Credible-Commitment Problem in the Center-Enterprise Relationship." *Journal of Comparative Economics* 13:359–82.

——. 1990. "How Polish Enterprises are Subsidized." School of European Studies, University of Sussex, U.K. Processed.

Sertel, Murat. 1982. *Workers and Incentives*. Amsterdam: North Holland.

Svejnar, Jan, and Janez Prasnikar. 1990. "Workers' Self-Management, Social Ownership and Government Policies: Lessons from Yugoslavia." Paper presented at the World Bank Conference on Privatization and Ownership Changes in East and Central Europe, 13–14 June, Washington, D.C. Processed.

Tyson, Laura. 1979. "Incentives, Income Sharing, and Institutional Innovation in the Yugoslav Self-Managed Firm." *Journal of Comparative Economics* 13:285–301.

Ursprung, Heinrich W. 1990. "Public Goods, Rent Dissipation, and Candidate Competition." *Economics and Politics* 2:115–32.

Vanek, Jaroslav. 1970. *The General Theory of Labor-Managed Market Economies*. Ithaca, N.Y.: Cornell University Press.

Vodopivec, Milan. 1989. "Productivity Effects of Redistribution in a
    Socialist Economy: The Case of Yugoslavia." Ph.D. dissertation,
    Department of Economics, University of Maryland, College Park.
    Processed.
———. 1990. "How Redistribution Hurts Productivity in a Socialist Economy
    (Yugoslavia)." Policy, Research and External Affairs Working Paper
    438. World Bank, Country Economics Department, Washington, D.C.
    Processed.
World Bank. 1989. "Yugoslavia. Financial Sector Restructuring: Policies
    and Priorities." Report 7869-YU. World Bank, Washington, D.C.
    Processed.

7

Enterprise Restructuring in the Transition from Hungarian Market Socialism

Arye L. Hillman

In 1990 the less than 1,000 or so socialist enterprises that comprised Hungarian industry confronted the need to restructure. This need derived from both domestic and external considerations. Domestically, the government had declared itself committed to policies that would replace the past "market socialist" economic system with a Western-type market economy. Externally, enterprises confronted liberalized international trade with the West and, as of the beginning of 1991, the impending end of the system of trade and payments of the Council for Mutual Economic Assistance (CMEA). The impending replacement of the CMEA transferable ruble clearing mechanism by convertible currency trade at world prices in particular introduced uncertainties regarding trade with the U.S.S.R.[1]

Whereas the other East European economies had maintained centrally planned systems, Hungary had in principle departed from central planning in 1968. The "New Economic Mechanism" introduced that year had sought to decentralize enterprise decision making and to facilitate market transactions. The market socialist system however failed to achieve Western standards of enterprise efficiency and output quality. Thus, after political reforms,[2] the need to restructure domestic industry remained. Restructuring could not be deferred, as past trade liberalization policies had been (Gacs

---

[1]See Martin Schrenk (this volume) on the importance of Soviet trade for Hungary under the CMEA system.

[2]Democratic elections took place in Hungary in March 1990.

David Tarr contributed helpful observations on this chapter.

1989 and Oblath 1989): the replacement of the "market socialist" system was a credible domestic policy objective, and while Hungary had been pressing for change from the CMEA trading regime, in the final analysis it was the Soviet Union that determined the timing of change and the nature of the post-CMEA regime.

The Hungarian economy would incur a substantial terms of trade loss as a consequence of the impending CMEA-related changes (Oblath and Tarr 1992). Individual enterprises would confront new relative prices in foreign and domestic markets and a changed structure of demand. Under the CMEA system, taxes and subsidies on CMEA trade that eliminated or contained price differences between domestic and foreign markets effectively muted direct price comparisons at the enterprise level of the relative profitability of different markets.[3]

Under the post-CMEA system, Soviet buyers would be required to find hard currency to maintain their traditional purchases from Hungarian enterprises, but the method of allocating hard currency in the U.S.S.R. was unresolved (or at least not known to Hungarian enterprises). Uncertainty regarding the future of traditional Soviet trade had been felt during 1990 with Soviet supply disruptions of oil exports and with the Soviet unwillingness to maintain past volumes of imports of Hungarian engineering goods and capital equipment. Other traditional CMEA trading relationships had also been disrupted, in particular as a consequence of the integration of the Democratic Republic of Germany into the Federal Republic of Germany.

Quality was a central issue. Stringent quality demands had not been placed on goods supplied by Hungarian enterprises to domestic or foreign CMEA customers.[4] If Hungarian enterprises were to be competitive with Western producers—whether in CMEA markets, domestically, or in world markets—quality improvement would be required to close the gap between the technology embodied in Hungarian "soft" goods and Western substitutes.

Managers of Hungarian enterprises believed that the new circumstances would not necessarily result in a wholesale shift away from CMEA markets. Indeed there were projections that Hungarian exports to the U.S.S.R. might increase under the new trade regime because of the favorable prices that enterprises could offer after the elimination of Hungary's CMEA export taxes. It was hoped that if enterprises applied Western technology to provide upgraded quality, Soviet sales could be maintained; even if Hungarian goods did not achieve technological parity with Western substitutes, low prices in

---

[3]The Hungarian version of the price equalization mechanism imperfectly arbitraged domestic and foreign prices. See Abel, Hillman, and Tarr (this volume).

[4]That is, the enterprises produced soft goods that because of low quality were inappropriate for sale in Western markets. See Schrenk (this volume) and Hillman and Schnytzer (this volume).

conjunction with past relationships and geographic proximity might compensate for quality differentials.[5]

This chapter is concerned with the Hungarian restructuring process, as enterprises confronted and perceived the need to reorganize and to bridge the technology gap with the West. In particular, this chapter (a) compares enterprise restructuring in Hungary with that in the West; (b) describes the adjustments that were required of enterprises in the transition to a Western market economy; (c) considers the role of markets in enterprise restructuring—asset markets, labor markets, and product markets—and distinguishes such markets from the markets of Hungarian market socialism; (d) relates restructuring to the technology gap; (e) considers the role of government in the restructuring process; (f) discusses proposals that enterprises with the best prospects for success be identified and targeted for special assistance; (g) reviews past Hungarian policies aimed at restructuring socialist industry; (h) looks at the effects of foreign resource transfers on the efficiency of enterprises; and (i) introduces enterprise-level perspectives by reporting on restructuring undertaken by several prominent Hungarian enterprises in 1990.

Enterprise restructuring in Hungary and the West

I begin with a consideration of the conception of enterprise restructuring. In Western market economies, restructuring involves changes in internal firm activities which, if successful, will increase a firm's market value. In the course of restructuring, redundant personnel and inefficient internal organization are eliminated, new technology is introduced, and units of the firm that do not have the requisite synergies with other parts of the firm's operations are sold off. The impetus for restructuring can arise in the West when a firm has lost an important market, or when demand has fallen off for a staple product line (either because of a change in international comparative advantage or a decline in domestic demand for the industry's output because of changed consumer preferences) or when the firm has simply been mismanaged. These circumstances are similar to those that confronted Hungarian enterprises in 1990.

A Western firm may decline or cease production,[6] or may rebound after successfully restructuring to reduce the costs of production, upgrade production technology, or change product mix. Whatever the outcome, the distinctive feature of Western restructuring is that at any one time only a small subset of all enterprises in the economy will be undertaking such

---

[5]Some specific enterprise responses are reported below. In fact, in the transition from the CMEA system, trade with successor states of the U.S.S.R. collapsed.

[6]There may be government intervention to ease the course of a firm's decline. On government policies toward senescent or declining industries in the West, see Hillman (1989).

activities. By contrast, in Hungary, the entire industrial sector with few exceptions confronted the need to restructure in 1990.

Because the need for enterprise restructuring in Hungary encompassed the entire industrial sector, successful restructuring would thus require policies directed toward the entire industrial sector rather than to specific enterprises in distress.

Making the transition from market socialism to a market economy

Restructuring Hungarian enterprises implied changing the conditions and behavior which had characterized the market socialist system. Excess demand in this system was manifested in a shortage economy which had absolved management of concern with maintaining market shares. Competitive pressures to improve the quality of output or to introduce new product lines were in general absent; the socialist enterprise in the socialist market did not confront price or quality competition, either from domestic sources or through foreign trade. Although the enterprise was in principle autonomous, in practice it was subject to substantial directives from government ministries.[7]

The new economic environment would be different; demand could no longer be assured, and the enterprise would be obliged to compete for the expenditures of consumers. Under these conditions, the assumptions that had guided managerial decision making would no longer be appropriate.

In particular, management in a shortage economy is reluctant to dispense with productive capacity. Restructuring to attain a Western-type enterprise, however, would require closure of unprofitable product lines or unprofitable plants, and scrapping of capital equipment. Capital specific to an enterprise earns a rent which can be decreased without changing the incentive to use the capital and, in the limit, capital can be valued at zero in computing the cost of production. There is still, however, an opportunity cost to maintaining old capital in place rather than introducing technologically superior equipment. It is in the nature of CMEA soft goods that low prices could not compensate for the low quality that resulted from using outdated technology. Soft good enterprises would therefore be obliged to write off capital, notwithstanding the physical life remaining for the equipment. This is contrary to managerial practice in a shortage economy; restructuring is inhibited by the insistence on maintaining capital that has "life left in it."

In a socialist system, enterprises take upon themselves social obligations to provide workers with housing, health services, entertainment, and employment security. These obligations increase enterprises' costs; in

---

[7]See the papers in Brada and Dobozi (1988), and also Kornai (1985), Hare (1990), and Newbery (1990).

particular, job security obligations can give rise to substantial on-the-job or hidden unemployment.[8] Because enterprises do not confront competition that would threaten the job security of workers, the additional costs are not a source of concern for management, so long as socialist paternalism is sustained; however, new approaches would be required with the introduction of a market economy.[9]

In addition to the barriers to entry that protected the socialist enterprise from competition, there were also barriers to exit. Bankruptcy was in principle feasible but was avoided by the authorities for a number of reasons. First, because of the prevalence of monopolies and high industrial concentration, closing an enterprise would deprive the economy of a sole or dominant domestic source of supply.[10] As well, since the CMEA state negotiators will have entered into commitments to supply output in exchange for necessary imports such as oil and other raw materials (Schrenk, this volume), the government's incentive was to subsidize an enterprise rather than let it fail. Second, bankruptcy was inconsistent with the government's commitment to provide workers with job security. And third, linkages among enterprises impeded the state's ability to permit bankruptcy. Debts could be maintained as assets for creditors only so long as the debtor enterprise remained in existence; bankruptcy by one enterprise would be detrimental to enterprises with whom the insolvent enterprise had vertical supply relationships, and would threaten a chain of bankruptcies that would undermine industry at large. The threat of bankruptcy therefore did not serve as an incentive to restructure.

Asset markets and restructuring incentives

Principal-agent problems arise within firms because of the different objectives of managers and owners.[11] In a Western market economy, managers are monitored directly by private owners, and indirectly by markets through claims to firms' assets and remuneration for managerial skills. In the West, the incentive to restructure enterprises derives from the presence of markets that permit the reflection of discrepancies between the potential and the current realized market value of the firm. The motive for restructuring

---

[8]Official unemployment was virtually nonexistent, with vacancies being multiples of unemployment. See Hillman (1990) on employment and other macroeconomic policies under Hungarian market socialism.

[9]Because these social responsibilities precluded cost minimization or attention to productivity improvement, enterprises could argue that they should not be asked to compete on an equal footing with enterprises motivated only by profit. On the responsibilities assigned to the socialist enterprise and the state's paternalistic policies, see Hillman (1991).

[10]On the high concentration of industry and the tendency toward sole production in socialist economies (which in a market economy would entail monopolization), see Ehrlich (1985).

[11]On principal-agent problems in Western firms, see Jensen (1990).

is the private claim to the potential increase in value: either incumbent management will defensively restructure in response to a decline in the value of the firm, or outsiders whose perceptions of the firm's potential profitability exceed the firm's market value will purchase some part (or all) of the firm and undertake restructuring.

Such ability of markets and private owners to impose discipline on enterprises was, however, not present under Hungarian market socialism. The legal changes that facilitated privatization (Milanovic, this volume) were not immediately followed by a substantial transfer of socialist enterprises to private ownership. In the absence of private property rights, markets in enterprises' assets could not develop. Without private ownership there can be no exchange of property rights, and hence no market disciplining.

Because it is difficult to value assets without a market, the absence of markets in itself impedes privatization. The sale of Hungarian enterprises that took place in 1988 and 1989 elicited controversy regarding estimates of fair value received for the enterprises by the legal owner, the state. Without private owners, but with decentralized enterprise decision making, managers could become de facto residual claimants, as could workers. The de facto residual claimancy was to income (and subsidies from the state). But managers could also secure part of the value of the assets through discretion exercised in the privatization process.[12]

There were thus claims that management did not seek to secure the maximum value for the state in conducting sales of state enterprises, but rather disposed of the enterprises' assets in ways that yielded personal gain. Devious and quasi-legal spontaneous privatizations that permitted management to reap the gains from successful restructuring inhibited further privatization and inflow of foreign investment.

The case for privatization is that private residual claimants with ensured property rights have incentives to bear the risks associated with enterprise restructuring. Privatization permits future returns from investments to be realized through sale of assets. Decisions regarding the introduction of new technologies, purchase of capital equipment, choice of product lines, and choice of which units of the enterprise to close down or sell are made under conditions of uncertainty. Efficient restructuring can occur when such decisions are consistent with the objective of increasing the market value of an enterprise; to provide an incentive for restructuring, however, the increased value has to be realizable by the agents who take upon themselves the risks. The realization of such gains is not possible in socialist industry.

---

[12]For example, enterprises could be sold to foreign investors with tied contracts that ensured managers' future positions in the enterprise and that provided for prespecified managerial incomes; new companies could be created and owned by managers to whom the assets of the state enterprise were transferred but not the liabilities.

Labor markets and workers' incentives

Workers, as well as managers and owners, have a role to play in restructuring. Workers' councils may object or refuse to cooperate in restructuring activities in order to protect jobs that are from an efficiency perspective redundant; workers may also object to the introduction of labor-saving capital equipment. Pressures by workers to resist change are familiar enough in Western economies and must be expected in socialist economies in transition. A social safety net therefore becomes a component of restructuring programs. Because restructuring will be occurring simultaneously in many enterprises, there will be overall high unemployment. If workers believe that unemployment will persist, they will resist restructuring, notwithstanding the promise of future efficiency.

The duration of unemployment itself depends upon the speed of restructuring—that is, on the speed with which managers adapt to new economic signals and take appropriate decisions under conditions of uncertainty. Unless industry is privatized, the risk/reward structure of socialist enterprises that discourages risk taking by managers will prolong the period of unemployment.

Human capital also plays a role in restructuring. Skilled and knowledgeable personnel are complementary with new, technologically sophisticated capital equipment. The absorption of new technology may, however, be limited not by lack of access to technology per se, but by a lack of personnel familiar with the technology and able to apply and integrate the technology into the firm. Hence, to facilitate restructuring, incentives are required to invest in human capital. Here again a departure from the norms of the socialist economic system is required. Wage or salary differentials in a market for labor provide incentives for individuals to undertake training in the skills required by industry, and to relocate in line with their highest value-adding activity. The market thereby directs individuals to enterprises that are the most promising candidates for successful restructuring. A socialist system is not consistent with the sort of income inequality that would reward human capital differentials. In Hungary, legal limitations on wage differentials limited the ability of enterprises to attract workers away from other employment. Workers remained in their current employment without regard for productivity differences among enterprises.

An efficient labor market also requires privatization: otherwise regulation of the labor market via legal limitations on wages remains necessary because of the disincentives for wage discipline in decentralized socialist firms controlled by workers.[13]

---

[13]Workers have an incentive to consume the capital of the socialist enterprise. See Hinds (1991), Hinds (this volume), and Saldanha (this volume).

Product markets

I have thus far considered the roles of asset and factor markets in facilitating restructuring activities. A competitive product market also facilitates restructuring, by subjecting mismanaged enterprises to the discipline of more competent new entrants. The entry barriers that protected socialist industry also diminished the incentive to restructure. Regulations in the 1980s permitted private enterprise but constrained the size of new ventures by limiting the number of employees and by inhibiting access to credit and real resources: the small private enterprises were not directly competitive with the large socialist enterprises (Tardos 1983).

A competitive product market also provides guidance for investment in new product lines. If product prices are distorted by protection or price controls, the incumbent firm confronts inappropriate signals regarding allocation decisions. Foreign investment can then also be welfare-reducing.[14]

The technology gap

Restructuring has, as a principal objective, closure of the technology gap with Western industry. This gap may in some instances have been discretionary. Enterprises may have produced soft goods to cater to CMEA demand, even though higher quality goods could have been produced, or there may have been a reluctance to use imported intermediate inputs acquired with convertible currencies to produce goods to be exchanged for clearing nonconvertible rubles.[15] But in other instances, and perhaps more generally, the need to transform soft good producers into producers of hard goods underlies restructuring efforts.

The transformation to higher-quality production requires new investment. The considerations raised above with respect to the relation between investment incentives and privatization pertain directly to bridging of the technology gap. Socialist industry did not provide the appropriate incentives. In particular, de facto residual claimancy to income flows but not assets biases intertemporal allocation away from investment toward current consumption. Because of the link between residual claimancy and incentives to bear risk, the pace of closure of the technological gap is constrained by the pace of privatization of socialist industry.

---

[14]Immiserizing growth can occur when the shadow price of a factor is negative because of domestic distortions. For an example of an estimate of this effect (in the case of Japanese investment in the U.S. auto industry under the U.S. quota on Japanese auto imports), see de Melo and Tarr (1992).

[15]Evidence presented below in a review of restructuring experiences of Hungarian enterprises suggests that in some instances softness was discretionary.

Asset markets facilitate foreign participation in domestic restructuring by allowing appraisal of the value of enterprises, thereby limiting opportunistic behavior in negotiation for the sale of enterprises to foreigners. As noted, opportunistic behavior in the sale of enterprises' assets had impeded privatization.

Government policy

What should the role of government policy be in enterprise restructuring? One view is that the government should take an activist role in targeting those enterprises and sectors that are perceived to have the greatest prospects for success. Research would thus be conducted to identify the potentially successful enterprises, and government officials would be presented with the results of this research. Enterprises targeted for assistance would receive preferential treatment in access to credit and convertible currency; they might also benefit from government subsidies and protection from foreign competition.

Such targeting assigns to government discretionary choice of beneficiaries of assistance; the assumption is that the choices made will be apolitical, and also that state officials have informational advantages relative to private investors risking their own capital.

The need for restructuring in Hungary is widespread and inconsistent with a focus by government on a few select enterprises. If restructuring through targeting were to take place on the requisite scale, it would not be targeting at all but a return to centralized direction of resources. Narrow targeting would require the state to decide on resource allocation, with no assurance that the political mechanism would not apply political criteria in designating the beneficiaries. It appears therefore inconsistent with the requisite change to propose a leading role for government in selecting or targeting investment projects.

Sequencing

Can successful internal organizational and technological restructuring precede privatization?[16] This sequencing is of course reminiscent of past attempts to restructure socialist enterprises. In these past attempts, restructuring was perceived as an organizational or technological issue devoid of ownership and incentive considerations.

---

[16]Sequencing problems also arise with respect to macroeconomic stabilization policies (see Hinds 1991 and Hinds, this volume). Hungary, in contrast to the former Yugoslavia and Poland, however, avoided destabilizing inflation.

The Hungarian economic reforms of 1968 had the objective of restructuring socialist enterprises by replacing central planning with decentralized decision making at the enterprise level.[17] Managers in decentralized socialist enterprises were to use newfound flexibility to improve enterprise efficiency and to cater to consumer demand. The reforms did result in growth of output and real wages. By the mid-1970s some 55 percent of investment had been decentralized to the enterprise level, subject to a central screening process. The role of the state in the economy, however, remained prominent. Although central planning had officially ceased, the visible hands of state ministries rather than the invisible hand of the market continued to guide the market socialist system. The state in particular exercised control over investment by imposing its preferences on the allocation of credit among enterprises. The evidence suggests that the change in procedures for investment allocation did not significantly increase the productivity of capital in the socialist enterprises.[18]

The new system sought to introduce a role for incentives by replacing the central determination of workers' incomes with a system in which each enterprise would meet its wage payments from its own earnings. Wage increases were to be linked to increases in enterprises' gross income; wage payments above the level allowed by the guidelines were subject to severe penalties.[19] Uneven productivity increases across enterprises, however, resulted in income inequality. Yet it was inconsistent with socialism for workers to be penalized or to benefit in accord within which state enterprise they happened to work. Wage equality across enterprises was thus eventually restored: in 1974, wages were once more centrally determined. Remuneration was therefore again divorced from enterprise productivity, and enterprises confronted the soft-budget constraints that reflected cross-subsidization, or income redistribution, among enterprises.[20]

Private ownership of enterprises would on the other hand have constrained wage increases to productivity gains through a non-negative profit constraint. In the absence of private ownership, the reform process moved unequally throughout the 1970s. In the 1980s a series of reforms introduced greater enterprise autonomy, but the state still remained the de jure owner of the enterprises. In 1984 self-management was introduced in over 80 percent of state-owned enterprises, which then were directed by enterprise councils. Self-management permitted enterprise managers and workers to become claimants to the returns from enterprise activities.

---

[17]For a detailed description of these and subsequent reforms, see for example Adam (1989).

[18]See, for example, Dezsenyl-Gueullette (1983) and Adam (1989). The evidence is also consistent with outcomes in other socialist economies. In general, socialist industry was not successful in integrating Western technology and improving productivity: see Fallenbuchl (1983), Kemme (1987), and Terrell (this volume) on the Polish case.

[19]There were progressive tax penalties ranging from 150 to 400 percent; see Adam (1989).

[20]See Vodopivec (this volume) for a discussion of a similar mechanism in Yugoslavia, and Schaffer (1990) on Poland.

Council members, elected by workers, could appoint management and determine remuneration; management could also make appointments to the councils. The Law on Association of 1989 facilitated the privatization of socialist enterprises by permitting the transformation of state enterprises to limited liability, joint stock companies in which shares could be sold to private purchasers. The State Property Agency was established in 1990 to monitor the sale of state-owned enterprise assets.

This sequencing of enterprise reform introduced ambiguities to the interpretation of ownership. Enterprise councils in many instances began to view themselves as owners, and undertook spontaneous privatizations. Renationalization was even proposed as a prerequisite for privatization, in order to preempt self-serving spontaneous privatizations. Because there were no markets to value the assets of enterprises and to counter claims that fair prices were not being received, privatization was controversial. The purpose of the State Property Agency was to eliminate controversy by appropriate monitoring.

In summary, market socialism in the 1980s did not transform socialist industry to Western-type enterprises responsive to price and quality competition. Enterprise autonomy was limited by the state as owner, and by political constraints (Kornai 1988). Since the state remained the ultimate de jure owner, there was little individual incentive to enhance the value of an enterprise. Enterprise managers found it in their interests to focus on the social objective of stable job security for workers, and to cater to the low-quality domestic and CMEA demand.

Foreign resource transfers

Hungary borrowed heavily from the West in the 1970s, and the resources were made available to the large state enterprises. Foreign borrowing left Hungary with a substantial debt but no long-term gain in productivity.

Hungary in particular benefitted in the 1980s from World Bank loans directed at facilitating industrial restructuring. The World Bank started lending to Hungary in 1983. The Bank's strategy for assistance was to support "Hungary's program of structural adjustment in the economy, to make it more efficient, flexible, market responsive and competitve in external markets, particularly in the convertible currency area" (World Bank 1989, p. 14). The Bank sponsored three industrial restructuring projects in the 1980s. The first two projects combined subsector and enterprise restructuring objectives with support for specified policy changes. The Industrial Export and Restructuring Project of March 1984 ($110 million) included support for 15 preappraised export-oriented and material saving projects. The first Industrial Restructuring Project of May 1986 ($100 million) included "specific measures in support of the policy reforms, as well as restructuring of promising subsectors" (World Bank 1989, p. 14). The second Industrial Restructuring Project of June 1987 ($150 million) "supported a deepening of the policy reforms, as well as the restructuring of several subsectors (rubber processing, and agricultural and food machinery manufacture) and a pilot component for the development of feeder industries" (World Bank 1989, p. 15). The Third Industrial Restructuring Project in 1989 was designed "to provide continuity and build on the first and second restructuring loans," so as to "help to accelerate the technological, managerial, physical, and financial restructuring of Hungarian industrial enterprises" (World Bank 1989, p. 15). In the first and second projects, there was a substantial targeting of "preappraised restructuring investments in selected priority sectors" (World Bank 1989, p. 15). The third Bank project was more generally directed to industrial restructuring and "devolved decision making and resource allocation authority to the banking system" (World Bank 1989, p. 15). The latter project also directed Bank assistance to the private small business sector and to employment creation and retraining.

It was the Bank's subsequent conclusion that "an early review of the implementation of the two industrial restructuring projects indicates the need to improve the understanding and application of the restructuring concept by the enterprises, the commercial banks, RPO (Restructuring Program Office), and the Ministry of Industry" (World Bank 1989, p. 16).

This external assistance did result in an improvement in the domestic enabling environment: tax and banking reforms were initiated, the manner of public procurement was changed, policies regarding the development of private small- and medium-sized enterprises were changed, and attitudes toward privatization improved. The flexibility exhibited by some Hungarian enterprises in sales to the West may be attributed to technical advice that was provided. However, although substantial resources had been made available through World Bank programs as well as through other foreign assistance and borrowing, when democratic pluralism replaced political monopoly in 1990, little substantial progress had been made in achieving technological parity with Western enterprises.

Enterprise case studies

In mid-1990, with the Hungarian economy in transition from the past system, enterprises were confronting changes in the manner of conducting international trade. This section reports on how leading Hungarian enterprises perceived they would be affected by these changes, and how the enterprises responded or projected that they would respond.

The machinery and electronics sectors were recognized to be soft good producers disadvantaged by a technology gap relative to Western competitors.[21] Yet, in contrast with pessimistic predictions of government officials, managers expressed optimism regarding future prospects in these sectors.

For example, rather than being concerned with the potentially adverse consequences of trading with the U.S.S.R. in convertible currency at world prices, the management of the electronics enterprise Videoton welcomed the impending changes because of projected continuing demand in the Soviet market. The management of Ikarus projected that Soviet demand for their buses would not be significantly reduced with changes in the trade and payments system; the managers indicated that as a fallback diversification of sales to Western markets could be achieved if Soviet demand did contract. Capital equipment producer SZIM and the locomotive producer Ganz undertook restructuring programs using foreign capital and technology, changed their ownership structures, and implemented programs to increase labor productivity by eliminating redundant labor.

Prominent among Hungarian industrial enterprises was the bus manufacturer Ikarus. The principal product was articulated buses sold to CMEA purchasers, although there were also CMEA sales of urban transportation buses and long-distance coaches. Ikarus had a 10 percent market share of the 100,000 unit CMEA annual demand. A declining market share was, however, attributed to Ikarus' relatively high CMEA price. In 1989 sales were around 12,000 buses, of which about 2,000 were exported to the West and 7,500 were sold to the U.S.S.R. Buses for the West and for the CMEA were produced on the same assembly line, but with engines, transmissions, internal fittings, and other components and parts differing depending on the vehicle's export destination. From Ikarus' perspective, there was no significant dichotomization of production, since the interchangeable components and parts were produced by outside suppliers. The price equalization system taxed Ikarus' sales to the U.S.S.R.: for every bus sold to the U.S.S.R., Ikarus received in Hungarian forint about 40 percent of the price it received from its sales to the West. Export sales to the Soviet Union were severely curtailed by licensing restrictions in the first quarter of 1990, because of policy measures taken in response to a Hungarian trade surplus with the U.S.S.R. Ikarus had developed substantial goodwill in the U.S.S.R.: there were approximately 100,000 Ikarus buses in service that required spare parts, and Ikarus maintained service centers in the U.S.S.R. for its buses.

Ikarus' managers projected that the Soviet demand for buses and spare parts would be sustained in the post-CMEA regime, and that Ikarus would be able to compete effectively in Soviet markets if freed from export licensing constraints and CMEA export taxes. There had been discussions with a potential Western joint venture partner. At various times in 1989 and

---

[21]This view was based on sectoral trade data revealing dependence on CMEA sales. By market designation, these sectors produced archetypical soft goods.

1990, however, Ikarus has been declared to be on the verge of bankruptcy. Ikarus nevertheless survived the transition from the CMEA system: the enterprise was able to maintain substantial sales to its traditional Soviet customers and also to diversify to other markets. The links that sustained former CMEA sales were aided by direct Russian investment in the enterprise.

Enterprises dependent on sales to Ikarus shared Ikarus' problems. Csepel Auto produced an integrated chassis for Ikarus that accounted for 80 percent of Csepel's sales. Ikarus' financial difficulties placed Csepel Auto on the verge of bankruptcy in early 1989. In the chain of vertical links, Csepel Auto made over 30 percent of its purchases from Raba, extending the dependency relationship. Raba's engines and axles were used by Csepel auto in assembling bus chassis for Ikarus. The CMEA had been the principal market for Raba engines. Raba in its heyday had 25,000 employees, but in 1990 this number had halved. Moreover, in the face of declining CMEA demand, a new 100,000 square meter production facility had been completed in 1990.

Raba initiated restructuring activities based on joint ventures with foreign participants. A joint venture with General Motors (67 percent General Motors) in Szentgotthard was planned to produce between 100,000 and 200,000 Opel engines per year; by 1992 10,000 to 20,000 Opel Kadet vehicles were to be assembled. Under the terms of the agreement, General Motors would provide the capital and technology and would itself buy the output of the new joint enterprise. The recovery of Ikarus also facilitated the continued viability of the enterprises to which it was vertically linked.

The SZIM enterprise accounted for some two thirds of Hungarian machine tool production. In 1987 SZIM had a turnover of 5 billion forint and had 4,700 employees. Machine tools accounted for 56 percent of turnover and brake equipment for road vehicles and railways accounted for 29 percent. SZIM was heavily dependent on CMEA trade: around 80 percent of output was exported, principally to the Soviet Union. SZIM's performance in previous years had contributed to the view that the machine tool industry was a potential casualty of the impending change in conditions of trade with the U.S.S.R. In 1988, however, SZIM initiated a major restructuring program; using a law more than 100 years old, it converted each of its eight plants to joint stock companies, with SZIM as the central holding company. Each separate company took on a West European partner in a joint venture, importing Western technology and reducing excess labor. SZIM maintained between 49 to 94 percent of the shares in the new companies. The remaining state company had in 1990 only 27 employees whose function it was to oversee the restructuring of the company through the operations of the new enterprises. Management claimed that the enterprise had undergone successful restructuring. Exports to the West were anticipated to be the prime source of sales in three to five years, and exports to the U.S.S.R. were projected to continue in the post-CMEA trade regime. It was envisaged that part hard currency part barter transactions would be used, to enable the Soviets to conserve hard currency. In the past, SZIM could not conduct such transactions with the U.S.S.R. because of Soviet restraints on nonconvertible currency transactions with Hungary, but the switch to hard currency settlement would eliminate this restraint on trade.[22]

The large Hungarian electronics enterprise Videoton had formerly produced electronics equipment for consumer and military use. A joint venture with a West German company had converted the facilities that had produced military equipment to production of telecommunications equipment, for which there was a demand in the U.S.S.R. Overstaffing problems remained and had been exacerbated by increased labor productivity in the new production plant. Videoton's computer division had had a French partner for many years. The French partner had not however maintained technological parity with Western competitors and had itself sought U.S. partners. Licensing constraints by the French firm's U.S. partner had prevented the transfer of technology to Videoton. Videoton had itself entered into licensing arrangements with U.S. and European companies. For example, a joint venture with Simera A.G. of Liechtenstein was to employ 1,000 workers to produce printers, industrial robots, flexible manufacturing systems and the control units of household appliances. Also, a Soviet enterprise had invested in Videoton in order to receive dividends in the form of Videoton consumer electronics products. Although in mid-1990 the management of Videoton expressed optimism regarding adaptation to the post-CMEA regime, Videoton was to encounter difficulties in the course of its adjustment from dependence on CMEA sales.

The Ganz enterprise produced locomotives. In August 1989, at which time losses were about U.S. $17,000 per day, Ganz formed a joint venture with the British firm Hunslet. Hunslet acquired 51 percent of the stock of Ganz Engineering for $20.4 million. The company was reorganized. A quality control unit was established, and redundant workers (around 30 percent of the work force) were laid off. Ganz Hunslet anticipated receiving quality certification to sell its products in the United Kingdom; under the rules of the 1992 European Single Market this would provide certification to sell throughout the European Community and the European Free Trade Association (EFTA) countries. The restructuring of Ganz was undertaken by separating assets from liabilities: in 1987 the Ganz Mavag group was reorganized into seven companies and four joint stock companies. The Ganz Locomotive, Wagon, and Machine Factory assumed all debts of the former company (around 20 billion forint) and declared itself insolvent on November 11, 1988. The company was liquidated and on December 19 the new Ganz that became the joint venture partner was established.

---

[22]A consideration stressed by SZIM management was that joint ventures with West European enterprises would permit SZIM to invite Soviet government officials and enterprise managers to visit the West European plants which SZIM would duplicate in Hungary, thereby avoiding compromise of SZIM sales by Soviet foreign travel preferences.

The Tungsram enterprise produced general household bulbs, energy-saving incandescent tubes, state-of-the-art gas discharge bulbs, miniaturized halogen bulbs, and infrared and quartz lighting in 12 plants with combined total sales of around $300 million per year, of which 85 percent derived from exports. In 1990 General Electric of the United States acquired 50 percent plus one share of Tungsram's stock, and took over management of the company. General Electric announced that it would modernize Tungsram's plant and equipment and introduce Western management techniques.

In these instances of restructuring, foreign participation provided the means to transfer technology and the impetus to internal reorganization. Foreign ownership also addressed the monitoring and incentive impediments of socialist industry: restructuring was undertaken without the direct involvement of government officials.

Conclusions

In the past, attempts had been made to restructure Hungarian industry, and foreign resources had been available for this purpose by international agencies and via other foreign borrowing. These restructuring attempts, however, failed. Foreign borrowing to facilitate technology transfer, price deregulation, and market liberalization, when sequenced before privatization, did not evoke restructuring responses consistent with adaptation to Western competition.

The end of the disincentives associated with the CMEA system of trade and consensus regarding the need to restructure could not in itself suffice to ensure the requisite transformation of the economy. Privatization would have a principal role, by ensuring the presence of residual claimants with incentives to undertake investments, bear risks, and monitor enterprise performance. In particular, private ownership introduced through foreign investment would facilitate the technology transfer and Western market access necessary for the successful transition to the post-CMEA era.

References

Abel, Istvan, Arye L. Hillman, and David Tarr. 1992. "The Government Budgetary Consequences of Reform of the CMEA System of International Trade: The Case of Hungary." This volume.

Adam, Jan. 1989. *Economic Reform in the Soviet Union and Eastern Europe since the 1960s*. Basingstoke, U.K.: Macmillan.

Brada, Josef C., and Istvan Dobozi, eds. 1988. *The Hungarian Economy in the 1980s. Reforming the System and Adjusting to External Shocks*. Greenwich, Conn.: JAI Press.

de Melo, Jaime, and David Tarr. 1992. *A General Equilibrium Model of U.S. Trade Policy*. Cambridge, Mass.: MIT Press.

Dezsenyl-Gueullette, Agota. 1983. "The Utilization and Assimilation in Hungary of Advanced Technology Imported from the West." *Soviet Studies* 35:196–207.

Ehrlich, Eva. 1985. "The Size Structure of Manufacturing Establishments and Enterprises: An International Comparison." *Journal of Comparative Economics* 9:267–95.

Fallenbuchl, Zbigniew M. 1983. *East-West Technology Transfer: Study of Poland 1971–1980.* Paris: OECD.

Gacs, Janos. 1989. "The Progress of Liberalization of Foreign Trade in Hungary." Paper presented at the World Bank Conference on Attempts at Liberalization: Hungarian Economic Policy and International Experience, 16–18 November. Budapest: Kopint-Datorg.

Hare, Paul G. 1990. "Reforming State-Enterprise Relationships in Hungary." In *European Economy: Economic Transformation in Hungary and Poland.* Brussels: Commission of the European Communities, 35–54.

Hillman, Arye L. 1989. *The Political Economy of Protection.* London and New York: Harwood Academic Publishers.

———. 1990. "Macroeconomic Policy in Hungary and its Microeconomic Consequences." In *European Economy: Economic Transformation in Hungary and Poland.* Brussels: Commission of the European Communities, 55–66.

———. 1991. "Liberalization Dilemmas." In Arye L. Hillman, ed., *Markets and Politicians: Politicized Economic Choice.* Boston and Dordrecht: Kluwer Academic Publishers, 189–207.

Hillman, Arye L., and Adi Schnytzer. 1992. "Creating the Reform-Resistant Dependent Economy: Socialist Comparative Advantage, Enterprise Incentives, and the CMEA." This volume.

Hinds, Manuel. 1991. "Incentives and Ownership in Socialist Countries in Transition." In Arye L. Hillman, ed., *Markets and Politicians: Politicized Economic Choice.* Boston and Dordrecht: Kluwer Academic Publishers, 138–68.

Hinds, Manuel. 1992. "Policy Effectiveness in Reforming Socialist Economies." This volume.

Jensen, Michael C. 1990. *Organizational Change and the Market for Corporate Control.* Oxford, U.K.: Basil Blackwell

Kemme, David M. 1987. "Productivity Growth in Polish Industry." *Journal of Comparative Economics* 11:1–20.

Kornai, Janos. 1985. *Contradictions and Dilemmas.* Budapest: Corvina.

———. 1988. "Individual Freedom and Reform of the Socialist Economy." *European Economic Review* 32:233–67.

Milanovic, Branko. 1992. "Privatization Options and Procedures." This volume.

Newbery, David. 1990. "Tax Reform, Trade Liberalization and Industrial Restructuring in Hungary." In *European Economy: Economic Transformation in Hungary and Poland*. Brussels: Commission of the European Communities, 67–95.

Oblath, Gabor. 1989. "Opening up in Hungary: The Relevance of International Experiences and Some Peculiarities." Paper presented at the World Bank Conference on Attempts at Liberalization: Hungarian Economic Policy and International Experience, 16–18 November. Budapest: Kopint-Datorg.

Oblath, Gabor, and David Tarr. 1992. "The Terms-of-Trade Effects from the Elimination of State Trading in Soviet-Hungarian Trade." *Journal of Comparative Economics* 16:75–93.

Saldanha, Fernando. 1992. "Self-Management: Theory and Yugoslav Practice." This volume.

Schaffer, Mark. 1990. "Taxation, Subsidization, and Regulation of State-Owned Enterprises in Poland." In *European Economy: Economic Transformation in Hungary and Poland*. Brussels: Commission of the European Communities, 183–201.

Schrenk, Martin. 1992. "The CMEA System of Trade and Payments." This volume.

Tardos, Marton. 1983. "The Increasing Role and Ambivalent Reception of Small Enterprises in Hungary." *Journal of Comparative Economics* 7:277–87.

Terrell, Katherine. 1992. "International Technology Transfer and Efficiency in Socialist Enterprises: The Polish Failure of the 1970s." This volume.

Vodopivec, Milan. 1992. "State Paternalism and the Yugoslav Failure." This volume.

World Bank. 1989. "Hungary, Third Industrial Restructuring Project." Staff Appraisal Report 7456. World Bank, Washington, D.C. Processed.

8

Life after the Polish "Big Bang": Episodes of Preprivatization Enterprise Behavior

Alan Gelb, Erika A. Jorgensen, and Inderjit Singh

In January 1990 the Polish government introduced a bold package of economic policy measures which became known as the "Big Bang." The government created a new economic environment for firms by simultaneously implementing stabilization and trade liberalization programs, freeing domestic prices, and eliminating subsidies. Industrial firms, however, were still formally state-owned. The Big Bang did not include privatization measures. This chapter explores how some firms fared in the aftermath of the Big Bang.

Firm-level data provide clear insight into agents' economic behavior. Aggregate data can obscure sectoral or subsectoral behavior. In socialist economies aggregate data may be of poor quality because of inaccuracies in collection; they are also often based on conceptual definitions that may be only vaguely related to market concepts (Hillman 1991). Furthermore, in a socialist economy under transition, the linkage between changes in policy tools at the macroeconomic level and microeconomic behavior is not well specified. An important ancillary role is therefore present for firm-level analysis. We report here on the behavior of a small number of firms. More detailed and quantitative analysis must follow on a larger sample of firms if the insights gained from our small sample are to be tested for generality. Nevertheless, the representative episodes that constitute our data source provide indications of the nature of microeconomic response.

We are indebted to Donna Schaller for her assistance in preparing data for this paper.

The series of economic shocks to Polish firms came in three overlapping waves: first, a period of severe macroeconomic instability; second, the Big Bang of stabilization, liberalization, and market reform; and third, the disruption and impending end of Council for Mutual Economic Assistance (CMEA) trade. The first wave gained strength through 1989 with sharply rising inflation and tightening credit. The January 1990 reforms (preceded by some preliminary policy changes in August and September 1989) transformed the environment in which firms operated. The CMEA system that had provided sheltered sales (Schrenk, this volume, and Hillman and Schnytzer, this volume) was evidently not to continue. As a result, in the first few months of 1990 there was uncertainty and chaos in the industrial sector. Firms were unsure about their markets for inputs and outputs; domestic demand continued to fall, credit remained tight, and expectations about CMEA sales became ever more pessimistic.

These negative shocks could have paralyzed firms. However, the sample of Polish firms studied generally revealed positive adaptation.

Because firms entered the Big Bang with relatively large financial cushions and because wages were not dominant in production costs, employment was cut only modestly. More assertive action was taken in two areas: firms pursued new markets, and in response to the severe credit squeeze receivables and payables increased, giving rise to a system of interfirm notes. There was a vacuum of ownership; the partial self-management that existed, however, was not a source of perverse behavior (Hinds, this volume, and Saldanha, this volume). Workers' councils and trade unions were constrained in their wage demands by the repression of the nominal wage that constituted part of the government's stabilization package.

The Big Bang policy package[1]

In 1981 Poland began a partial process of economic reform aimed at significantly diminishing the role of central planning in the economy. Enterprise autonomy increased, though with much variance across sectors.[2] A limited form of self-management was established with the introduction of workers' councils that had some decision-making power. Government control, however, was maintained through informal bargaining between enterprises and government financial authorities. Ad hoc negotiations determined prices, interest rates, and tax rates. This system discouraged

---

[1]For a more detailed analysis and description see Schrenk (1990), Lipton and Sachs (1990), Frydman and Wellisz (1991), Calvo and Coricelli (1992), Coricelli and Rocha (1991), and Schaffer (1990).

[2]Firms that produced consumer goods were allowed to determine most aspects of current operations.

financial discipline by firms and eventually created serious macroeconomic imbalances in the Polish economy. Further reforms introduced from 1987 to 1989 failed to improve macroeconomic conditions, though they did liberalize economic transactions.[3] By mid-1989 it was clear that macroeconomic conditions were unsustainable (Schrenk 1990 and Lipton and Sachs 1990). Inflation at the start of 1989 was already 100 percent (on an annual basis); in the last quarter of 1989 inflation was 2,000 percent. In response, the Solidarity government implemented the Big Bang in January 1990.

The stabilization component of this program was heterodox in nature, using both the wage and the exchange rate as nominal anchors for price stability. The predicted budget deficit for 1990 was reduced to 1 percent of GDP by cutting consumption and production subsidies. Tight credit was imposed through sharply higher interest rates and through a reduced quantity of credit. To create one nominal anchor, incomes policy was introduced in the form of repression of the nominal wage by levying a heavy tax on firms which exceeded government-mandated wage increases. The other nominal anchor for the economy arose from the pegging of the zloty to the dollar at a fixed rate, after a large devaluation (almost 60 percent) which allowed for trade liberalization. The foreign exchange market was unified, restrictions on access to foreign exchange were eliminated, and quantitative restrictions on imports were replaced with tariffs.

The Big Bang package also included important steps in the creation of a market economy. Remaining wholesale and retail price controls were lifted for all sectors except energy. In addition, the beginnings of a "safety net" to ease and encourage labor adjustment were created in the form of unemployment insurance. The unemployment insurance legislation which was passed in January 1990 also allowed firms to fire employees with one month's notice. The combination of openness to world markets and domestic price liberalization was intended to establish relative prices that reflected true scarcity value and to encourage the reallocation of resources toward more productive uses.

Firms had to cope both with these macroeconomic policy shocks and with other primarily microeconomic policy changes. The legal monopoly of the central distribution system was eliminated.[4] Several policies intended to harden the budget constraint of state-owned firms were instituted. For example, the existing levy on the fixed assets of state owned enterprises (the

---

[3]The central allocation system for inputs was scaled down to cover only five commodity groups, and firms were given greater freedom to set output prices. In August 1989 prices of agricultural inputs and products were freed. They accounted for approximately 20 percent of gross domestic product (GDP), pushing the share of goods with decontrolled prices to 50 percent of GDP.

[4]Antimonopoly legislation was prepared to counteract the high concentration of Polish industry.

so-called dividend tax[5]) was modified as of January: the enterprise assets that formed the base for the tax became inflation-adjusted and nonpayment was supposed to trigger rehabilitation procedures (similar to bankruptcy reorganization but initiated by the government as owner).

The five-year cycle of CMEA-planned trade ended in 1990, and it became clear during the spring of that year that negotiations with regard to the next five years of CMEA trade would not take place. The remaining contracts for 1990 came into question as doubts about delivery and payment grew and as governments withdrew subsidies to exporters that were part of the original bilateral agreements.[6] At that time 45 percent of exports, or 9 percent of GNP, were to the CMEA countries. The breakdown of CMEA arrangements thus affected a substantial portion of trade.

By March 1990 Big Bang measures had reduced inflation (as measured by the Consumer Price Index) to a steady monthly rate of 5 percent. Industrial production dropped sharply, contracting by 30 percent in the first five months of the year (compared to the same period in 1989).[7] Registered unemployment rose sharply, from near zero to 107,000 persons by the end of February and to 500,000 by the end of May. Real incomes fell by 35 percent from January through May. The trade account, however, improved. Total exports increased by 8 percent in real terms during the first five months of 1990 as compared to the same period in 1989, driven by hard currency exports which rose by 15 percent while exports to the CMEA remained unchanged. Over the same period, imports fell by 29 percent in volume, with a 32 percent contraction in imports from CMEA countries and 27 percent decline from convertible currency areas.

The important question was the following: when would a supply response occur? The resumption of growth had crucial political dimensions: the electorate could eventually lose patience with a lengthening and deepening recession. The political costs of deteriorating economic conditions would rise over time, especially in a country such as Poland where employment had been secure and many social benefits were tied to employment.

Behavioral responses to macroeconomic policy changes in a reforming socialist economy may differ from those in a market economy. Problems of ownership and control may dominate the reactions of state-owned industrial firms, because their objective functions are different from those of privately owned firms. However, obstacles to firms' adjustment may not be immediately evident in the aggregate analysis. The aggregate data may, by bundling together different sectors and firms, obfuscate the early individual

---

[5]This statutory tax on enterprise assets was introduced in 1989 for state-owned firms and called a dividend to be paid to the Treasury as owner.

[6]See Schrenk (this volume) on these price equalization payments.

[7]The industrial subsectors with the largest contraction were light industry, mining, food processing, and minerals.

firms' responses. A better way to learn how firms were affected by policy changes is to look at firm-level data. This is the approach we propose to use in this paper.

The responses of individual firms to the Big Bang

The firms in the sample

At the time of the Big Bang state-owned industrial enterprises in Poland accounted for almost 90 percent of net material product in industry and almost 90 percent of industrial employment. The response of state-owned firms to the Big Bang was crucial because private firms were too small to absorb much labor in the short run or to affect total production. State-owned firms were thus a major focus of our study's attention.

Nine firms were studied: seven state-owned enterprises, one cooperative, and one private joint venture. The firms covered a wide range of industrial subsectors—including capital goods, intermediate goods, and consumer goods—and the full range of product market orientations—domestic, CMEA export, and hard currency export.

Basic data on financial and real variables were collected during visits to each firm, and managers were interviewed. Conclusions derived from this small sample should be treated with caution, however.

Table 8.1 compares sample firms with the average firm in the Lista 500 (the top 500 state-owned firms ranked by sales) and the average firm in all of Polish state-owned industry. The average firm in our sample is close in size to the Lista 500 average in terms of sales, but larger in terms of employment, and is significantly larger on both counts than the average firm in all of industry. The sample firms also have significantly higher overall exports as a share of sales and somewhat higher profits in 1988 and 1989.

An overview of shocks and responses at the level of the firm

The following sections identify categories of firm behavior and responses. In general, the behavior of the sample firms reflected the overall industry response to Poland's Big Bang: firms reduced their output and employment. More interesting is the different ways firms identified the most important shocks and chose to respond to continuing uncertainty.

Managers of ailing firms, for example, identified demand conditions as the overriding concern. For firms with a domestic market orientation, depressed domestic demand was considered the most crucial. By contrast, the electronics firm studied, due to its heavy CMEA orientation, was affected most by the cessation of CMEA orders. Other issues were not as fundamental to survival. The firms that were best able to adjust were those with a preexisting orientation toward hard currency export markets.

8.1 Characteristics of sample of Polish industrial firms

Firm	Main product	Sector	Sales (millions of US$) 1989	Employment (thousands) 1989	Total exports (% sales) 1989	Exports to Zone II[a] (% sales) 1989	Sales growth[b] (percent) 1989	1990.I[c]	1990.05	Net profit before tax[c] (% sales) 1989	1990.I[d]	1990.05
State-owned firms												
1	Machine tools	Engineering	4	0.5	69	64	—	9	25	132	42	37
2	Computer printers	Electronics	27	3.1	80	0.2	—	-1	16	41	36	35
3	Electric generators	Engineering	13	3.3	15	3	—	19	68	33	16	21
4	Basic chemicals	Chemicals	77	6.2	26	23	—	18	55	36	27	23
5	Textiles	Light industry	18	3.8	11	7	—	-6	11	32	15	4
6	Garments	Light industry	8	2.4	19	12	—	n.a.	8	36	n.a.	22
7	Trucks	Transport equip.	76	13.8	4	0.4	—	-17	-11	16	11	7
State-owned cooperatives												
8	Food processing	Food industry	63	8.7	83	73	—	3	34	19	7	7
Private joint ventures												
9	Wood furniture	Wood and paper	44	5.5	21	21	—	n.a.	n.a.	32	n.a.	n.a.
Averages for firms in sample			36	5.2	36	23	n.a.	4	26	42	22	20
Average for Lista 500 firms[e]			31	3.2	21	n.a.	n.a.	n.a.	n.a.	34	n.a.	n.a.
Average for all industrial firms[f]			4	0.6	18	12	n.a.	17	n.a.	31	n.a.	n.a.

Notes: n.a. = not available.

a. Exports to Zone II are exports to hard currency areas.

b. Sales growth is change in sales from beginning of the year measured in U.S. dollars, where Polish zlotys have been translated to U.S. dollars at an average exchange rate of 3,502 zlotys per U.S. dollar for 1989 and 9,500 zlotys per U.S. dollar for 1990.

c. Net profit before tax is before company profits tax, excess wages tax, and dividend tax.

d. 1990.I represents data for the first quarter of 1990; 1990.05 is for end-May 1990.

e. Lista 500 firms are Poland's largest 500 state-owned firms ranked by sales, excluding mining.

f. All industrial firms are state-owned and include fuel and power, as well as industry.

Sources include interviews with firms, Central Statistical Office of Poland, and Central Planning Office of Poland.

The firms studied entered 1990 in a strong position, as did many Polish firms. In 1989 their profits were high relative to sales, averaging 42 percent for the nine firm sample while Lista 500 firms displayed profit of 34 percent of sales and total industry showed 31 percent (see Table 8.1). Profit as a share of sales doubled between 1988 and 1989 for all three groups of firms.

Oligopolistic market power may partially explain this pattern, but the near hyperinflation of the last quarter of 1989 was a far more important factor. Also, the firms in the sample generally had little net debt, due to state grants, the inflationary erosion of bank debt, and the passing on of foreign exchange losses to the government. The government-mandated dividend tax was modest relative to profits, averaging 2 percent of sales in 1989, partly because investments financed out of past retained earnings were excluded from the taxable base and the original capital of the firm on which the tax was levied had not been revalued in line with inflation. Wages were a low share of costs (13 percent of sales in 1989). Therefore, while firms reported a serious liquidity squeeze beginning at the end of 1989, most were cushioned against bankruptcy by high past retained profits.

In interviews conducted during June and July 1990, firms indicated that output for the first six months of 1990 averaged 20 to 30 percent below 1989 levels. There was considerable variation, however: some firms were operating at 50 percent of previous output levels, while others, notably in the garment and food processing industries, were operating at near full capacity. This general contraction is not evident in the simple measures of sales growth for the first quarter and for May 1990 shown in Table 8.1 for several reasons. First, nominal value of sales is deflated by the exchange rate (which was fixed), and second, many firms had strong seasonal sales patterns. In addition, production in many industrial branches (for example, for the maker of large electrical generators) is forward looking, based on orders for future delivery; production will thus fall more quickly than current sales.

The first six months of economic reforms were a period of turmoil. Most markets (except agricultural markets, where products had been freely traded since mid-1989) were volatile and highly segmented. Firms had difficulty estimating demand and pricing inputs and products. Border prices provided an imperfect guide. Some firms found that input supplies became more uncertain. State-controlled distribution channels were disrupted and firms sometimes had difficulty finding a replacement for a troubled or uncooperative monopoly domestic suppliers. Private distribution channels and markets were only in nascent stages of development.

Marketing and distribution activities

Behavioral responses of the sample firms to the creation of markets were extensive. Steps taken in purchasing, marketing, and distribution to adjust to the postreform environment included the following:

• creating sales departments, sometimes with travelling salespersons, and developing more direct links with clients, especially abroad;

• establishing factory shops selling at very low margins;

• sponsoring new distributors, for example, of clothing, to bypass the large state distributors which were forced in 1990 to widen margins to finance large and slow-moving inventories;

• holding special auctions and attending exhibitions and fairs;

• searching for foreign firms that could provide marketing expertise through joint venture arrangements (as well as providing technology and capital); and

• raising quality and product appeal, for example, by importing critical components from the West or acquiring licenses for high-visibility brand name products.

In some cases, efforts to develop a marketing strategy seem to have been effective. For example, the truck manufacturer had begun to sell 80 percent of output to individuals or small companies for cash, where such clients had previously accounted for no more than 20 percent of sales. The garment maker estimated that in 1990 it would be introducing 500 different garment products, compared with a few dozen the previous year, including high-value lycra bathing suits made under license. This behavior was a dramatic change from a product line previously dominated by low value standardized products, for which demand had fallen sharply.

Some firms, however, made significant marketing and distribution efforts with no effect. The electronics firm, for example, with most of its market in the U.S.S.R., had begun efforts to sell directly to past customers and was planning a trip to the U.S.S.R. to demonstrate its product line to previous purchasers. Yet the firm began to doubt that this bold move would pay off because of collapsing demand in the U.S.S.R. and the severe shortage of hard currency there. Similarly, the textile producer in our study reacted to strong import competition in a depressed domestic market by trying to coordinate closely with garment makers in order to increase specialization and customization; despite these actions the firm's costs remained too high to be competitive.

Export response

Difficulties with the CMEA markets compounded domestic problems. A number of factors limited the ability of Polish firms to export their products profitably to the CMEA market. The appreciation of the zloty against the transferable ruble lowered the profitability of exports. Expected profitability was also diminished for some firms by the exclusion of their products from intergovernment trade protocols and the elimination of export subsidies. For the computer printer manufacturer in the study, these changes caused it to lose money on exports sold at previously agreed-upon prices. Firms attempting to renegotiate price increases on existing contracts met resistance from foreign purchasers. By mid-1990, firms with long production cycles, such as the producer of electric generators, were facing the effects of a failure to negotiate another five-year CMEA agreement. In addition, general uncertainty, especially in eastern Germany, resulted in the suspension of orders to buy from Polish firms.

Firms continued to use state trade agencies (Foreign Trade Organizations or FTOs)[8] to export their products, even as they were moving away from a reliance on domestic state-owned distributors. Managers believed that because FTOs can sometimes operate effectively and cheaply, and because they often have valuable information and skills otherwise absent in Polish firms, these former export monopolies could continue to play an important role in exporting Polish products to both hard currency and CMEA markets.

In general, firms believed that exports to the West were more profitable than exports to CMEA, that Western markets had superior growth potential, and that such exports should be a central part of their strategy for survival. Virtually all of the firms had had some amount of exposure to Western markets before 1990 (although sometimes indirectly through FTOs). Those firms with greater previous exposure to Western markets appeared better able to formulate a viable strategy for survival, possibly because of an awareness of capitalist ways of doing business.

Cost-cutting measures: employment, wages, and material input costs

The profit margins of the firms studied were squeezed by sharp increases in input costs, notably for power and water, and by progressively more competitive product markets which limited firms' abilities to pass on higher costs to customers. Profits before tax as a percent of sales, which had doubled from 1988 to 1989, fell as a result from an average of 42 percent in 1989 to 22 percent for the first quarter of 1990 and 20 percent in May 1990, as is shown in Figure 8.1.

Policymakers expected that firms would respond to the Big Bang by firing labor. Employment in the industrial sector as a whole had declined by 3 percent already in 1989 (prior to the Big Bang), while Lista 500 firms reduced their labor forces by 8.4 percent. During the same period, the sample enterprises reduced employment by 7 percent. With these significant cutbacks in 1989 it is not surprising that firings in the first months of 1990 were modest. Employment declined in the sample firms by another 2 percent during the first quarter of 1990. By the end of May 1990 approximately 5

---

[8]See Schrenk (this volume) on the role of FTOs in CMEA trade.

percent of workers employed on January 1, 1990 had been laid off, far less than the reported reductions in production (26 percent).

Some firms, however, did significantly reduce employment. The textile firm and the truck manufacturer each laid off 18 percent of their workers. Firms were negotiating to reduce staffing even further. Workers approaching pensionable age and casual workers were laid off first. The private wood furniture manufacturer, responding to improved export opportunities and unburdened by the bias of state-owned firms toward overstaffing, stood out as the only firm to take on new labor in 1989 or 1990.

Figure 8.1 Poland: net profit before tax, 1988-90

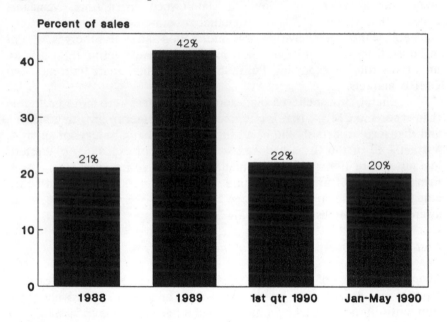

The unit cost of labor had also fallen since the Big Bang. Real wages had declined substantially, though the elimination of shortages of goods and related queuing provided some offsetting benefit for workers. The excess wages tax, in existence through the 1980s[9] but substantially increased in January 1990, constrained wages and bonuses, because of the financial cost to the firm and because payment of the tax was an indicator prompting government review of a firm's condition. The tax provided incentives to reduce the labor force so that the wages fund could be shared among fewer

---

[9]In an effort to reestablish financial discipline over firms, the government imposed a series of excess wages taxes in the 1980s which took the general form of progressively taxing wage increases above a government-mandated maximum. Frequent exemptions, however, undermined the impact of taxes.

employees. In the past, this seems not to have been a major incentive to lay off employees, though there are indications that by mid-1990 companies were considering layoffs to enable higher individual pay.

A parallel process occurred on the input side, as firms searched for more diversified suppliers. This search was complicated by the market dominance of a few producers and the higher costs of many imports. Firms had been revising their contracts with suppliers; they no longer desired the long-term and inflexible contracts that had been common and attractive in a shortage economy. Potential import competition held down prices, but in many cases domestic goods were still cheaper than close foreign substitutes. This gap offered an opportunity for adjustment to some firms hard hit by the abrupt transition from the protectionism of the CMEA system to the low protection system. For example, domestic steel prices were lower than international prices for comparable qualities, which provided a competitive advantage to the machine tool maker.

Credit and financing

A credit squeeze which began in the latter part of 1989 affected the balance sheets of even the most profitable firms. Since the firms in the sample were not heavily in debt, in most cases the rise in interest rates did not in itself seriously affect profits. An exception was the food processing firm, which had high credit costs because of its seasonal production cycle. Firms responded to tight credit in diverse ways. For example, the manufacturer of electrical generators, fearing that the high interest rates of January and February would continue, secured prepayment from a large client and paid off all debt.

More commonly, and of far more importance than bank credits, there was a sharp rise in payables, mirrored in rising receivables. For the sample firms, this pattern became evident between March and May of 1990 (see Table 8.2). Average payables stood at six weeks of sales for the *state-owned firms* in the sample in 1989, fell to 5 weeks during the first quarter, but rebounded to reach 7 weeks in May 1990. Almost all of the sample firms experienced a rise in receivables between March and May of 1990.

Did the Big Bang create a new "sink or swim" environment for firms?

The old regime for state-owned enterprises

There had been a gradual withdrawal by the government during the past 20 years from active ownership and management of firms. Decentralization in the 1970s left the government, however, with financial control over firms. For example, in 1988 one third of total subsidies went to enterprises. There were two types of enterprise subsidies: compensation for distortions in the pricing of output, in particular in the coal mining sector, and transfers to loss-making firms, prominently in the food and the fuel and power industries. More important for industrial firms in other sectors was the effect of indirect subsidies through a complicated system of subsidized credit and foreign exchange. Schaffer (1990) documented how government policies, such as firm-specific subsidies and tax rebates, caused the soft budget constraints of the Lista 500 firms. The almost total elimination of subsidies in 1990 removed the government from active involvement in industry except through its ongoing attempts to harden the budget constraint by initiating bankruptcy proceedings.

The credit crunch

Following the Big Bang, credit from the banking sector was tight and interest rates were high, reflecting the Big Bang's anti-inflationary focus; firms evaded this constraint, however, through the creation of negotiable interenterprise notes. It was expected that the cutoff from cheap credit would push inefficient firms toward bankruptcy and would encourage credit to be directed toward the most creditworthy borrowers. Banks, however, simply channeled remaining credit to their biggest borrowers. Other firms were left highly credit-constrained, but many found that their high 1989 profits left them in no immediate danger of bankruptcy. Interviewed managers said that their priorities were to first pay the government's dividend tax, then pay other taxes and wages, and pay suppliers last, since these latter liabilities could be forcibly stretched with no real penalty. Suppliers' credits thus became the buffer in the system, allowing firms a margin of adjustment during a period of credit tightening. The sample firms kept ahead of the interfirm credit game by delaying their own payables while accelerating receivables, thereby generating working capital for their own use.

The use of payables and receivables as a mechanism for financing interfirm transactions is not new. Socialist firms are notorious for accumulating unpaid interfirm commitments. Prior to the January reforms, payables plus receivables for the sample firms were around 17 weeks of sales. This sum dropped dramatically in the first quarter of 1990, suggesting that once firms were forced to be responsible for their own cash flows, they insisted on some clearing of interfirm accounts and an improvement of their own financial position. By the end of May 1990, however, the sum of receivables and payables increased again to 13 weeks of sales (see Table 8.2), while the receivables-to-payables ratio had fallen sharply. Managers reported that bank credit was generally unavailable and that they expected few or no losses from their own debtors. The presumption was that if debtors were pushed into bankruptcy by the government, the government would take on responsibility for the bankrupt firm's liabilities.

8.2 Financial variables for sample of Polish firms

Firm	Main product	Average receivables[a] (weeks of sales)			Average payables[b] (weeks of sales)			Inventories (% sales)			Liquidity[c] (% sales)		
		1989	1990.I[d]	1990.05	1989	1990.I[d]	1990.05	1989	1990.I[d]	1990.05	1989	1990.I[d]	1990.05
State-owned firms													
1	Machine tools	20.4	8.7	7.2	8.4	2.1	2.7	30	55	54	33	61	40
2	Computer printers	24.8	4.6	4.6	3.8	2.0	3.3	36	52	55	20	33	30
3	Electric generators	8.0	6.2	6.8	7.1	4.2	5.0	52	80	61	44	225	52
4	Basic chemicals	10.9	5.0	5.3	6.3	1.9	2.6	14	30	20	26	23	26
5	Textiles	11.0	9.9	10.9	7.8	8.2	10.5	38	93	79	30	109	78
6	Garments	7.0	n.a.	7.8	1.9	n.a.	5.9	20	n.a.	64	12	n.a.	57
7	Trucks	5.0	5.8	8.0	7.7	9.3	16.5	31	162	157	31	124	134
State-owned cooperatives													
8	Food processing	9.4	4.7	4.3	3.4	1.3	1.4	79	73	34	105	65	32
Private joint ventures													
9	Wood furniture	32.0	n.a.	n.a.	26.4	n.a.	n.a.	27	n.a.	n.a.	38	n.a.	n.a.
Average for firms in sample		14.7	6.4	6.9	8.1	4.1	6.0	36	78	65	38	92	56

Notes: n.a. = not available.

a. Average receivables is the average of beginning of year and current receivables, expressed in weeks of sales during the period.
b. Average payables is the average of beginning of year and current receivables, expressed in weeks of sales during the period.
c. Liquidity is working capital: the sum of working credits, payables, and foreign exchange bank accounts.
d. 1990.I represents data for the first quarter of 1990; 1990.05 is for end-May 1990.
Sources include interviews with firms, Central Statistical Office of Poland, and Central Planning Office of Poland.

In a significant development, suppliers' credits by the second quarter began being transformed into negotiable interfirm notes, costing far less than bank credit. Firms thus found an innovative way to avoid the disruption associated with the credit squeeze. Interfirm credits had benefits. In the face of rigidities in the banking system, firms could maintain a margin of flexibility for production and could also finance new distributors, thereby making markets more competitive. Continued growth of interfirm credit without regulation, however, limited the effectiveness of monetary policy and increased the risk of cascading bankruptcy. This latter concern had been present in 1989 before the Big Bang when the government considered a scheme to net out debts across all firms.

The pressure of import competition and the need to export

Changes in the international trade regime had a significant impact on markets, both for inputs and outputs. The extent of import competition varied by sector, but the continuing depreciation of the zloty against the hard currencies moderated foreign competitive pressure. The exchange rate alone, however, could not protect domestic producers. For example, the truck manufacturer's price was far below world prices for a truck of similar size, but since the quality of its trucks was also far lower, the firm continued to face strong competition from used trucks imported from Western Europe.[10]

The future of CMEA markets was highly uncertain. Doubts about payment, especially from the U.S.S.R., made firms hesitate to fulfill existing export contracts. According to the managers of the sample firms, the CMEA could be a viable market if trade were conducted at international prices, if the ruble rate were adjusted to reflect its true relative value, and if the uncertainty of payments was eliminated.

Bankruptcy policy for state-owned enterprises

The gradual implementation of the January 1990 bankruptcy law and the focus on privatization (Milanovic, this volume) shifted decisions on exit to individual firms, at least in principle. Yet, bankruptcy as an institution was not completely credible: firms in the sample believed that there was an implicit government guarantee to honor interfirm credit and to bail out lossmakers.

Nonpayment of the dividend tax was intended to initiate rehabilitation or bankruptcy procedures, according to the January 1989 law on finances of state enterprises. It was not until the threat of rehabilitation for nonpaying firms was reaffirmed in January 1990, however, that dividend payment

---

[10]This is an example of the soft/hard good distinction. See Schrenk (this volume) and Hillman and Schnytzer (this volume).

became a top priority for firms. From January 1990 the dividend became a fixed 32 percent of the capital base on which it was levied (a firm's Basic Assets Fund) and it was unrelated to profits or other performance measures. Because of the high inflation in 1989 the government also ordered a revaluation of enterprises' Basic Assets Fund in January by a factor of 14. The fixed nature of the payment means that it is less like a capitalist dividend as paid to shareholders and more similar to an interest payment on senior debt. Its importance for most firms was small: the dividend tax averaged only 3 percent of sales in the first quarter of 1990 for the sample firms and for no firm was it higher than 6 percent of sales.

Ownership, control, and privatization

At the time this study was conducted, ownership and control of the enterprises were ill-defined. The formal owner of the firm was clearly understood, at least by management, to be the Treasury. However, the control and supervision previously exercised by the Ministry of Industry had altogether ceased, even in strategic industries. The role of local government had expanded, but only in the areas of zoning, environmental control, and employee benefits. Some control was exercised within firms by workers' councils, but with few exceptions the general manager of the firm was the key decision maker. Nevertheless, job security for employees was usually also an objective of management. This is because the workers' councils were powerful enough to influence management and because some managers were formerly workers' council members and/or trade union activists.

All state-owned firms had elected workers' councils with formal powers covering all aspects of management. The workers' council approved profit distribution, the sale of fixed assets, and the appointment of deputy directors. Most important, it recommended a general manager from nominations made by the Ministry of Industry (subject to final approval by the Ministry). Management served at the pleasure of the workers' council, and all but two of the sample firms had very recently changed their general manager. The role played by the workers' councils, whether active or passive, however, depended on the individuals elected to them. Relations between management and workers' councils were described as good in all firms. Workers' councils were frequently cited as helpful, perhaps serving as a counterweight to trade unions. It should be noted that by constraining wages, the excess wages tax defused a potential area of contention among management, workers' councils, and trade unions.[11]

---

[11] The sample firms generally had two main unions, Solidarity and OPZZ (founded by the Communist party during the period of martial law in response to the rise of Solidarity), with roughly equal membership, and often a third small nonparty-affiliated union. The share of nonunion workers was sometimes as high as 40 percent. The trade unions' scope of activity was legally confined to approval of layoffs and wage agreements.

Workers' councils did not appear to consider themselves owners, though they exercised some rights that are, in a Western market economy, usually assigned to owners. Management usually doubted that workers wanted to be shareholders in the firm in which they worked. Unless firms were very secure and profitable, workers believed that ownership would bring them risk but little benefit. Only in the machine tool firm, which was well capitalized and had almost no liabilities, did workers express a desire to buy shares. Management and workers assumed without exception that in a privatization program, employees would have to purchase shares (perhaps at some discount) and would not receive shares without charge.

Joint ventures with foreign firms provided enterprises with an impetus to resolve the ownership issue. Strategies were various. Some involved breaking up the firm into different entities in order to facilitate joint ventures. The search for foreign partners, while not the sole element of a firms' adjustment strategy, was nonetheless intense. Firms believed that partners would offer advantages of market access and marketing expertise, technology and licenses, modern management methods, and new capital. Ironically, with ownership status unresolved, potential foreign partners were asking the government for guarantees on their investments. The terms of offers from foreign firms, however, were not always favorable to the Polish firm, especially if the firm was in great need of foreign assistance. For example, the electronics firm was negotiating a contract with a Western firm to provide new technology under license, joint production, and guarantees of distribution in Western markets; the prospective Western partner, however, was not providing any capital and was demanding a high fee for its services. On the other hand, the electrical generator maker was negotiating a favorable arrangement which would result in the acquisition of 75 percent of the firm by a Western firm in the same business. Overall, the favorable view of joint ventures among managers of Polish firms, and managers' eagerness to be able to commit to a joint venture, placed pressure on the government to resolve the ownership issue.

With ownership issues unresolved and privatization not proceeding, state-owned firms nominally belonged to the Treasury, local government exercised some regulatory powers, and management and workers' councils co-managed most aspects of these firms' operation. Firm decision making under these circumstances was subject to complex considerations and considerable uncertainty.

Conclusions

This chapter has described the adjustments and accommodations made by individual firms in response to the changes associated with the Polish Big Bang. These observations provide only a partial picture of the response, but it is possible to present some conclusions. In general, the extensive adjustment made by firms in the sample reflects flexibility in firm behavior.

In the aftermath of the demand shock and the product market liberalization shock associated with the Big Bang, there is evidence that state-owned firms in some industrial sectors made significant positive adjustments. Overall, the best-placed firms appeared to be those with previous exposure to Western markets.

One positive response was the rationalization of labor use. Firms were cutting input costs by searching for new suppliers and rewriting contracts with existing suppliers. They were actively searching for new markets and new products. Firms responded to the tightening of credit in the first semester of 1990 by expanding suppliers' credits and creating interfirm notes.

Some institutional features influenced firms' behavior. Workers' councils appeared to play a positive role; in some cases, they assisted management in its relations with trade unions. The excess wages tax, by placing an externally imposed ceiling on wage increases, might have allowed management, workers' councils, and trade unions to enjoy a form of honeymoon during the initial adjustment of firms to a post-Big Bang economy. The tax alleviated the wage pressure that could have built as the control of firms became decentralized and the ownership vacuum became apparent.

Uncertainty about firm ownership inhibited the implementation of longer-term survival strategies, especially as firms sought joint ventures with Western firms. It was becoming increasingly important to resolve this issue because continued delay would stall the adjustment.

The view of firm behavior that we have presented is based on observations when the transition to a market economy was far from complete. Uncertainty was extreme. The new tax structure (which included a personal income tax and a value added tax) had not yet replaced a socialist tax structure heavily dependent on revenues from payroll and turnover taxes; the social safety net still required further development and refinement; and the process by which privatization was to take place was not yet fully defined. Most important, firms required new investment, both from foreign and domestic sources in order to ensure medium-term success.

References

Calvo, Guillermo, and Fabrizio Coricelli. 1992. "Stagflationary Effects of Stabilization Programs in Reforming Socialist Countries: Enterprise-Side and Household-Side Factors." *The World Bank Economic Review* 6(1).

Coricelli, Fabrizio, and Roberto Rocha. 1991. "Stabilization Programs in Eastern Europe: A Comparative Analysis of the Polish and Yugoslav Programs of 1990." Policy, Research and External Affairs Working Paper 732. World Bank, Country Economics Department, Washington, D.C. Processed.

Frydman, Roman, and Stanislaw Wellisz. 1991. "The Ownership-Control Structure and the Behavior of Polish Enterprises during the 1990 Reforms: Macroeconomic Measures and Microeconomic Response." In Vittorio Corbo, Fabrizio Coricelli, and Jan Bossak, eds., *Reforming Central and Eastern European Economies: Initial Results and Challenges*. World Bank Symposium. Washington, D.C.: World Bank.

Hillman, Arye L. 1991. "Some Problems of Economic Measurement in the Transition from Planned Socialism." In Petr O. Aven, ed., *Economies in Transition: Statistical Measures Now and in the Future*. Laxenburg: International Institute for Applied System Analysis, 69-78.

Hillman, Arye L., and Adi Schnytzer. 1992. "Creating the Reform-Resistant Dependent Economy: Socialist Comparative Advantage, Enterprise Incentives, and the CMEA." This volume.

Hinds, Manuel. 1992. "Policy Effectiveness in Reforming Socialist Economies." This volume.

Lipton, David, and Jeffrey Sachs. 1990. "Creating a Market Economy in Eastern Europe: The Case of Poland." *Brookings Papers on Economic Activity* 75-147.

Milanovic, Branko. 1992. "Privatization Options and Procedures." This volume.

Saldanha, Fernando. 1992. "Self-Management: Theory and Yugoslav Practice." This volume.

Schaffer, Mark. 1990. "Taxation, Subsidization, and Regulation of State-Owned Enterprises in Poland." In *European Economy: Economic Transformation in Hungary and Poland*. Brussels: Commission of the European Communities.

Schrenk, Martin. 1990. "Poland: Reform of the Economic System." World Bank, Socialist Economies Reform Unit, Country Economics Department, Washington, D.C. Processed.

———. 1992. "The CMEA System of Trade and Payments." This volume.

II. Foreign Trade

A. The Legacy of Past Interdependencies

9

The CMEA System of Trade and Payments: Initial Conditions for Institutional Change

Martin Schrenk

The Council for Mutual Economic Assistance (CMEA) provided the principal framework for international transactions between socialist economies. This chapter describes the CMEA system and explains how changes to the system were necessary to facilitate the transition of East European countries from socialism.[1] The chapter begins with a summary of the history of the CMEA, the organizational structure and institutional principles, and the emergence of awareness of the need to reform the system. A brief statistical overview of the importance of CMEA trade for its members is then presented, followed by a description of the traditional "institutional model" of the CMEA system. Major practical defects of the CMEA regime are identified, and a summary evaluation is provided of the system's legacy.

---

[1]The CMEA system was never a major concern of Western literature; Western economists focused on issues of Western external debt, borrowing requirements and creditworthiness in convertible currencies. The paradigm of multilateral trade and currency convertibility was also not suited to an analysis of the CMEA regime of international trade and payments.

This is a revised version of World Bank PRE Working Paper 753, August 1991.

Organization and initiatives for reform

The CMEA was founded in 1949 as the trade and payments system of the socialist countries. Its European members were the U.S.S.R., Poland, the German Democratic Republic, Czechoslovakia, Hungary, Romania, and Bulgaria ("the Six"). Mongolia, Cuba, and Vietnam were non-European members of the Council; Yugoslavia was an associate member.

The highest level of the CMEA was the Council Session, the regular annual meeting of heads of governments. The CMEA's permanent board was the Executive Committee which consisted of government representatives. A number of council committees and standing commissions met regularly to discuss specific matters of sectoral planning and coordination. The core organization was the CMEA Secretariat. The CMEA created two special financial institutions, the International Bank for Economic Cooperation (IBEC), and the International Investment Bank (IIB), both located in Moscow, which was the CMEA's headquarters.

IBEC managed the complex clearing between the accounts of the members and short-term credits. Accounts were held and settled bilaterally in "transferable rubles" (TRs), the common currency for CMEA trade and payment transactions. IIB was mainly concerned with financing of joint projects; it also undertook external borrowing in convertible currencies for joint projects, and on a small scale financed investment projects in developing countries (principally in the non-European CMEA members). By end of 1987 IIB was reported to have committed a total of TR10 billion ($16 billion at the—meaningless—official exchange rate) to a total of 87 projects; 70 percent of total commitments were for the energy sector. While IIB participated in joint projects, not all joint projects relied on IIB financing. IIB loans typically had a maturity of between 5 and 15 years at interest rates of between 3 and 5 percent, with reportedly lower rates for "priority projects" and for lending to developing countries.

The political principle of the CMEA was "equality, sovereignty, and interest." Unanimity was required on all decisions of common concern. In contrast to the European Economic Community (EEC), the CMEA did not have an executive or legislative mandate. Common decisions were merely declarations of intent and were not legally binding, unless translated subsequently into (mostly bilateral) treaties. The unlimited veto power which the principle gave to every member was circumscribed merely by the "principle of interestedness," which excluded veto rights of countries not directly affected by the question. Nevertheless, the lack of supranationality in procedures and the emphasis on consensus tended to reduce the outcome of initiatives to their lowest common denominator, thereby impeding the CMEA's effectiveness; a case in point is the failure of the Soviet initiative during the Khrushchev era to institute an integrated CMEA-wide planning system.

In the more than four decades from its inception in 1948 until its demise in 1991, the CMEA developed an elaborate institutional framework for the planning and implementation of bilateral clearing trade between members. This did not create a "common market," but it did create a distinct "economic region" by fostering preferential relationships codified in bilateral treaties between governments.[2] This framework, which I refer to as the "CMEA regime," is an outgrowth of the traditional system of central planning. Rules and procedures differed fundamentally from those of convertible currency (CC) trade regimes.

Initiatives for system reform, in particular those emanating from the U.S.S.R., extended to the CMEA regime. By 1987 proponents of system reform considered the CMEA regime to be rigid and inefficient, and to have reached the limits of its usefulness. The 1987 session of the Council of Ministers passed a resolution advocating that the CMEA shift from a "plan coordination" to a "market relations" framework. The 1988 Session discussed a document referred to as the "collective concept." This document was not published in full, but its goal for CMEA transformation was:

> . . . *to overhaul the integration mechanism and to construct a qualitatively new model of intra-community cooperation . . . centered on the creation of a single market of the CMEA member countries, complete with free movement of goods, services, and other factors of production. The need for such a market stems objectively from the logic of economic reforms in the individual socialist countries, which are centered on the promotion of commodity-money (i.e., market) relations.*[3]

This radical shift in concept and terminology pointed to a fundamentally different vision of the role and function of the CMEA. Little however happened until the Forty-fifth Council Session in Sofia in January 1990, when the U.S.S.R. announced its intention to switch in January 1991 to an undefined framework of convertible currency accounting and some form of convertibility among members. This would end the CMEA.

The importance and pattern of CMEA trade

Table 9.1 gives an overview of the structure of global CMEA trade. The figures demonstrate the importance of intraregional trade for its members. Fifty-six percent of CMEA exports were traded within the CMEA region; for

---

[2]CMEA trade and payment agreements could in principle be multilateral. The difficulty of negotiating multilateral agreements with the degree of specificity dictated by the CMEA procedures of contracting and settlement made multilateral arrangements an exception in practice.

[3]Georgi Atanasov, Chairman of the Council of Ministers, during the Forty-fourth CMEA Council Session of the CMEA in Prague, July 6, 1988. FBIS-EEU-88-130, July 7, 1988, p. 15.

the U.S.S.R., intraregional trade accounted for approximately one half of total exports, and for the Six (in the aggregate and on average) accounted for approximately 60 percent.

Table 9.1 World structure of exports by area of trade, 1985 *(US$ billion)*

Area/country of origin	OECD	Developing countries	Yugoslavia	China	U.S.S.R.	Six	CMEA	World
			Area/country of destination					
OECD	909.4	269.2	6.0	27.0	20.6	15.2	(35.8)	1,247.4
Developing countries[a]	304.2	142.9	1.9	7.6	10.5	6.8	(17.3)	473.9
Yugoslavia	3.5	1.7	—	0.1	3.4	1.8	(5.2)	10.7
China	11.4	13.9	0	—	1.1	1.0	(2.1)	27.3
U.S.S.R.	21.3	15.7	0.2	0.9	—	40.8	(40.8)	78.9
Six	20.4	9.5	1.5	1.5	32.9	17.9	(50.8)	83.7
CMEA	(41.7)	(25.2)	(1.7)	(2.4)	(32.9)	(58.7)	(91.6)	(162.6)
World	270.2	452.9	9.6	37.1	68.4	83.5	(151.9)	1,921.7

— = not applicable.
a. Except for Yugoslavia and China.
Source: United Nations (1989).

The importance of intraregional trade and trade with the U.S.S.R. is highlighted in Table 9.2; the table shows that CMEA trade relations predominantly took the form of bilateral exchange between each of the Six and the U.S.S.R.[4]

CMEA trade exhibited a distinct pattern of commodity specialization. The U.S.S.R. supplied the Six with raw materials, including a high share of primary energy, mainly in exchange for manufactured goods. Hungarian data, which are representative for the Six, illustrate the commodity pattern in Table 9.3. The U.S.S.R. exported hard goods in worldwide demand in exchange for soft goods with only a limited, if any, market outside the CMEA; this established a high degree of dependency among the members. The commodity composition of trade indicates that the degree of dependency was quite different for the Six than for the U.S.S.R. While the latter could in principle shift trade to non-CMEA countries without major

---

[4]CMEA trade figures in Tables 9.1 and 9.2 are not strictly comparable with figures for other countries. They are computed from national data in national prices, converted at the official exchange rates between national currencies and the U.S. dollar. While these exchange rates were roughly in line with purchasing power parities for the Six, the official exchange rate between the TR and the U.S. dollar ($1.6/TR) was substantially overvalued. In addition, relative prices differed between CMEA and world market prices, with a general upward bias for manufactured goods and downward bias for raw materials. As a result, the numbers for the Six may be a reasonable approximation, whereas the numbers for the U.S.S.R. are likely to be overstatements (that is, the effect of an overvaluation of the TR exceeded the effect of underpricing).

economic disruption,[5] this was not feasible for the Six because of compelling structural supply-side constraints.[6]

Table 9.2 Shares of the CMEA in trade of member countries; shares of the U.S.S.R. in trade of member countries; 1989 *(percent)*

	CMEA in total		U.S.S.R. in CMEA		U.S.S.R. in total	
	X	M	X	M	X	M
Bulgaria	83	73	79	74	66	54
CSSR	54	55	57	54	31	30
GDR	42	38	57	58	24	22
Hungary	39	39	62	56	24	22
Poland	35	32	60	56	21	18
Romania	40	55	58	59	23	32
U.S.S.R.	46	50	—	—	—	—

— = not applicable.
Note: X = exports; M = imports.
Source: van Brabant (1990).

Table 9.3 Hungary: commodity composition (ruble and nonruble), 1985 *(percent)*

	Exports		Imports	
	Ruble	Nonruble	Ruble	Nonruble
Energy	0.8	8.1	31.6	11.3
Other raw materials	1.9	8.6	12.7	13.3
Semifinished goods	10.5	25.9	12.9	30.7
Machinery including spares	56.5	15.7	29.6	23.4
Other manufactures	17.2	13.2	10.5	10.3
Agricultural and food products	13.1	28.6	2.7	11.1

Note: "Ruble trade" is an approximation of CMEA trade; some CMEA trade transactions were denominated and cleared bilaterally in convertible currency (and, thus, were only superficially different from ruble trade); and a small percentage was denominated and actually "paid for" in convertible currency through a transfer of fungible funds. On the other hand, most trade with other socialist countries and some developing countries was denominated and cleared bilaterally in convertible currency.
Source: Central Statistical Office, Government of Hungary.

---

[5]As argued in the summary evaluation below, the U.S.S.R. would have benefitted from cutting itself off from the CMEA because of the relative ease with which it could transfer its CMEA exports to other markets; it would have, however, experienced some transitional difficulties with transport infrastructure and in obtaining spare parts for existing imported equipment.

[6]On how these constraints influenced CMEA trade, see Hillman and Schnytzer (this volume).

The institutional model of the CMEA regime

I consider now the traditional CMEA regime as an institutional model, identifying the main actors, principal rules, and interconnections.[7] The model presented here is a simplified picture of a more complex reality and will be subsequently refined. During the 1980s the difference between the model and reality widened, as it also did among countries, although often more in pronouncement than in fact.

Perceived advantages of integration

"Socialist integration" and a "socialist division of labor" were frequently cited objectives of the CMEA. The doctrine of static comparative advantage was, however, rarely invoked; the principal economic advantages of the CMEA were perceived as economies of scale realized by "cooperation" and "specialization." There could be capital cost savings from predictable output levels and composition, a concentration of research and development through coordinated programs with free exchange of results, and independence from exogenous cyclical disturbances. Achieving "security of supply" in the face of real or imagined political disruption of international trade was also a major goal, supporting a tendency toward regional autarky.

Industrial cooperation

Cooperation usually took the form of horizontal specialization agreements that gave the country of specialization a virtual monopoly on certain final products. Vertical specialization involving complex cross-country supply networks for parts and components was more difficult to organize through intergovernment agreements, and was accordingly rare. Supply of raw materials by the U.S.S.R. to the Six was a major exception. Cooperation agreements were mostly bilateral and long-term in nature.

Trade planning

CMEA trade was planned through a series of consultations or "plan coordination." The consultations were an integral part of the national five-year planning exercises, and focused on an exchange of information about national requirements and the availability of tradeables. Information was derived from national balances of supply and requirements. While participation in plan coordination was mandatory, extent and contents of

---

[7]As will be evident at the end of this section, the CMEA regime was not, as often thought, a random collection of irrational practices. Rather, it exhibited a great deal of internal logic and overall consistency, though its logic corresponded to the model of central planning from which it was derived rather than to the model underlying the conventional theory of international trade.

deliveries were voluntary. Bilateral medium-term government protocols set the precise planned volume and composition of trade. These agreements often included or were based on production cooperation. Over the planning cycle, the medium-term protocols were respecified further in annual protocols. The planned trade balances were broken down into a number of subcategories to be balanced separately. Since frequently both quantities and value balances were determined (either in absolute terms or in relation to past transactions), trade planning often set implicit transaction prices.

Quantity bias

The targets of bilateral protocols had a distinct quantity bias because of: (a) the origin of CMEA trade planning in traditional central planning through material balances, where trade is the "closing" item, and (b) the practice of breaking down a total into specific sub-balances. Even if *ex ante* balances were expressed in value terms for purposes of monitoring or statistical aggregation, value targets tended to become physical indicators because of understandings on commodity composition, or on quantity and price indices. This quantity bias, however, did not imply that CMEA trade was "barter trade."[8]

Hard/soft goods

The CMEA trade planning procedures and the nature of delivery commitments gave rise to the distinction between "soft" goods (that were uncompetitive in world markets, and tradeable only within the region and as part of bilateral quota regimes), and "hard" goods (that were fully tradeable in the competitive world market).[9] It was to the advantage of each country to maximize the exchange of CMEA imports of hard goods for CMEA exports of soft goods, in order to conserve convertible currency. This preference was referred to as "structural bilateralism." Incompatible country positions complicated the problem of setting and balancing subcategories of CMEA trade.

---

[8]Barter trade is inhibited by informational constraints. Under a pure barter arrangement, the number of specific commodity exchange ratios is $n[n - 1]/2$, where n is the number of commodities. For n=100, the number of ratios is 4,950. For any realistic number of commodities, and when the same pattern is extended to every pair of countries, the number of price ratios quickly approaches infinity (McKinnon 1979).

[9]According to an alternative definition "hard" goods were in shortage within the CMEA, and "soft" goods in surplus within the CMEA. Both definitions yield largely identical results, but there can be notable differences. For example, most agricultural products were "hard" according to the second definition, but "soft" according to the first because of the inability to access alternative markets.

Imported inputs

Many manufactured goods incorporated inputs in the form of raw materials, intermediate goods, and components imported from the CMEA and the West. If a country's average content of imported hard inputs of its exports to the CMEA exceeded that of its CMEA trading partner, and if the foreign exchange cost or benefit per unit of domestic currency differed between the two regimes, separate accounting and balancing were necessary to monitor hard-currency imbalances.

Trade management

In the CMEA regime, trade was managed by a small number of large Foreign Trade Organizations (FTOs) that operated under government supervision and had trading monopolies for designated products. This ensured that delivery contracts were concluded, and that deliveries were made in accordance with trade protocols. Central control over the maintenance of agreed delivery balances was thereby also facilitated, and the real economy was isolated from the effects of currency transactions.

Delivery priorities

CMEA trade was based on international treaties, so if current demand could not be met, CMEA exports had, at least in principle, the highest priority in the central allocation of output. Conversely, deliveries to convertible currency markets were, at least in principle, a residual after treaty obligations and domestic requirements were satisfied. Similarly, countries were legally bound to absorb agreed-upon CMEA imports, and to place the burden of adjustment on domestic deliveries and convertible currency imports in the case of an unplanned glut.[10]

Quotas

Because of bilateral treaty commitments, the need to maintain distinct sub-balances, and the lack of convertibility, an elaborate regime of import and export monitoring and control was required. *Ex ante* and *ex post* flows could be matched only through mandatory quotas, even if not described as such. Quotas could take the form of ceilings and/or floors on exports or imports, and were often enterprise-specific for each country (see Inotai

---

[10]Probably for no other element of the model was the difference between principle and practice as wide as that regarding relative priorities. The preferred practical response to such shortages was to default in bilateral agreements as long as retaliation in the form of withholding deliveries from the other side did not create prohibitive costs. Penalties for violations of protocols or contracts were often difficult to enforce.

1986). Ad hoc quota adjustments were required to manage emerging imbalances.

Prices

The CMEA tried but failed to develop its own set of regional relative prices based on the labor theory of value. In practice, each country had its own set of relative prices, reflecting domestic distributional and political priorities, that deviated from relative prices in both the competitive world market and other CMEA countries. Prices for CMEA trade were established with reference to world market prices. Moving five-year averages, converted into TRs (the so-called Bucharest principle), served as the basis for negotiations on the determination of regional transaction prices. As these negotiations were strictly bilateral, and aimed at bilateral balancing, the same good could be traded at different prices between different pairs of countries. CMEA prices therefore constituted sensitive information.

Price equalization

Since each CMEA country's internal relative prices were neither related to domestic supply and demand conditions, comparative advantage nor opportunity costs, domestic prices differed from both world market prices and CMEA transaction prices. Because of these inconsistencies, CMEA prices were pertinent for accounts of the large FTOs that were mandatory intermediaries in CMEA trade, rather than accounts of the export-producing and import-receiving enterprises. Domestic enterprises dealt with FTOs exclusively in domestic prices and domestic currency, and were thus completely isolated from external transaction prices. The inconsistency of relative prices created a potential for windfall profits and losses that was neutralized through the institution of "price equalization."[11]

Price equalization payments were ultimately settled through the government budget. The size and sign of the net balance could under certain conditions be adjusted by changes in internal prices, and/or by changes in

---

[11]Price equalization is used here as a generic term. The actual arrangement could work in a variety of ways—for instance, through the use of foreign trade "multipliers" or through "coefficients" in actual accounting, or through procedures which seemingly amounted to a multiple exchange rate system. In each case, the purpose and the effect were essentially as discussed above. An example of the actual outcome is the Hungarian "producers turnover tax" discussed below. See also Abel, Hillman, and Tarr (this volume).

exchange rates.[12] Price equalization was neither an amalgam of arbitrary distortions nor a trade management instrument, nor were there associated fiscal functions. It was rather a mechanism to maintain orderly financial relations in the face of the autonomous pricing practices of the CMEA countries that resulted in widely differing sets of relative prices. "Taxes" and "subsidies" may be convenient shorthand terms when used with reference to price equalization, but they can be misleading if used without reference to the specific systemic context. These were not the taxes and subsidies of the Western neoclassical international trade literature.

The payments system and convertibility

The CMEA system of bilateral clearing did not involve international payments through transfer of currency to or from accounts in another country. The TR lacked two major properties of money: it was neither a means of payment, nor was it a store of value (Ausch 1969, 1972). The total volume of TRs in the CMEA system was merely a measure of the volume of the outstanding bilateral surplus or deficit in national clearing accounts held by the countries with the IBEC (van Brabant 1977). A corollary of bilateral balancing and settlement through clearing is that the system functioned without currency reserves. By the same token, the system lacked financial convertibility. Predetermined commodity balances and domestic allocation regimes ruled out the possibility of using a surplus in clearing balances to "shop around" for procurement opportunities in the country with a debit; hence the "commodity inconvertibility" of the TR. This undermined a third function of money, that of an unambiguous measure of value. Surpluses in bilateral balances could be freely used in the deficit country only if bilateral subsidiary understandings existed, which specifically designated commodities and a quantitative ceiling for qualifying transactions. Of course, the lack of bilateral financial and commodity convertibility meant that financial multilateralism was also absent.

---

[12]The fiscal role of the exchange rate through the mechanism of price equalization is analyzed in the Appendix. In stark simplification, three cases can be distinguished: (a) If external transactions are in balance both in international (TR) and domestic currency, then the net balance of price equalization is zero; (b) if external transactions are in balance in international (TR) prices—that is, if the rules of bilateral clearing are adhered to—but the transactions are not in balance in domestic currency, then the aggregate net balance of all price equalization transactions has a specific value, reflecting the aggregate domestic imbalance, regardless of the exchange rate; (c) if external transactions in TR prices are not in balance—that is, if either a credit is involved, or trade planning and/or management miss the balancing target—then a change in the exchange rate changes the net balance, leading either to net budget revenue or expenditure in the amount of the net imbalance. See the Appendix for details.

Credits

Bilateral clearing of matching value balances, and the absence of properties of money for the common currency, also ruled out "commercial" trade credits for foreign trade. Because of currency and commodity inconvertibility, imbalances became "involuntary trade credits" which were of no value to the surplus country, unless there was mutual agreement for future clearing settlement. A major concern of prudent trade management was thus to avoid accumulating an unplanned surplus, and export quotas were the preferred instrument to prevent such an accumulation. Countries could, however, agree on medium-term commodity and long-term investment credits in the form of specified temporary surpluses and deficit positions in specific subaccounts. Interest and principal were in general settled in the same way, and the agreements were built into future commodity balances.

Balance of payments

The practice of establishing planned sub-balances and settling *ex post* through clearing made redundant macroeconomic management of the balance of payments between CMEA countries. External balance became a microeconomic task. Furthermore, because of the absence of fungibility across sub-balances, aggregate bilateral balances had no economic meaning, and could hide large partial surpluses and deficits that were not and could not be consolidated. The aggregate balance of a particular CMEA country with the region as a whole was an even less meaningful construct, as this could hide huge side-by-side bilateral surpluses and deficits that could not be cleared multilaterally.

Exchange rates

Exchange rates were used merely to facilitate statistical aggregation across CMEA currencies, because (a) trade flows were set in bilateral agreements and managed directly through government authorities or FTOs as their agents; (b) firms' financial claims and obligations from CMEA trade were denominated in domestic prices and currencies; (c) windfall gains and losses in the accounts of FTOs were neutralized through price equalization; and (d) external balance was not a macroeconomic management task. There was, however, as discussed above, a link between exchange rates and the aggregate fiscal balance.

Major practical defects of the CMEA regime

The CMEA system of rules and procedures, although internally consistent, had a number of endemic practical defects.

Consistency and reform

The CMEA trade regime impeded reform elsewhere in the economic system by locking member countries into a traditional system of economic management.[13] Countries seeking system reform would be "out of step" with their CMEA partners. Once the U.S.S.R. embarked on a drive for system reform, however, it was able, because of its economic weight, to convert CMEA institutions into a means of "transmission" of internal reforms to other countries. The interdependence, which was characteristic of the CMEA regime and which hampered reform in individual member countries, was reflected in the simultaneous end of the CMEA system for all members.

Deficiencies

Three deficiencies of the initial rationale for the CMEA became increasingly obvious. First, the traditional Marxist preoccupation with dynamic effects—according to which a country's comparative advantage is not given but rather is achieved through a process of "learning by doing"—was not matched by provisions to ensure a semblance of static efficiency. Second, the concern for achieving economies of scale through cooperative agreements was not balanced by a concern for maintaining competition. And third, as detente progressed, the concern for security of supply lost its earlier importance.

Assessment of gains from trade

Domestic and CMEA pricing conventions, and the lack of meaningful exchange rates, precluded any practicable means of evaluating domestic resource costs or assessing gains from trade. One consequence of this deficiency was the inability of governments to evaluate the economic efficiency of any particular exchange of goods.[14] The arbitrary pricing rules

---

[13]For elaboration of the consequences for trade dependence and agents' incentives, see Hillman and Schnytzer (this volume).

[14]Evaluation coefficients were reportedly used in some countries for this purpose. Most popular was the ratio of domestic currency units earned or spent per TR for a specific transaction. This coefficient is not, however, a measure of domestic resource cost, given pricing and exchange rate practices. Moreover, since the exchange rate between national currencies and the TR (which theoretically sets the dividing line between "efficient" and "inefficient" transactions) was in some instances reportedly a past ratio of currency valuation of all export transactions for a previous period, that is, the weighted average of all specific transactions, a circular analysis would result.

suggest that a sizeable portion of CMEA trade was "inefficient," while opportunities for efficient trade remained unrevealed.[15]

A related consequence was the suspicion each country had of having been a consistent loser from CMEA trade. This created a pervasive distrust of CMEA transactions. There is anecdotal evidence to suggest that each country experienced some instances of substantial "losses" as a result of CMEA transactions.

Complaints gave rise to an extended debate among Western economists about the extent of "implicit subsidies" by the U.S.S.R. to the CMEA Six during the 1970s and much of the 1980s, in the form of underpriced raw materials exchanged for overpriced manufactures. Estimates of the total implicit transfer differ widely. However, Western analysts are in general convinced that during this period the U.S.S.R. was by a wide margin the main "loser."[16] Supporting evidence is provided by the fact that the Eastern European Six—with the exception of Romania—did not make a determined effort to reduce the share of CMEA in total trade, though the principles of trade planning allowed for such a strategy.[17]

Procedures

A further shortcoming of the CMEA regime was that it required cumbersome and inherently inefficient clearing within bilateral sub-balances, for which export quotas were the major instrument of management. The

---

[15]As discussed below, even if world market prices were precisely known and product differences could be ignored, the Bucharest principle was still logically flawed, as these external prices did not reflect opportunity costs within the CMEA.

[16]Dawisha (1988, p. 90) notes: "The issues of economic leverage, exploitation, and subsidies were very troublesome in the Soviet-East European relationship. The East Europeans uniformly felt held back and constrained by the ties with Moscow, and the Soviets considered the East Europeans as ungrateful. In every crisis, these issues came quickly to the surface, along with charges and counter charges . . . ." According to the same source, the aggregate implicit transfers from the Six to the U.S.S.R. were around $14 billion (at the official exchange rate) for the period 1945–53, that is, of an order of magnitude comparable with Marshall Plan deliveries to Western Europe. Estimates of transfers in the opposite direction, which combine the effects of biased prices and the overvaluation of the TR, range as high as $80 billion for the period 1971–80 (Dawisha 1988, p. 88). There is evidence of continuing "subsidies" in Soviet oil deliveries—in spite of drastically lowered dollar-reference prices—due to the overvaluation of the TR. In addition to these "hidden" subsidies, the U.S.S.R. accumulated an aggregate trade surplus with the Six in the order of $50 billion between 1971 and 1986 (Machowski 1988, p. 440); a substantial portion was not part of formal credit arrangements and hence was, for all practical purposes, uncollectible.

[17]The nature of a strategy for a disengagement from CMEA were apparent from procedures of trade planning and from the need to maintain balance in the clearing account. A country which was determined to reduce its CMEA share merely had to systematically reduce its initial "offer" of demand and supply. This would have left the partner country, if it wanted to avoid running up involuntary trade credits, little choice but to settle on lower quantities of trade.

essentially bilateral nature of CMEA trade was the result of procedural complexity rather than a process of strategic decision making.

The cumbersome procedures depressed trade. In order to maintain bilateral balances for specific subcategories of goods, the obvious—if not only—means of assuring effective trade planning was to maintain export volumes "at safe levels," that is, at levels so low that both trading partners were reasonably certain that unplanned trade credits could be avoided.

The commodity specialization of FTOs was frequently determined in terms of export mix (serving a diverse clientele's import requirements), or by the import needs of the export-supplying producers (handling a broad spectrum of commodities which often paralleled other FTOs). In either case, the range of goods tended to be more diffuse on the import side than the export side, giving FTOs a predisposition to focus their expertise and initiatives on exports. The result was a systematic bias against CMEA imports and—because of feedback to trade planning—a volume of trade lower than might otherwise have been feasible, or desirable (Ausch 1969).

Trade patterns

The practice of having trade managed by a few large FTOs, and excluding thereby the export producing and import receiving firms, had a number of undesirable consequences for the trade structure. The generation and exchange of product information was suppressed, making CMEA trade informationally inefficient. It was unnecessary, and also impossible, for enterprises to develop an export marketing infrastructure. Because exports were guaranteed and underwritten by bilateral treaties—and this was particularly the case with bilateral specialization agreements—monopolies were created which gave export producers no incentive to be concerned with product standards, delivery terms, and customer satisfaction, when combined with sellers' market conditions. The practice of trade planning and reliance on detailed bilateral protocols also tended to restrict changes in the composition of trade to incremental adjustments in past negotiated quantities and prices; this limited trade-expansion opportunities from product development.

Production structure

Access to low-cost imported raw materials and assured exports, regardless of production costs, were advantageous to CMEA producers in the short run, in that domestic enterprises were shielded from exogenous disturbances and could achieve consistently high output levels and acceptable financial results. In the long run, however, structural change was inhibited. Continued access in the 1970s and much of the 1980s to cheap crude oil and natural gas from the U.S.S.R. caused CMEA members to neglect energy conservation needs. The ease with which CMEA members disposed of manufacturing output in the U.S.S.R. led them to not upgrade output mix and process technologies in line with world market standards. Production activities were maintained for goods that were not viable in non-CMEA trade. The isolation of the domestic economy from changes in world relative prices and from product and process technological innovation ossified the industrial structure, making industries increasingly uncompetitive and further restricting trade possibilities to bilateral CMEA agreements. Enterprises were therefore often almost exclusively dependent on CMEA transactions.

Incentive structure

Price incentives to increase exports were eliminated in the CMEA trading framework by the practice of determining trade flows *ex ante* in intergovernmental bilateral protocols, and because traded goods were valued in domestic prices after all "windfall" gains and losses were neutralized by price equalization. Lack of financial rewards and assured export sales also discouraged product development.

Price formation

The Bucharest pricing principle was unworkable, except in the case of a few homogenous commodities for which prices were publicly quoted. The principle was particularly infeasible in the manufacturing sector, where products were rarely comparable, reliable price information was nonexistent, and sheer numbers overwhelmed any attempt to apply the principle.[18] The procedures amounted to an open invitation to resort to deceptive information practices and excessive bargaining, even though the price equalization mechanism compensated enterprises for "losses" due to discrepancies between domestic prices. More dysfunctional practices reportedly occurred. For example, prices were adjusted retroactively in order to correct *ex post* imbalances. "Unrealistic" or otherwise objectionable prices for some deliveries were offset by price concessions for other goods.[19] In the absence of price negotiations between exporters and importers, trade cannot be considered to have entailed "commercial" transactions.

Even if international prices could be determined, application of the Bucharest principle was inappropriate on efficiency grounds. World market prices reflect market power, scarcity, and opportunity cost at the degree of convertibility and multilateralism prevailing in the world market. As long as

---

[18]For example, CMEA cooperation in the production and trade of ball bearings reportedly recognized some 50,000 distinct specifications. This lack of reasonably detailed and reliable information makes the claims of some CMEA countries to have based domestic prices on "world market prices" implausible.

[19]For example, Soviet crude oil priced under the Bucharest principle and converted from U.S. dollars to TRs at the IBEC exchange rate, was substantially underpriced. This advantage was offset by the practice of setting artificially low export prices for food exports to the U.S.S.R.

the same conditions did not apply for the CMEA, market clearing prices within the CMEA would necessarily be different. World market prices, even if determined accurately, provided a poor indication of CMEA "opportunity costs."

Payments system

The CMEA was not a "payments union" because national currencies were excluded from CMEA transactions, and the TR lacked those key functions of money that would have made it a genuine instrument of payment. The lack of currency and commodity convertibility restricted the payments system even bilaterally. Settlement of unplanned credits in *ex post* imbalances was difficult or impossible in the short run, and could not necessarily be achieved in the long run.

Convertibility

There was some convertibility in three special cases. First, under the rules of bilateral trade between the U.S.S.R. and Finland, Finnish exporters could sell their export receipts (in rubles) to the Finnish National Bank at the official Soviet exchange rate (Oblath and Pete, 1986). The total amount for conversion, however, was tightly controlled on the Finnish side through export licenses, which were established in a planning procedure that closely resembled that used among CMEA countries. Under such conditions, bilateral balance was assured, and the settlements amounted to clearing in all but name.[20]

Second, the U.S.S.R., Bulgaria, Poland, and Czechoslovakia permitted firms with "direct links" (that is, firms cooperating under long-term contracts) to freely convert funds from one national currency to the other at special "investment exchange rates." The privilege was limited to transactions specified in the contract.

Third, some CMEA countries shifted part of their CMEA trade from accounting in TRs to accounting in convertible currency. This, however, amounted merely to a change of the unit of account in bilateral clearing, unless imbalances could be settled through a transfer of convertible currency. Even if this were part of the arrangement, such transfers were often restricted to pre-agreed "swings." Such pseudoconvertibility made sense only if all deliveries made according to this mode of settlement were agreed to be considered "hard."

In none of these three cases was there convertibility in the sense understood in the West.

---

[20]Similar arrangements were in force for Finnish trade with other CMEA countries. This solution supports the contention that CMEA trade required compatible rules on both sides, even if they were alien to the internal economic system.

Exchange rates

Exchange rates between national currencies and the TR had no apparent rational basis.[21] There is evidence that in some countries at least exchange rates were computed as the ratio of total exports valued at domestic prices to the value in TRs for some base period; this made exchange rate determination a historical "purchasing power parity" rate computed for exports. Even so, such a ratio would reflect centrally regulated trade, and not market values or comparative costs.

Mismatched cross-rates were a natural consequence of this system. For example, in the summer of 1987 the National Bank of Hungary's exchange rate for convertible currency transactions was 47 forint/dollar. For CMEA trade, the commercial rate was 28 forint/TR; in combination with the IBEC rate of 0.65 TR/dollar, the implicit forint rate under the CMEA regime was only 18 forint/dollar. Differences in relative prices (the overpricing of Hungarian manufacturing exports and underpricing of Soviet raw materials) and offsetting price adjustments elsewhere reduced this discrepancy, but a significant difference remained.[22]

Macroeconomic policies

Centrally planned economies neither had—nor needed—a macroeconomic policy framework for managing internal and external balance, which were maintained through central micromanagement of transactions. The principles

---

[21]"The exact guidelines that underlay the determination of exchange rates in centrally planned economies are quite obscure and sources differ on their rationale" (van Brabant 1987, p. 201). Van Brabant (1977, 1985, 1988), and Wolf (1988), among others, survey the array of exchange rate concepts used in practice or for analytical purposes; there appears to have been confusion among Eastern economists as well. The concept of "exchange rate," thus, is very "soft" in this paper, as well as in the context of the CMEA.

[22]PlanEcon (volume 5, p.2) arrived at a numerically compatible evaluation: using "typical operational commercial cross-exchange rates in countries with fairly realistic commercial exchange rates (Hungary and Poland) [the cross-rate] was only $0.48/ruble, or less than one third of the official rate" of $1.53/ruble. The overvaluation of the TR implied in the comparison of the text (47/18 = 2.61) is in the same order of magnitude. The reference to "fairly realistic" implies that PlanEcon considered the imputed rate between dollar and ruble a reasonable estimate of a "realistic" rate. In the same context, and relating to Soviet oil exports to the Six, PlanEcon observed: "No wonder the East Europeans have refused to walk away from this nominally overpriced bargain." The Hungarian differential producers turnover tax also reflected a gain from unrealistic exchange rates, and at the same time illustrated the roundabout way in which the institution of price equalization worked in practice. In order to prevent Hungarian importers of Soviet crude from enjoying a windfall, a special tax was levied, which captured the difference between the actual import value (computed according to CMEA rules), and the price of competing crude oil from CC markets and paid at the official exchange rate applicable for CC transactions. The existence of this tax supports again the presumption of continued subsidies transmitted through the CMEA exchange rate rules and disproves the claim that crude oil from the U.S.S.R. was overpriced.

of the CMEA expressly excluded obligations for international coordination, or for cooperation on other than strictly microeconomic matters as specified in bilateral treaties. The common currency was unsuitable for regional monetary coordination or management, because of the limitations of automatic creation and contraction of aggregate TR stocks through aggregate temporary imbalances in the accounts of IBEC, and the lack of currency reserves and fungibility. Also, the tendency of the CMEA to view fiscal policy as an instrument for financing budgetary expenditures made cross-country coordination less relevant than would have been the case if fiscal policy were concerned with internal demand management.

Currency links

Trade under the CMEA regime and convertible currency trade were conducted separately. This separation caused many misconceptions. With convertible currency more valuable than TRs,[23] it was advantageous to shift hard exportables from the CMEA to convertible currency markets. Even if protocols had permitted this, however, there would not necessarily have been a gain. Under CMEA trading practices, export reductions tended to trigger matching export reductions by the trading partner, so the partner could avoid export surpluses, and retaliation against a breach of commitment. This response, in turn, made it necessary for the initiating country to counter the decline in CMEA imports by acquiring additional imports from convertible currency sources, which in turn required matching export proceeds in convertible currency. The initiating country may or may not have benefitted from convertible currency savings. The outcome depended on the real exchange ratios for the goods deleted from CMEA exchange.

Imported inputs

A related effect appeared in the form of imported inputs used in export production. Table 9.4 shows an example based on Hungarian data on the import content of exports. The estimates, which are derived from input-output data, reveal that Hungary transferred three times the amount of convertible currency incorporated in exports to CMEA countries than it received (25.6 percent vs. 8.5 percent).

Trade agreements could take account of such export-embodied currency arbitrage by specifying special arrangements for exports with a high convertible-currency content, by supply in kind by the importing country, or

---

[23]Convertible currency was more valuable because of the overvaluation of the TR. Under the rules of the CMEA regime, however, the exchange rate between domestic currency and the TR was an almost irrelevant policy variable. More importantly, export proceeds in convertible currency were, in contrast to those in TRs, fully convertible. This fungibility permitted convertible currency proceeds to be allocated to imports that yielded the highest economic return.

Table 9.4 Hungary: imported input content of exports, 1974

	As percentage of exports under	
Inputs imported from	TR regime	CC regime
TR regime	11.2	8.5
CC regime	25.6	21.5

Source: Pecsi (1981).

by direct reimbursement for convertible currency outlays. In many instances, however, such special arrangement were not feasible; consequently, there were proposals to idle CMEA export capacity if CMEA exports of a certain good constituted a net drain on the convertible currency balance (see, for example, Koves 1985).

Summary evaluation

This chapter has shown that the traditional CMEA regime was not a random accumulation of ad hoc rules. Although the regime was not derived from a comprehensive theoretical blueprint, it nonetheless exhibited a great deal of internal logic. The system evolved heuristically over several decades of bureaucratic trial and error. As a result, the institutions of the traditional CMEA regime were fundamentally compatible in several ways. First, the rules were consistent with one another. Second, systematic interdependencies were internalized, that is, the principles and rules of the regime were consistent with the model of traditional central economic planning from which the CMEA regime was derived, and within which it operated; these rules were also, though to a somewhat lesser extent, consistent with a "modified" version of central planning. Frictions began to emerge, however, once the interdependent framework of central planning was compromised through the partial reform of other systemic rules. Third, in order to conduct mutual trade, member countries adopted essentially identical rules and procedures for CMEA trade planning, implementation, and settlement. Unilateral changes out of step with other countries would create frictions which in turn would result in a need to introduce corrective measures, thereby leading to further frictions and inconsistencies. The CMEA regime was, in short, in a powerful sense self-perpetuating for systemic reasons alone. In the 1980s these consistency properties increasingly became barriers to reform.

Because of its consistency, the CMEA regime effectively managed a large volume of trade without breaking down or allowing excessive cyclical disruptions. In addition to generally stifling system reform, however, it exhibited two other systemic defects which became increasingly obvious.

First, there was often a need to resort to complex and awkward procedures and practices to make the principles of the model operational; also, the built-in incentives to maintain the bill of traded goods established in intergovernmental protocols eliminated short-term flexibility, and subjected medium-term changes to cumbersome bilateral negotiations.

Second, the CMEA model could not ensure an efficient pattern of trade. The principle reason for this was that the system did not identify static gains from trade, let alone establish a feedback between economic gains and economic decisions. The evident inefficiency of the system was reflected in the pattern of specialization in exports of hard raw materials and imports of soft manufactured goods, which in conjunction with biased price formation practices, disadvantaged the U.S.S.R.

For the Six, the trade pattern offered a short-term advantage and incentive to retain and strengthen underlying production structures, regardless of changes in relative prices in world markets. Furthermore, monopolistic domestic and regional markets removed all incentive for the Six to keep up with international standards of product and process technology, and to develop effective marketing expertise and infrastructures outside the CMEA. These mutually reinforcing, cumulative effects were reflected in a secular decline of exports to competitive markets together with a down-market shift of the export mix. Table 9.5 illustrates how the Six gradually lost world market shares and became increasingly less competitive.

Several decades of symbiotic relations within the CMEA, combined with the weight of intraregional transactions, led to a pervasive structural dependency among the countries. The degree of structural dependency, however, differed among the countries. The U.S.S.R. could in the short run divert a large share of exports of raw materials to convertible currency markets (either in the West or for convertible currency payment to CMEA countries).

The inherent risk of this structural dependency for the East European economies was revealed in 1990, when the U.S.S.R. led the CMEA into the decision to phase out the TR trade and clearing system and to switch to convertible currency accounting and world market prices. These changes resulted in the dual shock of (a) terms of trade adjustment and (b) reduction in trade flows. The aggregate loss of the five remaining ex-CMEA countries (the German Democratic Republic having ceased to exist) vis-à-vis the U.S.S.R. as a result of terms of trade adjustment is variously estimated at between $10 and $16 billion. Adjustment of trade flows entailed substantial trade destruction, largely in the exports of manufactured goods, which could not, at least in the short run, be diverted from the U.S.S.R. to world markets because of uncompetitive quality and/or the lack of an effective marketing infrastructure.

The CMEA was terminated on January 1, 1991. The adjustment concerns of the Five led them, however, to search for bilateral transitional arrangements with the U.S.S.R. Consideration was given to two, if not three, not mutually exclusive regimes. One regime was mutually balanced deliveries in accordance with *ex ante* agreements; these would be similar to the past traditional CMEA deliveries, except that denomination of trade would be in

Table 9.5 World export shares *(percent)*

	1970	1980	1987
East European Six			
Share in world exports total trade	6.8	4.5	3.0
Share in world exports, engineering products	0.8	0.7	0.4
Share in world exports, high and advanced technology engineering products	1.6	1.2	0.7
Share of high and advanced technology products in engineering exports	31.5	26.8	25.9
Asian NICs (Korea, Taiwan, Singapore, Hong Kong)			
Share in world exports, engineering products	2.1	9.3	14.7
Share in world exports, high and advanced technology engineering products	1.0	3.9	6.3
Share of high and advanced technology in engineering exports products	53.8	44.9	54.0

Note: NICs = newly industrializing countries.
Source: ECE: Economic Survey of Europe in 1989-1990, New York, 1989.

convertible currency and exports to the U.S.S.R. would meet more demanding quality standards. A second approach was transactions regulated by "indicative lists"—that is, a framework of advance trading licenses within which individual firms would agree on quantities and prices, again denominated in convertible currency.[24]

In order to economize on scarce foreign exchange reserves, the regime would in both instances have been under an aggregate bilateral clearing arrangement, with or without a settlement of balances by transfer of convertible currency.

---

[24]By the fall of 1990, the U.S.S.R. had extended trading rights to approximately 20,000 organizations, in effect eliminating all FTO monopolies except for raw material exports.

A third approach was transactions concluded under conditions of international free trade. As the necessary currency reserves would be accumulated over time and as the economy proceeded with adjustment, the first two subregimes could make way for the third.

These were proposals for ameliorating the burden of adjustment of the end of the CMEA. As the following chapter makes clear, these burdens of adjustment could be expected to be substantial.

Appendix. Price equalization

Computation of total net price equalization

Net Price Equalization is expressed by

(9.1)
$$NPE = XPE + MPE$$

XPE denotes export price equalization given by

(9.2)
$$XPE = \sum_i q_{Xi} p'_{Xi} r - \sum_i q_{Xi} p_{Xi}$$

where for export item i, q_{Xi} denotes quantity, p'_{Xi} denotes TR price, p_{Xi} denotes domestic price, and r is the exchange rate.

MPE denotes import price equalization given by

(9.3)
$$MPE = \sum_i q_{Mi} p_{Mi} - \sum_i q_{Mi} p'_{Mi} r$$

where for export item i, q_{Mi} denotes quantity, p'_{Mi} denotes TR price, and p_{Mi} denotes domestic price. Accordingly,

(9.4)
$$NPE = r \sum_i \left[q_{Xi} p'_{Xi} - q_{Mi} p'_{Mi} \right] - \sum_i \left[q_{Xi} p_{Xi} - q_{Mi} p_{Mi} \right]$$
$$= r\, TB' - TB$$

where TB' is the trade balance in TRs and TB is the trade balance in domestic currency.

Interpretation

If the two systems of relative prices (p'_{Xi}, p'_{Mi}) and (p_{Xi}, p_{Mi}) are identical, then *TB'* and *TB* differ by the same factor as the relative prices, i.e., by *r*, and *NPE* is zero. As stated, relative prices were not equal, and one has to consider several cases:

Case 1: if *TB'* = 0 and *TB* = 0,
then *NPE* is automatically zero, regardless of the exchange rate;

Case 2: if *TB'* = 0 and *TB* ≠ 0,
then *NPE* has a definitive fixed value, regardless of the exchange rate, and *NPE* is equal to *TB*;

Case 3: if *TB'* ≠ 0 and *TB* = 0,
then the size and sign of *NPE* can be positive or negative depending upon both the size and sign of *TB'*, and the exchange rate;

Case 4: if *TB'* ≠ 0 and *TB* ≠ 0,
then the size and sign of *NPE* can be positive or negative depending upon both the size and sign of *TB'* and *TB*, and upon the exchange rate.

Conclusions

(1) As *TB'* and *TB* can be equal only by accident, case 1 can be ignored. Similarly, as *TB* = 0 would require a calibration of the whole domestic price system, it can be expected to occur only by accident; case 3 can therefore be ignored. Case 2 describes the outcome of a perfect match and realization of balanced trade plans; in this case the exchange rate is irrelevant. In case 4 there is either planned imbalance of CMEA trade or accidental imbalance resulting from deviations between *ex ante* and *ex post* quantities and/or prices. In this instance, a change in the exchange rate alone, while not establishing balance, changes the size and can change the sign of NPE. Since NPE is consolidated with the budget, however, the only effect of the exchange rate is fiscal. Nevertheless, serious domestic price distortions, as for instance substantive underpricing of some important import categories, do affect NPE, so that a supplementary adjustment of domestic prices can contribute to correction of a highly negative outcome. This is what happened in Poland in the early 1980s when domestic food prices were far below international prices.

(2) In all cases, any change in the exchange rate changes all payments made to or received from producers of exports and consumers of imports.

References

Ausch, Sandor. 1969. "Possibilities of Developing Market Relations in the Cooperation of the CMEA Countries." In T. Foeldi and T. Kiss, eds., *Socialist World Market Prices*. Budapest: Akademiai Kiado.

Ausch, Sandor. 1972. Theory and Practice of CMEA Cooperation. Budapest: Akademiai Kiado.

Clement, Hermann. 1988. Transfer-Rubel und Hartwaerungsverrechnung im Intra-RGW und im Ost-West Handel. Munich: Osteuropa-Institut.

Dawisha, Karen. 1988. *Eastern Europe, Gorbatchev and Reform: The Great Challenge*. Cambridge, U.K., and New York: Cambridge University Press.

Hillman, Arye L., and Adi Schnytzer. 1992. "Creating the Reform-Resistant Dependent Economy: Socialist Comparative Advantage, Enterprise Incentives, and the CMEA." This volume.

Inotai, Andreas, ed. 1986. "The Hungarian Enterprise in the Context of Intra-CMEA Relations." Hungarian Scientific Council for World Economy, No. 52.

Koves, Andras. 1985. *The CMEA Countries in the World Economy: Turning Inwards or Turning Outwards*. Budapest: Akademiai Kiado.

Machowski, Heinrich. 1988. "Aussenwirtschaft." In G. Buetow, ed., *Laenderberichte Sowjetunion, Studien zur Geschichte und Politik*. 263, 431-48.

McKinnon, Ronald. 1979. *Money in International Exchange: The Convertible Currency System*. New York and Oxford, U.K.: Oxford University Press.

Oblath, Gabor, and Peter Pete. 1986. "The Development, Mechanism, and Institutional System of Finnish-Soviet Economic Relations." *Vienna Institute for Comparative Economic Studies* 111.

Pecsi, Kalman. 1981. "The Future of Socialist Economic Integration." *Eastern European Economics* 19:2-3.

———. 1985. "Intra-CMEA Cooperation: Interest Patterns in the Extractive and Energy Industries and their Future Prospects." Hungarian Scientific Council for World Economy, No. 53.

PlanEcon. N.d. *PlanEcon Report* 5(32-33). Washington, D.C.: Plan Econ.

Savor, M. 1969. "Price Formation in CMEA Intertrade: Problems and Solutions." In T. Foeldi and T. Kiss, eds., *Socialist World Market Prices*. Budapest: Akademiai Kiado.

UNCTAD (United Nations Conference on Trade and Development). 1988. *New Management Mechanisms in Foreign Economic Relations*. New York: United Nations.

United Nations. *World Economic Survey 1989*. New York.

van Brabant, Josef M. 1977. *East European Cooperation: The Role of Money and Finance*. New York: Praeger.

———. 1985. *Exchange Rates in Eastern Europe: Types, Derivation, and Application*. World Bank Staff Working Paper 778. Washington, D.C.

——. 1988. *Adjustment, Structural Change and Economic Efficiency.* Cambridge, U.K., and New York: Cambridge University Press.

——. 1990. *Remaking Eastern Europe: The Political Economy of Transition.* Boston and Dordrecht: Kluwer Academic Publishers.

Wolf, Thomas A. 1988. *Foreign Trade in the Centrally Planned Economy.* London and New York: Harwood Academic Publishers.

10

Creating the Reform-Resistant Dependent Economy: Socialist Comparative Advantage, Enterprise Incentives, and the CMEA

Arye L. Hillman and Adi Schnytzer

The institutional principles and structure of the Council for Mutual Economic Assistance (CMEA) trade are described in the previous chapter. This chapter focuses on the role of comparative advantage in the CMEA system of trade and the incentives of enterprises to restructure and reorient in a manner consistent with participation in international trade in the broader world market. The CMEA mechanism was replaced in January 1991 by trade at world prices and payment in convertible currency, but as the countries of Eastern Europe make the transition from socialism, they confront the legacies of the pattern of trade and incentives associated with the CMEA system.

The analytical framework employed in this chapter is the specific factors model of international trade. This model distinguishes those factors of production that are intersectorally mobile within an economy and that earn the value of their marginal product in different uses, from factors that are specific to a particular sector and that earn residual rents—although in a limiting case all factors might be specific.[1] The interest of an enterprise is associated with the residual claimants to whom residual rents accrue. The

---

[1]See for example Mayer (1974).

This is a revised version of World Bank PRE Working Paper 505, September 1990.

model has been extensively applied to investigations of protectionist policies in Western economies where industry-specific capital is subject to private ownership.[2] The model and behavioral implications are also applicable to cases of socialist industry, where the state may formally own an enterprise, but management and workers can be residual claimants, in particular in cases of self-management where management is not subject to the formal monitoring of planners or private owners.[3]

We introduce into this model the concept of transaction-specific capital.[4] Much of the capital of East European socialist enterprises—both human and physical capital—was suited for producing output acceptable only in CMEA transactions. In the theory of the Western firm, the concept of transaction-specific capital explains why certain transactions between agents are conducted within a single organization (the firm) rather than through external market transactions. External transactions are avoided because of the potential for opportunistic behavior: for if capital is specific to a particular transaction, the seller confronts a monopsonistic buyer. *Ex ante* the seller can contract with the buyer for future exchange that acknowledges the cost of the specific investment that facilitates the transaction; *ex post*, however, the seller is dependent on the buyer and is vulnerable to opportunistic recontracting. Hence the incentive is to internalize the transaction within a single ownership organization. This explains the institution of the firm.

Although capital was transaction-specific, however, CMEA trade was not internalized, but rather conducted through negotiation between distinct parties. A predictable monopsonistic dependence relationship resulted; capital that produced "soft" goods for CMEA sale could not readily be transformed to produce "hard" goods that could be sold for hard currency in Western markets.[5] Although governments may at certain times have sought to encourage domestic enterprises to adopt a Western orientation, close the technology gap, and provide hard currency, enterprise incentives were to maintain soft goods production.

The link between the CMEA mechanism of trade and payments and enterprise incentives through CMEA transaction-specific capital introduces income distribution considerations into the analysis of the socialist system of international trade. In contrast, the more traditional "distortions" perspective emphasizes the inefficiencies associated with the planned socialist economic system, and the failure to improve efficiency by

---

[2]For a survey of this literature, see Hillman (1989).
[3]See Hillman (1991), Hinds (this volume), and Saldanha (this volume).
[4]See Williamson (1983, 1985).
[5]See Schrenk (this volume) for elaboration.

introducing markets for decentralized transactions between socialist enterprises.[6]

We shall begin with a description of how CMEA trade was determined. This was central to the strategic negotiation of the trade pattern and enterprise incentives. We then proceed to review prior perspectives on CMEA trade—the perceived irrationality of CMEA exchange, CMEA as a customs union, studies of the CMEA trade pattern, and studies of how the U.S.S.R. subsidized other CMEA economies through CMEA terms of trade. Subsequent sections consider "socialist comparative advantage," quality and the CMEA pattern of trade, and attempts to orient enterprises away from the CMEA. The failure of these attempts is linked to CMEA-related enterprise incentives.

Determination of CMEA international trade

Although CMEA trade was, in principle, a multilateral trade and payments arrangement, in practice it was determined by bilateral negotiation. Under negotiated protocols, trade was planned to be bilaterally balanced in units of transferable rubles. "Payment" was made through a bilateral clearing system.[7]

Since understanding the manner in which CMEA trade was determined is necessary for understanding the behavioral and analytical implications of the system, we proceed with a brief description of the system emphasizing its strategic aspects.[8]

The determination of the commodity composition and quantities of goods traded began with negotiations intended to "harmonize" the five-year plans of individual CMEA economies. Hungary was a special case, since after 1968 no central plan was binding on enterprises; it nevertheless conducted its CMEA trade negotiations in much the same manner as the centrally planned CMEA economies. Harmonization, in principle at least, took place two or three years prior to the first year of the upcoming five-year plan. The structure, volume, and balance of trade for basic commodity groups was determined via an iterative bargaining process during this harmonization stage.[9] The sequencing of bilateral negotiations allowed the U.S.S.R. a preeminent position: each East European country undertook

---

[6]For perceptions influenced by the distortions literature, see, among others Adam (1989), Fallenbuchl (1986), Marer (1986), Marer and van Veen (1987), Brada and Dobozi (1988), and Wolf (1988).

[7]This system was therefore not one of decentralized multilateral market exchange in convertible currencies as in Western international trade.

[8]For a broader description, see Schrenk (this volume).

[9]Socialist international trade was thus not directed at satisfying contemporaneous "needs" that could not be met by the domestic plan. International trade commitments were in principle contemporaneous with the plan.

negotiations with the U.S.S.R. before negotiating with other CMEA trading partners, and the U.S.S.R. was the dominant trading partner for each country.[10]

While there were rules for price determination,[11] procedures for determining the prices of manufactured goods were complex; the prospective buyer was required to present the seller with a price quotation from a Western supplier for a similar product. Negotiations at the ministerial level then determined price adjustments warranted by quality differences between the Western and CMEA good. The prices thus determined, however, only provided guidelines for more detailed negotiations that took place in the course of annual foreign trade planning. In the end, with the exception of fuels and raw materials, there was often little relation between the pricing guidelines established in the initial negotiations and the prices at which CMEA exchange took place.[12]

The quantities of goods to be traded were negotiated on the basis of the disaggregated output targets of the negotiating countries' five-year plans, before each country began its annual domestic planning. Different teams of negotiators attended to the physical flow of different commodity groups. The perceived importance of a commodity determined the seniority of the foreign trade ministry officials involved in the negotiations. Outcomes of negotiations were collated over time to ensure approximate adherence to five-year plan targets and a bilateral zero net balance of trade between negotiating countries. No adjustments were made for quality differences. The one-year protocols did not necessarily fulfill five-year plan trading commitments, either because CMEA-designated goods were diverted to hard currency markets or because they were used to address domestic supply needs. The U.S.S.R. as supplier of fuels and minerals in particular had alternative hard currency markets for its predesignated CMEA exports.

The CMEA unit of account, the transferable ruble, was transferable neither over time nor between countries. A transferable ruble surplus did not therefore imply that the deficit trading partner was obliged to balance trade through future supply, nor did it imply that a country with a surplus could apply the deficit of another country to secure trilateral trade balance. It was in general not possible to secure compensation for a trade surplus

---

[10]See the data in Schrenk (this volume).

[11]Until 1976 the prices at which CMEA trade took place were based on the average of world prices over the previous five years. Prices, once computed, remained fixed throughout the five-year plan period. Subsequent to 1976 prices were based on a moving average of past prices. For raw materials, price determination rules were directly established with reference to world markets. For example, the price of a particular grade of oil was that prevailing in Rotterdam, plus half the cost of transportation from that port to the importing CMEA country.

[12]For discussions of CMEA prices, see Hewett (1974) and van Brabant (1987). Toth (1988) and Zalai (1988) provide the sources for the account in this section.

arising from the failure of a trading partner to comply with supply commitments.[13]

Prior perspectives on CMEA trade

This review of the manner in which prices and quantities in CMEA trade were determined provides background for a consideration of prior perspectives on the nature of CMEA trade.

Economic irrationality

Analyses of CMEA trade, in particular in Western international economics textbooks, have often presented the view that there was no rational economic basis for CMEA exchange. It has been proposed that because of the distortions and inefficiencies resulting from the absence of a market mechanism, socialist international trade could only fortuitously reflect true comparative advantage. For example, Caves and Jones (1985) take the position that "it is surprising if East-West trade achieves any rationality in relation to the basic forces of comparative advantage." Ethier (1988) observes that "in centrally planned economies domestic relative prices do not reflect opportunity costs and do not guide the actions of foreign trade organizations." The view that CMEA trade lacked economic rationale because of distorted domestic prices was widely held in the West.

CMEA as a customs union

A number of authors have suggested that the CMEA can be considered rational when understood within the framework of customs union theory.[14] Pelzman (1977) thus, for example, based his empirical investigations of CMEA trade creation and trade diversion on this perspective. He took the position that the CMEA could be considered a customs union because its annual bilateral negotiations were a proxy for the accepted common external tariff.

The CMEA, however, differed from a customs union in a number of significant ways. There was no common external tariff; indeed there was no

---

[13]International trade was conducted by enterprises with the mediation of exclusive foreign trade organizations (FTOs). Since domestic prices differed among CMEA trading partners, a price equalization mechanism that taxed or subsidized imports and exports assured that prices of domestic and foreign goods were equalized. Again Hungary was an exception. Hungary's CMEA trade taxes and subsidies did not necessarily equalize the prices received by an enterprise for domestic and export sales, and were determined by negotiation between the state and the enterprise. See Abel, Hillman, and Tarr (this volume).

[14]The view of CMEA as a customs union was developed by Holzman (1974, 1976, 1985) and Bergson (1980).

need for protectionist tariffs in the Western market sense, because planning ensured that trade was not disruptive to domestic enterprises.[15] The import taxes that were components of the price equalization mechanism[16] did have the effect of a tariff in raising import prices to the level of domestic prices. The purpose of these taxes, however, was to prevent foreign trade organizations (FTOs) from making arbitrage gains. The FTOs were also protected from losses by import subsidies.

Customs union theory also does not include consideration of the types of strategic asymmetries that characterized CMEA trade negotiations and that influenced incentives to adhere to or depart from agreed trade flows. The theory assumes voluntary market exchange, which did not apply without reservation to CMEA trade.

Nor was the CMEA a free trade area. Because relative prices for CMEA exchange resulted from bilateral negotiations, there was no set CMEA price for a particular good.[17] The *ex ante* balanced trade constraint also resulted in actual prices deviating from the price offers with which bilateral bargaining was initiated. The same goods could therefore have different prices in different bilateral CMEA exchanges.[18]

The CMEA did have the attribute of a customs union, that it constituted a market-segmenting discriminatory trading arrangement, with bilateral terms of trade that differed from world prices. The discriminatory terms of trade have the been the subject of several empirical studies. Before we review these studies, we will consider evidence concerning patterns of trade.

The Heckscher-Ohlin Theorem?

Rosefielde (1974, 1981) found somewhat remarkably that the pattern of Soviet trade during the years 1955–68 was consistent with the predictions of the Heckscher-Ohlin Theorem.[19] This outcome could not have resulted from a competitive market mechanism efficiently allocating resources; it was rather the outcome of planning.

Rosefielde chose to interpret his results as reflecting rational economic calculation on the part of CMEA planners, even if not in accord with principles of market valuation. He acknowledged that "whatever special ideological forces may be at work in determining the composition of Soviet

---

[15]See Hillman (1991).

[16]See Schrenk (this volume) and Abel, Hillman, and Tarr (this volume).

[17]Although CMEA pricing rules provided a starting point for bilateral bargaining, trade flows and prices for different commodities were, as noted above, negotiated separately.

[18]The nonuniformity of prices is also apparent in the long-term contracts for fuel supplies signed by the U.S.S.R. and both the German Democratic Republic and Czechoslovakia outside the CMEA framework, and the aid provided to Poland by the U.S.S.R. in the wake of the Solidarity crisis.

[19]The Theorem predicts that the factor content of trade will reflect domestic relative factor abundance.

trade with the socialist bloc, they are seemingly subordinate to the dictates of pure theory . . . . Several possibilities can be entertained ranging from perfect planning to the semi-divine intervention of Stalin's not too invisible hand" (p. 678). Rosefielde proposed that we consider "the least implausible of a wide variety of implausible explanations, that the Soviet results are the outcome of comparative advantage, labor value, accounting price calculations" (p. 678).

Rosefielde's results could be explained by factors other than perfect planning or Stalin's economic judgment; for example, the many explanations offered for the "Leontief Paradox," that the pattern of U.S. international trade has not been consistent with the predictions of the Heckscher-Ohlin Theorem. We reserve judgment on the puzzle as to why the Heckscher-Ohlin Theorem might predict the comparative advantage of the Soviet planned economy, but not of the U.S. market economy.

The commodity composition of trade

The Heckscher-Ohlin Theorem can be formulated in both factor-content and commodity-composition versions. Evidence on the commodity composition of Soviet trade is provided by Joseph Pelzman (1980). Pelzman observed sustained systematic relationships in Soviet trade flows during the decade 1963–73: for most product groups, the U.S.S.R. exported to Eastern Europe intermediate inputs that were required for industrialization programs, and imported goods that reflected East European supply capabilities. Pelzman (1978) also studied intraindustry trade between 1958 and 1973 and found that such trade was prominent in the machinery, equipment, and chemicals sectors. His interpretation of the intraindustry trade flows was that "in the early stages of their development (late 1940s and 1950s), the East European economies were dependent on the Soviet Union to purchase the machinery output of their new heavy industries in exchange for basic raw materials" (p. 301). The Soviets, however, did not wish to have this pattern of trade persist. In the early and mid-1960s they exchanged raw materials for East European machinery, only if the East Europeans were willing also to provide them with semimanufactures, consumer goods, and foodstuffs—hence giving rise to the intraindustry trade observed by Pelzman.

There is evidence, then, of a definitive commodity trade pattern, and evidence, too, that the U.S.S.R. was responsive to the composition of trade. CMEA trade appeared to have had some rational basis; for at least the U.S.S.R. could by its principles distinguish a pattern of trade that it wished to encourage from one that it did not.

CMEA trade after 1973 and into the 1980s reflected the same basic commodity pattern of specialization. There was a persistent systematic pattern of trade between the U.S.S.R. and the six East European CMEA countries.[20] Soviet exports consisted principally of oil, other mineral raw materials, and metals, in return for which the East European economies supplied chiefly manufactured goods.

CMEA terms of trade

For this trade pattern, we can identify general terms of trade between raw materials and CMEA manufactured goods. Studies undertaken by Marrese and Vanous (1983a, 1983b) reveal that the U.S.S.R. subsidized East European economies via the CMEA terms of trade[21] by exchanging fuel and nonfood raw materials for manufactured goods at relative prices higher than world market terms of trade.[22]

Marrese and Vanous suggested that underlying these subsidies were national security objectives, and that the preferential terms of trade rewarded East European countries for contributing to Soviet national security.[23]

In the next section, we link the preferential terms of trade in the CMEA system to enterprise incentives. Background is provided by an account of the development of the role of comparative advantage and specialization in CMEA trade.

Comparative advantage and specialization in CMEA trade

According to the Stalinist model of economic development, economic progress was achieved by countries pursuing parallel industrialization along balanced growth paths.[24] The classical notion of comparative advantage did not play a role in this model. The CMEA was established in a manner consistent with the model, and not as a customs union or free trade area. It

---

[20]For details, see Schrenk (this volume).

[21]Marrese and Vanous (1983a and b) estimate the value of the Soviet subsidy to East European economies between 1960 and 1980 to have been $87.2 billion. Of this amount, $75.5 billion was estimated to have taken place between 1971 and 1980.

[22]Some economists have had reservations about the Marrese-Vanous calculations, and have offered recomputations and updates. For comments and qualifications see Brada (1985, 1988), Holzman (1985), and Desai (1986). Poznanski (1988) has downgraded the Marrese-Vanous estimate of the Soviet transfer during the period 1972–84 and finds evidence of periodic shifts in the direction of transfer. Marrese and Wittenberg (1989) have made another computation of the implicit terms of trade subsidy for Hungary. An estimate of Hungary's terms of trade loss has also been made by Oblath and Tarr (1992). For an earlier interchange see Menderson (1959) and Holzman (1962).

[23]Marrese and Vanous suggest that this compensation was covert in that it was known to the CMEA governments, but not to the population at large. The East European population was "worse off due to its association with the Soviet Union," but not "the East European government that shared the preferences of the Soviet government to a greater extent than its East European population."

[24]See Schnytzer (1982).

was established precisely as its name indicates, as a "council for mutual economic assistance," for the purpose of cooperation to achieve the objective of balanced industrialization.[25]

Comparative advantage became, however, an acceptable guiding principle for international trade in the post-Stalinist period when the benefits of production specialization were recognized. The U.S.S.R. sought at various times from the second half of the Khrushchev era to establish a supranational CMEA planning body that would guide member countries into specific patterns of specialization. Supranational planning was, however, resisted by the East Europeans.

Romania offered the first resistance to this form of planning. In 1957 the CMEA was in its first wave of Soviet-directed specialization in engineering. Romania was producing a type of truck not allotted to it; the U.S.S.R. responded by threatening to cease all steel deliveries to Romania, and not only the intermediate inputs for production of the truck. The next conflict concerned the Galati steel mill. In late 1960 the Soviets agreed to assist Romania with the steel project by providing machinery and equipment, to be delivered between 1961 and 1968. Following the decision at the Twenty-second Communist Party of the Soviet Union (CPSU) Congress in October 1961 to foster international socialist specialization, however, it was decided that Romanian comparative advantage did not lie in steel production. The Romanians were pressured by both the Soviets and the East Germans to abandon the steel project, but they refused to comply. The conflict assumed ideological overtones: Romania had to choose between adhering to the principles of Stalinist development strategy and abandoning these principles. Romania's chief planner, Gaston-Marin, justified Romania's position as consistent with orthodox socialist principles of development, declaring at the November–December 1961 plenum of the Central Committee:

> *Our Party has always resolutely opposed and has always combatted from a Marxist-Leninist standpoint those erroneous "theories" which while defending the keeping of proportions between branches of the national economy and the priority development of a heavy industry on the scale of the whole socialist camp rather than within the framework of the individual socialist country, in fact deny the necessity of creating the technical and material base of socialism and present in a distorted manner the principles of specialization and cooperation within the framework of the socialist international division of labor.[26]*

By November 1962, Romania was placing orders for steel machinery in the West. What had begun as an economic dispute took on political dimensions, with Romania adopting its "independent line."

---

[25]On the CMEA in its formative years, see Kaser (1967).

[26]Cited in Wiles (1968, p. 325).

Quality and the CMEA pattern of trade

Although the Soviets were unsuccessful in efforts to dictate a pattern of comparative advantage and international specialization for CMEA trade, tendencies toward specialization evolved. These tendencies were influenced by two characteristic features of central planning: static technology and the absence of quality competition.

In the traditional Soviet model, growth was planned in terms of physical output targets. Prices had a controlling rather than allocative function. In the quest to ensure plan fulfillment, planners offered enterprise managers bonuses tied exclusively to the physical quantities produced. Thus, for the manager, there was no incentive to be concerned with output-mix or product quality. Substitutes for Western-style quality competition were sought via incentive schemes that met with little success.[27] The consequent quality differentials segmented CMEA and Western markets. Within the CMEA, low quality goods were purchased by domestic consumers because consumers lacked alternatives, and were supplied to foreign consumers via CMEA trade. For these low quality or soft goods, the unit cost of production exceeded the price obtainable on the world market, or Western consumers could simply not be induced to forego the higher quality Western substitute. Although cost advantages for soft goods could not compensate for the inferior CMEA quality in competition with Western goods, market segmentation nevertheless allowed soft goods enterprises to survive.

Western consumer goods were imported into Hungary and Poland during the 1980s. The limited supplies of Western goods, however, catered to privileged consumers and were not directly competitive with domestic production of soft goods. In the CMEA beyond Hungary and Poland, only soft consumer goods were available.

Capital and intermediate goods were also soft. There was demand for these goods in a central planning context (and in market socialist Hungary) in each CMEA country. Because membership in the CMEA—and hence trading at some minimal level—was mandatory, soft intermediate goods were, in the early years at least, traded partly to ensure bilateral trade balances. The U.S.S.R. contracted to receive soft capital and intermediate goods via CMEA protocols. Once soft intermediate and capital goods were embedded in CMEA enterprises, there was further demand for (soft) spare parts. Workers also became familiar with the use of soft inputs.

---

[27]The Central Institute of Quality Control was established in the U.S.S.R. in 1987. An enterprise's output had to pass inspection by the Institute before it could be credited to plan fulfillment. Products that did not meet standards were not delivered to the planned user, and for the purposes of plan fulfillment this output was regarded as having never been produced. In the first quarter of 1987, however, quality controls in the machine-building sector impeded the delivery of goods to the extent that, by the end of the year, the screening function of the Institute had in effect been eliminated.

The CMEA economies thus became committed to the production of and international trade in soft goods. The trade pattern was such that, on a net basis, the U.S.S.R. exported hard goods, Eastern Europe economies exported soft goods, and there was also substantial intraindustry trade in soft goods.

Attempts to orient economies away from the CMEA

The soft/hard goods pattern of trade posed difficulties if CMEA governments wanted to increase hard currency export earnings. The market segmentation between the CMEA economies and Western markets meant that domestic CMEA enterprises were able to avoid competing against more technologically sophisticated Western goods. Yet there were potential benefits to the CMEA economies if the inefficiencies of the domestic socialist enterprises and the quality differentials between domestic and Western goods could be moderated or eliminated.[28] Still, outside of Hungary and Poland there were no attempts to shift to a Western market orientation. Czechoslovakia and the former Democratic Republic of Germany, which produced the most sought after soft goods in the CMEA, took a position consistent with Marxist-Leninist ideology, that it was possible to improve the efficiency of the centrally planned economy and to resolve the quality problem without recourse to domestic markets and Western technology. Hungary and Poland, on the other hand, sought to improve the efficiency of their socialist enterprises. Hungary undertook reforms in 1968 that in principle replaced central planning with markets, while Poland imported Western capital for its centrally planned socialist enterprises. The CMEA system, however, inhibited reform attempts because of enterprise disincentives that were associated with costs of disengaging from the system.

Poland

In the early 1970s the Polish leader Edvard Gierek implemented a modernization program for Polish industry based on borrowing in the West to import technologically sophisticated capital equipment. Substantial quantities of Western capital were made available to Polish enterprises. This restructuring attempt has been studied by Terrell,[29] who found no evidence that this infusion of Western capital improved productivity. In some sectors the marginal product of Western capital was negative, whereas the marginal product of CMEA capital was invariably positive.

---

[28]Excluded from the East European reform discussions of the 1960s were the implications of the high concentration of socialist industry. Competition was considered inconsistent with cooperative relationships among socialist enterprises. See Hillman (1991).

[29]See Terrell (1990) and Terrell (this volume).

Polish enterprises thus failed to utilize the Western capital that was made available to them. CMEA capital remained more useful to enterprises than imported Western capital.

When this modernization attempt was abruptly halted in the mid-1970s, Poland's CMEA-oriented socialist enterprises continued to emphasize the production of soft goods, and Poland was left with Western debt obligations it could not honor. The subsequent Jaruzelski regime refocused on the development of CMEA trade.

It could be said that the Polish modernization program failed because of attributes inherent in the planned socialist economy: in the absence of domestic prices reflecting opportunity costs, it is impossible to determine comparative advantage and impossible, hence, to penetrate Western markets. Even if the planners could not determine comparative advantage, however, enterprises still could have increased factor productivity by absorbing the technologically advanced Western capital made available to them. Instead, the evidence is that Western capital was put aside and not used.

Western capital could facilitate transition from international trade based on negotiated CMEA protocols to competition in Western markets. Existing incentives however encouraged state enterprises to resist disengagement from the CMEA. Risk-averse management in socialist enterprises had little to gain from turning away from the traditional CMEA demand to inherently more uncertain Western market competition. The availability of Western capital was therefore irrelevant to enterprises that could participate in CMEA trade.

Hungary

Hungary's New Economic Mechanism, which in 1968 abolished central planning, was the first of a sequence of policy steps directed at effecting a transition to a market economy. The Hungarian economy, however, continued in the subsequent two decades to be dominated by large state enterprises, and, even though the state bureaucracy was, in principle, no longer responsible for directing enterprise planning, close ties persisted between the former planners and the enterprises. Enterprises did not transform themselves into Western-type firms, and they did not significantly absorb Western capital and technology. As the end of the CMEA approached, enterprises still continued to concentrate primarily on the production of soft goods.[30]

---

[30]There is a substantial literature on Hungarian reforms. See Bauer (1983, 1988)), Dezsenyi-Gueullette (1983), Tardos (1983), Gacs (1986), Inotai (1986), Kornai (1985, 1986, 1988), Marer (1986), Brada and Dobozi (1988), Hare (1990), Newbery (1990), Hillman (1991), and Hillman (this volume).

Although domestic central planning formally ceased in Hungary after the New Economic Mechanism, CMEA trade, planned and negotiated by the state, continued to play a prominent role. The industrial composition of Hungarian exports to the U.S.S.R. and Organisation for Economic Co-operation and Development (OECD) countries remained remarkably stable throughout the 1970s and 1980s; whereas almost half of industrial exports to the U.S.S.R. consisted of machines and vehicles, the share of these goods in Hungarian exports to the OECD remained around 10 percent. The Hungarian trade pattern continued to reflect the dichotomy between soft and hard goods, with soft manufactured goods exchanged for hard oil and raw materials.

Hungary had by the end of the 1980s accumulated a substantial foreign debt (but unlike Poland, it did not default). Despite the foreign resources reflected in the debt, Hungarian enterprises in the market socialist system did not adopt Western technology, and in 1990 had yet to confront the adjustment problems associated with the impending end of the CMEA system of trade and payments.[31]

Albania

The case of Albania illustrates the cost of disengaging from the CMEA. In 1961, during the first year of the Albanian Third Five-Year Plan, the U.S.S.R. severed all economic relations with Albania and imposed a boycott. Even though the Chinese government offered to replace Soviet aid, Albania was still tied to the CMEA system by the technology of local construction plants, machinery, and spare parts. The Third Five-Year Plan was a disaster. It was not until 1966 that the relatively simple Albanian economy, facing no foreign debt difficulties and with the willing assistance of China, recovered from the disruption that resulted from its disengagement from the CMEA.[32]

Of course, the Albanian experience does not provide complete counterfactual evidence to be matched against the experience of economies that did not disengage from the CMEA because Albania did not orient itself toward the West on leaving the CMEA. The Albanian case does, however, illustrate the magnitude of disruption caused by disengagement from the CMEA.

CMEA-specific capital

The private claims to industry-specific capital that underlie enterprise incentives in the West are absent in socialist enterprises. De facto residual

---

[31]See Hillman (this volume).
[32]For a detailed account of the Albanian experience, see Schnytzer (1982).

claimancy in state-owned enterprises, however, did not reside exclusively with the state. The socialist enterprise had social responsibilities toward its employees, and discretionary expenditures could be made to collectively benefit employees and their families. There were also discretionary expenditures of which enterprise managers were beneficiaries. Benefits provided by the enterprise to workers and management thus extended beyond wages, which were subject to regulation.

In instances of self-management in Hungary and Poland, where enterprise councils controlled an enterprise, the de facto residual claimancy of management and workers was more directly established.[33]

Because CMEA export sales were planned to ensure balanced bilateral trade, enterprises did not need to engage in the sort of marketing efforts associated with exports to the West in order to sustain CMEA sales. The specialization in soft manufacturing nurtured by predictable CMEA demand made the socialist enterprises' capital transaction-specific to CMEA trade. The Western practice of avoiding market transactions by internalizing transactions within a firm, however, had no parallel in the CMEA trade regime, which was dependent on bilateral bargaining. There was scope for *ex post* opportunistic behavior in this bargaining process, in decisions made regarding subsequent deliveries. The relationship was asymmetric, since the East European economies depended on the U.S.S.R. to purchase their soft goods, whereas the Soviets had alternative markets for their hard goods.

Soviet strategic positioning and monopsony power were not, however, used to the disadvantage of the East Europeans; the empirical studies indicate that, on the contrary, the soft/hard goods terms of trade for CMEA exchange disadvantaged the U.S.S.R. as hard goods supplier and advantaged the East European soft goods suppliers.

A dependency relation was therefore established through CMEA trade. This relation arose out of the shift in emphasis from balanced parallel socialist development to a conception of socialist comparative advantage. The demand of the U.S.S.R. for East European soft goods in turn sustained East European enterprises and permitted them to fulfill their social responsibilities toward their workers, particularly with regard to job security.

Dependence relations influence decisions to specialize in international trade.[34] In the case of the CMEA, the inferior technology embodied in the enterprises' transaction-specific capital constrained the East European economies to trade primarily with the U.S.S.R. or among themselves. The U.S.S.R. had to be relied upon to deliver oil and other natural resources in exchange for East European soft goods.[35]

---

[33]See Grosfeld (1990), Schaffer (1990), Hinds (1991), and Milanovic (this volume).
[34]See Arad and Hillman (1979), Cheng (1987).
[35]Transaction-specific investment was also associated with imports. For example, Hungary invested in pipelines within the U.S.S.R. to supply imports of Soviet natural gas.

The Hungarian enterprise

The circumstances of Hungarian enterprises were different from those of enterprises in the centrally planned economies. The Hungarian enterprise was in principle an autonomous entity operating in a market setting. The Hungarian market was somewhat different from Western markets: there were in effect no factor markets, and product markets were monopolistic, with barriers to entry that protected the large established socialist enterprises.

Within Hungarian market socialism, the resistance to change that stemmed from the CMEA trading relationship was compounded by the role of the state as centralized international trade negotiator on behalf of the enterprise as decentralized supplier. The state would make a commitment in CMEA trade negotiations to export the output of an enterprise, which in general was a domestic monopoly.[36] The enterprise was not disadvantaged by its soft goods products. On the contrary, the state's commitment to supply an enterprise's soft goods allowed the enterprise to negotiate with the state for favorable tax, subsidy, and price levels and also regarding price determination, taxation, and subsidization.[37]

There was therefore a direct link between CMEA trade and the soft budget constraint (see Kornai 1985) of the socialist enterprises.

The CMEA system was also advantageous to Hungarian enterprises from the perspective of import management. Imports in a planned economy are by their nature not competitive with domestic output. In Hungary, CMEA imports were likewise planned via the trade protocols. CMEA trade thus provided protection for domestic enterprises, because CMEA imports were noncompetitive with domestic output.

Since Hungary had a market economy rather than planned economy, domestic enterprises potentially confronted competition from Western imports. The viability of domestic enterprises required that market segmentation with respect to the West be maintained. There was no assurance that a particular tariff could compensate for soft/hard goods differences in quality, and exchange controls and quantitative restrictions on Western imports were thus required. CMEA trade was easier to manage than Western trade, because CMEA imports were negotiated through trade protocols and did not require surreptitious noncompliance with international accords.[38]

---

[36]The FTO acted as an intermediary.
[37]See Schaffer (1989) for a formalization of this strategic relationship.
[38]See Gacs (1989), Oblath (1989).

Concluding remarks

This chapter has demonstrated how the CMEA trading system created trade-dependent economies whose socialist enterprises had incentives to resist Western orientation. An enterprise's physical and human capital was transaction-specific to CMEA trade, thereby binding the enterprise to transactions within the CMEA and in particular with the U.S.S.R. as monopsonistic purchaser of soft goods in exchange for hard goods—at terms of trade advantageous to East European soft goods producers.

The U.S.S.R. strategically benefitted from CMEA exchange via (a) the hard/soft structure of the commodity pattern of trade that gave the U.S.S.R. potential monopsony power; (b) the option to redirect to the world market hard goods that had been committed as exports to the CMEA; (c) the nontransferability of transferable ruble surpluses that arose if hard goods were diverted for sale for hard currency; and (d) the sequential bilateral bargaining nature of CMEA trade negotiations.

Yet from an economic point of view, the system was unfavorable to the U.S.S.R. The U.S.S.R. would have reason to advocate an end of the CMEA if it changed its estimation of the value of geopolitical benefits—as, in fact, happened. The benefit of the CMEA system to the U.S.S.R. was hegemony. If hegemony was a diminished concern, or if the cost of hegemony came to be viewed as too high—and if Western substitutes could be obtained by exporting the same hard goods that secured, at disadvantageous terms of trade, inferior East European goods—there was little incentive for the U.S.S.R. to sustain the CMEA system.

The U.S.S.R. closed down the CMEA in January 1991, insisting that trade take place at world rather than CMEA prices, and that payment be made in convertible currency. The costs of disengagement for East European economies were the terms of trade losses. But also the structure of trade that had sustained the past dependency relationship, and had led to resistance to reform, now became a point of departure for required adjustments. CMEA-specific capital was diminished in value by the end of the socialist system of international trade. The still unprivatized socialist enterprises remained, adapted to a CMEA system that had previously nurtured them, but which had now disappeared.

References

Abel, Istvan, Arye L. Hillman, and David Tarr. 1992. "The Government Budgetary Consequences of Reform of the CMEA System of International Trade: The Case of Hungary." This volume.

Adam, Jan. 1989. *Economic Reform in the Soviet Union and Eastern Europe since the 1960s*. New York: St. Martin's Press.

Arad, Ruth, and Arye L. Hillman. 1979. "Embargo Threat, Learning and Departure from Comparative Advantage." *Journal of International Economics* 9:265–76.

Bauer, Tamas. 1983. "The Hungarian Alternative to Soviet-Type Planning." *Journal of Comparative Economics* 7:304–16.

———. 1988. "Economic Reforms within and beyond the State Sector." *American Economic Review, Papers and Proceedings* 78:452–60.

Bergson, Abram. 1980. "The Geometry of COMECON Trade." *European Economic Review* 14:291–306.

Boot, Pieter A. 1987. "East-West Trade and Industrial Policy: The Case of the German Democratic Republic." *Soviet Studies* 39:651–71.

Brada, Josef C. 1985. "Soviet Subsidization of Eastern Europe: The Primacy of Economics over Politics." *Journal of Comparative Economics* 9:80–90.

———. 1988. "Interpreting the Soviet Subsidization of Eastern Europe." *International Organization* 42:639–58.

Brada, Josef C., and Istvan Dobozi, eds. 1988. *The Hungarian Economy in the 1980s*. Greenwich, Conn.: JAI Press.

Caves, Richard, and Ronald Jones. 1985. *World Trade and Payments*. Boston: Little Brown.

Cheng, Leonard. 1987. "Uncertainty and Economic Self-Sufficiency." *Journal of International Economics* 23:167–78.

Desai, Padma. 1986. "Is the Soviet Union Subsidizing Eastern Europe?" *European Economic Review* 30:107–16.

Dczsenyi-Gueullette, Agota. 1983. "The Utilization and Assimilation in Hungary of Advanced Technology Imported from the West." *Soviet Studies* 35:196–207.

Ethier, Wilfred. 1988. *Modern International Economics*. New York: Norton.

Fallenbuchl, Zbigniew M. 1986. "The Economic Crisis in Poland and Prospects for Recovery." In *East European Economies: Slow Growth in the 1980s*. Washington, D.C.: U.S. Government Printing Office.

Gacs, Janos. 1986. "The Conditions, Chances, and Predictable Consequences of Implementing Step by Step Liberalization of Imports in the Hungarian Economy." *Acta Oeconomica* 36:231–50.

———. 1989. "The Progress of Liberalization of Foreign Trade in Hungary." Paper presented at the Conference on Attempts at Liberalization: Hungarian Economic Policy and International Experience, 16–18 November. Budapest: Kopint-Datorg.

Grosfeld, Irena. 1990. "Prospects for Privatization in Poland." In *European Economy: Economic Transformation in Hungary and Poland*. Brussels: Commission of the European Communities.

Hare, Paul G. 1990. "Reforming State-Enterprise Relationships in Hungary." In *European Economy: Economic Transformation in Hungary and Poland*. Brussels: Commission of the European Communities.

Hewett, Edward A. 1974. *Foreign Trade Prices in the Council of Mutual Economic Assistance*. Cambridge, U.K.: Cambridge University Press.

Hillman, Arye L. 1989. *The Political Economy of Protection*. London and New York: Harwood Academic Publishers.

———. 1990. "Macroeconomic Policy in Hungary and its Microeconomic Consequences." In *European Economy: Economic Transformation in Hungary and Poland*. Brussels: Commission of the European Communities.

———. 1991. "Liberalization Dilemmas." In Arye L. Hillman, ed., *Markets and Politicians: Politicized Economic Choice*. Boston and Dordrecht: Kluwer Academic Publishers.

———. 1992. "Enterprise Restructuring in the Transition from Hungarian Market Socialism." This volume.

Hinds, Manuel. 1991. "Markets and Ownership in Socialist Countries in Transition." In Arye L. Hillman, ed., *Markets and Politicians: Politicized Economic Choice*. Boston and Dordrecht: Kluwer Academic Publishers.

Hinds, Manuel. 1992. "Policy Effectiveness in Reforming Socialist Economies." This volume.

Holzman, Franklyn D. 1962. "Soviet Foreign Trade Pricing and the Question of Discrimination: A Customs-Union Approach." *Review of Economics and Statistics* 44:134–47.

———. 1974. *Foreign Trade under Central Planning*. Cambridge, Mass.: Harvard University Press.

———. 1976. *International Trade under Communism: Politics and Economics*. New York: Basic Books.

———. 1985. "COMECON: A Trade-Destroying Customs Union?" *Journal of Comparative Economics* 9:410–23.

Inotai, Andreas. 1986. "Economic Relations between the CMEA and the EEC: Facts, Trends, and Prospects." *Acta Oeconomica* 36:307–27.

Kaser, Michael. 1967. *COMECON*. Oxford, U.K.: Oxford University Press.

Kornai, Janos. 1985. *Contradictions and Dilemmas*. Budapest: Corvina.

———. 1986. "The Hungarian Reform Process: Visions, Hopes, and Reality." *Journal of Economic Literature* 24:1687–1737.

———. 1988. "Individual Freedom and Reform of the Socialist Economy." *European Economic Review* 32:233–67.

Marer, Paul. 1986. "Economic Reforms in Hungary: From Central Planning to Regulated Market." In *East European Economics: Slow Growth in the 1980s*. Washington, D.C.: Government Printing Office: 3, 233–97.

Marer, Paul, and van Veen, Pieter. 1987. *East European Economic Trade and East-West Trade: U.S., West and East European Perspectives*. London: JAI Press.

Marrese, Michael, and Jan Vanous. 1983a. *Soviet Subsidization of Trade with Eastern Europe*. Berkeley: University of California Press.

———. 1983b. "Unconventional Gains from Trade." *Journal of Comparative Economics* 7:382–99.

Marrese, Michael, and Lauren Wittenberg. 1989. "Implicit Subsidies within the CMEA: A Hungarian Perspective." Department of Economics Working Paper. Northwestern University, Evanston, Ill.

Mayer, Wolfgang. 1974. "Short-Run and Long-Run Equilibrium for a Small Open Economy." *Journal of Political Economy* 82:955–67.

Menderson, Horst. 1959. "Terms of Trade between the Soviet Union and the Smaller Communist Countries." *Review of Economics and Statistics* 41:106–18.

Milanovic, Branko. 1992. "Privatization Options and Procedures." This volume.

Newbery, David. 1990. "Tax Reform, Trade Liberalization and Industrial Restructuring in Hungary." In *European Economy: Economic Transformation in Hungary and Poland.* Brussels: Commission of the European Communities.

Oblath, Gabor. 1989. "Opening up in Hungary: The Relevance of International Experiences and Some Peculiarities." Paper presented at the World Bank Conference on Attempts at Liberalization: Hungarian Economic Policy and International Experience, 16–18 November. Budapest: Kopint-Datorg. Processed.

Oblath, Gabor, and David Tarr. 1992. "The Terms-of-Trade Effects from the Elimination of State Trading in Soviet-Hungarian Trade." *Journal of Comparative Economics* 16:75–93.

Pelzman, Joseph. 1977. "Trade Creation and Trade Diversion in the Council of Mutual Economic Assistance, 1954–1970." *American Economic Review* 67:713–22.

———. 1978. "Soviet-COMECON Trade: The Question of Intra-Industry Specialization." *Weltwirtschaftliches Archiv* 114:297–304.

———. 1980. "Economic Determinants in Soviet Foreign Trade with Eastern Europe." *European Economic Review* 14:45–59.

Poznanski, Kazimierz Z. 1988. "Opportunity Cost in Soviet Trade with Eastern Europe: Discussion of Methodology and New Evidence." *Soviet Studies* 40:290–307.

Rosefielde, Steven. 1974. "Factor Proportions and Economic Rationality in Soviet International Trade, 1955–1968." *American Economic Review* 64:670–81.

———. 1981. "Comparative Advantage and the Evolving Pattern of Soviet International Commodity Specialization 1950–1973." In Steven Rosefielde, ed., *Economic Welfare and the Economics of Soviet Socialism.* Cambridge, U.K.: Cambridge University Press.

Saldanha, Fernando. 1992. "Self-Management: Theory and Yugoslav Practice." This volume.

Schaffer, Mark. 1989. "The Credible Commitment Problem in the Center-Enterprise Relationship." *Journal of Comparative Economics* 13:359–82.

Schaffer, Mark. 1990. "Taxation, Subsidization, and Regulation of State-Owned Enterprises in Poland." In *European Economy: Economic Transformation in Hungary and Poland*. Brussels: Commission of the European Communities.

Schnytzer, Adi. 1982. *Stalinist Development Strategy and Practice*. Oxford, U.K.: Oxford University Press.

Schrenk, Martin. 1992. "The CMEA System of Trade and Payments." This volume.

Tardos, Marton. 1983. "The Increasing Role and Ambivalent Reception of Small Enterprises in Hungary." *Journal of Comparative Economics* 7:277–87.

Terrell, Katherine. 1990. "Productivity of Western and Domestic Capital in Polish Industry." Working Paper. Department of Economics, Graduate School of Public and International Affairs, University of Pittsburgh, Pittsburgh, Pa. Processed.

———. 1992. "International Technology Transfer and Efficiency in Socialist Enterprises. The Polish Failure of the 1970s." This volume.

Toth, Tamas. 1988. Personal communications on CMEA trade. University of Economic Sciences, Budapest.

van Brabant, Josef M. 1987. *Regional Price Formation in Eastern Europe: Theory and Practice of Trade Pricing*. Boston and Dordrecht: Kluwer Academic Publishers.

Wiles, Peter J. D. 1968. *Communist International Economics*. Oxford, U.K.: Basil Blackwell.

Williamson, Oliver. 1983. "Credible Commitments: Using Hostages to Support Exchange." *American Economic Review* 73:519–40.

———. 1985. *The Economic Institutions of Capitalism*. New York: Free Press.

Wolf, Thomas A. 1988. *Foreign Trade in a Centrally Planned Economy*. London and New York: Harwood Academic Publishers.

Zalai, Erno. 1988. Private communications on CMEA trade. University of Economic Sciences, Budapest.

11

International Technology Transfer and Efficiency in Socialist Enterprises: The Polish Failure of the 1970s

Katherine Terrell

During the 1960s and the 1970s, the centrally planned economies (CPEs) of the U.S.S.R. and Eastern Europe emphasized research and development and industrial technological innovation as the means of achieving economic objectives. Reflecting this emphasis, Western licenses were purchased, and Western machinery and equipment were imported. Poznanski (1985) reports that the number of Western licenses purchased by socialist countries rose from 300 during the 1960–65 period to 1,200 in the 1971–75 period. Hungary and Poland were significant importers of capital-embodied Western technology; the U.S.S.R. imported somewhat less such technology. According to Gomulka (1986, pp. 52–53), imports of Western machinery as a proportion of total machinery investments averaged 3 percent to 8 percent in the U.S.S.R. and 10 percent to 30 percent in Eastern Europe in the early 1970s.[1]

In spite of this investment, enterprises in Eastern Europe and the U.S.S.R. technologically lagged behind the West. A body of microeconomic evidence reveals a high degree of inefficiency and misallocation of resources.[2] These findings raise the questions: What was the nature and extent of inefficiency and resource misallocation? And why were socialist industries unable to absorb Western technology?

---

[1] These proportions, however, are small in comparison with developing countries and the Republic of Korea.

[2] See for example, Gelb, Jorgensen, and Singh (this volume), Fallenbuchl (1983), Hanson (1982), and Poznanski (1985).

This chapter addresses the first of these questions in the context of the Polish experience with the 1971–76 "new development strategy" which was based on large-scale imports of Western capital. The section on the new development strategy describes the political-economic background and the goals of this strategy. The following sections report the empirical evidence from production function estimation comparing the efficiency of Western and domestic (or Council for Mutual Economic Assistance (CMEA)) inputs. The results indicate that Polish industry failed to use Western capital efficiently. Reasons for this failure are considered in the concluding section.

The new development strategy

During Eastern Europe's industrialization drive in the 1950s, attempts were made to construct a comprehensive industrial structure with the long-term objective of achieving self-sufficiency. Priority was given to highly capital-intensive heavy industries which required large investment outlays. To a considerable extent this strategy imitated that of the U.S.S.R. in the 1930s, and ignored developments in the more developed countries at that time. Poland followed this pattern.

By the mid-1960s, however, when the rate of growth of industrial output had slowed, modernization of productive capacity became a central objective. In 1968 a strategy of "selective development" was adopted. Priority was given to developing certain branches of industry and certain groups of commodities. The designated branches of industry were to receive priority in the allocation of investment funds, research and development facilities, and imports of machines and equipment. The policy encountered serious difficulties because the share of saving was raised to unsustainable levels, and the policy was abandoned after the workers' riots of December 1970.

At the beginning of the 1970s, Western capital became more readily available to the centrally planned economies. Because of the world recession, Western exporters were more willing to offer credit. After the 1973 oil price shock, banks were also more liquid. Most CPEs increased their imports of Western capital and technology.

Against this background, Poland in 1971 launched its "new development strategy." The objective of the strategy was to promote the rapid expansion of modern, efficiently produced commodities by using Western credits and imported Western technology. It was envisaged that production would take place in new or modernized plants, and would utilize the most modern Western equipment, in accordance with contemporary Western standards. The large current account deficit that would ensue would for a time be financed by borrowing from the West, facilitating investment growth in the medium term without pressure on consumption. The plan was that in the long run a portion of the technologically advanced commodities would be exported to Western markets. Another portion would satisfy domestic demand, thereby saving hard currency imports. By containing the growth of external debt, the process could be continued without foreign currency constraints.

In 1972 Poland thus embarked on an unprecedented increase in investment in machinery and equipment. The rate of growth of fixed capital investment averaged 21.3 percent per year during 1972–75 as compared to an average annual rate of about 7.6 percent during the preceding 15 years.[3] The share of imports of machinery and equipment from nonsocialist countries in total machinery and equipment imports rose from an average of 21.2 percent during 1961–71 (never rising above 26 percent) to an average of 43.3 percent during 1972–76, reaching a peak of 52 percent in 1975 (Fallenbuchl 1983, p. 105).

The two branches of industry emphasized in the modernization process were chemicals and engineering. These two branches received over half (59.1 percent) of the total value of imported completed plants in 1972–79. They received by far the largest amount of Western technology (defined as the value of machinery, equipment and completed plants imported from nonsocialist countries) during this period.

By the mid-1970s internal and external disequilibria appeared and it became clear that the new development strategy was not sustainable. The strategy was replaced in 1976 by a "new economic maneuver," which imposed a drastic reduction in the rate of investment and in the growth of hard currency imports. This was accompanied by a return to an even higher degree of centralization than had previously existed and a greater use of administrative controls. A gradual reduction of the trade deficit with nonsocialist countries could have allowed the completion of existing projects. However, imports from the West were sharply curtailed. These cuts were effected by administrative commands in an arbitrary manner. Imports of machinery and equipment from nonsocialist countries, which had been growing at an average annual rate of 59.8 percent during 1972–75, slowed to a 2.2 percent increase in 1976 and fell by 8.5 percent in 1977 (all in nominal zloty terms). By 1980 the value of imports of machinery and equipment from nonsocialist countries was less than two thirds (65 percent) of the 1976 level. The actual annual rate of growth in investment in 1976–78 (2 percent) fell below the planned rate of 8 percent. Despite the draconian import cuts in 1976, however, it was not until 1980 that the trade deficit with nonsocialist countries was reduced substantially, from $3.0 billion in 1975 to $70 million in 1980 (Fallenbuchl 1983, p. 104).

During 1971–80 Poland received $38.6 billion in long- and medium-term credit. Debt servicing increased from 12.4 percent of the value of exports to nonsocialist countries in 1971, to 83.2 percent in 1980 (Fallenbuchl 1983, p. 20). The new development strategy was largely responsible for this debt,

---

[3]The only other period when the rate of investment in capital approximated the rates of the 1971–75 period was during 1950–55, when the rate averaged 15.4 percent per year (Fallenbuchl 1983).

partly because of the magnitude of hard currency imports, but also because of failure to increase hard currency exports within the projected time.

The political, social and economic crisis that followed the collapse of the new development strategy remained unresolved in the 1980s. A recession, similar in magnitude to that experienced in the West during the 1930s, made evident the need for far-reaching and comprehensive reform. A reform was eventually launched on January 1, 1990 (see Gelb, Jorgensen, and Singh, this volume).

Evidence on the effect of technology transfer

The new development strategy was thus characterized by a rapid and large increase in industrial sector investment which was based on hard currency imports of Western technology and capital financed by Western credit. The policy was short-lived because of the external disequilibria it produced.

The evidence indicates that the transfer of Western technology during this period, as well as generally during the 1960s and 1970s, failed to achieve the intended goals of increasing efficiency and increasing industrial exports. The analysis of light and heavy industries presented here, as well as other disaggregated studies that I have carried out (Terrell 1990a, 1990b), indicate that resources were misallocated and that there was virtually no technical progress during the 1961–83 period. Moreover, there is little revealed connection between technology transfer to particular industries and export performance.

The new development strategy and productive efficiency

My findings here and elsewhere (Terrell 1990a, 1990b) are drawn from production function analysis using 1961–83 time series of annual data on output (global product) and three inputs (domestic capital, Western capital, and labor). Western capital is a newly constructed series. A brief description of these data and the formal methodology used is presented in the Appendix.

If the transfer of technology modernized industry, a positive correlation would be revealed between productive efficiency and the rate of accumulation of Western technology. One would expect a generally positive rate of technical change, especially in those industries that had acquired relatively larger amounts of Western technology.

Table 11.1 presents statistics on the relative share of Western capital to total capital in eight industries, as well as aggregated light and heavy industries, during the 1961–83 period. The share of Western capital to total capital is higher in light industry (4.2 percent) than in heavy industry (2.4 percent). This is the result of the more rapid rate of growth of Western capital accumulation in light industry (12.4 percent per year) in comparison with heavy industry (10.2 percent per year), and a slower average annual rate of growth of domestic capital accumulation in light industry (7.6 percent) relative to heavy industry (8.2 percent). As the figures in Table 11.1 indicate, however, there is considerable variation in the rate of growth of Western capital among the eight industrial branches.

Table 11.1 Selected descriptive statistics for eight Polish industries, 1961-83

Industry	Average $\left(\dfrac{K_w}{K_w + K_d} \right)$	Average annual growth rate (in percent)			
		Q	K_w	K_d	L
Light (aggregate)	*4.2*	*6.1*	*12.4*	*7.6*	*1.7*
Food and tobacco	1.6	4.3	14.5	7.3	1.7
Light industry	4.9	5.7	11.4	7.1	1.3
Wood and paper	4.9	5.8	9.9	7.4	1.2
Chemicals	4.3	8.9	13.6	8.4	2.6
Heavy (aggregate)	*2.4*	*6.6*	*10.2*	*8.2*	*1.7*
Engineering	3.4	10.2	10.4	10.4	3.1
Fuels and energy	2.8	5.3	3.6	7.0	1.3
Minerals	1.6	5.8	9.4	6.5	0.9
Metallurgy	0.9	5.6	17.4	9.0	1.7
Total industry	*3.1*	*6.4*	*11.9*	*8.0*	*2.0*

Note: Q = output (global product); K_w = Western capital; K_d = domestic capital; and L = labor (number of workers). The growth rates are calculated on the basis of OLS regression of the logarithm of the dependent variable on a constant term and time.

Rate of technical change. Parameters estimated from an augmented translog production function for light and heavy industry (see Appendix Table 11A.1) permit the calculation of the rate of technical change for each industry.[4] The rates were calculated for three important years: (a) the first year of the period under analysis (1961); (b) the year the new development strategy was formulated (1971); and (c) the year before the economy went into major crisis (1979). The results in Table 11.2 indicate that almost no technical progress occurred in Polish industry during these years. This finding is supported by more disaggregated analysis in Terrell (1990b) for seven of the eight industries.

In light industry the rate of technical change appears to have been negative—showing technical regression—for the entire period. In 1961, however, the estimate was not statistically significant. In 1971 the rate of

---

[4]See the Appendix for the specification of the estimated translog production function (Equation (1)) and the rate of technical change (Equation (2)).

technical change was –1.2 percent, and statistically significant at the 10 percent level. In 1979, the negative rate remained approximately the same (–1.1 percent) but at a higher (5 percent) level of significance. Heavy industry, on the other hand, exhibited a positive rate of technical change in 1961 (5.7 percent). The rate fell to zero in 1971 and then fell further to –2.4 percent in 1979. There was, therefore, a clear decline in the rate of technical change in heavy industry, from a positive rate to technological regression.

Table 11.2 Poland: rates of technical change and output elasticities for light and heavy industries

	Light industry	Heavy industry
Rate of technical change		
1961	-0.033	0.057[a]
1971	-0.012[b]	0.012
1979	-0.011[a]	-0.024[a]
Output elasticity of domestic capital		
1961	0.711[a]	0.203
1971	0.677[a]	0.393[a]
1979	0.733[a]	0.455[a]
Output elasticity of Western capital		
1961	-0.042	-0.001
1971	-0.063	0.038
1979	0.009	0.093
Output elasticity of labor		
1961	1.179[a]	0.111
1971	0.720[a]	0.307[a]
1979	0.324[a]	0.491[a]

a. Significant at 5 percent confidence interval.
b. Significant at 10 percent confidence interval.

Shifts in total factor productivity. The overall rate of technical change incorporates the effects of "embodied" and "disembodied" technical change. There is also evidence of shifts in the disembodied portion of technical change (or total factor productivity) in specifications wherein time does not interact with inputs.[5] If the new development strategy increased productive efficiency, one would expect to find an upward shift in, or increase in the growth rate of, total factor productivity during 1972–76 for all industries, or, at the very least, for those industries that imported relatively large amounts of Western technology. The results from Terrell

---

[5]That is, in specifications that exclude the $\Sigma \lambda_i t \ln X_i$ term in Equation (1) in the Appendix, but which, however, include a dummy for the period under study or such a dummy interacted with time.

(1990a) suggest that total factor productivity did not always rise in the industries that imported larger amounts of Western technology or whose shares of Western capital to total capital were among the largest and growing. For example, minerals was one of the three industries that experienced an increase in total factor productivity in 1972–76, but which ranked last among the eight in expenditures on Western capital.

These findings are confirmed by Kemme's (1987) production function analysis of eight major Polish industries.[6] Kemme tested the hypothesis that the rate of growth of total factor productivity rose during 1973–77 in comparison with 1960–72 in those branches that had acquired relatively more Western technology licenses. He found that the growth of total factor productivity and investment in Western licenses were not correlated.

The new development strategy and allocation of resources

Ideally one would like to assess the allocative efficiency of Polish industry by comparing the value of the marginal product of each input to its price. Input price data are not available; one can, however, base an empirical investigation on the fact that Western and domestic capital can be measured in the same cost units (millions of constant 1961 zlotys). A necessary allocative efficiency condition that one can therefore seek to verify is that domestic and Western capital have identical marginal products. If marginal products differed, total product could have been increased by reallocating resources. One can also seek to ascertain whether the marginal products, or output elasticities of the inputs, were positive. A zero or negative marginal product or output elasticity would signify that the given input had been used excessively.

Output elasticities. The customary means of assessing the contribution of inputs to output is to examine output elasticities. In Table 11.2, the estimated output elasticities are presented for each of the three inputs, at three points in time (1961, 1971, 1979). The gain in output from a 1 percent increase in Western capital is revealed to be zero throughout the period for both heavy and light industry. This evidence is rather damaging to the argument that there were beneficial effects from the injection of Western capital, in particular since the output elasticities of domestic capital and labor are positive throughout for both sectors.

Once again, these findings are similar to those obtained in my earlier disaggregated analysis (Terrell 1990a), except that here the output elasticity for Western capital is actually found to be negative in three light industries:

---

[6]It should be noted that Kemme's functional specification differs from that which I have employed (he uses Constant Elasticity of Substitution (CES) and Cobb-Douglas specifications), and capital in his study is not disaggregated by source.

food and tobacco, other light industry, and chemicals.[7] The results suggest that Western capital was wastefully employed (on the margin) in these three industries. This is particularly distressing in the case of chemicals, since this industry was given priority status by the new development strategy and accumulated Western capital at a rate of 13.6 percent per year during 1961–83.

Linkages to other sectors. Another aspect of resource allocation is the general equilibrium linkage through which investment in given sectors can affect the rest of the economy. Svejnar and Chaycowski (1991) find from an input-output analysis of Polish industry that investment was not always allocated to sectors that had high linkages with the rest of the economy, and was often allocated to sectors with high import requirements.

The new development strategy and hard currency exports

As I have indicated, it was expected that the debt incurred as a consequence of the new development strategy would be paid by exports to the West by those sectors receiving imported Western technology. Several researchers (including Fallenbuchl 1983 and Hanson 1982) have concluded that imported Western technology had no more than a limited impact on the expansion of exports to nonsocialist countries.

Fallenbuchl (1983, p. 39) found that the four most important earners of foreign exchange at the end of the 1970s (in terms of per unit of traded output with nonsocialist countries) were producers of raw materials or intermediate products: fuels and energy, metallurgy, food and tobacco, and wood products. Three of these industries were ranked at the lower end of the scale (fifth, sixth, and seventh) in terms of the amount of Western capital received during 1972–76.

Hanson (1982) found little correlation between the size (or growth) of technology imports by industrial branches and the size (or growth) of the branches' dollar exports. About 30 percent of Western technology imports was absorbed by sectors producing nontradable goods.

Although total exports to Western countries did rise somewhat during the period of the new development strategy, there was insufficient growth of exports to hard currency markets to avoid the accumulation of a substantial foreign debt. It was therefore necessary to reverse the import-led strategy in order to achieve external balance.

It should be noted that external factors contributed to the internal (systemic) difficulties encountered in achieving the sought growth in exports

---

[7]It should be noted, however, that the output elasticities for the eight industries were calculated with parameters estimated from a production function that did not include input-time interaction terms and with means of the logarithmic value of the inputs and output over a period of several years (that is, 1961–71, 1972–76, 1977–83) as opposed to specific years (1961, 1971, 1979).

to the West. Poland attempted to expand exports at a time when the newly industrialized countries were increasing world market shares.[8] The Polish planners underestimated (or did not perceive) the difficulty of competing with these countries for exports to nonsocialist countries.

Why did the new development strategy fail?

The findings for heavy and light industry presented in this paper, as well as the findings of other disaggregated analyses, indicate that the new development strategy failed to achieve its objectives of increasing the productivity of Polish industry and increasing exports to nonsocialist countries. In the face of massive imports of Western technology, there was a significant decline in the rate of technical progress; light industries even experienced technological regression in the 1970s. Moreover, those industries that were provided with the greatest access to imported Western technology increased neither total factor productivity nor the rate of productivity growth.

One approach to explaining these results (for example, Gomulka 1986, Fallenbuchl 1983) has been to propose that the Polish economy of the 1970s was not "capable" of absorbing the greatly increased levels of technology transfer because of the excessive pace of investment. Another reason proposed for the collapse of the new development strategy is that the economic system remained basically unchanged. As Brus (1980, p. 43) notes:

> *In the East European case the system seems to have acted as a powerful brake both on the generation and the diffusion of technological innovations. This is one of the reasons why the otherwise apparently sound idea of massive injections of Western technology bought on credit to be paid back from the output of the newly created industrial base ran into such serious difficulties, notably in Romania in the second half of the 1960s and in Poland in the 1970s.*

Numerous systemic obstacles in Poland indeed prevented the transfer of technology from achieving its objectives. The overcentralized and rigid system of planning and management caused delays in the construction and expansion of plants. Buildings meant to house new machinery were not constructed on time; there were delays supplying complementary parts and there were shortages of experienced managers and technical personnel. Management-level systemic factors also inhibited innovation and modernization: managers of state enterprises accustomed to incentives which

---

[8]For example, Eastern Europe's share in Organisation for Economic Co-operation and Development (OECD) imports of machinery and transport equipment increased from 0.1 percent in 1970 to 0.7 percent in 1980, while Poznanski (1985, p. 42) reports that the share of six newly industrialized countries increased from 0.1 percent to 4.1 percent during the same period.

rewarded the achievement of plan goals worried that the introduction of new technology would disrupt production.

Given the incentive structure, there was no demand for the technological change that effective use of Western capital would have provided. In Poland, as in other centrally planned economies, state enterprises often perceived technology transfer as a means of solving short-term problems or eliminating current bottlenecks, rather than as a means to long-term technological progress.[9]

A further reason for the lack of interest in technological change was lack of cost consciousness. The soft budget constraint reduced the incentives of managers to seek out new and cheaper production methods. Capital investment in socialist countries was financed through budget subsidies or credits that often did not have to be repaid on strict terms.

The centralized system of planning and management led to mistakes in investment policy which were at least partly responsible for the inability of enterprises to expand profitable exports to nonsocialist countries. The planners who selected lines of specialization for export and who allocated investment resources and imports of foreign technology were detached from the actual needs of production and foreign trade. As Fallenbuchl (1983, p. 17) notes:

The priority allocation of investment, imported machines and licenses to sectors which could not become profitable exporters, but on the contrary, induced additional imports of fuels, materials, and parts, and were heavily capital-, material-, and energy-intensive, created additional balance of payments pressures.

The lack of success in expanding of exports to the West also stemmed from a lack of experience with Western trade. The Poles lacked personal contacts. An adequate distribution network takes time to develop. Independently of these considerations, however, a reorientation of trade toward the West involved risks that managers under the existing incentive structure were not inclined to take, in particular given the security of the CMEA system (see Hillman and Schnytzer, this volume).

Marxian theory of economic development and social change emphasizes that economic efficiency and productivity growth are key factors that, in the course of history, determine the outcome of the competition between different forms of organization of economic activity (Elliot 1976, pp. 151–84). The irony is that the lack of economic efficiency and the absence of productivity growth are the very factors that brought an end to the socialist centrally planned system.

---

[9]See Fallenbuchl (1983, p. 87) and Gomulka (1986, p. 46) for elaborations on this issue.

Appendix

Data

The data for this study were collected from Polish statistical yearbooks. Output and capital are measured in millions of 1961 zlotys. Labor is measured as number of people working. The data for Western capital (technology) are a new series, constructed from the *Foreign Trade Yearbook* statistics on the value of machinery, equipment and completed plants imported from nonsocialist countries. The Western capital stock was constructed by summing and depreciating the real value of these annual imports to each industry. (See Terrell 1990b for details on the construction of this variable.)

Methodology

Treating time as the variable capturing technical change, I estimate the following translog production function:

$$
(11.1) \quad \ln Q = \ln \alpha_0 + \alpha_1 t + \alpha_2 t^2 + \sum_{i=1}^{3} \beta_i \ln X_i
$$
$$
+ 0.5 \sum_{i=1}^{3} \sum_{j=1}^{3} \gamma_{ij} \ln X_i \ln X_j + \sum_{i=1}^{3} \lambda_i t \ln X_i + \mu
$$

for four light and four heavy industries, where Q = output, t = time, $X_1 = K_d$, $X_2 = K_w$, $X_3 = L$ (labor), and $\gamma_{ij} = \gamma_{ji}$.

This specification allows the calculation of the rate of technical change,

$$
(11.2) \quad \frac{\partial \ln Q}{\partial t} = \alpha_1 + 2\alpha_2 t + \sum_{i=1}^{3} \lambda_i \ln X_i
$$

which incorporates both the effect of "disembodied" technical change (α_1 and α_2) and the effect of any bias in technical change on the use of each of the factor inputs (λ_i). The λ_i coefficient indicates the extent to which technical change is biased toward the particular factor input. That is, technical change is factor i-using, -neutral, or -saving as the estimate of λ_i is positive, zero, or negative, respectively.[10]

---

[10]See Jorgenson, Gollop, and Fraumeni (1987, p. 242).

Technical bias clearly affects the output elasticities of each factor input, which are also examined in this paper:

$$(11.3) \qquad \frac{\partial \ln Q}{\partial \ln X_i} = \beta_i + \sum_{j=1}^{3} \gamma_{ij} \ln X_j + \lambda_i t$$

Equation (11.1) is estimated with 1961-83 data for four heavy and four industries. The eight industries have been aggregated into the two major industrial groups referred to be planners in order to facilitate the analysis and discussion. The four heavy industries are engineering, fuels and energy, minerals, and metallurgy; the four light industries are food and tobacco, other light industry, wood and paper, and chemicals.[11]

To increase the efficiency of estimation, the method of "seemingly unrelated regression" (SUR) was used. The parameters were constrained to be identical across the four light and four heavy industries. The equations were corrected for first-order serial correlation.

It was first of interest to determine whether technical change significantly affected total factor productivity and/or the factor inputs. The parameter estimates are used to test the hypotheses that (a) there was no disembodied technical change ($\alpha_1 = \alpha_2 = 0$) and (b) there was no technical bias in the factor input ($\lambda_1 = \lambda_2 = \lambda_3 = 0$). The Wald test statistics indicate that in light industry one cannot reject the hypothesis of no disembodied technical change and in heavy industry one cannot reject the hypothesis of no technical bias in all three factor inputs.[12] The equations were reestimated with these constraints in force and the results are presented in Table 11A.1.

---

[11]The chemicals industry is included in light industry, although part of this industry may not be considered light, for purposes of the estimation procedure.

[12]For light industry, the chi square statistic for the first hypothesis is 2.46 and for the second is 8.03. For heavy industry, the chi square statistic for the first hypothesis is 14.87 and for the second is 2.40.

Table 11A.1   Poland: parameter estimates for light and heavy industry production functions

	Light		Heavy	
	β	(SE)	β	(SE)
Constant	6.093[a]	(1.529)	12.456[a]	(3.583)
T	...	...	0.057[a]	(0.023)
T^2	...	...	-0.002[a]	(0.001)
$\ln K_d$	0.059	(0.592)	-0.094	(1.025)
$\ln K_w$	-0.189	(0.556)	-0.385	(0.415)
$\ln L$	4.678[a]	(0.630)	-1.820[a]	(0.542)
$\ln K_d \cdot t$	-0.011[b]	(0.006)	...	...
$\ln K_w \cdot t$	-0.009	(0.011)	...	...
$\ln L \cdot t$	0.021[a]	(0.008)	...	...
$(\ln K_d)^2$	0.103[a]	(0.068)	-0.007	(0.076)
$(\ln K_w)^2$	-0.018	(0.019)	0.002	(0.019)
$(\ln L)^2$	0.139	(0.086)	0.210[a]	(0.094)
$\ln K_d \cdot \ln K_w$	0.063	(0.088)	0.068	(0.068)
$\ln K_d \cdot \ln L$	-0.603[a]	(0.111)	0.232[a]	(0.078)
$\ln K_w \cdot \ln L$	-0.182[a]	(0.058)	-0.056	(0.062)

	Rho	R^2	D.W.	Rho	R^2	D.W.
IND 1 (5)	0.794[a]	0.986	1.27	0.179	0.998	1.62
	(0.105)			(0.197)		
IND 2 (6)	0.881[a]	0.993	1.43	1.000[a]	0.988	1.38
	(0.316)			(0.015)		
IND 3 (7)	0.381[a]	0.994	1.91	0.967[a]	0.989	1.81
	(0.156)			(0.015)		
IND 4 (8)	0.784	0.996	1.14	0.939[a]	0.989	1.41
	(0.743)			(0.050)		

a. Significant at 5 percent confidence level.
b. Significant at 10 percent confidence level.
... Variable not included in equation.
Note: Data in parentheses are standard errors.

References

Brus, Wlodimierz. 1980. "Political System and Economic Efficiency: The East European Content." *Journal of Comparative Economics* 4:40–55.

Elliot, J. E. 1976. "Marx and Contemporary Models of Socialist Economy." *History of Political Economy* 8:151–84.

Fallenbuchl, Zbigniew M. 1983. *East-West Technology Transfer: Study of Poland 1971-1980*. Paris: OECD.

Gelb, Alan, Erika Jorgensen, and Inderjit Singh. 1992. "Life after the Polish Big Bang: Episodes of Preprivatization Enterprise Behavior." This volume.

Gomulka, Stanislaw. 1986. *Growth Innovation and Reform in Eastern Europe*. Brighton, Sussex, U.K.: Wheatsheaf.

Hanson, Philip. 1982. "The End of Import-Led Growth? Some Observations on Soviet, Polish and Hungarian Experience in the 1970s." *Journal of Comparative Economics* 6:130–47.

Hillman, Arye L., and Adi Schnytzer. 1992. "Creating the Reform-Resistant Dependent Economy: Socialist Comparative Advantage, Enterprise Incentives, and the CMEA." This volume.

Jorgenson, Dale W., Frank M. Gollop, and Barbara M. Fraumeni. 1987. *Productivity and U.S. Economic Growth*. Cambridge, Mass.: Harvard University Press.

Kemme, David M. 1987. "Productivity Growth in Polish Industry." *Journal of Comparative Economics* 11:1–20.

Poznanski, Kazimierz Z. 1985. *The Environment for Technological Change in Centrally Planned Economies*. World Bank Staff Working Paper 718. Washington, D.C.

Svejnar, Jan, and Richard Chaycowski. 1991. "Optimal Export Oriented Economic Policies in Poland." In D. Kemme, ed., *Economic Reform in Poland: The Aftermath of Martial Law 1981-1988*. Greenwich, Conn.: JAI Press.

Terrell, Katherine. 1990a. "Productivity of Western and Domestic Capital in Polish Industry." Unpublished manuscript, Department of Economics, Graduate School of Public and International Affairs, University of Pittsburgh, Pittsburgh, Pa. Processed.

———. 1990b. "Technical Change in Socialist Industry: Evidence from Poland." Working Paper 263, Department of Economics, Graduate School of Public and International Affairs, University of Pittsburgh, Pittsburgh, Pa. Processed.

12

The Government Budgetary Consequences
of Reform of the CMEA System
# of International Trade:
The Case of Hungary

Istvan Abel, Arye L. Hillman, and David Tarr

Previous chapters have been concerned with the consequences of the end of the Council for Mutual Economic Assistance (CMEA) from directly trade-related perspectives of specialization and comparative advantage, the technology gap, enterprise incentives for adjustment, changes in the terms of trade, and international payments arrangements. This chapter draws attention to a further impact of the end of the CMEA, that of the effect on government budgets.

CMEA trade and the government budget

The price equalization mechanism

Revenues and expenditures deriving from taxes and subsidies on imports and exports link an economy's international trade to the government budget. Within the framework of the CMEA system of trade and payments, a price equalization mechanism insulated domestic prices of internationally traded goods from the prices at which the economy secured its imports or sold its exports. Domestic prices were determined and maintained in accordance with the perceived needs of the population. The criteria for determining domestic prices had little to do with domestic costs of production or world prices, and domestic prices differed among CMEA economies.[1] The price equalization mechanism enforced the law of one price for socialist trade.

The foreign trade organizations (FTOs), which under the CMEA system of socialist international trade were responsible for managing export sales and import purchases of particular goods, would have incurred windfall gains and losses from their conduct of the economy's international trade as set out in the CMEA protocols, had there not been a compensatory mechanism that eliminated price differentials between markets. In the absence of a price equalization mechanism, FTOs would have confronted incentives to undertake profitable transactions from within the CMEA-negotiated international trade protocols, and to limit or eliminate unprofitable transactions. The price equalization mechanism facilitated the functioning of the CMEA system of trade by eliminating such arbitrage opportunities.

Changes in the terms of trade

In a centrally planned economy, changes in the terms of trade are directly reflected in changes in revenue or expenditure in the government budget, through adjustments via the price equalization mechanism. If imports of a good were taxed to assure equality of the price of a domestic good and the imported substitute, and the foreign price of the import were to decline, the import tax on that good would be increased in order to maintain the established domestic price. The improvement in the terms of trade would thus generate revenue for the budget. Conversely, a deterioration of the terms of trade via an increase in the price of an imported good would result in a decline in government revenue.

The same link between changes in the terms of trade and the government budget applied to exports. If the terms of trade deteriorated because the price received for an export good declined, and the export was taxed because the foreign price exceeded the domestic price, government revenue declined. If the export price increased, so would government revenue. If the export was subsidized because the price at which the good was sold to the CMEA trading partner was below the domestic price, the improved terms of trade would decrease subsidy expenditures, which would again be reflected in the budget.

As of the beginning of 1991 the system of bilaterally negotiated "transferable ruble" (TR) trade protocols at CMEA prices was replaced by convertible currency exchange at world prices. This change involved a terms of trade loss for East European economies, equal to former Soviet subsidies

---

[1]See van Brabant (1987).

derived from the difference between the CMEA terms of trade and world prices.[2]

The terms of trade loss would be directly reflected in the government budget via the adjustments of the price equalization mechanism, if that mechanism were maintained. Trade at world prices in conjunction with the transition to a decentralized market economy eliminates the need, however, for a price equalization mechanism to prevent arbitrage, since markets perform the arbitrage function.

CMEA reform and the government budget

The elimination of the price equalization mechanism has macroeconomic consequences via the impact on the government budget. The significance of these consequences depends on the magnitude of tax revenues and subsidy expenditures associated with a country's CMEA trade. The impact on each CMEA economy is a matter for quantitative investigation. This chapter reports on the measurement of the budgetary impact on Hungary of the change from the CMEA system of trade. The calculations indicate a quantitatively significant effect on the government budget.

The Hungarian CMEA trade tax and subsidy scheme did not precisely arbitrage domestic and CMEA foreign trade prices in the manner of classical price equalization. Trade taxes and subsidies were established by direct negotiations between an enterprise and government authorities. The tax or subsidy partly reflected the profitability of the enterprise, although taxes and subsidies were formally defined by product, not by enterprise.[3] In principle, the (imperfectly arbitraging) CMEA trade taxes and subsidies could have been a source of either net revenue or net expenditure for the budget, depending on the configuration of domestic prices in Hungary and in its CMEA trading partners.

To evaluate the effect on the government budget of Hungary of the end of the CMEA trading system, we ask, counterfactually, what the effect on the budget would have been had the CMEA system been replaced by trade at world prices at the beginning of 1990. In Hungary, CMEA trade taxes and subsidies prior to the move to world prices were a source of net revenue for the budget. Calculations based on 1990 budgetary projections and some revised 1990 estimates indicate that the elimination of CMEA-trade taxes and subsidies would have resulted in a net loss to the government budget of

---

[2]On the historical Soviet subsidization of Eastern Europe via CMEA terms of trade, see Marrese and Vanous (1983) and Brada (1985). For updates see Oblath and Tarr (1992), Marrese and Wittenberg (1989), Marrese (1991), and Kenen (1990). Estimates of the magnitude of subsidization (or conversely of the terms of trade loss from the switch to world prices) vary, and are in particular contingent on the world price of oil and the extent to which the U.S.S.R. fulfilled its oil supply quota as specified in CMEA trade protocols.

[3]Because of high industry concentration, there was often coincidence between enterprise and product.

approximately 55.4 billion forint (or 2.7 percent of gross domestic product (GDP)).[4] For trade with the U.S.S.R. only, the loss of revenue to the state budget in 1990 would have been 49.4 billion forint (or 2.4 percent of GDP).

Policy significance of the budgetary impact

The estimated revenue loss from the CMEA system of trade taxes would move the budget from a small surplus of 0.5 percent of GDP (measured on a Government Financial Statistics basis) in 1990 to a deficit of about 2 percent of GDP in the absence of offsetting measures. The fiscal impact of the end of the CMEA system is thus of substantial policy significance.

In the period of transition to a market economy, it is understandable that a government will have as an objective of policy the preservation of fiscal stability. This will require restricting the size of the budgetary deficit to manageable levels. The government may, however, confront declining revenues because of falls in real output, and also increasing social safety net expenditure obligations. The end of the CMEA system of trade and payments introduces further fiscal consequences via the budgetary impact that are pertinent for policies to contain the budget deficit.

Distinguishing the budgetary impact from the terms of trade loss

Calculations of the terms of trade loss are to be distinguished from calculations of the budgetary impact of the change from the CMEA system of trade. As we shall demonstrate,[5] calculation of the budgetary impact is based on a comparison between domestic forint prices of CMEA imports and exports and transferable ruble (TR) prices converted at the prevailing forint per TR exchange rate. Trade taxes and subsidies arbitrage these prices. The net revenue lost (or, in principle, gained) from an elimination of these trade taxes and subsidies yields the impact on the government budget from the end of the CMEA transferable ruble clearing system of trade and the switch to world prices.

The terms of trade loss from the switch from CMEA to world prices, on the other hand, involves comparing TR prices and world (or dollar) prices. For this computation, goods traded at TR prices are revalued at dollar prices. The computation of the budgetary impact is, however, at given TR prices, and dollar prices thus have no role in this computation.

Dollar prices would be relevant to the budgetary impact if the TR reference-price taxes and subsidies of the CMEA system were replaced by new taxes and subsidies that arbitraged forint and dollar prices.[6] Under such

---

[4]The loss of government revenue is increased to 66.9 billion forint (or 3.2 percent of GDP) if the associated loss of tax revenue from domestically produced oil is included.

[5]See Equations (12.1)–(12.4).

[6]See Equation (12.5).

a scheme[7] price equalization[8] would persist with dollar rather than TR reference prices. A comparison between TR and dollar arbitraging taxes and subsidies at given domestic prices and exchange rates links the budgetary impact and the terms of trade loss, via the difference between the net revenue lost by the budget from the elimination of CMEA price and dollar price arbitraging taxes and subsidies. While the terms of trade loss incurred as a consequence of the switch from CMEA to world prices could in principle be computed by this method, it is more straightforward to compare TR and dollar prices without the intermediating forint valuation.[9]

Arbitrage and enterprise transactions

The elimination of trade taxes and subsidies would transfer the tax revenue lost by the budget to enterprises if domestic and TR prices and the exchange rate were not to change. Thus, if counterfactually the CMEA trade taxes and subsidies had been eliminated in 1990, the values that we calculate as lost to the budget would have been transferred to the enterprises.

The imperfect arbitrage of the Hungarian system of CMEA trade taxes and subsidies was also a source of gain or loss to enterprises engaging in CMEA trade—that is, producers or FTOs. The nonarbitraged part of the forint per TR price difference for goods subject to an export tax was a source of gain for the exporting enterprise, as were increased subsidies for goods for which the forint price exceeded the foreign price; hence, the significance of the negotiations between the government and enterprise in determining the levels of CMEA trade taxes and subsidies.

Changes in the price of imported raw materials and intermediate goods directly affect enterprise profits. In order to provide a comparison with the revenue loss experienced by the government, we also present an estimate of the costs to enterprises of the shift to dollar import prices. Again, this is a counterfactual estimate pertaining to 1990.

Additional fiscal effects

The end of the CMEA system resulted in additional fiscal effects which are beyond the scope of this study. Enterprise profits from export sales changed, for example, thereby changing tax revenue. For our purposes, the change in enterprises' export proceeds cannot be quantified with certainty, and there is considerable range in official estimates. Our calculations do not account for changed tax revenue from enterprise profits associated with export sales to CMEA countries, nor do they account for expenditures on social safety net outlays, infrastructure, and other expenditures made necessary by the

---

[7]Which is neither anticipated nor recommended.

[8]Or, in the case of imperfect arbitrage, the tendency to equalize prices.

[9]See Oblath and Tarr (1992).

adjustment of the economy to a market system. We confine ourselves to asking how the elimination of the CMEA system of trade taxes and subsidies would have affected the government budget had it occurred in 1990.

Price equalization

Classical price equalization[10]

The classical model of price equalization was employed to insulate CMEA economies from intra-CMEA arbitrage of grossly distorted prices. The state either received or paid out in domestic currency taxes or subsidies on traded goods. The difference for each good between the domestic price and the transferable ruble price converted at the TR exchange rate determined the magnitude of the tax revenue or the subsidy expenditure associated with CMEA trade in a good.

To be specific, let p_M^{TR} and p_X^{TR} denote the vectors of import and export prices in transferable rubles for Hungarian CMEA trade with the U.S.S.R., and let M and X respectively denote the quantity vectors of Hungarian imports from and exports to the U.S.S.R. Let t_{Mi} and t_{Xi} denote the percentage or ad valorem import and export taxes, respectively in sector i (these parameters take negative values when they refer to subsidies), let t_M and t_X be their vectors, and let p_{Mi} and p_{Xi} be the forint prices of the goods imported and exported, and p_M and p_X their vectors. Thus, if e is the number of forint per transferable ruble received or paid by Hungarian agents for exports or imports in the CMEA (that is, the forint per transferable ruble exchange rate), then the domestic forint prices and transferable ruble prices are related via

$$(12.1) \qquad p_{Mi} = e(1 + t_{Mi})p_{Mi}^{TR}, \quad p_{Xi} = e(1 - t_{Xi})p_{Xi}^{TR}.$$

Let p_i be the forint price of the domestically produced goods of sector i and p be the vector of these prices. Under classical price equalization, the import and export tax or subsidy rate would equalize the import and export prices with the price of the domestically produced goods in the sector, such that[11]

$$(12.2) \qquad\qquad p_i = p_{Mi} \quad \text{and} \quad p_i = p_{Xi}.$$

---

[10]See also Schrenk (this volume).
[11]Competition would also lead Equation (12.2) to hold for homogeneous goods in an open market economy.

Combining Equations (12.1) and (12.2), we have for a domestically produced traded good within the CMEA:

$$(12.3) \quad p_i = p_{Mi} = e(1+t_{Mi})p_{Mi}^{TR}, \quad p_i = p_{Xi} = e(1-t_{Xi})p_{Xi}^{TR}.$$

Thus, if the good is exported and the export price is greater (less) than the domestic price at the prevailing exchange rate, then exports are taxed (subsidized). Similarly, if the good is imported and the import price is less (greater) than the domestic price, then imports are taxed (subsidized). Equation (12.3) establishes the relationship between the transferable ruble exchange rate, the tariff or subsidy rate, and the foreign and domestic price. For classical price equalization, the exchange rate and the tariff or subsidy rates are tied together. A devaluation, which makes imports more expensive, implies a reduction in the tariff rate or an increase in the subsidy rate for imports. Similarly, a devaluation will imply an increase in export taxes or a decrease in export subsidies. If domestic prices are increased, through a reduction in price controls for example, then export taxes will be decreased and import taxes will be increased. Without these accommodating adjustments, the domestic economy is open to arbitrage possibilities.

The net revenue in forint to the government budget from the system of taxes and subsidies on CMEA trade under classical price equalization is determined by summing taxes and subsidies over all sectors:

$$(12.4) \qquad \sum_i e(t_{Mi}M_i p_{Mi}^{TR} + t_{Xi}X_i p_{Xi}^{TR}) = R^f.$$

There is no systematic relationship between the trade balance in transferable rubles and the net contribution R^f of the system of trade taxes and subsidies to the government budget. In particular, balanced trade in transferable rubles does not imply a zero net payment to the budget. Moreover, although Equation (12.4) could appear to suggest that a devaluation would increase government revenues from price equalization, in fact, as noted above, there are offsetting changes in the import and export taxes under classical price equalization.

If a shift to dollar-denominated prices were to occur in the CMEA region, then Equation (12.1) would be replaced by

$$(12.5) \qquad p_{Mi} = e^\$(1 + t_{Mi})p_{Mi}^\$, \quad p_{Xi} = e^\$(1 - t_{Xi})p_{Xi}^\$,$$

where $e^\$$ is the number of forint received or paid for a U.S. dollar (the forint per dollar exchange rate) and $p_M^\$$ and $p_X^\$$ are the dollar prices of the vector of goods in the CMEA region. In principle it would be possible to impose import and export taxes on the dollar prices in the CMEA region to equalize prices and prevent arbitrage. That is, Equation (12.2) could still be valid after the shift to dollar-denominated prices even in the presence of noncompetitive domestic prices, if tax and subsidy policy were applied to achieve price equalization. Such a policy would have a budgetary impact which, given the anticipated terms of trade loss, would entail loss of government revenue. Such a policy is, however, incompatible with an opening of the economy to international competition. Rather, it is expected that, as a result of international competition and domestic restructuring, domestic prices will adjust so that Equation (12.2) will remain valid (with allowance made for quality differences).

The Hungarian price equalization system

The Hungarian CMEA trade tax and subsidy scheme did not precisely arbitrage domestic and CMEA foreign trade prices in the manner of the above model. Trade taxes and subsidies were determined by negotiation between enterprises and the government authorities with reference to the profitability of the enterprise and other considerations. With regard to the terms of trade loss, part of the deterioration in Hungary's terms of trade from the shift to world prices will be reflected in direct increases in enterprises' costs of imported inputs and in lower prices of exports.[12] This is because of the imperfect arbitrage of the Hungarian system.

Table 12.1 presents representative magnitudes of Hungarian CMEA ad valorem import and export taxes and export subsidies in 1989.[13] The exchange rate between the forint and the ruble was set low enough (at 27.5 forint per ruble) that the need for import subsidies for price equalization purposes was avoided. Excluded from the sample in Table 12.1 are oil and other energy-related imports. Oil was not taxed on an ad valorem basis, but in a manner that we shall describe below.

Many domestic prices were neither fixed by a central planning authority nor independently set by enterprises, but were determined by negotiation between enterprises and the Government Price Office. Successive domestic liberalization policies decreased the proportion of prices regulated by the Government Price Office. Table 12.2 describes the extent of price regulation during 1988–90. Enterprises not subject to price regulation could adjust prices in response to changes in the foreign prices of inputs or exchange rate changes. Regulated prices were responsive to influences such as changes in enterprises' costs of imported intermediate inputs and raw materials. Subject to such changes, prices were determined by bargaining between the Price Office and the enterprises. Since both domestic prices and CMEA trade

---

[12]In aggregate; individually, of course, some enterprises may gain.

[13]These are specifically CMEA trade taxes and subsidies. For the complete listing from which Table 12.1 is drawn, see Hungary, Hungarian Official Bulletin 1989a. In addition to the CMEA subsidies, there was a combined subsidy of approximately 10 billion forint on food and agricultural exports to other non-CMEA markets; this was reported as a production subsidy in the budget.

taxes and subsidies were in many cases subject to negotiation with the enterprises, there was imperfect price equalization.

Table 12.1 Hungary: ad valorem taxes and subsidies on CMEA trade, 1990 *(sample)*

Surcharge on TR imports	
Coal	40%
Nonferrous metal	90%
Inorganic raw material	90%
Organic RM	89%
Plastic RM	105%
Synthetic fibers	100%
Leather	30%
Lada car 1500 L/2107	150,000 forint each
Surcharge on TR exports	
Household appliances	24%
Electronics	24%
Rubber products	20%
Detergents	30%
Machines	19%
Subsidy on TR exports	
Metallurgy	88%
Aluminum	97%
Shoes	51%
Textiles	48–79%
Beef meat	350%
Canned meat	220%
Chicken	290%
Canned vegetables	150%
Grain	130%
Corn	132%

Source: Hungary, Hungarian Official Bulletin (1989b).

Computing the impact on the budget

Aggregate CMEA trade

Table 12.3 presents the 1990 values of revenue from trade taxes and outlays
on export subsidies by sector, as in accord with planned trade as of
January 1, 1990.[14] Column 1 gives sources of import tax revenue. The two
largest sources of import tax revenue are in the extractive and trade

Table 12.2   Hungary: extent of price regulation *(percentage of total final
consumption)*

| Year | Administered prices[a] | Specific regulation | | Total regulated |
| | | Product[b] | Company[b] | |
(1)	(2)	(3)	(4)	(5 = 2 + 3 + 4)
1988	22	21	5	48
1989	19	12	7	38
1990	16	6	1	23

a. Administered prices were set by the Price Office.
b. Product-specific regulation: An enterprise that wished to change a price was obliged to report
this in advance to the price authority. In certain cases, the authority could initiate negotiations
with the company.
c. Company-specific regulation: The price authority together with the company and suppliers or
users of company products specified price guidelines for the year. The company was obliged to
adhere to the guidelines on average. It could increase the price of some products only if other
prices were lowered.
Source: Hungary, Reform of the General Government (1990), p. 38.

categories. The Foreign Trade Organizations and wholesalers appear under
the category "trade," because taxation of many imports took place at this
level; as the table indicates, 32 percent of import taxes on CMEA trade were
levied on the FTOs or wholesalers. An additional 41 percent of taxes on
CMEA imports derived from the mining and extractive sector: the 31.9
billion forint of revenue from this category of imports includes the revenue
from oil imports from the U.S.S.R. These two categories together accounted
for 73 percent of the revenue from import taxes. The total budgetary loss
associated with the elimination of all CMEA import taxes is 77.4 billion
forint.

---

[14]These values were revised during 1990. In May 1990 projected revenue from import taxes
had increased to 84.32 billion forint. This figure, however, would be decreased because of
reduced Soviet supply of oil. The source for the disaggregated CMEA data in Table 12.2 is the
Budget Report to Parliament.

Column 2 indicates the revenue associated with taxation of domestic production.[15] Oil comprises the principal part of the extractive category, and the tax on domestic oil production is referred to as a "natural monopoly" tax. The difference between the domestic price of domestically extracted oil and the domestic cost of production was entirely appropriated as tax. The cost of domestically extracted oil in the first quarter of 1990 was 5,891 forint per ton and the average domestic price was 7,170 forint per ton. The tax on domestic oil was therefore 1,279 forint per ton. Projected 1990 revenue from the "natural monopoly" tax on domestically extracted oil was 10.7 billion forint, which together with the "natural monopoly" tax on the domestic chemical industry of 0.8 billion forint resulted in total domestic

Table 12.3 Hungary: taxes and subsidies on CMEA trade, 1990 *(planned as of December 1989; billions of forint)*

Sector	1 Import tax	2 Tax on domestic production[a]	3 Export tax	4 Export subsidy	5 Net effect (I) (1+2+3–4)	6 Net effect (II) (1+3–4)
Extractive	31.9	10.7	—	—	42.6	31.9
Electricity	5.9	—	—	—	5.9	5.9
Metallurgy	5.9	—	—	3.8	2.1	2.1
Machinery	0.1	—	16.0	—	16.1	16.1
Building materials	—	—	—	—	—	—
Chemical industry	4.7	0.8	3.7	1.0	8.2	7.4
Light industry	3.1	—	—	3.9	–0.8	–0.8
Food processing	0.1	—	—	24.3	–24.2	–24.2
Industry total	51.7	11.5	19.7	33.0	49.9	38.4
Agriculture	0.2	—	—	2.6	–2.4	–2.4
Trade	25.1	—	0.8	7.3	18.6	18.6
Other	0.4	—	0.6	0.2	0.8	0.8
Total	77.4	11.5	21.1	43.1	66.9	55.4

Note: — = not applicable. In net effects, subsidies are indicated by (–) sign.
a. Domestic natural monopoly tax.
Source: Hungary, Ministry of Finance (1989).

---

[15]In 1989 Hungarian domestic production of oil was 1.9 million tons; 6.5 million tons were imported from the U.S.S.R., tax revenue from which appears in Table 12.2 in the extractive category.

natural monopoly revenue of 11.5 billion forint. The domestic natural monopoly tax was not a tax on CMEA trade; it would, however, be affected by the change to trade at world prices to the extent that the domestic price of oil would change. If the shift were to raise (lower) the domestic price of oil, then these revenues would increase (decrease).

Column 3 indicates export taxes. The principal source of export tax revenue was the machinery sector. Column 4 indicates export subsidies. Here the dominant sector was food processing. A substantial component of outlays for export subsidies appears in the "trade" category, reflecting the export activities of FTOs.

Excluding the domestic natural monopoly tax, the total loss to the budget is 55.4 billion forint (column 6). Using an estimate of 1990 Hungarian GDP of 2,071 billion forint in current prices,[16] the revenue loss to the state budget is 2.7 percent of GDP.

Soviet trade

Table 12.3 refers to total CMEA trade. Table 12.4 presents projected magnitudes in forint of taxes in 1990 on imports from the U.S.S.R. only, divided into three categories: energy, raw materials, and machines and consumer goods. These data were provided by the Ministry of Finance, and are based on 1990 Hungarian-Soviet trade as projected by the Ministry of Trade in May 1990. The data make allowance for revisions of planned 1990 trade, based on the expectation that there would be shortfalls in Soviet deliveries relative to the balanced trade protocols. The import tax revenue is 74.4 billion forint.[17]

---

[16]This is based on 21 percent nominal and –4 percent real growth (that is, inflation of 25 percent). It is close to the estimate of the Hungarian National Planning Office of 2,035 billion forint. (See Hungary, National Planning Office 1990, Table 3.)

[17]Some minor discrepancies arise in comparisons between the CMEA numbers in Table 12.5 and the Hungarian-Soviet trade tax and subsidy data. The Hungarian budget data are composed on a cash basis while income statistics for consumers and enterprises are composed on an accrual basis. The value of 74.4 billion forint for revenue from taxes on imports from the U.S.S.R. refers to the dominant component of the same tax proceeds as the 77.4 billion forint import tax revenue for total CMEA trade reported in Table 12.5: the latter value is based on planned CMEA trade on a cash basis, and the former value is based on expected Hungarian-Soviet trade on an accrual basis. The accrual basis permits the effects on the budget and the incomes of enterprises and households to be identified.

Table 12.4 Hungary: net change in budgetary revenue, 1990 *(expected as of May 1990; billions of forint)*

	Import taxes	Export taxes	Export subsidies	Total
Energy	44.02	—	—	—
Raw materials	26.75	—	—	—
Machines and consumer goods	3.63	—	—	—
Total	74.40	9.1	34.1	49.4

— = not available or not applicable.
Source: Hungary, Ministry of Finance (1990).

Taxes on energy imports (oil and natural gas) account for 59 percent of the revenue from import taxes, with 36 percent deriving from taxes on raw materials. Thus, taxes on energy and raw material imports together account for 95 percent of import tax revenue.

Table 12.5 focuses on the dominant energy component of revenue and further disaggregates revenue sources. Taxes on crude oil accounted for 35.5 percent of total revenue from taxes on Soviet imports. The tax on imported oil was the difference between the domestic regulated price and the import price. For example, for the period January–March 1990, the average domestic price was 7,170 forint a ton, and the import price was 96.3 TR a ton or 2,648 forint.

Table 12.5 Hungary: import taxes on energy-related products, 1990 *(expected; billions of forint)*

Imports	Expected taxes
Crude oil	26.38
Heating oil	0.77
Diesel oil	4.52
Petrol	1.10
Kerosene	0.25
Natural gas	5.43
Coke	0.60
Electricity	4.97
Total energy	44.02

Source: Hungary, Ministry of Finance (1990).

The value for expected revenue from taxes on exports to the U.S.S.R. in 1990 was 9.1 billion forint. Subsidies to exports to the U.S.S.R. in 1990 were expected to be 34.1 billion forint.[18] With regard to trade with the U.S.S.R., the net budgetary impact of the change from the CMEA system of trade to free trade at world prices is therefore 49.4 billion forint.[19] The budgetary impact of the loss of this revenue in 1990 would have been 2.4 percent of Hungary's GDP.

Tax revenue from exports

The changed conditions for conducting trade with the U.S.S.R. as of the beginning of 1991 would affect the volume and value of exports, thereby influencing enterprises' earnings and their tax liabilities, and therefore affecting budgetary revenues. The effect of the change from the prior CMEA system of trade and payments on the value of Hungarian exports to the U.S.S.R. was uncertain.[20] Ministry of Finance estimates suggested an increase in enterprise income from exports to the U.S.S.R. ranging from 15 to 73 billion forint.[21] Thus, for example, an increase in enterprise income of 30 billion forint, at prevailing tax rates on enterprise profits, would yield the budget an additional 13 billion forint in tax revenue.

Other budgetary impacts

The domestic adjustment associated with the change from the CMEA system of trade and payments imposes budgetary burdens via social safety net outlays. We have not estimated the magnitude of these outlays, which are subject to considerable uncertainty and are contingent on the extent and duration of labor unemployment and need for retraining of labor.

Trade policy

Trade in convertible currency at world prices with the U.S.S.R. did not imply free trade. The agreement between Hungary and the U.S.S.R. related to the prices at which they would trade with each other as of 1991, but did not specify that the domestic prices confronting Hungarian purchasers of Soviet

---

[18]These figures are derived from the Ministry of Finance. Disaggregated data on goods taxed or subsidized were not available.

[19]That is, the import tax revenue (74.4 billion forint) plus the export tax revenue (9.1 billion) minus export subsidy outlays (34.1 billion).

[20]The effect on exports to the U.S.S.R. would depend upon whether there would be substitution, and if so the extent thereof, in Soviet demand away from Hungarian goods.

[21]The range in calculations derives from different assumptions regarding future exports and from the different exchange rates used. The Ministry of Finance estimated the lower value via calculations based on the dollar profitability in Western markets of the goods that would be sold to the U.S.S.R., assuming no change in the volume or structure of exports to the U.S.S.R. The higher figure is based on Ministry of Trade estimates that exports to the U.S.S.R. would decline from 3.5 billion rubles in 1990 to 2.9 billion in 1991, with export revenue based on an exchange rate of 67 forint per dollar to obtain a dollar value of exports of $2.65 billion.

Table 12.6 Hungary: increases in enterprises' costs, 1990

Product	Domestic price (forint) 1	World market price (U.S. dollars) 2	Volume 3	Cost increase (thousands of forint) (2e − 1)3 (e≡63 ft/$)
Coal	4,726	83	700	352,000
Foundry coke	6,000	140	500	1,410,000
Oil	7,170	116	6,200	855,600
Diesel fuel	9,740	177	740	1,044,140
Fuel oil	5,130	94	200	158,400
Gas	4,837	85	5,900	3,056,200
Jet kerosene	11,290	187	110	54,010
Electricity	3,000	40	10,000	−4,800,000
Energy				*2,130,350*
Asbestos	14,000	600	32	761,600
Cement	1,600	40	500	460,000
Pig-iron	6,630	168	250	988,500
Ferro alloy	29,800	830	44	989,560
Rolled-material	18,920	325	600	933,000
Cold-rolled steel	36,800	600	1	1,000
Lead	36,560	627	5	14,705
Nickel	840,000	13,557	3	42,273
Aluminum	76,549	2,536	105	8,737,995
Polyethylene m.	42,000	1,200	10	384,000
Polyethylene a.	36,000	1,133	30	1,061,370
Ethylene	20,000	666	60	1,317,480
Polystyrene	59,370	1,425	10	361,050
Methanol	9,240	189	60	205,380
Synthetic rubber	45,200	1,339	41	1,605,437
Ammonium nitrate	5,940	95	118	5,310
Carbamid	5,187	83	371	15,582
Phosphate	5,557	89	120	6,000
Potash fertilizer	2,200	110	568	2,686,640
Log	3,000	92	760	2,124,960
Timber	7,500	155	844	1,911,660
Cellulose	22,352	653	86	1,615,682
Paper	22,400	668	79	1,555,036
Cardboard	14,300	562	62	1,308,572
Cotton	75,900	1,548	40	864,960
Viscose	57,300	1,951	10	656,130
Raw materials				*30,613,882*
Lada parts	1,179,750	37,000	1	1,299,250
Agricultural machines	841,500	27,600	0.5	503,850
Metallurgical machines	426,250	16,000	1	645,750
Trucks	573,787	13,950	1	305,063
Other machines	1,405,250	50,000	1	1,744,750
Machines				*4,498,663*
Total cost increase of enterprises				*37,242,985*

Source: Hungary, Ministry of Trade (1990) (authors' calculations).

goods would equal world prices. Issues relating to trade policy therefore arise. Our calculations of the budgetary impact of the elimination of the CMEA trade taxes and subsidies are based on the assumption of no substitute revenue from trade restrictions imposed as part of a commercial policy response.[22]

The enterprises

If the only projected change were the elimination of trade taxes and subsidies, then the amount lost by the government budget would be transferred to enterprises. Enterprises, however, were also to confront world (or dollar) prices, rather than the given TR prices and given exchange rate.

Table 12.6 presents illustrative computations of direct cost increases of imported raw materials and intermediate inputs encompassing approximately 75 percent of domestic transactions. The calculations should be regarded as illustrative because price estimates for a number of the categories are uncertain. For each input the difference between the domestic forint price and the world dollar price converted at the official exchange rate and quantity weighted was computed. The increased costs to enterprises for imports totaled 37.2 billion forint or 1.8 percent of GDP.[23]

Conclusions

The computations reported in this chapter demonstrate how the elimination of CMEA trade taxes and subsidies can have a significant budgetary impact. The results are based on counterfactual consequences of deviating from planned 1990 data. Had the CMEA come to an end in 1990 (rather than 1991), the projected government deficit would have changed from a surplus of 0.5 percent to a deficit of approximately 2 percent of GDP. This points to the potential importance of the fiscal impact of the end of the CMEA system of trade.

---

[22]Because of General Agreement on Tariffs and Trade (GATT) requirements of nondiscrimination, Hungary, for example, could be obliged to impose duties on Soviet imports equal to the tariffs Hungary levies on Western imports.

[23]A prominent item in Table 12.6 is aluminum, which accounts for 23.5 percent of the cost increase. Aluminum was subject to a special agreement whereby Hungary provided bauxite to the U.S.S.R. and in return received refined aluminum. The domestic forint price of aluminum ($1,215 at 63 forint per dollar) was less than half of the world price ($2,536). Under an agreement with the U.S.S.R., Hungary reimported refined bauxite. Higher prices for bauxite would reduce the cost burden on Hungarian industry. Eliminating aluminum from the calculations reduces the cost increase for Hungarian industry to 28.5 billion forint or 1.4 percent of GDP.

References

Brada, Josef C. 1985. "Soviet Subsidization of Eastern Europe: The Primacy of Economics over Politics." *Journal of Comparative Economics* 9:80–90.

Hungary, Hungarian Official Bulletin (Magyar Kozlony). 1989a. "Decree of the Government 148/89." 28 December.

Hungary, Hungarian Official Bulletin (Magyar Kozlony). 1989b. No. 98.

Hungary, Ministry of Finance. 1989. "Budget Report to the Parliament." December.

———. 1990. Internal memorandum.

Hungary, Ministry of Trade. 1990. *Official Statistics*.

Hungary, National Planning Office. 1990. "Economic Policy Programme of the Hungarian Government for 1990—Summary." January.

Hungary, Reform of the General Government. 1990. *Vol. 4, Competition and the Price System* (in Hungarian). Budapest: Perfect Publisher.

Kenen, Peter. 1990. "Transitional Arrangements for Trade and Payments among the CMEA Countries." IMF Discussion Paper. Washington, D.C.

Marrese, Michael. 1991. "The Cost to Central-East Europe of the Disintegration of the CMEA and the 1990 Oil Price Increase." Paris: OECD.

Marrese, Michael, and Jan Vanous. 1983. *Soviet Subsidization of Trade with Eastern Europe*. Berkeley: University of California Press.

Marrese, Michael, and Lauren Wittenberg. 1989. "Implicit Subsidies within the CMEA: A Hungarian Perspective." Working Paper. Department of Economics, Northwestern University, Evanston, Ill. Processed.

Oblath, Gabor, and David Tarr. 1992. "The Terms-of-Trade Effects from the Elimination of State Trading in Soviet-Hungarian Trade." *Journal of Comparative Economics* 16:75–93.

Schrenk, Martin. 1992. "The CMEA System of Trade and Payments." This volume.

van Brabant, Josef M. 1987. *Regional Price Formation in Eastern Europe: Theory and Practice of Trade Pricing*. Boston and Dordrecht: Kluwer Academic Publishers.

B. The Adaptation of International Transactions

13

Proposals for Post-CMEA Trade and Payments Arrangements

Constantine Michalopoulos and David Tarr

This chapter discusses interim institutional arrangements for trade and payments among previous Council for Mutual Economic Assistance (CMEA) members. Three problems have resulted from the end of the CMEA system. First, there has been a breakdown of trade relations and a reduction of trade volume among former CMEA members. Currency inconvertibility and the absence of a free market system have hampered transactions. The question that arises is what interim arrangements can best facilitate international trade given that former CMEA countries are at different stages in the transition process.

Second, the denomination of international trade at international rather than CMEA prices implies a deterioration in the terms of trade of East European economies, because of the relative undervaluation of energy products in former CMEA trade.[1] To the extent that payments are settled in hard currencies, financing requirements are raised at a time when East European countries confront overall foreign exchange shortages.

Third, recognizing that full currency convertibility may not be reached for all countries in the near term, and that continuation of the former CMEA arrangements is not possible, the question is raised: what interim payments arrangements can be made for former CMEA members and for successor states of the U.S.S.R.

---

[1]The estimates include Oblath and Tarr (1992), Rosati (1990), Marrese (1991), and Kenen (1990).

This is a revised version of World Bank PRE Working Paper 644, April 1991.

Trade arrangements in the post-CMEA era

Legacy of central planning and CMEA trade

As described in previous chapters,[2] trade within the CMEA was conducted as an outgrowth of the central planning process. Under the planning mechanism, enterprises in Eastern Europe and the U.S.S.R. were given quantity targets; prices did not play a role in resource allocation. Total imports and exports were coordinated under the plan; prices were so misaligned with world prices that conducting trade according to market forces would have been too disruptive. Even when central planning was formally abandoned, as in Hungary in 1968, price controls, price equalization, and other taxes and subsidies sustained misaligned relative prices.

Trade among CMEA members was conducted almost exclusively through bilateral agreements (or protocols).[3] The annually negotiated agreements obligated signatory governments to export and import specified quantities of particular goods. Enterprises were then required by their government to supply goods for the purpose of meeting the export requirement of the protocol. Upon delivery of the goods, the commercial bank account of the exporting enterprise was credited in domestic currency by its own central bank. Consequently, the customer of the producing enterprise was not a foreign firm, but its own government which both placed the order for the goods and paid the enterprise. Moreover, if the firm was obligated under the plan to provide goods for export, it felt justified in asking for subsidies if it incurred losses in production.

Transferable ruble (TR) balances were in principle redeemable for goods from the partner countries, though when denominated in TR, trade was supposed to be bilaterally balanced. Several East European countries, however, did accumulate significant export surpluses in TR, because of two types of opportunism in trade. First, countries failed to meet their delivery obligations under the protocols. During 1989 and 1990, the U.S.S.R. was reducing deliveries as domestic shortages and production problems increased. Another type of opportunism occurred at the transactions level. Because firms received payment from their own government, they found it in their own interest to export even if, because of the TR trade surplus, this was not in the interest of the country.

---

[2]See Schrenk (this volume) and Hillman and Schnytzer (this volume).
[3]See Schrenk (this volume).

Desirable features of a new trade regime in Eastern Europe

The objective of East European countries must be to establish a trading system unfettered by the controls and distortions that characterized the CMEA regime. Interim trade arrangements to facilitate trade should be based on the following principles.

• Wide ranging reforms of the price system are necessary. Without such reforms, trade reforms are not likely to be meaningful.

• The state-granted monopoly of foreign trade organizations (FTOs) in the former CMEA region should be eliminated to prevent FTOs from distorting prices to enterprises.

• Price equalization practices should be abolished. Such practices prevent resource reallocation in accordance with comparative advantage.

• East European countries should develop the legal basis to impose product-specific tariffs or export taxes, provided the taxes are not discriminatory or inconsistent with the General Agreement on Tariffs and Trade (GATT). Export taxes are not recommended, but they may be necessary when the domestic product is subsidized and the subsidy applies to all production. For example, the price of agricultural exports in some countries may be less than the cost of production, leading to welfare-reducing exports. The optimal policy would be to reduce the subsidy and allow exports; in the presence of subsidies, however, an export tax may be required on all exports and not just exports to former CMEA members.

• To encourage product development and cost-saving technological development in enterprise decision making, it is necessary to allow exporting or importing enterprises to deal directly with agents in the countries with which they are trading, to enter into contracts and to bear the risk of their contracts. This can only be accomplished if the governmental obligation to supply or purchase items from other countries is discontinued. An essential feature of a desirable trade regime for Eastern Europe is thus the termination of state-determined quantity or price levels of the past protocols.

• CMEA trade should not be replaced by a system in which governments conduct trade in dollar terms at world market prices. Government negotiation of trade at world market prices is difficult to implement for products subject to quality differences. The exporting government will claim that its product is of high quality. Prices in market economies are determined through firm-level negotiation, and if a firm does not like a price, it is free to seek other offers. Through seeking or obtaining the best offer on world markets, the world market price for products of a particular quality is found. When the government intervenes in decentralized decision making regarding the nature of the contract (such as steel reference prices or agricultural policies in the European Community), the consequence is usually a barrier to trade. The government cannot be a substitute for the market in the determination of market prices. An essential reform of the CMEA is thus to remove governments from determination of the prices and quantities at which trade is conducted. It then becomes redundant to propose that trade be conducted at world market prices.

• Refusal by partner countries to allow direct negotiation with their enterprises should not deter governments who wish to reform their own policies. If successor states of the U.S.S.R. do not move forcefully to establish market economies, East European countries should allow their own enterprises to negotiate with agents such as FTOs. Austria and Finland have shown that small, market oriented countries can successfully trade with centrally oriented economies without introducing central control in their own economies.[4] The U.S.S.R. made price offers to Austria and Finland; they in turn were able to maximize their gains from trade by allowing their firms to trade with the U.S.S.R. according to the prices and financial arrangements negotiated with the relevant Soviet agent. It did not matter that the price bid or offered by the U.S.S.R. was distorted by central planning.[5]

• East European governments should not agree to anything more binding than "indicative" lists of products. Some countries may prefer to see a continuation of the binding intergovernmental protocol lists of the past, but this arrangement is not in their best interest. If a product appears on the indicative list, the government only agrees to allow it to be freely imported and exported. Products not on the lists can still be traded, because placing the product on the lists only means that licensing requirements are relaxed and that foreign exchange is available for products on the lists; the lists would not restrict the licensing of other products. It is crucial, however, that the presence of a product on the list should not in any way obligate a government or a particular enterprise to supply this product. An enterprise wishing to sell a product must find a buyer in the other country and enter into a contract. Trade based on indicative lists was employed in trade between the U.S.S.R. and Finland for many years.[6]

• Trade should be conducted in hard currency and all deficits should be settled in hard currency. True hard currency settlement is the best mechanism for solving the problem of unredeemable surpluses. Individual enterprises should negotiate the financial arrangements of a transaction with foreign enterprises and bear the risk of that transaction. Because of the potential for opportunism by foreign governments, the settlement period or credit limit between countries must be carefully restricted. An extensive system of bilateral credit arrangements could lead to the proliferation of quantitative restraints on trade (as happened in Western Europe around 1950).

---

[4]See Oblath and Pete (1985).

[5]For example, if the delivered price of Soviet oil to East European countries is low by international standards, their enterprises will attempt to buy it, and it is in the interest of the government to allow them to do so.

[6]The proposed system is not identical to the Soviet-Finnish system, in which trade was denominated in rubles and no hard currency was exchanged. See Oblath and Pete (1985).

In summary, if these recommendations are implemented, East European enterprises will conclude contracts directly with foreign firms (or other authorized agents) in former CMEA countries, they will be under no state obligation, and the role of licenses and FTOs will be minimized. This trading environment would be an improvement over arrangements of the past CMEA, because there would be enterprise autonomy, trade would be conducted according to world prices, and settlement would be made in convertible currency. The principal difference between this approach and trade between firms in market economies is that, because many East European countries do not have convertible currencies, transactions would be denominated and settled in the hard currency of third countries. This practice is common among developing countries.

Potential trade deficit problems and transition arrangements

In the final months of 1990 it became apparent that the costs to former CMEA countries of the switch to hard currency trade were greater than previously estimated. The U.S.S.R.'s failure to decide on a method by which foreign exchange would be allocated meant that, despite "demand," Soviet importers were unable to sign contracts with East European exporters. Because the central authority was losing control of the Soviet economy, it became more crucial to convert to hard currency trade and enterprise-to-enterprise transactions. An exporting enterprise would otherwise be reluctant to export to Eastern Europe, because the payment it would receive under an intergovernmental protocol would be the delivery of goods through the plan, rather than the immediate and more certain direct payment of hard currency.[7] Payments issues are thus central to the future evolution of trade among these countries. The establishment of appropriate transitional clearing and payments arrangements is the subject of the remainder of the paper.

Institutional alternatives for payments arrangements

The ideal arrangement for international payments in the post-CMEA era is full currency convertibility. Recognizing that this will take time to achieve and that the pace of change will vary among countries, two alternatives for interim monetary cooperation have been suggested: (a) simple clearing arrangements with a relatively short interval between settlement dates (of between one and three months) and the provision of solely interim financing; and (b) payments arrangements, where clearing is supplemented by a facility providing short- (for example, one year) or perhaps even

---

[7]Thus, when production of oil declined in 1990, Soviet deliveries to Eastern Europe declined more than proportionately.

medium-term credit—in a manner similar to that provided by the European Payments Union (EPU).[8] For each of these alternatives, variations are suggested with respect to the financial contributions of nonparticipants, credit terms, terms of settlement, and types of transactions covered. What are the potential advantages and disadvantages of these proposed arrangements for trade among former CMEA members?

A clearing arrangement between two or more countries establishes a centralized system of mutually compensated settlements for intragroup transactions, using an agreed-upon unit of account. Net balances arising from transactions (which could include trade in both goods and services) would be settled periodically in agreed upon convertible currencies. For example, in the Central American Common Market (CACM) clearing arrangement, participants originally extended credit up to $12 million to each participant, with a six-month settlement period and settlements made in U.S. dollars. Shorter settlement periods have been in place in other clearing arrangements among developing countries.

The basic distinction between a payments union and a clearing arrangement is that, with the former, credit is provided for more than an interim period (that is, exceeding three months). The union could be based on mutual credit extended only among members, or could be financed in part by outside contributors. The EPU was just such a mixed arrangement: the United States made a contribution, but did not otherwise participate in the arrangement. The use of outside assistance allows creditors to be paid in part or in full, with larger credit extended to the debtors than would be otherwise possible.[9]

Many countries have tried to replicate the apparent success of the EPU, but have failed. The EPU trading region encompassed the entire sterling area; the overseas dependencies of France, Belgium, and Portugal; and the West European members themselves. It accounted for 35 percent of world exports in 1950 (in contrast to less than a 4 percent share of the CMEA in 1988).[10]

East European countries should probably look to the developing world for models for collaborative payments arrangements. In developing countries, as with the CMEA, intraunion trade has represented a relatively small portion of world trade. The most successful of these arrangements was the one established in Central America in support of the CACM. It functioned with some outside assistance for over two decades, until it de facto suspended operation in 1987 for reasons to be discussed below. Payments

---

[8]Other arrangements, for example reserve pooling, are also possible, but require greater monetary and economic integration.

[9]See Michalopoulos (1973).

[10]Kenen (1990).

arrangements have also been in place in Francophone Africa as part of Communauté Financière Africaine arrangements.[11]

The role of clearing arrangements in post-CMEA Eastern Europe

Clearing arrangements have been established typically in a regional context, among countries with inconvertible currencies. A clearing arrangement is intended to provide two kinds of benefits to its members. First, there would be foreign exchange savings because each country would require fewer liquid foreign exchange reserves to back its trade and because transaction costs arising from payments through third country banks would be reduced. The second and by far the most important benefit would be support of a mutual expansion of trade. Clearing can stimulate intragroup trade if two conditions are satisfied: (a) exchange rates are and continue to be overvalued substantially and in different degrees and, as is typical, there is foreign exchange rationing; and (b) trade is hampered by strictly bilateral arrangements that lead to inconvertible balances.

Can clearing arrangements make a contribution in Eastern Europe? A clearing arrangement can provide limited foreign exchange savings by reducing transaction costs. The key issue is the relationship between clearing and international trade. Trade among CMEA countries was hampered by the maze of CMEA bilateral agreements.[12] It is unclear how trade will develop when unimpeded by these constraints. It is possible that, if prices and trade were fully liberalized, the countries would trade less rather than more with each other.[13] If this happened, expansion of mutual trade, a key objective of previous clearing arrangements, would not occur in former CMEA countries. The main concern is how to cushion reductions in exports to the former U.S.S.R. and the adverse terms of trade that resulted from the end of the CMEA regime.

The contribution of clearing arrangements would be reduced if more realistic exchange rates were introduced and a significant degree of

---

[11]A number of earlier proposals in the Economic and Social Commission for Asia and the Pacific (ESCAP) region (which were not implemented) called for a payments union financed without outside credit (although the option of contributions from developed countries was left open), on the basis of initial positions. In a payments union based on initial positions, credit is provided only with respect to increments in trade among member countries. A country thus would be asked to participate in the arrangement not with respect to all its trade, but only with respect to changes from its original position. How these original positions are established presumably would be the subject of negotiations among the members (Michalopoulos 1973).

[12]Because a surplus earned in trade with one country could not be used to import goods from another CMEA country, trade under CMEA protocols was bilateral.

[13]See also Ethier (this volume) on the prospective trade pattern.

convertibility were achieved.[14] For example, if former CMEA countries introduced a system of foreign exchange auctions (or a variant thereof) that provided firms with foreign exchange for most of their foreign trade transactions, a clearing mechanism for intragroup trade would not be necessary.[15] Firms could buy foreign exchange at auction.

Another suggestion is that Russia preallocate a negotiated amount of hard currency for purchases from former CMEA economies. A country would purchase a specified value of Russian goods and in return Russia would purchase the same specified value of the other's exports. It is important to emphasize that if a country's authorities wish to negotiate a level of aggregate Russian purchases in order to ensure Russian demand, these aggregate hard currency purchases should not limit the autonomy of the country's enterprises in their trade with Russia. It is also crucial that such purchases not be targeted in bilateral negotiations toward specific products. This would result in the protection of certain exports at the expense of other industries.

Moreover, if bilateral agreements were reached on aggregate hard currency trade, it would be desirable eventually to reduce the amount of trade determined through such agreements to avoid a permanent bias in the bilateral aggregate amount of trade. For example, Russia and an East European country might agree to purchase a minimum $3 billion worth of goods and services from each other. Trade above this amount would be permitted, but would be discretionary. That is, there would be no guarantee that trade above the $3 billion minimum would be balanced. In subsequent years, however, the value of guaranteed hard currency purchases between the countries would be reduced—for example, to $2.5 billion in the second year and $2 billion in the third year, and so on. Total Russian purchases of the other country's exports, however, might not decrease if discretionary trade increased. In this manner, the aggregate value of trade would over time become market-determined, and a restructuring of trade among former CMEA countries or toward the West would be possible.

A system that permits settlement of balances in hard currency would allow trade to be multilateral. If countries agree to periodically settle their trade balances in convertible currencies, then trade surpluses earned with one country could be used to purchase goods elsewhere. It is thus possible to make interim arrangements for countries without convertible currencies and so permit fully multilateral trade without a clearing or payments union.

---

[14]By the end of the CMEA, several countries in Eastern Europe had made a commitment to introduce some degree of currency convertibility. Poland had essentially already done so. Hungary was moving in that direction. Czechoslovakia had indicated a desire to achieve substantial convertibility in 1991. Others, notably the successor states of the U.S.S.R., were lagging.

[15]Such arrangements were in place in Poland in 1989. See Tarr (1990) for a description and quantitative assessment of the consequences.

Nonetheless, if currency convertibility is introduced at different times in different countries, and significant foreign exchange controls continue to exist in most of these countries, clearing arrangements in foreign exchange with short settlement periods (of up to three months) can be a useful, strictly interim measure. They can provide small foreign exchange savings in transactions costs and a means of monitoring evolving patterns of trade. Their stimulus to trade can be expected to be small, as was the case with previous arrangements of this kind. These arrangements can be phased out as soon as countries achieve a modicum of convertibility.

Such arrangements should not be confused with the suggestion that a "clearing dollar" be established. According to this proposal, trade would have to be balanced in dollars and intergovernmental protocols and state obligations would continue. The only change that would take place, then, would be that the unit of account would be the U.S. dollar and not the transferable ruble, and prices would be negotiated between governments at "world market levels." In particular, the problem of how to redeem a TR surplus is not solved, but merely transformed into the problem of a clearing dollar surplus, and the many inefficiencies of state trading remain.

It is of course conceivable that clearing arrangements could be used not to expand trade, but rather to regulate its reduction over time and thus to cushion the adjustment of firms previously oriented to CMEA markets. Depending on the design, bilateral clearing arrangements could insulate and protect certain industries in each country from international competition. While such an arrangement could ease the transition to international competition, it is clearly an inferior means of cushioning the adjustment. Protection through clearing arrangements could involve nontariff barriers and make the cost of protection nontransparent. Interim and declining industry protection should be provided when needed through tariffs and subsidies.

The role of enhanced credit arrangements: general considerations

Simple clearing arrangements are potentially useful transition mechanisms, but they are not by themselves likely to substantially benefit participants or materially affect their trade. Proposals for clearing arrangements, therefore, frequently become proposals to enhance arrangements through the type of short- to medium-term credit characteristic of a payments union. When considering the usefulness of enhanced credit arrangements for countries in Eastern Europe, issues of both feasibility and desirability arise.

Mutual credit

The fundamental problem with a payments arrangement that allows for mutual credit is that it is difficult to find countries willing to become creditors within the union, since potential creditors are typically large

debtors in their overall balance of payments. This is precisely the problem
in Eastern Europe.

A country's willingness to participate in a payments scheme as a creditor
depends on the likelihood that its position as a creditor within the group
will change to debtor, and that its trade will expand more rapidly as a result
of its membership in the union. Unless reversals in imbalances are
anticipated, there is no incentive for a creditor country to participate.[16]
Trade balance reversals, however, may not occur.[17]

To some extent, a reversal in existing positions can be effected by
provisions that guide the extension of credit and repayment. In general, two
approaches can be used: repayments can be based on the reversal of position
or on a prearranged time schedule.

The EPU used the first approach. Repayment was made on a monthly
basis, partly in cash and partly in the form of credit under a quota system.
(Originally a sliding system of cash and credit was utilized; it was later
changed to a uniform fifty-fifty rate.) Any payments in excess of the quota
were settled in cash—with some exceptions relating to extreme debit or credit
cases. Under this system, a debtor country could enjoy continued credit for
an indefinite period as long as it remained within its quota, and repayment
hinged on a reversal of its position.[18] The same applied to creditors. Such
a system spreads the onus of adjustment between debtors and creditors, but
at the same time quotas limit the credit that is extended to or received by
any single country to predetermined amounts.

The second method requires repayments on the basis of a prearranged
timetable regardless of position. A country may have large negative balances
in intragroup trade because of exchange rate overvaluation or other
ineffective macroeconomic policies. A prearranged timetable places the onus
of adjustment more heavily on the debtor, who must either take actions that
force a reversal within the union or yield a surplus on trade with the rest of
the world.

The feasibility of these approaches depends on the extent of cooperation
among members of the union. If there is considerable agreement between
debtors and creditors on general economic policy questions such that
reversals of position are assured, then the former method is preferable. If,

---

[16]If all countries similarly identify the countries likely to be creditors and debtors, then in
principle it is possible to devise complicated credit arrangements (which limit the exposure of
the likely creditor), that will provide an incentive for all countries to join as long as the likely
creditor has some positive probability of becoming a debtor. See Ethier (this volume) for an
elaboration. As mentioned above, however, credit arrangements are difficult to negotiate, and
complications such as these might aggravate those difficulties.

[17]In intra-CACM trade, for example, there was only one trade balance reversal among the
five countries in the five-year period from 1964 to 1969. There were several reversals in the
1970s. In the 1980s Nicaragua emerged as a large persistent debtor and Costa Rica and
Guatemala as persistent creditors.

[18]A description of such a settlement scheme for Eastern Europe has been elaborated by
Ethier (this volume).

on the other hand, such cooperation cannot be assured, then the generally more demanding terms of the second approach may have to be imposed to reduce the amount of credit extended by participants to persistent debtors.[19]

Even if there is policy coordination, there is no guarantee that intragroup trade will not leave some countries with large persistent credit or debit positions. It would then make little sense for an East European country to participate in a payments arrangement as a creditor, particularly if that country, though a creditor in the union, were an overall debtor, requiring foreign transfers to maintain satisfactory growth performance.

The basic problem of a payments arrangement for intragroup trade and payments is that it focuses on only a segment of the overall balance of trade and payments. Because surpluses within the region may not be converted automatically for the purpose of importing from outside the region, the arrangement falls short of allowing multilateral trade. This is why the Economic and Social Commission for Asia and the Pacific (ESCAP) abandoned the idea of a payments union. It is also why the CACM clearing arrangement was ultimately suspended. Nicaragua ran large deficits in intragroup trade because of its ineffective macroeconomic policies; these deficits amounted to over $500 million by the end of 1987. Costa Rica and Guatemala emerged as persistent creditors within the CACM at a time when both countries faced severe balance of payments and debt servicing difficulties in their overall international accounts. Guatemala in 1986 and Costa Rica in 1987 suspended their involvement in the clearing mechanism; CACM is still in existence, but it cleared only 1 percent of intraregional trade in 1987. The CACM experience is also instructive because it suggests that, once a payments arrangement is established, the pressure by debtors to raise credit ceilings increases, as do the number of requests by the payments union for outside credit to augment available resources.[20]

To avoid the problem of large and persistent debtor or credit positions and the need to finance substantial intraregional (as opposed to global) deficits, it has been suggested that payments arrangements be established on the basis of initial positions (see above). The problem with this suggestion, however, is that in Eastern Europe it is precisely the initial trade positions that need to be changed, since the price relations on which trade positions were initially based were distorted. Thus, payments arrangements based on these initial positions are not desirable.

A payments union's prospects for success are enhanced if creditors anticipate large increases in their exports as a result of membership in the union. For this to occur, however, the payments union must either require

---

[19]Michalopoulos (1973).

[20]In response to such requests the European Commission approved a new credit to the CACM of 120 million ECUs tranched over three years. This credit was to support future trade expansion among these countries and not to settle past balances (European Commission 1989).

participants to undertake trade liberalization, or provide an incentive to undertake trade liberalization. This is a very important condition which, if not fulfilled, is likely to render any payments arrangement inoperative. It should be recalled that members of the EPU were required to liberalize their intra-European trade. Members were obligated to eliminate all quantitative restrictions over a five-year period, as well as to adopt other measures facilitating intra-European trade. Greater trade liberalization within the region than is undertaken externally, however, would induce some costly trade diversion. Given the desire of East European countries to increase their trade integration with the rest of the world, a payments arrangement that focuses on expanding intraregional trade would provide incentives in the wrong direction.

Perhaps more important than the EPU code itself were the conditions that prevailed in Western Europe at the time of the EPU's formation. A network of bilateral credit arrangements among Western European countries had evolved, and most countries were in debt to some countries, but had credit with others. There is an incentive in such a situation for bilateral discrimination in trade. For example, suppose country A is a creditor to country B, but country A is also a debtor to country C. Country A then has an incentive to impose trade barriers against imports from country C in favor of imports from country B. Importing from country B allows country A to import goods and services at less than their full cost by reducing credits to country B; importing from country C, on the other hand, involves full payment of convertible currency or goods.

Without a network of bilateral credit and debit positions, a country facing a convertible currency deficit will gain equally by reducing imports from any country. A dollar's worth of imports from country B has the same value as a dollar's worth of imports from country C. Country A will thus have no incentive to discriminate in its trade barriers. A country with nonconvertible currency generally imposes trade barriers including foreign exchange rationing, but there is no marginal gain from rationing against countries with which it runs a bilateral deficit.

The EPU removed the incentive to impose country-specific trade barriers because credit or debit positions were defined regionally within the payments union. In Eastern Europe, however, at the end of the CMEA, there was no network of significant debit or credit positions among the countries. East European countries thus had no incentive to discriminate bilaterally in their trade with each other. The initial conditions which were important to the success of the EPU in reducing trade barriers were therefore absent in Eastern Europe. The Western European experience does indicate, however, that it is important to limit extensive bilateral credit arrangements, because such arrangements may evolve into an excessively regulated pattern of trade.

The role of outside assistance

The usefulness or desirability of outside participation in payments arrangements varies considerably with the nature of the arrangement. In clearing arrangements, strictly defined, foreign participation is not needed; participants can themselves extend the necessary amount of short term credit. Foreign participation has not been a necessary component of clearing arrangements in the past, and its absence did not inhibit the setting up of clearing arrangements. Foreign participation has been considered crucial to the establishment and successful operation of payments unions, however. It has often been pointed out that the success of the EPU was in part due to an original U.S. grant, which helped the union solve the problem of persistent debtors. Outside aid eases the problem of financing credit positions within the union. Aid funds can pay creditors in part or in full, while a certain amount of credit can be extended to other participants. The incentive for a creditor to participate is then the benefit that it derives from potential trade expansion.

A basic issue raised by a payments union with outside credit involves the criteria for allocating credit. Persistent debtors enjoy the benefits of outside credit (that is, they enjoy transfers of resources) while other countries benefit only to the extent that exports increase as a result of the union. A fundamental problem, then, is whether or not aid funds are rationally allocated by a payments union. Debtors, whoever they are, automatically obtain credit according to certain rules, the stringency of which can vary with the amount of credit requested. The extension of credit relates to a balance of payments position with respect to the region and not the world as a whole; it is, however, the position with respect to the world and not the region that should be considered when assistance is extended on balance of payments grounds, as is the case in the context of an International Monetary Fund (IMF) standby arrangement or a World Bank structural adjustment loan. More important, it may be that the need for credit results from inappropriate macroeconomic policies, such as overvalued exchange rates; if this is so, the aid will not reward countries that have adopted desirable policy reforms.

Enhanced credit arrangements for Eastern Europe

We now look at payment arrangements with more than interim credit and with foreign participation. We will first consider an arrangement limited to Eastern Europe. It would be undesirable to provide external support (from outside the union or, in particular, from European or Organisation for Economic Co-operation and Development (OECD) countries) for a payments arrangement that provides interim credit for intraregional trade balances. Indeed, this would be counterproductive, as provision of such credit would reduce the incentive of Eastern Europe to reorient trade toward the rest of the world; beneficiary countries would be chosen regardless of their economic policies, and only if they have a negative balance within the region, which in and of itself is of little economic significance.

Suppose, however, that Russia were to participate and provide credit. Still, no external support from outside the group would be justified, again for the reasons discussed above. Could such an arrangement, however, ease the adjustment of Eastern Europe to the terms of trade loss?

If Russia agreed to participate in a payments arrangement with Eastern Europe and to provide interim financing for negative balances on intragroup trade, this would clearly ease terms of trade losses. In the course of confronting adjustment problems of its own, Russia is unlikely to be willing to finance the unlimited deficits of others. Credit limits (quotas) would have to be imposed. The allocation of credit from Russia would be inefficient, as it would again be guided by intragroup payments balances—which would include, in addition to payments resulting from terms of trade losses, other factors that affect intragroup trade.

If Russia were willing to provide credit, it would gain more if it did so in the form of an export credit arrangement.[21] Such an arrangement, especially for capital goods, would facilitate its own exports in competition with Western exports.

An alternate arrangement has been elaborated by Ethier (this volume). He describes the establishment of a clearing arrangement with credit (either mutual credit or credit augmented by outside resources) in which trade with Russia is included in the settlement balances of East European members, but Russia neither receives nor provides credit.

The inclusion of trade with Russia addresses, at least in part, the criticism that payments arrangements for Eastern Europe that exclude Russia provide financing for deficits arising in a small and arbitrarily segmented part of the total trade of participating countries. Inclusion of Russian trade, however, would still result in automatic financing of a component of total trade, regardless of the policies that give rise to the deficit, and as such may be criticized for its inefficiency.

Inclusion of Russia also raises questions about (a) the nature of the ensuing pattern of payments and (b) the incentives of different countries to participate. Two alternatives can be envisaged: (a) that all East European countries end up in a net deficit position, or (b) that some will be creditors and some debtors. If all participants become net debtors, why establish such an arrangement in the first place? Provision of outside credit, presumably from the European community (EC) or other donors, would finance deficits with Russia, while Russia would not bear any financing burden. If this were to happen, the clearing arrangement would permit East European countries

---

[21]As noted by a multiagency task force study of the (former) U.S.S.R. See International Monetary Fund et al. (1991, p. 30).

to present a united front against Russia. If the objective is to present a united front, however, why create an arrangement that includes trade?

It may be proposed that if an East European country were a creditor in such an arrangement, it might still want to join, because the alternative could be a bilateral surplus with Russia which Russia would find unacceptable. This assumes that Russia would wish to maintain bilaterally balanced trade with all its trading partners and that it would therefore force a potential surplus country to restrict exports. A creditor in this arrangement, it is argued, would provide credit to the union as a whole, to avoid having to reduce its own exports. The rationale for discrimination by Russia is, however, not well elaborated, because, as argued above, no country, including Russia, has an incentive to bilaterally balance or bilaterally discriminate in trade before it has developed a network of credit and debit positions.

Conclusions

We offer the following recommendations about post-CMEA trade and payments arrangements.

• We recommend the following changes in the trade regime: East European enterprises should have autonomy to conclude contracts directly with foreign firms (or other authorized agents) in former CMEA countries; they should be under no state obligation; and they should bear the risk of their contracts. The role of licenses and price equalization should be minimized or eliminated and foreign trading organizations should not enjoy monopoly trading privileges. Trade should be conducted according to world prices and denominated and settled in convertible currencies.

• We recommend that competitive exchange rates with a degree of convertibility be eventually introduced. Because countries will achieve this goal at an uneven pace, we recommend that clearing arrangements with short settlement periods—that is, less than three months—be considered an interim measure, strongly preferred to a system in which bilateral balancing of trade is forced. Such arrangements can be established without outside contributions.

• We recommend that clearing arrangements not become vehicles for continued protection. Clearing and payments arrangements have been useful in circumstances where a network of existing bilateral credit arrangements has led to bilateral trade discrimination or where the objective of participating countries is to increase mutual trade. This is not the case in East European countries as they emerge from the CMEA system; these countries have only small debts to each other and the focus is on better integration of their economies in the worldwide trading system.

• We recommend that outside credit to support payments arrangements among East European countries not be provided, whether such arrangements include or exclude Russia and other successor states of the U.S.S.R.

Payments arrangements involving credit pose problems when the credit is provided solely by the participating members. Outside credit can be helpful in overcoming some of these problems. But the allocation of such credit is inefficient because with little economic justification it automatically assists countries in the financing of intraregional balances, which could have resulted from ineffective macroeconomic policies of participants.

References

European Commission. 1989. Press Release P(89) 830, November 8. Brussels.

Ethier, Wilfred. 1992. "International Trade and Payments Mechanisms: Options and Possibilities, Another View." This volume.

Hillman, Arye L., and Adi Schnytzer. 1992. "Creating the Reform-Resistant Dependent Economy: Socialist Comparative Advantage, Enterprise Incentives, and the CMEA." This volume.

IMF (International Monetary Fund), IBRD (International Bank for Reconstruction and Development), OECD (Organisation for Economic Co-operation and Development), and EBRD (European Bank for Reconstruction and Development). 1991. *The Economy of the U.S.S.R.: Summary and Recommendations.* Washington, D.C.: World Bank.

Kenen, Peter. 1990. "Transitional Arrangements for Trade and Payments among the CMEA Countries." IMF Discussion Paper presented at the OECD-World Bank Conference on the Transition to a Market Economy in Central and Eastern Europe, 28–30 November, Paris. Processed.

Marrese, Michael. 1991. "The Cost to Central-East Europe of the Disintegration of the CMEA and the 1990 Oil Price Increase." Paris: OECD.

Michalopoulos, Constantine. 1973. *Payments Arrangements for Less Developed Countries: The Role of Foreign Assistance.* Essays in International Finance 192. Princeton, N.J.: Princeton University.

Oblath, Gabor, and Peter Pete. 1985. "Trade with the Soviet Union: The Finnish Case." *Acta Oeconomica* 35:165-94.

Oblath, Gabor, and David Tarr. 1992. "The Terms-of-Trade Effects from the Elimination of State Trading in Soviet-Hungarian Trade." *Journal of Comparative Economics* 16:75–93.

Rosati, Dariusz. 1990. "Impact of Replacing CMEA Trade Regime by a Market Trade Regime: Poland." Foreign Trade Research Institute, Warsaw. Processed.

Schrenk, Martin. 1992. "The CMEA System of Trade and Payments." This volume.

Tarr, David. 1990. "Second Best Foreign Exchange Policy in the Presence of Domestic Price Controls and Export Subsidies." *World Bank Economic Review* 4:175–93.

International Trade and Payments Mechanisms: Options and Possibilities, Another View

Wilfred J. Ethier

Multilateral trade and payments arrangements in Eastern Europe were once the concern of the Council for Mutual Economic Assistance (CMEA), although CMEA trade was not in practice multilateral but bilateral. This chapter will discuss what, if anything, could take the place of the CMEA.

General goals and outlook

Although there are differences among East European countries, there is consensus that East European trade should eventually be characterized by the following features:

• Currencies should be convertible to hard currencies after a moderate transition period. Countries have different views about the importance of this goal, the optional length of a transition period, and even the meaning of "convertibility." There is, nonetheless, widespread support for this idea.

• East European economies should be integrated into the world (that is, Western industrial) trading system. Again, East European countries have differing attitudes about how quickly and to what extent integration should occur, but a desire to "join the West" is pervasive.

• Trade among East European economies should be conducted by individual enterprises. Enterprises should negotiate prices and financing and

My conversations with David Tarr of the World Bank have been of great benefit. I have also benefitted from discussion when the paper was presented at a World Bank seminar.

should be fully accountable for their decisions. The former system of state trading should not be replaced by a system of quantitative restrictions or indirect state controls.

• Trade among East European countries should be conducted at world prices, and imbalances should be settled in hard currencies. This feature would follow automatically from the others were they to be attained, but it should be mentioned separately because this is the agreed procedure for many transactions, including the paramount bilateral exchanges of Russia and other republics with the East European countries. Thus, this change will characterize much Eastern trade well before the time when it will be but an innocuous consequence of other reforms.

If the above goals were realized, the East European countries would successfully conduct multilateral trade with little distinction between East and West. The goals are widely accepted, but we emphasize that there is much diversity in the approaches of different countries to these goals. In view of this, two conclusions about the outlook for East European trade are warranted. (a) In an interim period (say, three to five years), progress toward these goals will be significant but incomplete; (b) progress achieved will vary considerably, both across countries, and across goals.

These conclusions provide the motivation for this paper. During the intermediate term, the East European currencies will be less than completely convertible, so some mechanism of payments settlement will be needed to facilitate trade among these countries.

Another clear implication of these conclusions is that, in the intermediate term, barriers and distortions related to East European trade with the West will fall relative to the barriers and distortions related to trade among the East European countries themselves. This needs to be kept in mind when reviewing the nature of East European trade.

Intra-CMEA trade was conducted by large foreign trade organizations (FTOs) that operated in centrally planned economies and were protected from world markets.[1] This trade was thus highly distorted. Mutual trade was to a large extent bilaterally managed. For each country, trade with the U.S.S.R. was most important. There were significant bilateral flows between the other East European economies, but very little triangular (or essentially multilateral) trade.[2] The expansion of intra-CMEA trade will not be emphasized in the foreseeable future as much by these countries as either the development of trade with the West or the preservation of trade with Russia. Furthermore, future trade also involves the continued exploitation of trading opportunities that exist now by virtue of installed capacity, but whose continued existence over a long period may be neither likely nor

---

[1] Schrenk (this volume).

[2] The bilateral character is perhaps the single aspect of East European trade emphasized most often over the years in Western treatments. See Holzman (1987) and numerous references cited therein.

desirable.[3] Nevertheless, all this does not imply that multilateral issues do not matter for the former CMEA economies.

There is little multilateral trade because of the distortions of the former system. Efficiency will require that significant trade be conducted among East European countries: the extent of future trade is difficult to estimate because of the lack of relevant historical experience, but it is obvious that these countries are important natural trading partners. Current reforms aim to achieve economic restructuring; if restructuring takes place subject to distorting constraints on trade, restructuring will be ineffective, and reforms will have to be repeated at great cost.

Because there is so little nondistorted Eastern trade, the marginal returns from restructured Eastern trade will be great. Eastern Europe has clearly not yet experienced great benefits as a result of mutual trade. It is crucial to recognize, however, that benefits result from an efficient restructuring of trade and not from expanding or maintaining the current inefficient flows. Large benefits would thus result from substantial reduction of East-East trade in the intermediate term, provided that this involves efficient restructuring.

A marginal diversion of resources from East-West trade into restructured East-East trade will be beneficial, and the benefits will increase in the intermediate term. This is because East-West trade, already conducted in hard currencies at world prices, is more efficient than East-East trade; this discrepancy will only increase as the emphasis on enterprise accountability increases. This is a classic economics-of-the-second-best situation, such as arises from economic integration. The argument is a familiar one: if East-West trade were relatively undistorted, marginal benefits would be in line with marginal costs, and little would be lost by a small cutback; if East-East trade remains relatively distorted, the marginal benefits from an increase in nondistorted trade significantly exceed marginal costs, and much would be gained by a small increase.[4] The more successful Eastern European countries are in integrating their economies with the West, the greater the payoff will be from diverting resources from East-West trade to restructured East-East trade.

Conventional though this argument may be, care should be taken not to misuse it. First, it is crucial to recognize that this argument does not present a case for maintaining or expanding existing distorted arrangements in the East: benefits will result from developing new nondistorted trade patterns. Second, from a practical point of view, it will be difficult to maintain momentum in expanding East-West trade and restructuring East-East trade; considerations such as the above should not be allowed to hinder East-West integration. Such considerations should only remind us of the importance of (nondistorted) East-East trade: while the prospect of increased East-West

---

[3]Hillman and Schnytzer (this volume).
[4]A relevant formal discussion may be found in Ethier and Horn (1984).

trade is attractive, we cannot forget that in the long run East European countries will remain each other's most important trade partners. The above argument also instructs us not to reject out of hand arrangements that only correct distortions in East-East trade (and not in East-West trade), provided these arrangements do not hamper East-West trade. Such arrangements would be discriminatory but beneficial.

The balance of this paper discusses three means of reforming, or replacing, the CMEA. These alternatives include default bilateralism, the most likely development in the absence of any explicit multilateral initiative; a multilateral trading and settlements system for clearing payments and fostering nondistorted trade; and an East European Payments Union (EEPU) to provide credit for payments imbalances. A concluding section ranks the alternatives.

Default bilateralism

It is possible, and probably desirable, that replacement of the CMEA will be addressed in an explicitly multilateral fashion. It is also possible, however, and perhaps likely, that East European trading relationships will develop through bilateral negotiations.

There are significant political constraints to the establishment of a formal East European multilateral payments system. Dissatisfaction with the former CMEA system is widespread, not only because of its obvious inadequacies as a trade and payments mechanism, but also because of a wide perception that it served as an instrument of Soviet domination. The preference of many East European countries is to avoid multilateral arrangements, and even multilateral negotiations, and instead to conduct bilateral negotiations when opportunities arise for mutual benefit.

In addition to these political concerns, East European countries experience economic temptations to favor bilateral arrangements that ignore multilateral possibilities. There are three principal reasons for this preference: (a) Lack of experience with multilateral East-East trade. CMEA trade flows were typically bilateral, to a large degree involving bilateral trade with the U.S.S.R.[5] (b) Interest in expanding trade with the West. (c) The view that in the medium term, the volume of East-East trade relative to total trade is more likely to decrease than increase.

In the absence of a concerted effort to foster multilateral trade, East European trade policy will probably (continue to) emphasize bilateral trade by default. What are the pros and cons of such an approach?

The major advantage of bilateralism by default is that it sidesteps the political concerns described above. Also, if there is no attempt to establish multilateralism in Eastern Europe, there will be no attempt to establish

---

[5]See Schrenk (this volume).

multilateral institutions; and if there are no multilateral institutions, there is no danger that aspects of the CMEA system will be preserved.

There are two major disadvantages of bilateralism by default. The first is that critical multilateral issues will not be addressed. Second, a reliance on bilateral agreements may perpetuate the old system of state trading and the old trade patterns: the temptation to negotiate bilateral agreements will be greatest in sectors dependent on soft goods (that is, in sectors with installed capacity for the production of goods that cannot be sold outside Eastern Europe, or sectors that are dependent on East European goods).

In view of this, it is important that East European governments guard against bilateral arrangements that reintroduce distortions, quantitative restraints and state-managed trade. In the absence of an explicit commitment to nondiscriminatory trade, the temptation to slip into bilateralism by default will be accentuated by the adoption of world prices and hard currency settlement. This is because the world prices of raw materials, largely exported by Russia, are more definitively determined than the prices of the manufactured goods for which they are exchanged. Thus East European countries facing a terms of trade loss vis-à-vis Russia will be tempted to negotiate bilaterally with regard to prices and terms of sale of their exports. Having done this, they will then be tempted to negotiate with one another, bilaterally, to try to eliminate the discrepancies produced by negotiations with Russia, with the result that much of the CMEA mechanism will be preserved, although without its formal organizational framework. This will further set back the process of economic reform in Eastern Europe.

A multilateral trade and settlements system

There has been semantic confusion regarding the term *clearing arrangement*. Within the CMEA, the transferable ruble system was known as a clearing arrangement. There was discussion within Eastern Europe of adopting in the aftermath of the CMEA a clearing system with prices denominated in convertible currency, by which it was meant that trade should be planned to be bilaterally balanced, with no convertible currency actually used to settle balances. In effect, the transferable ruble would be replaced with a transferable dollar, and no structural changes would be made in the nature of trade except for changed terms of trade. However, in the West a clearing arrangement means a method of multilateral settlement of accounts in convertible currency through a common facility or clearinghouse. In this section, the term *clearing arrangement* will be used in the Western sense of convertible currency settlement of outstanding balances handled through a multilateral clearinghouse.

A clearing arrangement could serve as the kernel of a multilateral settlements system for Eastern Europe. The arrangement would have four components. The first would be the clearing arrangement itself, which would consist of a clearinghouse that would cancel offsetting multilateral balances and that would allow each country periodically to settle its net position in hard currencies.

Second, each country would stipulate how its central bank would provide foreign exchange service to enterprises conducting trade with participating countries. If East European currencies were fully market convertible, foreign exchange would be provided automatically and unconditionally. Foreign exchange access in Eastern Europe, however, is likely to be limited (for example, via rationing or an auction market with limited access), at least in the short term, when full convertibility would not be attained. Conditions placed on foreign exchange access should be spelled out. The countries would also agree that trade credits among themselves, if any, would be extended only through the clearinghouse. Bilateral credit arrangements between individual East European countries would be prohibited as a condition of participation in the settlements system. If significant credit were to be extended through the clearinghouse, the arrangement would become what we call a *payments union*. Discussion of this possibility is deferred to the next section.

The arrangement might provide reciprocal foreign exchange access to enterprises from different participating countries. For example, foreign exchange auctions can be held as part of a program of partial convertibility;[6] participation in such auctions might be permitted for foreign enterprises that are trading with enterprises in the country conducting the auctions. Alternatively, such foreign enterprises might be allowed access to the foreign exchange market in a country, so that its currency would become internally convertible, as is the case in Poland. Although some form of reciprocal access is desirable, however, it is not necessary for the success of a multilateral trade and settlements system.

Third, participating countries would stipulate that neither their central bank nor their government would assume the risk of foreign trade contracts. An exporter signing a contract with a foreign firm must assume the risk that the contract might not be honored. This is a critical aspect of conducting trade with individual enterprises. If exporters receive domestic currency payment for their goods from officials when goods are shipped (leaving to government officials the problem of collecting payment from foreign customers), as was CMEA practice, exporters will not take into account the full social cost of the transactions they negotiate.

Fourth, there would be an agreement to limit mutual trade barriers. As East European economies continue to shift from state trading to trading by independent and accountable enterprises, they will adopt systems of tariffs and other trade barriers. The agreement should establish limits to such barriers to trade among participating countries. At a minimum, they should extend most-favored-nation status to each other, so that trade is

---

[6]See, for example, Rosefielde and Pfouts (1990).

nondiscriminatory. The analysis of the above section on general goals and outlook indicates the advantages of tariff preferences.

Two benefits of this form of multilateral trade and settlements system, characteristic of a clearing arrangement, should be emphasized:

• *Automatic canceling of triangular balances.* Triangularly balanced positions are automatically canceled when individual countries settle with the clearinghouse. Countries need not attend to such matters: in a system of bilateral agreements, triangular balances would needlessly prevent mutually beneficial trades.

• *Freedom from bilateral balancing.* Countries settle their net positions with the clearinghouse, and not with trading partners. Authorities in each country have no reason to distinguish in any way a dollar obligation to Poland, say, from an equal dollar obligation to Czechoslovakia. Bilateral balances are thus no longer a matter of policy concern. This is especially convenient for a country attempting to restructure its trading system toward nondiscrimination and convertibility.

These benefits of a clearing arrangement may be small, insofar as they relate to existing East European trade. Of greater importance are two other advantages of such a settlements system (of which a clearing arrangement is but one component). First, such triangular patterns do not characterize actual East European trade because former CMEA arrangement could not accommodate multilateral trade: East European countries were in effect forced to structure their economies to ensure bilateral balance. The purpose of transitional arrangements is to allow countries to restructure their economies in ways consistent with efficiency. If this is attempted through transitional arrangements that also impose bilateral balance, restructuring will not occur: countries will not only forego some transitional trade gains, but they will also prolong the adjustment process and needlessly magnify its cost. Second, the multilateral trade and settlements system requires a commitment to avoid bilateral credit arrangements and to practice enterprise-to-enterprise trade. It would thus inhibit continued state trading and/or discriminatory practices in East European transactions.

An East European payments union

There have been proposals to establish an East European Payments Union (EEPU), modeled after the European Payments Union (EPU). The settlements system outlined in the previous section can be expanded into an EEPU by the addition of credit facilities.

The interest in an EEPU has arisen because the situation that faced Western Europe during the postwar period is in important respects analogous to that currently facing former CMEA countries. In 1950 there was a need to adopt a multilateral payments clearing arrangement in Western Europe to make better use of the region's limited collective stock of gold and dollar reserves and to promote multilateral exchange unfettered by discriminatory trade restrictions. Similarly, Eastern Europe faces a collective "dollar shortage" as it attempts to adopt hard currency settlement at a time when significant further borrowing is inhibited by large outstanding debts.

Furthermore, the EPU was successful principally because of its ability to counter the proliferation of bilateral credit arrangements, which had given rise to incentives to discriminate bilaterally against imports. In post-CMEA Eastern Europe, no such formal credit arrangements exist, but an analogous distorted, bilateral structure was imposed by the former CMEA regime. It is necessary to change this structure and to avoid bilateral credit arrangements, or other devices, that perpetuate it. Thus, there is again a strong historical analogy.

If an EEPU is formed by adding credit facilities to a multilateral settlements system such as was discussed in the previous section, East European countries would enjoy the following additional benefits of a payments union.

Automatic recycling of scarce hard currency balances

This is, of course, a payments union's central purpose. It is possible to question the feasibility of such a union: creditor countries would seem to have nothing to gain from participation. It is argued that countries that can identify themselves in advance as creditors and that believe their status will not change have no incentive to join. It is true that trade balance reversals are not common, but we are not discussing normal times here: the countries of Eastern Europe are experiencing mammoth regime changes and it is impossible to predict what their mutual imbalances will be over the next three to five years. A union could thus offer insurance to all. Countries confident of running surpluses would be reluctant to accept exposure to the possibility of extending large credit positions, and may need to be compensated with the prospect of receiving substantial credit in the unlikely event they actually run deficits. As long as countries are risk averse, however, some set of arrangements can be found that will confer at least some benefit on all.

If an EEPU were formed, not all East European countries would have to participate. The pace of transformation in East European countries will differ, and it is likely that some countries would not be able to participate. An EEPU would offer additional benefits if its clearing and credit facilities could be used to offset its members' balances with other East European countries, as well as among themselves (see the Appendix for further details).

Reduced need for bilateral balancing with East European countries outside the EEPU

One participant's deficit against a nonparticipant (Russia, say) could be settled against another participant's surplus with Russia. Individual participants could be less concerned than they would otherwise be about bilateral balances with nonparticipating East European countries—less concerned, but not unconcerned. To the extent that the EEPU in the aggregate is unbalanced in its trade with nonparticipants, the imbalances of participants cannot be canceled against each other. In effect, such an arrangement would provide automatic financing by EEPU members of each other's trade with other East European countries. Each member in essence obtains insurance from the others for its trade with nonparticipant countries.

Automatic removal of reasons for other East European countries to discriminate among members' trade

To make this point as clearly as possible, suppose now that the imbalances with other East European countries are basically imbalances with Russia, net imbalances with other nonparticipants being small. This is the potential outcome of greatest current policy concern. As long as Russia kept its total dollar trade with the EEPU countries in balance as a group, the latter would settle any individual imbalances. This means that the Russians also have no reason to care about their individual bilateral balances with these countries. Individual bilateral balances are now no different from the Russian point of view than huge individual imbalances with these countries that aggregate out. This means that Hungary, for example, need have much less fear that the prospect of a large Hungarian trade surplus with Russia will induce discrimination against Hungarian goods in order to achieve bilateral balance.

If an EEPU were established, it could prove useful for several reasons apart from its function of providing a payments mechanism. The EEPU might, for example, find itself paying more hard currency to surplus countries than it was receiving from deficit countries, and so would require an initial endowment of hard currency. This endowment could come from members' contributions and/or from outside sources.

Consider the possibility of outside credit. Outside credit, from whatever source, would increase the feasibility of an EEPU because it would give all East European countries, including potential surplus countries, added incentive to join. An EEPU could receive Western aid in the form of contributions to the EEPU's hard currency endowment. Such contributions could provide leverage with which to encourage change: credit could be made conditional on the adoption of measures to restructure trade, such as the institution of enterprise-to-enterprise transactions with full enterprise accountability and nondiscriminatory access to hard currency. Countries could, for example, be required to commit to reforms, or imbalances might be restricted to such transactions. There is a countervailing argument, however. Western sources hoping to use aid to spur change might be reluctant to channel such aid through an EEPU if they suspected that the net effect would be to force them to deal with an insulating level of international bureaucracy when they would prefer to pressure national officials directly.

The discussion thus far has focused on the potential advantages and disadvantages of an EEPU. Yet there are additional reservations that must be raised.[7] First there is the concern that an East European organization, especially one endowed with credit from outside, might act to forestall change rather than foster it.

The second concern is that the advantages of an EEPU can also be obtained in other ways. For example, inducing change through the provision of conditional credit requires credit, but it does not require an EEPU. More generally, the availability of credit is what sets a payments union apart from other arrangements, and outside credit is crucial for East European economies as they undergo transition. But there may be more efficient ways to direct scarce credit than through an EEPU. There is reason to favor a restructuring of East-East trade relative to East-West trade, but if the objective of credit is to foster the economic development of these countries, it should not be directed toward payments imbalances at all, but instead be granted in response to overall needs or used to induce general economic reform. If the objective is to foster a restructuring of East-East trade, then providing credit to an EEPU could be useful, but it would certainly not be necessary. With regard to credit supplied by the East Europeans themselves, the main concern is that this credit not be supplied in a bilateral fashion.

Concluding comments

In emphasizing the importance of multilateral issues, we should not overemphasize the need for multilateral institutions. What is really necessary is that the East European countries, and all interested parties, move steadily in the direction of nondistorted, nondiscriminatory trade and that they do not ignore or deemphasize the multilateral implications of the institutions and initiatives (bilateral or otherwise) they recommend or establish. This requires that they think ahead and adopt a multilateral perspective from the start. The danger is that, by not doing this, they will fall into a web of ad hoc bilateral responses to successive situations that, in the aggregate, are irrational and hinder restructuring and transformation.

The following specific points therefore deserve emphasis:

• East European countries should explicitly address multilateral issues during the transition of their currencies to full convertibility, and individual

---

[7]For a further discussion of the disadvantages of an EEPU, see Michalopoulos and Tarr (this volume).

East European countries should at all times be aware of the multilateral consequences of bilateral arrangements.

• Incentives should be provided for East European countries to restructure their mutual trade in an efficient, nondistorted fashion.

• East European (and international) policymakers should realize that as East-West integration proceeds more rapidly than East-East integration, there will be an increasing benefit at the margin from favoring a restructuring of East-East trade relative to East-West trade.

Of the three alternatives presented in this chapter, default bilateralism appears the least desirable according to the above criteria, and a multilateral trade and settlements system the most desirable. The possibility of an EEPU has received widespread attention, but the response has been ambivalent.[8] The analysis in this chapter suggests reasons for the ambivalence. The attractiveness of such an arrangement depends on the counterfactual. If the alternative is simply default bilateralism, an EEPU has much to recommend it. But if a new system can be designed, an EEPU offers little that cannot be obtained more directly.

Appendix

This appendix describes the details of a hypothetical EEPU arrangement. The aim is to assist readers not familiar with payments unions and to illustrate issues that arise if some East European countries were not to participate. We will suppose that our hypothetical EEPU were to consist of Hungary, Poland, and Czechoslovakia.

The mutual trade of participating countries will be denominated and settled in hard currencies, for example, the dollar. Trade will be negotiated and consummated by individual firms. In conducting trade, exporters will acquire the dollar obligations of their trading partners, and importers will incur dollar obligations. These obligations are to be reported to the respective central banks as they are incurred. Central banks can extend domestic currency credit, either directly or through commercial banks as intermediaries, to firms conducting such trade. Neither the central bank nor the government, however, should assume such obligations. The purpose of the central bank in this context is to provide foreign exchange service.

As a result of the agreement between Hungary, Poland, and Czechoslovakia, each country will have designated (or created) a common agent for their central banks. We will suppose this agent is the Bank for International Settlements (BIS), in Basle, Switzerland. The BIS is an example of an appropriate agent, since it is not an institution associated with the old CMEA. The BIS will maintain dollar-denominated accounting for each of the three central banks.

---

[8]See Michalopoulos and Tarr (this volume).

At the start of each month, each of the three central banks communicates to the BIS the figure it has compiled for its previous month's net export surplus to Eastern Europe as a whole. The first column of Table 14.1 shows hypothetical figures for the three countries. The BIS calculates the joint net export surplus for the preceding month for Hungary, Poland, and Czechoslovakia with the rest of Eastern Europe. In the example in Table 14.1, the three countries together have jointly exported $150 million more to the rest of Eastern Europe (plus Russia) than they have imported.

The agreement between Hungary, Poland, and Czechoslovakia provides for the clearing (in one way or another) of mutual trade balances, and also for the clearing of offsetting imbalances with the rest of Eastern Europe. The three countries' joint imbalance with the rest of Eastern Europe, however, cannot be cleared through the agreement, because the rest of Eastern Europe is not participating. Thus this joint balance must be left to the relevant countries to deal with individually. In Table 14.1, there is a joint positive net export surplus of $150 million that cannot be cleared through the agreement. Because Hungary and Czechoslovakia are the surplus countries, and because Hungary's surplus is twice that of Czechoslovakia, two thirds of the $150 million will remain with Hungary and one third with Czechoslovakia. The fact that $100 million of the $400 million surplus with Eastern Europe will not be cleared through the agreement means that this $100 million is treated just like Hungary's trade with the rest of the world other than Eastern Europe: it is up to Hungary to arrange settlement.

Table 14.1 East European trade: hypothetical monthly situation *(millions of U.S. dollars)*

Country	Net export surplus	Amount cleared	Amount not cleared
Hungary	+400	+300	+100
Poland	−450	−450	0
Czechoslovakia	+200	+150	+50
Total	+150	−450, +450	+150

Because no country's account can exceed preset limits, in both positive and negative directions, each central bank settles the amount of its imbalance that is to be cleared with the agent, settling a certain proportion with a dollar transaction and the remainder with an adjustment to its account balance. To illustrate, suppose that the proportion settled by cash is one half, and that in the case depicted in Table 14.1, settlement would leave each country within its preset limits. The BIS would then pay Hungary $150 million and would increase Hungary's account balance by an equal amount; Poland would pay the BIS $225 million and the BIS would lower Poland's account by that amount; the BIS would pay Czechoslovakia $75 million and increase Czechoslovakia's balance by an equal amount.

The agreement between Hungary, Poland, and Czechoslovakia described here differs from other payments unions in that it applies not only to the mutual trade of the three participants among themselves, but also to their offsetting trade balances with the rest of Eastern Europe, including Russia. This feature is included in recognition of the fact that the countries have not only trade with each other in common, but also large distorted trade volumes with other East European countries. The implications of this feature will be discussed in more detail below.

In this example, the total dollar value that the BIS pays equals the total it receives, and the total change in account positions is also zero: the agent's net position with the three countries as group does not change. This need not be the case, however. Suppose, for example, that Czechoslovakia already has a positive balance with the BIS equal to its preset limit. Because such circumstances can arise, the agreements between the three countries must provide for an initial contribution of dollars to a reserve account for use by the agent.

We now discuss the implications of such a payments framework for East European trade. We will suppose that the example used above resulted from the pattern of multilateral trade shown in Table 14.2.

Table 14.2 East European trade: hypothetical net export surpluses *(millions of U.S. dollars)*

	Hungary	Poland	Czechoslovakia
Hungary	—	−200	+400
Poland	+200	—	−300
Czechoslovakia	−400	+300	—
Other Eastern Europe	+600	−550	+100
Total Eastern Europe	+400	−450	+200
BIS dollar settlement	+150	−225	+75
BIS account change	+150	−225	+75

— = not applicable.

The two bottom rows show each country's settlement with the BIS in accordance with the provision that no country will reach its preset limit and that one half of the settlement is made in dollars. We will now use this example to illustrate properties of the payments framework.

Automatic recycling of scarce hard currency balances

Hungary and Czechoslovakia are running monthly surpluses in their East European trade, while Poland is running a deficit. Because the BIS settlement is only half in dollars and half in account balances, Hungary and

Czechoslovakia are in effect jointly lending a portion of their dollar earnings to Poland to finance its East European trade, thereby more effectively utilizing the three countries' joint dollar holdings.

This raises a problem characteristic of payments unions. Countries want access to credit when they experience deficits, but they do not necessarily want to extend credit when they run surpluses. Surplus countries have no incentive to participate, and such a proposal will not be feasible unless there is a source of outside credit. The distinctive feature of Eastern Europe, however, is that it is in a period of change: it is impossible to forecast future Eastern imbalances, and it is likely that at least some countries will experience significant trade balance reversals with each other.

It is accordingly possible to devise credit arrangements that confer *ex ante* benefits to all, even without an outside credit source. Suppose, for example, that the chances are three in four that Hungary will experience a net excess demand for goods from Poland in the amount of $1,000, and only one chance in four that Hungary will instead have a net excess supply of $1,000. The expected disequilibrium, then, is a Hungarian excess demand of $500, and the chances are three out of four that if a payments union were established, it would cause Poland to extend credit to Hungary. Consider, however, a union in which Hungary extends credit up to a maximum of $300 and in which Poland extends credit up to a maximum of $100. Then there are three chances in four that Hungary will develop an excess demand of $1,000 for Polish goods and that $100 of this will be financed through the union, leaving a net disequilibrium of $900 and a Polish credit position of $100.

Similarly, there is one chance in four that the arrangement will lead to a disequilibrium of $700 (in the form of a Polish excess demand for goods) with a Hungarian credit position of $300. Each country's expected net credit position is thus zero, and the expected disequilibrium remains equal to a Hungarian excess demand of $500. What is the net effect on each country's welfare? The conclusion is that *ex post* there will have been agreement that the country with the lesser need for commodities will supply some to the country with the greater need, and the expected disequilibrium will remain unchanged. The net effect is thus that the real uncertainty faced by each country is reduced: both countries gain. Outside credit is not required, and indeed, both countries would gain *ex ante* even if they knew that there was no chance that outstanding debit positions would ever be redeemed.

Though such an agreement would benefit both countries, it would not necessarily be adopted. This is because the medium through which national welfare is raised—the balance sheets of the central banks—becomes subject to increased uncertainty. Central bankers may not like the proposal. Two points are worth noting: (a) there is no reason for the Polish central bank to be less favorably disposed than the Hungarian central bank, because the proposal would have no effect on either banks' expected position and would raise uncertainty in the same way for both; and (b) as long as each central bank gives at least some weight to its country's welfare, it should be willing to participate on at least some level.

Reduced need for bilateral balancing with nonparticipating East European countries

This (limited) advantage is a result of the unique aspect of the present arrangement identified above. In Table 14.2, Hungary has a total surplus of $600 million with East European countries other than Poland and Czechoslovakia. Of this amount, $500 million is settled through the BIS and $100 million is not. The settlement is made partly by canceling Hungary's imbalance with Poland and Czechoslovakia ($200 million), partly through a payment of dollars from the BIS ($150 million), and partly by an increase in Hungary's account balance with the BIS ($150 million). The outcome is the same regardless of whether the $500 million was earned via modest surpluses with most other East European countries, or whether it resulted from an enormous surplus in Russian trade accompanied by deficits in Hungary's other Eastern trade. Thus Hungary need be less concerned than it would otherwise be about its bilateral balances with other East European countries.

Part of Hungary's surplus ($100 million) is not cleared through the BIS, however. Hungary must make arrangements with nonparticipating countries individually for settlement or for prevention of future imbalances. Hungary, then, cannot completely ignore the bilateral structure of trade with nonparticipating East European countries, but involvement in an EEPU still greatly decreases the importance of such bilateral balances.

Automatic financing by Hungary, Poland, and Czechoslovakia of each other's trade with other East European countries

In Table 14.2, Hungary has a surplus of $600 million with other East European countries, Poland a deficit of $550 million, and Czechoslovakia a surplus of $100 million. To the extent that surpluses offset each other and so can be cleared through the BIS, they are used to finance the deficit. Arrangements with Poland and Czechoslovakia, for example, allow Hungary to finance imbalances with Russia, for example, without Hungary having to involve itself in a clearing arrangement with that country. This will not matter *ex post* if Russia ends up with a surplus with each individual member country. Nevertheless, because Soviet trade was in the past the dominant part of each country's East European trade, and with the outlook with regard to future trading behavior uncertain, insurance such as that provided by an EEPU is *ex ante* very important.

Automatic removal of reasons for other East European countries to discriminate among members' trade

We will suppose that imbalances with nonparticipating East European countries are basically imbalances with Russia, and that net imbalances with Yugoslavia, Bulgaria, and Romania are small. As long as Russia balances total dollar trade with Hungary, Poland, and Czechoslovakia, the BIS will settle any individual imbalances. This means that Russia also has no reason to be concerned about individual bilateral balances with these countries. Individual bilateral balance with Hungary, Poland and Czechoslovakia is now no different from the Russian point of view than huge individual imbalances with these countries that aggregate out. This means that Hungary, say, need have much less fear that the prospect of a large Hungarian trade surplus with Russia will induce Russian discrimination against Hungarian goods in order to achieve bilateral balance: reducing Russian imports from Hungary is not different from reducing imports from Poland or from Czechoslovakia. This benefit of an EEPU may be the incentive needed to attract potential creditor countries that might otherwise be reluctant to join a payments union.

The fact that they need to be less concerned about Russian balances with East European countries individually, and only be concerned about the aggregate balance, would also make life considerably easier for Russia. That is, such an agreement is also in the interest of Russia, even it were not directly involved.

References

Ethier, Wilfred, and Henrik Horn. 1984. "A New Look at Economic Integration." In Henryk Kierzkowski, ed., *Monopolistic Competition and International Trade*. Oxford, U.K.: Oxford University Press. Reprinted in Alexis Jacquemin and André Sapir, eds., 1989, *The European Internal Market: Trade and Competition*. Oxford, U.K.: Oxford University Press.

Hillman, Arye L., and Adi Schnytzer. 1992. "Creating the Reform-Resistant Dependent Economy: Socialist Comparative Advantage, Enterprise Incentives, and the CMEA." This volume.

Holzman, Franklyn D. 1987. *The Economics of Soviet Bloc Trade and Finance*. Boulder, Col.: Westview Press.

Michalopoulos, Constantine, and David Tarr. 1992. "Proposals for Post-CMEA Trade and Payments Arrangements." This volume.

Rosefielde, Steven, and R. W. Pfouts. 1990. "Ruble Convertibility: Demand Responsive Exchange Rates in a Goal-Directed Economy." *European Economic Review* 34:1377–97.

Schrenk, Martin. 1992. "The CMEA System of Trade and Payments." This volume.

About the Editors and Contributors

Istvan Abel is a member of the faculty of the Budapest University of Economic Sciences. He has been a visiting professor of economics at Wesleyan University, Connecticut, and a visiting researcher at the Department of Applied Economics, the University of Cambridge. His principal area of research is the economy of Hungary, on which he has published extensively.

Željko Bogetić is an economist at the World Bank in the Europe and Central Asia Region. Since 1990 he has been working primarily as a macroeconomist for Bulgaria. He articles have been published in journals such as *Economic Analysis and Workers' Management* and the *Journal of Economic and Social Geography*. His topics of interest are applied general equilibrium analysis, regional economics, economics of labor management, and employee ownership and privatization in the context of East European transition.

Kang Chen has been a consultant to the World Bank and is now on the faculty of the National University of Singapore. His research interests are Chinese economic reform, economic transition in Eastern Europe, and dynamic multisectoral models. He has written *The Chinese Economy in Transition* (Singapore University Press. 1992). His recent articles include "The Failure of Recentralization in China: Inter-play among Enterprises, Local Governments, and the Center" (in Arye L. Hillman, ed., *Markets and Politicians: Politicized Economic Choice*, Kluwer, 1991); "China's Economic Reform and Social Unrest" (in Jia Hao, ed., *The Democracy Movement of 1989 and China's Future*, 1990); and "Modelling China's Economy in Transition," (*Economic Systems Research*, No. 1, 1991).

Wilfed J. Ethier is professor of economics and director of the International Economics Research Center at the University of Pennsylvania, Philadelphia. He authored *Modern International Economics* (Norton, 1988) and has published widely in professional journals, including the *American Economic Review*, the *Journal of Political Economy*, the *Quarterly Journal of Economics*, and the *Journal of International Economics*. His research interest is international economics. He is editor of the *International Economic Review*.

Alan Gelb is chief of the Transition and Macro-Adjustment Division in the Country Economics Department at the World Bank. His areas of research include employee ownership and incentives in cooperative structures, macroeconomic theory and modelling, financial systems, and socialist economics. He has authored several books (*Worker Capitalism: The New Industrial Relations*, written jointly with K. Bradley, Heinemann, 1983; *Oil Windfalls: Blessing or Curse?* written with associates, Oxford University Press, 1990) and numerous articles in economic journals. Recent publications include "Issues in Socialist Economies Reform" (with Stanley Fischer, the *Journal of Economic Perspectives*, Fall 1991), and "Public Sector Employment, Rent Seeking and Economic Growth" (co-authored with J. B. Knight and R. H. Sabot, *Economic Journal*, September 1991).

Arye L. Hillman is William Gittes Professor of International Economics at Bar-Ilan University in Israel. He has been a visiting professor of economics at the University of California at Los Angeles and at Princeton University, and has been associated with the World Bank under the Visiting Research Fellow Program and as a consultant on Eastern Europe. He is author of *The Political Economy of Protection* (Harwood, 1989) and editor of *Markets and Politicians: Politicized Economic Choice* (Kluwer, 1991). He has published widely on issues relating to international economics and on the role of government in the economy in professional journals, including the *American Economic Review*, the *Quarterly Journal of Economics*, *Public Choice*, *Economics and Politics*, the *Journal of International Economics*, and the *Journal of Public Economics*. His research interest is international economics, in particular international trade policy and the transition from socialism.

Manuel Hinds is chief of the Trade, Finance and Private Sector Development Division for the Europe and Central Asia, and Middle East and North Africa Regions at the World Bank. Before joining the Bank, he was minister of the economy in El Salvador. He has written on issues of financial reform and transition to market economy. Recent publications include "Issues in the Introduction of Market Forces in Eastern European Socialist Economies" (World Bank, 1990), "Markets and Ownership in Socialist Countries in Transition" (in Arye L. Hillman, ed., *Markets and Politicians: Politicized Economic Choice,* Kluwer, 1991), and "Prospects for Perestroika: Privatization as a Requisite for Reform" (in Douglas D. Purvis, ed., *Economic Developments in the Soviet Union and Eastern Europe,* John Deutsch Institute, 1990).

Gary H. Jefferson is associate professor of economics at Brandeis University, Massachusetts. As a consultant to the World Bank, he coordinated research for the project Industrial Reform and Productivity in Chinese Enterprises. His recent articles include "The Impact of Reform on Socialist Enterprises in Transition: Structure, Conduct and Performance in Chinese Industry" (*Journal of Comparative Economics,* January 1991) and "Growth, Efficiency, and Convergence in China's State and Collective Industry" (*Economic Development and Cultural Change,* January 1992).

Erika Jorgensen is an economist in the East Asia and Pacific Region of the World Bank. Her research interests encompass the areas of financial markets, corporate debt, and industrial development. She has recently published articles on Latin American debt and financial markets.

Constantine Michalopoulos is senior adviser for the Europe and Central Asia Region in the World Bank. In this capacity, he advises Bank management on issues of economic policy in successor states of the Soviet Union. Since joining the Bank in 1982, his assignments have included those of senior economic adviser to a vice president, and director of Economic Policy Analysis and Coordination. Before joining the Bank, he was chief economist of the Agency for International Development and deputy director of the International Development and Cooperation Agency. He has published extensively on trade and financial policy issues related to development. Recent publications include *Aid and Development* (Johns Hopkins University Press, 1989).

Branko Milanovic is a senior economist in the Transition and Macro-Adjustment Division in the Country Economics Department at the World Bank. Previously, he worked as country economist for Turkey and Poland. His areas of interest include income distribution, privatization, and system reform in Eastern Europe. He is the author of two books: *Income Inequality in Yugoslavia* (1989, in Serbo-Croatian) and *Liberalization and Entrepreneurship: Dynamics of Reform in Socialism and Capitalism* (M.E. Sharpe, New York, 1989). Recent articles have appeared in the *Journal of Comparative Economics, Soviet Studies,* and *Review of Income and Wealth.*

Fernando Saldanha is a financial officer in the Financial Operations Department at the World Bank. Previously, he served as an economist in the Europe, Middle East and North Africa Region. Before joining the Bank, he held teaching positions at the University of Arizona, the University of Paris XII, and Catholic University of Rio de Janeiro. His main areas of interest are comparative economic systems, corporate finance, and economic psychology. He has published several papers and monographs on these and other subjects, including "Fixprice Analysis of Labor-Managed Economies" (*Journal of Comparative Economics*, June 1989).

Adi Schnytzer is on the faculty of the Department of Economics at Bar-Ilan University, Israel. His recent articles were published in the *Economic Journal* and *Social Choice and Welfare*. He has written extensively on the Albanian economy, including a book, *Stalinist Economic Strategy in Practice: The Case of Albania* (Oxford University Press, 1982). His research interests include the study of how the heritage of planning impedes transition to a capitalist market economy, and the economics of cooperation.

Martin Schrenk is a consultant in the Transition and Macro-Adjustment Division in the Country Economics Department at the World Bank. He has worked in the Bank since 1968 as industrial and country economist on Yugoslavia, Romania, the Republic of Korea, and China. He has published numerous articles on these countries, including a book, *Yugoslavia: Self-Management Socialism and the Challenges of Development* (co-authored with C. Ardalan and N.A. El Tatawy, Johns Hopkins University Press, 1979). His areas of interest are industrial economics and foreign trade.

Inderjit Singh is lead economist in the Transition and Macro-Adjustment Division in the Country Economics Department at the World Bank. His activities in the Bank have covered a variety of operational and research assignments. He has been an advisor on agriculture and rural development to a vice president, industry economist in the South Asia Department, and principal economist on industry and finance in the China Department. He was a co-author of the Bank's first *World Development Report*. He has published several books and many professional papers. His books include *Agricultural Household Models: Extensions, Applications and Policy* (Johns Hopkins University Press, 1986) and *The Great Ascent: The Rural Poor in South Asia* (Johns Hopkins University Press, 1990). Presently, he heads a major research initiative that is examining the impact of reforms in socialist economies (China and Eastern Europe) on enterprise behavior and performance.

David Tarr is a principal economist in the Trade Policy Division of the Country Economics Department at the World Bank. He has written extensively on the quantitative effects of trade reforms. His books include *A General Equilibrium Analysis of U.S. Foreign Trade Policy* (co-authored with Jaime de Melo, MIT Press, 1992). Recent articles were published in the *Review of Economics and Statistics*, the *Journal of International Economics*, and the *Journal of Comparative Economics*.

Katherine Terrell is an assistant professor of economics at the Graduate School of Public and International Affairs, with a joint appointment in the Economics Department, at the University of Pittsburgh, Pennsylvania. Her recent publications include "Productivity of Western and Domestic Capital in Polish Industry" (*Journal of Comparative Economics*, September 1992), *The Industrial Labor Market and Economic Performance in Senegal* (co-authored with Jan Svejnar, Westview Press, 1989), and *A Methodology for Analyzing the Effects of Stabilization and Structural Adjustment Policies on Labor Markets of Developing Countries* (Cornell University Press, 1989). Her areas of research interest are public policy and theoretical issues in labor economics and comparative economic systems.

Milan Vodopivec is an economist in the Transition and Macro-Adjustment Division in the Country Economics Department at the World Bank. Before joining the Bank, he worked as a researcher in the Economic Institute of the Law School of the University of Ljubljana, Slovenia. His research focuses on labor market and industrial organization issues in postsocialist economies. Recent articles have appeared in *Journal of Comparative Economics*, *Economic Development and Cultural Change*, and *Soviet Studies*.

Index